*Black Hawks Rising* – the title of this book – acknowledges the formation and deployment of the African Union Mission to Somalia (AMISOM) in March 2007. Initially confined to peacekeeping within the Mogadishu enclave, it transformed into a peace-making mission. Many – including the author, who predicted the mission was DOA (Dead on Arrival) – gave the mission little chance of success. As a fighting force, however, AMISOM took on the Somali insurgents in 2010; expelled them from Central Mogadishu on Saturday, 6 August 2011; and expanded control of territory under the Somali Government in the succeeding years to most of Somalia.

The opening chapters of the book take the reader behind the scenes to highlight the inconsistent – and sometimes disastrous – US policy in the Horn of Africa generally, and in Somalia (specifically dating back to the Kennedy administration in the early 1960s). Under President George Bush, the US strongly and vigorously opposed deployment of regional African troops in Somalia – instead sponsoring Somali factions to fight against each other and, when that flopped, egged on Ethiopia to invade Somalia in December 2006, which caused the rise of violent insurgency that spilled across borders.

Young jihadists streamed from the heart of USA to fight the invaders. To clean up the mess, the Bush administration finally supported the deployment of regional troops. Black Hawks Rising captures intimately the stories of the men and women who made up AMISOM: their triumphs, setbacks and victories.

The spotlight focuses on the Uganda People's Defence Forces (UPDF), whose Herculean efforts supported by Burundi National Defence Forces (BNDF) – and later the Kenya Defence Forces (KDF), *Forces Armées Djiboutiennes* (FAD) , Ethiopian National Defence Forces (ENDF) and Republic of Sierra Leone Armed Forces (RSLAF) – were pivotal to the success of the mission. Their dedication, professionalism, ideological commitment, hard work and humanity turned Somalia from a wasted nation to one with hope for peace, stability and a better future for the Somali people.

Like Heru – the Hawk-God of Ancient Egypt – AMISOM's new breed of African peace-warriors have demonstrated the capacity to work across borders regionally, continent-wide and globally to help resolve conflicts whenever and wherever they arise – protecting lives and property, and preventing genocides before they happen.

Opiyo Oloya is an educator, researcher and published author. Born and raised in Gulu in Northern Uganda, he became involved in national political activism for democratic reforms during the early 1980s. As President of the Makerere University Student Guild, he publicly condemned the 1980 National Election as fraudulent. He was asked to surrender, but he chose exile: first in Kenya, and subsequently as a refugee in Canada. He completed his BA Hons and Bachelor of Education at Queen's University, Kingston; M.ED at the University of Ottawa; and PhD at York University.

Opiyo Oloya's areas of interest include child-inducted soldiers; conflict and war in Africa; regional, continental and global security; and counter-terrorism and international affairs. He currently works with the York Catholic District School Board, north of Toronto. His book, *Child to Soldier* (University of Toronto Press, 2013), was the culmination of research conducted in the war zone in Northern Uganda – and for which he was awarded his aforementioned PhD in October 2010.

Beginning in August 2010 to the present, he has travelled every summer to Somalia as a war and peace researcher – working alongside the African Union Mission in Somalia (AMISOM) troops based in the country.

In April 2013 York University awarded Opiyo Oloya an Honorary Doctorate of Laws (LLD) for work in Africa generally and Somalia specifically. His popular column, 'Letter from Toronto', has been published weekly since 1996 in the *New Vision Newspaper*, Uganda. His writing informs on security and defence; education; social and scientific issues on Continental Africa; and global politics. Many of his articles are used as teaching tools in major universities across East Africa. He is married to Emily and they have two sons, Oceng and Ogaba.

# BLACK HAWKS RISING

## THE STORY OF AMISOM'S SUCCESSFUL WAR AGAINST SOMALI INSURGENTS, 2007–2014

Opiyo Oloya

This book is dedicated to my friend, the late General Aronda Nyakairima (July 7, 1959—September 12, 2015) whose gentle vision saw a continent where all live in peace; the men and women of Uganda People's Defense Forces (UPDF), and other troops contributing countries to the African Union Mission in Somalia (AMISOM) whose dedication and sacrifices gave Somalia a second chance.

# BLACK HAWKS RISING

## THE STORY OF AMISOM'S SUCCESSFUL WAR AGAINST SOMALI INSURGENTS, 2007–2014

Opiyo Oloya

Helion & Company

Helion & Company Limited
26 Willow Road
Solihull
West Midlands
B91 1UE
England
Tel. 0121 705 3393
Fax 0121 711 4075
email: info@helion.co.uk
website: www.helion.co.uk
Twitter: @helionbooks
Visit our blog http://blog.helion.co.uk

Published by Helion & Company 2016
Designed and typeset by Farr out Publications, Wokingham, Berkshire
Cover designed by Paul Hewitt, Battlefield Design (www.battlefield-design.co.uk)
Printed by Gutenberg Press Limited, Tarxien, Malta

Front cover photograph taken by Stuart Price
Rear cover photo: Uganda Battlegroup troops participate in Operation Free Shabelle (OFS)
in Daynile on May 21, 2012. (UPDF Archives)
Text © Opiyo Oloya 2016
Illustrations © as individually credited
Maps drawn by George Anderson © Helion & Company Limited 2016

ISBN 978-1-910777-69-5

British Library Cataloguing-in-Publication Data
A catalogue record for this book is available from the British Library

For details of other military history titles published by Helion & Company Limited contact
the above address, or visit our website: http://www.helion.co.uk

We always welcome receiving book proposals from prospective authors working in military
history.

# Contents

# List of Photographs

## Colour section 1

## Colour section 2

# List of Maps

# List of Abbreviations and Acronyms

| | |
|---|---|
| ACOTA | Africa Contingency Operations Training and Assistance |
| ACRI | African Crisis Response Initiative |
| AF | African Affairs |
| AIAI | Al-Itihaad al-Islamiya |
| AMIB | African Union Mission in Burundi |
| AMIS | African Union Mission in Sudan |
| AMISOM | African Union Mission in Somalia |
| APC | Armoured personnel carrier |
| ARPCT | Alliance for the Restoration of Peace and Counter-Terrorism |
| ASWJ | Ahlu Sunna Waljama'a |
| AU | African Union |
| AWSS | Authorized weapons storage site |
| BG | Battle Group |
| BN | Battalion |
| BNDF | Burundi National Defence Forces |
| CENTCOM | The United States Central Command |
| CHOGM | Commonwealth Heads of Government Meeting |
| Civpol | Civilian police |
| CJOA | Combined Joint Operational Area |
| CJTF-HOA | Combined Joint Task Force—Horn of Africa |
| Contico | Contingent commander |
| ECOMOG | Economic Community of West African States Monitoring Group |
| ENDF | Ethiopian National Defence Forces |
| FAO | Food and Agriculture Organisation |
| FLS | Frontline states |
| GOT | Government of Tanzania |
| GWOT | Global war on terror |
| ICU | Islamic Courts Union |
| IGAD | Intergovernmental Authority on Development |
| JSOC | Joint Special Operations Command |
| KDF | Kenya Defence Forces |
| LAS | League of Arab States |
| MFA | Ministry of foreign affairs |
| MSF | Médecins Sans Frontières |
| NRA | National Resistance Army |
| NSS | National Security Services |
| ONUB | United Nations Operation in Burundi |
| OPD | Outpatient department |
| PAF | Pakistan Armed Forces |
| poloff | political officer |
| PSC | Peace and Security Commission |

| | |
|---|---|
| QRF | Quick Reaction Force |
| RDF | Rwanda Defence Forces |
| Reftel | reference telegraph |
| RPG | rocket-propelled grenade |
| SADC | Southern African Development Community |
| SMG | Somali Manifesto Group |
| SNA | Somali National Army |
| SNDF | South African National Defence Force |
| SOAR | Special Operations Aviation Regiment |
| SPM | Somali Patriotic Movement |
| SRRC | Somalia Restoration and Reconciliation Council |
| SSF | Somalia Salvation Front |
| TFR | Task Force Ranger |
| TPDF | Tanzania People's Defence Force |
| UAV | unmanned aerial vehicle |
| UGABAG | Uganda Battlegroup |
| UN | United Nations |
| UNAMID | United Nations–African Union Mission in Darfur |
| UNCHR | United Nations High Commission for Refugees |
| UNICEF | United Nations Children's Fund |
| UNITAF | United Task Force |
| UNOSOM | United Nations Operation in Somalia |
| UNSCR | United Nations Security Council Resolution |
| UNSOA | United Nations Support Office for AMISOM |
| UNSOM | United Nations Assistance Mission in Somalia |
| UPDF | Uganda Peoples Defence Forces |
| USAU | US Representative to African Union |
| USC | United Somali Congress |
| USG | United States Government |
| USSR | Union of Soviet Socialist Republics |
| WFP | World Food Program |
| WHO | World Health Organization |
| WSLF | Western Somali Liberation Front |

# Preface

Despite echoing another famous book, *Black Hawk Down*, this book is not about the US helicopter named after the famous American native chief Black Hawk who defied and went to war against the US government in 1832 in Illinois,[1] and which featured prominently in the deadly debacle on the afternoon of Sunday, October 3, 1993 when 18 American troops were killed and US helicopter pilot Michael Durant was taken prisoner of war trying to capture two Somali leaders from the heart of Mogadishu. Rather, the title of this book acknowledges that in many African cultures the hawk symbolizes the protection and welfare of the people. Among the Zulu of southern Africa, the hawk was seen as the symbol of courage, truthfulness and fighting for the right cause.[2] In ancient Egyptian culture, Heru (also known as Horus in Greek), the hawk-god, was believed to unite the people, protect the Pharaoh and by turn, the kingdom.[3] *Black Hawks Rising*, the story you are about to read, is based on a series of historical events that led to the formation and deployment of the African Union Mission to Somalia (AMISOM) in March 2007. Initially confined to peacekeeping within the Mogadishu enclave, it transformed into a peacemaking mission after the devastating twin bomb suicide attacks on AMISOM forces base on September 17, 2009 in which 21 troops were killed. As a fighting force, AMISOM took on the Somali insurgents in 2010, expelled them from Mogadishu on Saturday, August 6, 2011, and expanded control of territory under the Somali government in the succeeding years to most of Somalia.

The story is written with three goals, firstly, to highlight the inconsistent and sometimes disastrous US policy in the Horn of Africa generally and in Somalia specifically dating back to the Kennedy administration in the early 1960s. Following 9/11, under President George Bush, while pursuing the policy of global war on terror (GWOT), the US strongly and vigorously opposed deployment of regional African troops in Somalia, using instead Somali factions to fight against each other and later Ethiopia to fight what it perceived as radical Somali Islamists. When it became clear that the US-supported invasion of Somalia by Ethiopian troops in December 2006 had turned into a catastrophic failure, the Bush administration suddenly became the champions of the deployment of regional troops, finally allowing Uganda first, then Burundi and later Djibouti, Kenya, Ethiopia and Sierra Leone to clean up the mess created by its policies and restore order in Somalia.

The second objective of the book, therefore, is to narrate the stories of the men and women who made up AMISOM, focusing on the Uganda People's Defence Forces (UPDF) whose Herculean efforts were pivotal to the success of the mission. Their dedication, exceptional professionalism, ideological commitment, hard work and humanity, was able to turn Somalia from a wasted nation to one with hope for the future. How they did it, and why they were successful where others including the US had previously failed and their continued concerted efforts in Somalia give meaning to the book's title *Black Hawks Rising*. Like the hawk-god of Ancient Egypt, the UPDF is the new breed of African peace-warriors with demonstrated capacity to work across borders, regionally, and continent-wide to help resolve conflicts whenever and wherever they arise, protecting lives and property, and preventing genocides before they happen.

The mission, of course, was possible with massive logistical and resource support from the international community, the United Nations and the US. But the grunt work of making Somalia a peaceful place with a functioning central government for the Somali people after three decades of chaos was done by the African themselves.

The final goal of the book is to show the resilient nature of the people of Somalia. This resilience was evident during the difficult transitional period, first under President Abdullahi Yusuf Ahmed and, beginning in early 2009, under President Sheikh Sharif Sheikh Ahmed. The work of rebuilding Somalia continues apace under the current leadership of President Sheikh Mahmoud Hassan. The names of the individuals and places in the story are retained to reflect their true identities, except where the individuals themselves used pseudonyms.

AMISOM Forces Base Camp,
Halaane, Mogadishu,
Thursday, July 18, 2013, 5:37 p.m.

# Acknowledgments

A chance encounter at a small restaurant in Kampala, the Ekitoobero, launched the beginning of this research. The date was Saturday, August 14, 2010. I ran into then Commander of Land Forces of Uganda Peoples' Defence Forces (UPDF) Major General Katumba Wamala. The general invited me to accompany him to Somalia the following Tuesday, August 17, 2010. I did. And began a remarkable journey into the world of peacemaking, something I had very little knowledge about.

Foremost, my sincerest gratitude to H.E. President Yoweri Museveni for providing space to discuss security and peacekeeping issues, and to H.E President Sheikh Sharif Sheikh Ahmed, and H.E. President Sheikh Mohamud Hassan for taking the time from their busy schedules to meet with me to talk about Somalia.

For their unwavering support of this project, my sincerest appreciation to the men and women of UPDF, especially the Chief of Defence Forces (CDF) General Katumba Wamala, his predecessor, the late General Aronda Nyakairima (RIP), Joint Chief of Staff (JCOS) Gen. Wilson Mbadi, UPDF Spokesperson Lt. Col. Paddy Ankunda, Lt. Col. Anthony Mbuusi, Maj. Chris Magezi, Maj. Deo Akiiki, Maj. Henry Obbo, Maj. Ronald Kakurungu, Capt. Lawrence Draga, Capt. Isaac Oware, Lt. David Kamya, L/Cpl. Robert Amia and Grace Kigo. I am also thankful to Burundi Information Officer Capt. Gilbert Nitunga for information provided that enabled me to identify key personnel of the Burundi contingent.

I am also grateful to AMISOM force commanders—Gen. Nathan Mugisha, Gen. Fred Mugisha, Gen. Andrew Gutti and Lt. Gen. Silas Ntigurirwa—for exceptional accommodation and safe passage to all corners of Somalia where operations were taking place. A special thank you to Ambassador Gen. Nathan Mugisha for providing valuable feedback to the manuscript. Although busy with leading operations, the contingent commanders—Brig. Ondoga, Brig. Paul Lokech, Brig. Kayanja Muhanga, Brig. Dick Olum, and Brig. David Kavuma—were readily accessible and very open.

I am deeply indebted to Director, York Catholic District School Board, Patricia Preston for being accommodating, my dear friend school principal Sandra Tuzi-Decaro for reading and providing insightful feedbacks to the many drafts of the manuscript, and my amazing assistant Claire Ceci for her support as the work developed. I am also thankful for Italian translation by Professor Roberta Provenzano, York University, and Somali translation by Hussein Adani of Bilan Restaurant, Toronto.

All work involving the written word is possible only with a first rate publishing team—I am very grateful for the generous guidance and support of the Helion Publishing team, especially Duncan Rogers and Charles Singleton.

Last, but not the least, my dearest family—Emily, Oceng and Ogaba—for putting up with days, even weeks when Daddy was too busy writing to cook, join family gathering or go out for a fun evening. Your love and support is the bedrock on which everything is possible. I love you dearly.

# Introduction

## 9/11

For most of its 104 years, except for a period of about twenty years when it was silenced by disrepair in the late 1950s through to 1979, the giant clock with four-sided faces of frosted glass in the Clock Tower Building at 346 Broadway Street in Manhattan unfailingly struck exactly on the hour. Installed in 1897 by the E. Howard Clock Company of Boston, New York and Chicago, few New Yorkers paid much attention to the ancient timekeeper as they went about their day.[1]

On the clear Tuesday morning of September 11, 2001 as the Old Warrior marked exactly 8 o'clock, the familiar innocent chimes floating above the din of New York's early morning traffic, the breeze carried the sound a mile away to the foot of the cloud-high Twin Towers at the World Trade Center in Lower Manhattan.

Unknown to many New Yorkers, the clock had tolled for the last time for many hurrying to or already at work inside the Twin Towers. Hundreds of Americans would lose their lives violently within the hour. By day's end, the death toll would rise to 2,977.[2]

At that precise moment, 19 terrorists had infiltrated four US continental planes. In excruciating details, minute by minute, the devastating attacks that followed were laid out in the voluminous report titled *The 9/11 Commission Report: Final Report of the National Commission on Terrorist Attacks Upon the United States*.[3] Chaired by former New Jersey Governor Thomas H. Kean, the report noted that the terrorists "had defeated all the security layers that America's civil aviation security system then had in place to prevent a hijacking."[4] The chain of events on that fateful morning began a minute earlier, at 7:59 a.m., when American Airlines Flight 11 took off from Logan International Airport in Boston on a scheduled flight to Los Angeles. On board were 81 passengers, of whom five were terrorists on a suicide mission to turn the Boeing 767 into a flaming missile. The leader of the group Mohamed Atta, and two others, Abdul Aziz al Omari and Satam al Suqami sat in business class. Two brothers, Wail al Shehri and Waleed al Shehri sat in first class. With the exception of Atta who was an Egyptian national, the others were Saudi Arabian citizens.

As American Flight 11 gained altitude in the peaceful sky, on the ground United Airlines Flight 175, also bound for Los Angeles, inched forward for takeoff in heavy morning traffic at Logan International Airport. Inside the Boeing 767, the crew of 9 serving 56 passengers busily prepared for the six-hour flight. The plane finally took off at exactly 8:14 a.m., climbing quickly into the clear blue sky. As on Flight 11, this flight too carried five terrorists with the same objective, to use the plane as a missile. Marwan al Shehhi, the designated pilot-hijacker and Fayez Banihammad hailed from United Arab Emirates (UAE). The other three, Mohand al Shehri, Ahmed al Ghamdi and Hamza al Ghamdi were Saudi citizens.

Six minutes later, at 8:20 a.m., seven hundred and forty-four kilometers South-West of Boston at Dulles International Airport in Virginia, American flight 77 took off. Six crews responsible for 58 passengers handled the 757 Boeing flight to Los Angeles that morning. A five man all-Saudi hijacking team was on board this flight. In first class, designated pilot-hijacker Hani Hanjour sat with two brothers Nawaf al Hazmi and Salem al Hazmi. Khalid al Mihdhar and Majed Moqed, the musclemen, rode coach.

Twenty-two minutes later, at 8:42 a.m., a delayed United Flight 93, headed for San Francisco, took off from Newark Liberty International Airport, New Jersey. Two crew and five flight attendants serviced the 37 passengers on board. Four hijackers sat up front in first class. Ziad Jarrah, the designated pilot hijacker was a citizen of Lebanon. The other three, Saeed al Ghamdi, Ahmad al Nami and Ahmad al Haznawi were all Saudi Arabian nationals.

By the time United Flight 93 gained altitude at full throttle, American Flight 11 was approaching its fiery violent end. The hijackers on that flight had subdued the crew. At the controls, Mohamed Atta made a detour toward New York City. He brought the plane low over Manhattan. At exactly 8:46:40 a.m., the fuel-laden aircraft ploughed into the North Tower of the World Trade Center, instantly killing all aboard and many inside the tower.

Barely eighteen minutes later, at 9:03:11 a.m., as shocked onlookers watched in horror, United Flight 175 rammed into the South Tower of the World Trade Center. All on board and many inside the tower were instantly killed. Before officials could fully appreciate the scale and magnitude of the terror attack, at 9:37:46 a.m., Hanjour crashed Flight 77 into the Pentagon at over 800 km/hr., killing all on board and 125 people on the ground.

US President George Bush was getting ready to read *The Pet Goat* to a class of second-graders at Emma E. Booker Elementary School in Sarasota, Florida when the second plane hit the South Tower. White House Chief of Staff Andrew Card briefly interrupted the reading with the urgent news. He made it clear America was under attack. President Bush carried on with the story, for a while anyway, and was later evacuated to Sarasota International Airport. At 9:57 a.m. events hundreds of kilometers apart were simultaneously reaching their climaxes. In Florida, Air Force One with President Bush on board climbed steeply into the eerily quiet sky.

Half an hour earlier, at around 9:27 a.m., the four hijackers on board commandeered United Airlines Flight 93. Ziad Jarrah took control of the 757-200 aircraft. Several passengers on board were aware of the fate of the two aircrafts that crashed into the World Trade Center. At 9:57 a.m., after voting in defiance of the terrorists, passengers on United Flight 93 rushed the cockpit in one last heroic act to regain control of the aircraft. Feverishly, they worked to break open the reinforced cockpit doors. Jarrah dipped the plane from side to side, attempting to knock the passengers off their feet.

Moments later, as the courageous rebellious passengers began their final assault on the cockpit door, Jarrah attempted one last desperate manouver. He jerked the nose of the plane up and down. Then, finally, realizing that his goal to fly the plane to Washington had failed, the Lebanese terrorist flipped the plane upside down, sending it into spiraling plunge to earth at over 800 km/h. United Flight 93 crashed in an empty field in Shanksville, Pennsylvania, killing all on impact. The time was 10:01:11 a.m.

Two minutes earlier in Manhattan, as millions of viewers gasped in collective horror, the South Tower of the World Trade Centre began imploding on live television. The collapse was total at 9:59:04 a.m.

That morning, America had suffered a singular apocalyptic attack. The seismic reverberation of those events would be felt in the weeks, months and years that followed, far beyond its borders, in the dusty streets of far-flung corners of the world. In addition to the thousands that died that morning at the World Trade Center, the Pentagon and Shanksville, Pennsylvania, hundreds of thousands more lives would be lost around the globe.

The world could never be the same again.

## The Usual Suspects

In the immediate aftermath of 9/11, US authorities were under extreme public pressure to find those responsible for the attacks on US soil, and to preempt future attacks on the homeland. Somalia was quickly fingered as a breeding ground for terrorists eager to do harm to the world's most powerful nation.[5] This was to be expected. For almost a decade and half, mostly over cups of cappuccino in cafes in Nairobi or Addis Ababa, Western media reporters filed tailor-made stereotypical reports of Somalia's badass image. These reports, even at their most positive, often portrayed the country as one of the most dangerous places on earth.[6] In time, the media painted vivid images of the distant African dustbowl nation, its streets filled with stick-thin starving black children while murderous clan militia goons wearing flip-flops, and armed with AK-47 rode the backs of ratty-old pick-up 'technicals', shooting at anybody who got in the way of their greedy American-hating fat-bellied warlords. So the story went.

Following 9/11, not surprisingly, in the relentless pursuit of real or imagined terrorists in Somalia, the Bush administration singularly ignored one simple historical fact: Somali people did not hate America. Post-colonial leaders of emerging Somalia, if anything, genuinely admired America, and deliberately sought the superpower's friendship and support to help nurture the fledgling democracy. To successive US presidents, from John F. Kennedy to George W. Bush, however, Somalia only mattered when it suited America's overall strategic interests in the Horn of Africa. Instead of helping Somalia, US policies from the early 1960s hastened the chaos that would later consume the African nation like wild bushfire and which, in time, returned to haunt the US. America's role in Somalia reads like a movie script and, indeed, movies were made about the country's devolution into the abyss.[7]

# Ruined Beginnings

## Wanted: Best Friend For Life

On the chilly morning of Tuesday November 27, 1962, US President John Fitzgerald Kennedy beamed as he welcomed on the South Lawn of the White House Dr. Abdirashid Ali Shermarke, the first Prime Minister of the Somali Republic. Fresh from his historic triumphant blockade of Soviet ships carrying nuclear warheads to Cuba during the Cuban Missile Crisis, President Kennedy wasted little time welcoming the Somalia prime minister, telling his guest why Somalia mattered to America. "We are glad to have you here, Prime Minister, because your country occupies a most strategic area on the horn of Africa," Kennedy said with no irony.[1] Two years earlier, freshly independent from colonial Italy, Somalia had reached out to the US for support, but the overture was ignored. The newly independent nation felt naked, exposed and vulnerable not only from inside saboteurs but from Ethiopia, the bigger archenemy to the west. For generations, both countries staked direct claim to the territory that straddled the Ogaden. Arbitrary colonial demarcation sliced apart kin ties that predated the coming of Europeans in the region.

Prime Minister Shermarke, his hands thrust deep in the pockets of his heavy overcoat, responded extemporaneously. "I am looking forward to our meeting which I am sure will contribute on the creation of good relations between our two countries. Thank you."[2] A pragmatist like most Somali people, Dr. Shermarke hoped to return home with something to show his people that the trip to America was worthwhile.

At the birth of Somalia on July 1, 1960, the Italian colonial administrators had left some parting gifts of military hardware barely adequate to defend itself from possible Ethiopian aggression. These were mostly miserably antiquated World War ll aircrafts that included eight F-51D Mustangs, six C-47 Dakota military transport, and six Beech C-45s that formed the core of the new Somali Air Corps (SAC).[3] Post-independence Somalia needed better protection than these weapons could provide. America, a powerful democracy, seemed a natural ally to help build an independent, stronger and better protected Somalia.

Unknown to Somali leaders, Italy, the former colonial master, was busy behind the scene telling America to give the least possible help to the new nation, and America seemed to listen.[4] Scorned by the world's most powerful democracy, extremely poor and experiencing a Cinderella-like disappointment, reluctantly, Somalia drifted elsewhere. The new African nation soon attracted the attention of communist Union of Soviet Socialist Republics (USSR). Eager for a footprint in the Gulf Region and along the eastern shorelines of Africa, the USSR wasted little time signing a treaty for economic and technical assistance on June 2, 1961.[5]

Then the US-USSR superpower Cold War rivalry heated up. USSR tried to place ballistic missiles in Cuba, sparking a showdown that lasted from October 14, 1962 to October 28, 1962 when the Soviets finally backed down in the face of American challenge. The premier's first official visit to the US, therefore, was well timed. The US would not play second fiddle to the Soviets in the Horn of Africa.

Keen to make a good first impression on his host, Dr. Shermarke came loaded with gifts. Highly educated but humble, the premier had left nothing to chance. He gracefully presented President Kennedy with exotic wooden carvings of a rhinoceros, a giraffe and a camel, and a most exquisite eight-piece ivory desk set.[6] With the help of an Italian interpreter, the two leaders then sat down for discussion at noon. Prime Minister Shermarke engaged in "frank and direct" conversation with Kennedy, telling the American leader that US arms provided to Ethiopia were being used against defenseless Somali people.[7] Moreover, Somalia could use some help getting military assistance as well. Kennedy was noncommittal, saying that arms to Ethiopia started before Somalia attained independence. Still, Kennedy left the door open for helping Somalia.

The next day, still courting Kennedy's support for his country, Dr. Shermarke sent yet another gift. This time it was a framed portrait of the young Somali premier, looking handsome and hopeful.[8] It was a reminder to Kennedy never to forget the people of Somalia. Tragically, by the time of his assassination a year later on Friday November 22, 1963, Kennedy had not shifted American foreign policy in favour of Somalia. Nor did Kennedy's successor, Texan Lyndon Baines Johnson.

Instead, under the leadership of Nikita Khrushchev, the USSR began an ambitious program of supplying aircrafts to the fledgling Somalia including 40 MIG-17 and MIG 15UTIs. As the relationship blossomed between the USSR and Somalia military, Dr. Abdirashid Ali Shermarke, still keen to be a friend of America, did not have a long future. Shermarke, like Kennedy whom he admired greatly, was felled by a fatal bullet fired by his bodyguard while visiting the northern town of Las Anod on October 15, 1969. Six days after Shermarke's assassination, on October 21, 1969, a group of Somali army officers took power in a military *coup d'état*. Major General Siyaad Barre was appointed the leader of the Supreme Revolutionary Council (SRC), and moved quickly to cement relationship with Moscow. He declared Somalia a socialist state in 1970, all the while aggressively cultivating the Soviets for increased military hardware. The overture paid off. The USSR-Somalia Treaty of Friendship and Cooperation was signed on July 11, 1974.

In exchange for port docking privileges and rights in Berbera, Mogadishu and Kismaayo, Moscow beefed up SAC with additional 40 MIG-21MFs and MIG-21Ums fighter jets, and some M-8 helicopters. Hundreds of Russian military advisors, technicians and trainers, meanwhile, converged on Somalia.[9] There was more from where that came. The Somali National Army (SNA) also received 250 Soviet-built T-34 medium tanks, and T54/55 variant tanks. Well over 300 battle-ready Soviet-supplied BTR-40, BTR-50 and BTR-152 armoured personnel carriers (APC) were at the disposal of over 20,000 SNA troops. Such was the dizzying pace of arms built-up in Somalia that at the start of the acrimonious ill-fated Ogaden war against Ethiopia in 1977, the SNA boasted a robust attack force comprising an air force corps, armoured divisions and large infantry. At least 3000 SNA soldiers were fighting alongside the Western Somali Liberation Front (WSLF) as early as May 1977.[10] When Somalia crossed into the Ogaden on July 23, 1977, its robust air force made lightning advances deep inside Ethiopia and, on the ground, SNA troops pressed forward, taking the towns of Gode, Gabridaharey, and Jijiga, before besieging for two months the town of Harer.

For weeks after war broke, Moscow plied arms to both Somalia and Ethiopia. Toward the end of September 1977, in a quick about face, Moscow turned against Somalia. The previous Soviet President Nikolai Podgorny who was closer to Siyaad Barre, even dropping in for an unscheduled visit in early April 1977,[11] was ousted from the Soviet politburo on May 21, 1977. President Leonid Brezhnev, the newly appointed Soviet leader, was less sympathetic to Somalia's claims in the Ogaden. In September 1977, at a Moscow luncheon honouring visiting Angolan leader Agostinho Neto, Brezhnev publicly blasted Somalia for allowing 'imperialists' to split African unity.[12]

President Siyaad Barre was livid at what he felt was a betrayal by the Soviet Union. On November 13, 1977, the Somali leader ordered all Soviet citizens out of Somalia in seven days. Somali Information Minister Addulqadir Salad Hassan announced the expulsion.[13] The Cubans fared even worst—they had 48 hours to leave Somalia. In December 1977, rubbing salt into the wound, Brezhnev ordered airlifts of more than 600 battle-tanks and as many as 69 MIG jet fighters in support of flagging Ethiopian forces.[14] Exhausted, without armour and its supply routes cut off by constant aerial assaults from a rejuvenated Ethiopian air force manned by Cuban pilots, Siyaad Barre withdrew his forces from the Ogaden in March 1978. It was a most bitter and humiliating defeat for Somalia.

A shrewd desert survivor, Siyaad Barre lived by the old Somali saying, *'Either be a mountain or lean on one'*.[15] Without the support of Soviet arms, Barre quickly sent smoke signals for help from Western nations. Italy immediately stepped forward to fill the vacuum left by the Soviets, providing more than $520 million worth of arms between 1978 and 1985.[16] Barre also worked hard to get America's supply of armament to feed the military machine that had ballooned into one of the largest in sub-Sahara Africa.

This time, America showed up in Somalia. In the post-World War II Cold War, instead of a coherent foreign policy in the Horn of Africa that focused on democratic reforms in Barre's Somalia, the US needed to go head to head with the ambitious USSR in arming Africa's dictatorial regimes. Having watched with growing alarm the looming presence of the Soviets in Iran, Afghanistan, next door in Ethiopia, and elsewhere in sub-Sahara Africa, the expulsion of the Russians from Somalia gave the Americans the opportunity to step into the dance. Starting in 1981, the US supplied small arms to Somalia, sending in American M16 rifles and ammunitions. By 1984, the US was spending well over $120 million annually on various projects including education, agriculture and, of course, military aid. M.W Kellogg was contracted to spruce up the port left by the Soviets at Berbera to the standards of taking in big civilian vessels and warships.[17] There were even talks in Washington in the early 1980s of building US Central Command (CENTCOM) in Ras Hafun on the Horn to counter Soviet threat in the Gulf regions, although it was eventually located at MacDill Air Force Base, in Tampa, Florida.[18]

America's sudden interest in Somalia was too little, too late. The stinging defeat of Siyaad Barre in the Ogaden War had removed the cult of mysticism he so carefully cultivated to cling to power. In the eyes of the Somali people, Barre gambled and lost. His popularity dimming, the president became insular, increasingly relying on a dwindling circle of advisors and supporters. In the wake of the disastrous war, the National Security Service (NSS) aggressively targeted critics of the regime. Hundreds of real and imagined political dissidents were tossed into and forgotten at the notorious Labataan Jirow and Lanta Buur prisons. *The Mourning Tree—An Autobiography and A Prison Memoir* by Mohamed Barud Ali, a former political detainee at Labataan Jirow in the early 1980s, is required reading.[19]

The regime's clampdown of critics backfired badly. Emboldened rather than cowed, militancy spread inside the Darood clan to which Barre belonged and other major clans like the Isaaq in the north, Hawiye in south-central Somalia, and Dir in the west. On April

9, 1978, a group of disaffected officers in the SNA, most of them from the Majerteen, a sub clan of the Darood, staged an unsuccessful coup against the regime.[20] The coup was brutally put down by the fearsome special force known as the Duub Cas, the Red Berets, mainly recruited from the president's Mareehaan clansmen, and whose violent methods included wiping out whole villages and livestock.[21] The coup leader Colonel Mahammad Shaykh Usmaan "Cirro" and sixteen others were publicly executed by firing squads in October 1978.

Within a year, one of the coup-plotters Lieutenant Colonel Abdullahi Yusuf Ahmed who escaped to Kenya before moving to Ethiopia, founded the Majerteen-dominated Somali Salvation Front (SSF), later renamed Somali Salvation Democratic Front (SSDF) after merging with smaller anti-Barre movements. The Somali National Movement (SNM), formed mainly by the northern Isaaq clan in April 1981, fired its first volley against the regime in the first week of January 1982. Six years later, in February 1988, the SNM gained a toehold within Somalia territory, capturing three villages around the Togochale refugee camp along the northwestern border of Somali and Ethiopia. In 1989, the United Somali Congress (USC) was formed, bringing into play two major Hawiye sub-clans, the Habar Gidir commanded by General Mahammad Farah, and the Abgaal fronted by Ali Mahdi Mahammad, a businessman. Meanwhile a mostly Ogadeen army officers broke away from Siyaad Barre's SNA in March 1989 to form the Somali Patriotic Front (SPM), operating mostly around the capital Mogadishu.

With the insurgency now on full throttle, a group of 114 Somali intellectuals and elites later known as Somali Manifesto Group (SMG) led by Somalia's first president Aden Abdulle Osman, met in Mogadishu on May 15, 1990, and drafted a document outlining how Siyaad Barre could save Somalia and, in turn, himself.[22] Instead President Barre responded to SMG by arresting 44 of the signatories, including Aden Abdulle Osman and Professor Ibrahim Mohamud Abyan, president of the Somali Institute for Development Administration and Management (SIDAM), putting them through a show trial in June, before directing the court to release them in July.

Already teetering like a bull elephant that suffered one sharp spear too many, there was no reasoning with the dictator, now using brutish violence to suppress dissent.[23] On July 6, 1990, in what became known as the Stadium Incident, the Red Beret, Barre's presidential guards, fired randomly at a section of the crowd that jeered at President Barre while he was speaking at Mogadishu Soccer Stadium.[24] More than sixty people were killed and over three hundred wounded. In November 1990, united by their intense opposition to the regime, the various armed groups cobbled together a unified front against Barre. By the beginning of December, the roads leading north out of the city were cut off. Insurgents soon began laying siege on Mogadishu. Already for weeks, in all the districts around Mogadishu, there was acute shortage of water, food, and fuel. Power was sporadic if at all, and telephone link with the world was cut. Somalia was falling apart, fast.

### Hyenas Outside the Gate

On Thursday December 27, 1990, James Keough Bishop, the US Ambassador Extraordinary and Plenipotentiary to Somalia sat in a plush chair in the cabinet meeting room at Villa Somalia, waiting.[25] His appointment with the 80-year old President Mohammed Siyaad Barre was running late. A career diplomat, Bishop knew his way around troubled spots in Africa. He served in Niger from 1979 to 1981, and Liberia from May 1987 to March 1990, just as the country's first civil war was nibbling at the edges of the countryside. War was nothing new to him. Here, in the cavernous space inside the presidential palace bathed in soft beautiful glow of the morning sun, perched on a hilltop in the middle of the city surrounded by exquisite aging Italian architecture, it was easy for Bishop to forget for a moment that Somalia was engaged in the bloodiest civil war since independence.

Three months earlier, on September 19, 1990, Ambassador Bishop had presented his credentials to President Siyaad Barre. The Somali leader seemed in firm control of the situation. The ceremony was one of those inconsequential events peppered with the usual diplomatic platitudes and niceties of working together and so forth. Siyaad Barre, already in power for two decades since the military coup of October 1969, seemed reassured that America would stick with his regime for a while longer.

The situation had deteriorated fast. The conflict had gained momentum, becoming almost unstoppable. Anti-Barre rebels were pressing toward the capital and, cornered, the regime was acting erratically, brutally. Bishop was aware of the incident three weeks earlier, on December 6, 1990, when a pick-up truck with five uniformed men armed with a Browning sub-machinegun, pulled up at the livestock market in northeast Mogadishu, and fired on unarmed civilians.[26] The uniformed men sped back to the garrison of the 77th Battalion, leaving twelve dead, and several wounded. The violence was reaching a climax. This meeting, Bishop's second with the aging Somalia's leader, was arranged on the request of the ambassador. Bishop needed to know what President Barre's future plans were. More precisely, however, the ambassador carried a message for the president. The priorities of the US government had shifted somewhere else.

Without fanfare, President Barre strode confidently into the room, Bishop rising to greet him. Slightly gaunt, his face pinched tightly around his high cheekbones, Barre otherwise looked crisp and attentive for his age. Accompanying the president was vice minister Bashir from the foreign ministry, and another statehouse official the ambassador could not recall seeing before. After a firm handshake, Barre waved the ambassador to sit down. The president ordered some orange juice for his guest, and then turned to face Bishop, waiting for the ambassador to speak. The American envoy got straight to the point. He requested the meeting to get an assessment from the president on the escalating fighting in Somalia. The Americans had begun to take precautionary measures. Recently, non-essential American staff was evacuated from Mogadishu. With fewer hands to go around, the US also suspended civil and military programs in Somalia. "We are also reassigning fuel, equipment and contract personnel from Berbera to the Persian Gulf where they are needed," added the ambassador.[27]

President Barre listened carefully, then his face relaxed. Surrounded by the excesses and opulence of two decades of unbridled dictatorship there was no hint of the noose tightening around his regime. "Oh, good, I thought you were coming to say goodbye and to tell me the other Americans also were leaving," said the president at last with feigned relief. Barre added that he understood why the US had taken the preemptive move of evacuating their non-essential personnel. The current situation was bad, Barre admitted, "And I am too old," he added as an afterthought. Then the president clammed up, and although Bishop tried to get him into a conversation, the Somali leader bit his tongue.

Barre knew that Bishop came to say farewell. The Somali leader was not about to display for the world his desperation. Instead he put on a brave face. The Americans, it was true, had a fight on their hands in the Gulf. President Saddam Hussein, the grandiose Iraqi leader, had invaded neighbouring oil-rich Kuwait on August 2, 1990, prompting President George H. Bush to build a coalition to drive the invaders out. At that very moment while Ambassador Bishop spoke to President Barre, war with Hussein's army was less than 72 hours away. All US military assets in the region including warships were steaming toward the Persian Gulf.[28]

Barre knew the Americans would still bail out of Somalia even without a pressing war to fight in the Gulf, now that the rebels were closing on Mogadishu. The Americans had used him to get even with the Soviet Union in the Horn. Like the relic of the Cold War that he had become, Barre was expendable, abandoned to the hyenas whining at the gate. The Somali people had a saying for precisely this moment. *Aroos lagama raago, lagumana raago*, one should neither be late for a wedding nor stay too long at it.[29] The US was late coming to Somalia, but was the first to run for cover, abandoning the people of Somalia to their own fate.

That very evening after his last meeting with President Siyaad Barre, Bishop cabled US Secretary of State James A. Baker in Washington. The Ambassador had a lot to say about his last encounter with Siyaad Barre early that morning. "He was anxious to terminate the meeting and probably would have done so, except for the fact that the juice he had offered had not yet arrived," wrote the ambassador.[30]

Bishop further added in the cable, "My general impression was that I was dealing with a worried man who does [not] feel he has a gameplan which will allow him to overcome the problems before him. Nevertheless he seemed intent to muddle on, giving no hint that he might be thinking of heading toward the exit."[31]

Three days later, while on New Year Day jog within the US Embassy compound in Mogadishu, Ambassador Bishop dove for cover when the outside perimeters of the diplomatic complex came under small arms fire.[32] The insurgents had arrived at the gate. Bishop cabled for the immediate evacuation of Americans at the Embassy. The following night the US launched Operation Eastern Exit to ferry to safety American and other nationals from Somalia.[33] Two US warships, the USS Trenton and USS Guam, were dispatched from the North Arabian Sea. From hundreds of miles out from Mogadishu, USS Trenton launched CH-53E helicopters with 60-man SEAL and Marine evacuation force, while a wave of CH-46 helicopters took off from Guam to begin airlifting to safety 281 men and women from as many as thirty different nations including Russians and Chinese.

In the early hours of January 27, 1991, exactly thirty days following the morning meeting with Ambassador Bishop, Mohammed Siyaad Barre fled the presidential bunker near Aden Abdulle airport. His convoy of military vehicles and tanks headed for southwestern Somalia toward the province of Gedo, and eventually setting base in the town of Garba Harre. Although he would soldier on for a year, rallying the remnants of his loyal troops under the banner of Somali National Front (SNF) to engage the militia armies in asymmetric warfare, even fighting to within 40 kilometres of the capital in April 1992, Barre's reign was finished. On the early morning of Wednesday, April 29, 1992, the former policeman fled to Kenya with 1,200 supporters, crossing through the border town of El Wak, before travelling to the northern town of Wajir.[34] Denied asylum by Kenya's President Daniel Arap Moi, Barre travelled in May 1992 to Lagos, Nigeria where he eventually died of a heart attack on January 2, 1995.

## Things Fall Apart

Five years earlier before the overthrow of Siyaad Barre, on a hot day in July 1985, Professor Ibrahim Mohamud Abyan, former president of SIDAM, and later a member of the Manifesto Group, sat down for a chat with Blaine Harden, the Washington Post correspondent covering Africa.[35] Blaine was curious to know why Somalia was free of the fervent Islamic fanaticism that was the hallmark of Khomeini's Iran at the time. Harden later wrote in a news story how Prof. Abyan laughed heartily at Harden's observations, before explaining, saying, "All of us are nomads or descendants of nomads. A nomad does not know if tomorrow the water well will dry up or if his goats will be eaten by hyenas. This gives us an instinctively pragmatic approach to life."[36] It does a Somali no good, Abyan added between fresh burst of mirth, to be a fanatic.

On the same day Siyaad Barre was deposed from power, Prof. Abyan supported the installation of Ali Mahammed Mahdi as interim president of Somalia.[37] But with Barre gone, and everyone scrambling for the seat of power in Mogadishu, the pragmatics of clan unity that sustained the war began unraveling. Mahdi's Hawiye/Abgaal clan went into overdrive to consolidate its power, growing suspicious of non-Abgaal nationalists like Prof. Abyan. A few days later, in early February 1991, barely a week after Siyaad Barre fled Mogadishu, Prof. Abyan and a number of other Darood/Dulbahante men including Abdi Tuhe, a chemist and Muse Yusuuf Ali, an educator (after whom Muse Yusuf Secondary School in Las Anod is named) died violently, among the first post-Barre casualties. Their murders were poignant because Ali Mahdi, seated with a group of Hawiye/Abgaal elders mere meters away in the compound controlled by General Mohamed Nur Galal, said nothing as Prof. Abyan and others were rounded up and shot.[38]

Meanwhile, to the clan leaders of Hawiye/Habar Gidir/Sa'ad, to which Gen. Farah belonged, Mahdi's power maneuver was seen as slamming the door in the face of General Aidid, the former Somalia ambassador to India who joined the struggle against the Barre regime later in June 1990. Aidid's militia dominated by the Habar/Gidir/Sa'ad clan had distinguished itself in the final push against the former regime. Feeling cheated by Mahdi, Gen. Aidid began using his well-armed militia to undermine Mahdi for the ultimate prize, politically strengthening his claims by getting elected as chairman of the United Somali Congress (USC), also doubling as the minister of defence and army chief-of-staff.

Ali Mahdi, in any case, was formally recognized at the Djibouti peace conference attended by all the factions on July 15, 1991, and he was sworn for a two-year period on August 18, 1991 in Mogadishu. Yet, tension and suspicion dogged the relationship with his restless army chief Gen. Mahammed Farah. Violence was never far from the surface as Habar Gidir clan worked to uproot Mahdi's Abgaal clan from Mogadishu. After months of simmering feud, clashes broke out on September 8, 1991 between the opposing Hawiye clans. In the ensuing chaos that became part of daily life in Mogadishu and much of Somalia, clan-based armed militias wielding automatic weapons roamed the streets, looking for those from opposing clans.[39]

For the next three months thousands were killed and over 8,000 injured. So intense was the fighting in November and December that the only three working hospitals in Mogadishu, Medina, Digfer, and Benadir run by the French Médecins Sans Frontières (MSF), were using 1000 liters of blood plasma everyday.[40] Somalia's endless wars, meanwhile, were compounded by an extended drought that soon caused a deadly famine. As early as February 1991, MSF was raising the alarm about the severe malnutrition in the population.

By mid-year 1991, domestic animals and, later, people were dying from hunger. Mass exodus ensued with waves of walking skeletons searching for safe refuge from both bullets and hunger. Nearly 1 million refugees crossed into neighbouring Ethiopia and Kenya, while a further 2.8 million people were displaced internally. Children, women, men, old and young were all victims. On October 15, 1991, the World Food Program (WFP) announced that as many as 300,000 had died, while a further 4.5 million Somali risked starvation.[41]

The unfolding crisis in the Horn finally got a world response. On January 23, 1992, the UN Security Council unanimously adopted Resolution 733, placing a complete embargo on sale of arms to Somali factions.[42] The resolution also called on the various fighting armies to guarantee safe passage for humanitarian personnel and assistance for starving population. Representatives of the warring factions, meanwhile, were invited to the United Nations in New York and, following three weeks long mediation brokered by the UN, League of Arab States (LAS), Organization of the Islamic Conference (OIC), and Organization of African Unity (OAU), a ceasefire deal was inked on March 3, 1992 in Mogadishu by Gen. Aidid and interim president Ali Mahdi.

The UN Security Council moved quickly to shore up the ceasefire agreement by unanimously adopting Resolution 746, on March 17, 1992, asking Somali factions to "honour their commitment under cease-fire agreement signed at Mogadishu on 3 March 1992," and continue supporting humanitarian effort by various relief agencies.[43] Then on April 24, 1992, the UN Security Council unanimously passed resolution 751 that established United Nations Operation in Somalia I (UNOSOM I). The goal was to oversee the ceasefire, and authorized the deployment of 50 unarmed troops to Somalia in July 1992.[44] The unenviable task was given to UN Chief Military Observer, Brigadier-General (later Lt. Gen.) Imtíaz Shaheen of the Pakistan Armed Forces (PAF), who arrived with an advance party in Mogadishu in early July 1992. In New York, meanwhile, UN Secretary General Boutros Boutros-Ghali announced on August 12, 1992 that the factions agreed to a further 500 UN troops.

By then, six major UN agencies, the Food and Agriculture Organization of the United Nations (FAO), the United Nations Development Programme (UNDP), UNICEF, the Office of the United Nations High Commissioner for Refugees (UNHCR), WFP and the World Health Organization (WHO), and as many as three dozen NGOs were working flat out to provide food, shelter and basic health for the millions of Somali people. But in the volatile country where men armed with Kalashnikovs shot at anything they did not like, safe passage was needed for the trucks carrying the bags of food and aid workers to where they were needed. Deteriorating security in Mogadishu and elsewhere in the country meant food and medical supplies were routinely looted from storage depots, in some cases as soon as the ships or planes carrying them docked at the port or landed at the airport. Already agencies working in Mogadishu like the ICRC, MSF, British Save the Children and American International Medical Corps (IMC) were shelling out as much as 60 dollars daily for armed Somali escorts in cobbled-together jalopies rigged with heavy machineguns, as one French writer put it, worthy of "Mad Max", riding shotgun on mercy runs in the city.[45]

For many starving Somali people, the situation grew dire by the hour. In central and southern Somalia, the fighting continued apace. On December 3, 1992 the UN Security Council adopted Resolution 794, authorizing the use of "all necessary means to establish as soon as possible a secure environment for humanitarian relief operations in Somalia."[46] President George H. Bush did not need further convincing to answer UN's desperate plea for help to send troops to Somalia. The public mood in the US was still giddy and euphoric following the highly successful Operation Desert Storm that ousted Iraqi troops from Kuwait. Television replayed endlessly the images of victorious US General H. Norman 'Stormin' Schwarzkopf walking with a swagger on March 4, 1991 into the town of Safwan where he dictated the terms of surrender to the humiliated Iraqi forces. Lieutenant General Sultan Hashim Ahmed, the boyish-looking Iraqi commander with the thick dyed-black mustache, waited meekly to sign Iraqi surrender. America was the toast of the world at that moment.

Bush authorized the deployment of 25,000 US troops to support humanitarian effort, adding US troops were "doing God's work."[47] The mission was codenamed Operation Restore Hope. Bush assured the American people he was confident the troops would support food delivery in Somalia, hand over command to UN forces, and still be home in time for Inauguration Day on January 20, 1993 when Americans welcomed to the White House President-Elect William Jefferson Clinton. It was the least he could do in the twilight days of his presidency. "We will not fail," Bush concluded.

## Operation Restore Hope

United Task Force (UNITAF) mission, under the command of the US, began auspiciously in the early morning of December 9, 1992. Television footage showed US Marines wading ashore from ships anchored off the Somali shoreline in the Indian Ocean. Less prominent was the entry into Somalia of troops culled from diverse nations including Australia, Belgium, Botswana, Canada, Egypt, France, Germany, Greece, India, Italy, Kuwait, Morocco, New Zealand, Nigeria, Norway, Pakistan, Saudi Arabia, Sweden, Tunisia, Turkey, United Arab Emirates, United Kingdom and Zimbabwe. Altogether, by the end of December, 37,000 troops blanketed most of central and southern Somalia, almost 40 percent of the entire country. Relief supplies began to reach those desperately affected by the famine.

The New Year, too, seemed to bring better fortune for Somalia. The presence of US troops appeared to have a calming influence on the warring clan factions, bringing much needed respite to the beleaguered people. A conference on national reconciliation in Addis Ababa, Ethiopia that started on March 15, 1993, meanwhile, concluded two weeks later, on March 27, 1993 with all major players to the Somali conflict including Gen. Farah signing the agreement to finally end the bloodletting.

A day earlier, on March 26, 1993, the prospect of peace in Somalia brightened as the UN Security Council forged ahead by passing resolution 814 (1993), replacing UNITAF with UNOSOM II. Innocuous was the addition of the mandate to facilitate nation building, restore law and order, re-establish the ruined institutional structure and forge reconciliation in the country.[48] Shrewdly, the resolution radically expanded the mandate of the UN from purely humanitarian program to facilitating the nation-building process. To achieve the mandate, the resolution eagerly endorsed the Addis Ababa agreement aptly named the Agreement of the First Session of the Conference of National Reconciliation in Somalia, which among others required the surrendering of all militia weapons and ammunitions to UNITAF and UNOSOM II within 90 days.[49]

A tall order in a country where it was easier to buy an AK47 on the street than a loaf of bread, yes, but one that seemed achievable for the increasingly bullish UN. Meanwhile, convinced that America had done its share of charity work in Somalia, fresh-faced President Bill Clinton ordered the withdrawal by June 1993 of all US troops except 1,300 Quick

Reaction Force (QRF) and a further 3,000 logistics support troops. UN Secretary General Boutros Boutros-Ghali immediately appointed US Admiral Jonathan Howe as Special Representative of the Secretary General (SRSG) to Somalia to oversee the transition from UNITAF to UNOSOM II. Reporting directly to Admiral Howe was Lieutenant-General Çevik Bir of Turkey, appointed as Force Commander of UNOSOM II, and to whom the US formally handed over the leadership of the Somalia mission on May 4, 1993. A tough no-nonsense by-the-book workaholic who graduated with an engineer degree from the Turkish Military Academy in 1958, he climbed the military ladder before serving in NATO from 1973 to 1985. The Deputy Force Commander of UNOSOM II was Lieutenant General Thomas Montgomery, who also doubled as the commander of the remaining US forces in Somalia. A decorated Vietnam War veteran, Gen. Montgomery was awarded the Silver Star for saving his troop while serving as a commander in the 11th US Armored Calvary Regiment in Vietnam. On that day, February 26, 1969, while commanding Company H, 2nd Squadron, near Tan Bihn village, east of Saigon, the lead tank in his convoy took a direct hit from enemy anti-tank grenade. Acting quickly, Montgomery used his tank to shield the disabled tank, enabling his men to be evacuated safely to another tank.[50] He repeated the same daring maneuver when a second tank was knocked out, all the while taking enemy fire himself. He was a soldier's general, dependable, practical and brave.

Gen. Bir began his job with great energy, focusing on preventing further violence among the warring Somali clans. For a short time, the clans cooperated by storing away their heavy weapons and technicals in authorized weapons storage sites (AWSS). It did not take long before tension began building between UNOSOM II troops and the militias. Gen. Bir directed his blue-helmet troops to inspect the weapons depots. General Aidid, who incorporated smaller militias within the United Somali Congress (USC) in June 1992 to create the offshoot the Somali National Alliance (USC-SNA), resisted Bir's effort to inspect the arms caches. The mood changed as USC-SNA started using Radio Mogadishu (also known as Radio Aidid) to broadcast anti-UNOSOM II messages, while its militias took potshots with small arms at UNOSOM II troops, which did little harm since the UN troops moved in armored vehicles.[51]

The cat and mouse between UNOSOM troops and USC-SNA militias turned deadly on the morning of June 5, 1993 when Pakistani troops went to inspect five weapons storage sites in south Mogadishu belonging to the USC-SNA militias. The entire operation had been announced a day earlier to USC/SNA commanders to prevent any misunderstanding and, in fact, the sites were inspected that morning as planned without much incident. By mid-morning, however, USC/SNA used women and children as shields to hem in Pakistani troops guarding feeding centers in Mogadishu, causing the disciplined UN troops to hold fire, and quickly fell victims to the ruse as Somali men wielding knives and AK-47 assault machineguns emerged from behind the unarmed civilians, hacked and shot at the defenseless peacekeepers. By the end of the day, USC/SNA attacks had killed 24 Pakistani troops and wounded another 76 others.[52]

Angry, the UN Security Council reacted swiftly to the attack on UNOSOM II troops. It met through Saturday night until early Sunday morning, June 6, 1993, before adopting Resolution 837. The toughly worded ultimatum reaffirmed the ending of hostilities by the militias, and authorized the use of all necessary measures to apprehend and bring to justice the individuals responsible for the attacks of the previous day.[53] UN Secretary General Boutros Boutros-Ghali requested support from President Clinton for additional US troops, leading to the deployment of Task Force Ranger (TFR) to Somalia in August 1993. In the meantime, from June 12 to August 29, UNOSOM II troops led by the US began attacking various weapons and command sites used by USC/SNA militias, with AC-130 gunships pounding compounds belonging to Aidid and his top lieutenants. On June 17, as on June 5, the UN suffered further casualties when USC/SNA used the same strategy by deploying children and women ahead of armed militias. This time Moroccan troops near Digfer Hospital were surrounded and attacked, leaving four dead and 41 wounded.[54]

With a $25,000 bounty placed on his head in late June, and fighting for his very survival, Gen. Farah was fully engaged at war with the UN by August 1993. Daily tit for tat clashes grew between USC/SNA militias and the various troops of UNOSOM II, now numbering almost 30,000 strong from 29 nations worldwide. USC/SNA militias planted mines along roads used by UNOSOM II troops, and succeeded in blowing up a US military Humvee on August 8, near Medina market, killing 4 American military police (MP) personnel, leaving a gaping 8-foot crater in the ground.[55] On September 5, while replacing Italian contingent along Balaad Road, Nigerian forces also suffered serious casualties. On September 9 and 16, Pakistani and American QRF forces engaged in intense firefights with USC/SNA along Maka al-Mukarama Road. On September 21, 1993, US Rangers working with UNOSOM II captured Aidid's financier, businessman Osman Hassan Ali Atto, while he was visiting an associate near Digfer Hospital. The militias threatened to attack UN installations if Atto was not released within four hours, but that deadline came and passed without the attack. The USC/SNA, using the strategy described by US forces as "shoot and scoot", often fired on UNOSOM II forces, and withdrew before a counter-attack was launched.[56] The hit-and-run tactic was supplemented with the more deadly offensive of placing women and children at the front of a large crowd. In almost every case, the multinational forces were unable to defend themselves for fear of killing civilians.[57]

## Black Hawk Down
In late August, US Task Force Ranger consisting of Bravo Company 3rd Battalion, 75th Ranger Regiment, 1st Special Forces Operational Detachment-Delta (Delta Force) and the 160th Special Operations Aviation Regiment (SOAR), arrived in Somalia. Almost immediately, the scene was set for a big showdown between the well-armed US forces and the scrappy USC/SNA militias. That moment came on the afternoon of October 3, 1993, and would elevate to mythology the fighting prowess of Somali militias while at the same time creating a lasting aversion of Somalia in the minds of Western nations, especially Americans. Early that morning, intelligence indicated that senior advisors to Gen. Aidid were meeting in a building near the Olympic Hotel in Mogadishu. In the surprise mid-afternoon operation, after first softening the target building with TOW-anti tank missiles fired by AH-1 Cobra gunship helicopters, about 120 Task Force Ranger and Delta Force special operations team rappelled down from hovering UH-60 Black Hawk helicopters, moved in quickly and detained 24 men including two of Aidid's top officials.[58] The mission, however, spilled into a disaster. A rocket-propelled grenade (RPG) fired by a militia brought down a Black Hawk helicopter call sign Super 61 piloted by Chief warrant officer, three (CW3) Clifton "Elvis" Wolcott and CW2 Donovan "Bull" Briley. Twenty minutes later a second Black Hawk, call sign Super 64, piloted by CW3 Michael Durant was shot down by RPG fire. In the mad dash to rescue the crews of the downed helicopters, the US Quick Reaction Force used soft-bodied vehicles that came under intense fire from militias.

Casualties mounted quickly. The multinational forces endured several hours of fierce firefights until the mechanized Pakistani and Malaysian troops executed a rescue in the early hours of the following morning. The list of casualties told the story of the devastating battle; 18 American Special Forces killed, 84 injured, and helicopter pilot Durant taken prisoner of war.[59] Meanwhile, one Malaysian was killed and 10 wounded, and two Pakistani wounded. Estimates run from a low 315 to a high 800 Somali civilians and militia killed, and as many as 3,000 wounded.

The battle that entered popular Somali folklore as the Battle of Mogadishu, but often referred to as Black Hawk Down, was more than the American public had stomach for. The sights of rowdy Somali crowds dragging through the streets naked corpses of Americans soldiers infuriated Americans. Washington was miffed. Barely a year in office, President Bill Clinton pulled out American forces altogether from Somalia beginning February 7, 1994 and, a month later, on March 6, 1994, all UNOSOM II troops also quit the troubled country. Such was the haste of US withdrawal from the Horn of Africa that there was never a proper moment to fully honour, let alone atone the deaths of so many colleagues killed on that horrible afternoon in Mogadishu. Clinton's abrupt decision to pull out was maddening for US troops still keen to carry on with the fight in Somalia.[60] There was no going back; America had turned its back on Somalia.

Two years later warlord Gen. Faraah Hussein Aidid also suffered reversal of fortunes. First, he had a falling out with his once most trusted confidant and financier Osman Hassan Ali Atto. The two were set on a collision course after Aidid declared himself president. Not to be outdone, and feeling confident enough to challenge his mentor, Atto staked his claim as the new Chairman of the USC/SNA. As the Somali saying goes, *Ciirtaa-dhamaa ceebtaa yaqaan*, the person who drank your precious sour-milk knows how to anger you deeply.[61] Starting April 1996, and for the next three months, clashes intensified between militias loyal to the two former allies. The other shoe dropped for Gen. Aidid on July 24, 1996. During one of the skirmishes in the Medina neighbourhood, Gen. Aidid was wounded in the shoulder and liver. The gunman who fired the fatal shots was believed to be one of Atto's militia fighters.[62] On Friday August 2, 1996, the USC/SNA controlled Voice of the Somali People radio announced that Gen. Aidid died of an apparent heart attack the previous day while undergoing a surgery for the infected liver. It was the end of an era.

Thousands of weeping Mogadishu residents jammed the streets around the Al Rahma Mosque where a memorial was held. Gen. Aidid was buried in a simple Muslim ceremony in South Mogadishu.[63] The following day, the Voice of the Somali Republic radio operated by Aidid's archrival Ali Mahdi announced a unilateral ceasefire. In the days that followed, the Hawiye Habar Gidir/Sa'ad named Aidid's 35-year old son Hussein Mohamed Aidid, a naturalized American, living in California as his father's successor. The handsome looking former US Marine who served with Battery B, 14th US Marine Regiment in Pico River, California, took over a week after his father was buried, inheriting the enemies that the elder Aidid had cultivated over the years including Ali Mahdi and Osman Hassan Ali Atto.

The US was not sorry to see the last of Aidid. A White House press briefing was held the same afternoon Aidid's death was announced. When asked what the Clinton Administration intended to do now that Aidid was dead, Senior Director for Press and Public Policy Administration David Johnson answered simply, "We clearly hope that while we regret the demise of any of God's creature, that his removal from the scene can set the foundation for a more peaceful future for Somalia."[64] Johnson did not need to say it. The

US was still deeply wounded from the October 1993 fiasco in Mogadishu. The opportunity for redeeming America's humiliation in Somalia, instead, would come six years after the demise of Gen. Aidid, not from the impoverished nation itself, but from the Middle and Far East, in Saudi Arabia and Afghanistan, where a group of radical Islamists plotted carefully to use commuter planes to bring terror onto US soil on September 11, 2001.

The Somalis, of course, had nothing to do with it.

# 2

# War on Terror Somalia (WOTS)

*You don't go searching for bones in a lion's den.*
Somali Proverb

Nine days after the horrific and unprecedented terror attacks on US soil that became known simply as 9/11, President George W. Bush declared global war on terror (GWOT). Bush, angry and defiant, spelled out what the new world order looked like after the attack. Addressing the joint session of Congress in Washington on Thursday, September 20, 2001, he said, "And we will pursue nations that provide aid or safe haven to terrorism. Every nation in every region now has a decision to make: Either you are with us or you are with the terrorists."[1] Three days later, on September 23, 2001, President Bush signed Executive Order 13224, giving the power to declare as terrorist foreign person known "to have committed, or to pose a significant risk of committing, acts of terrorism that threaten the security of U.S. nationals or the national security."[2] Prominent on the list was Osama bin Laden and al-Qaeda. The list of terrorists and terror entities was continuously updated, six times in 2001 alone; October 12, November 2, November 7, December 4, December 20 and December 31, 2001. Two EO 13224 updates were especially significant for Somalia. America's enemies were suddenly rediscovered in Somalia. On the November 7 list were Somali individuals, businesses and organisations suspected of supporting terror including Abbas Abdi Ali, general manager of the Barakaat Bank in Mogadishu, Ahmed Nur Ali Jim'ale, a leader in the Islamic Court Union, Abdullahi Hussein Kahie, CEO of Barakaat Telecommunications, and Sheikh Aweys.[3] But, as will be revealed later in the book, one particular name stood out in the update released on October 12: Fazul Abdullah Mohammed. He lived in the shadows, and liked it that way.

The designation of Sheikh Hassan Dahir Aweys as a terrorist, however, seemed an overreach by the US State Department. One of several hundreds of Somali veterans who participated in the Afghanistan war against the Soviets in the 1980s, Aweys fought alongside other Muslim brothers. He was one of the founders of the Somali offshoot of al-Itihaad al-Islamiyya (AIAI), the transnational Muslim brotherhood organisation with branches in many Muslim countries.[4] With roots dating back to the mid 1980s, AIAI support cut across traditional Somali clan loyalty. A resilient bunch with deep religious convictions about a Caliphate that would unite Muslims everywhere, it made up with sheer motivation what it lacked in military armaments. Its members saw themselves as Muslim brothers first, and were involved in the final uprising against Barre in the 1990s.

Evidently, the focus of Somalia-based AIAI was to assert political and religious influence within the borders of Somalia and, although it became one of the first organisations to be designated as a terror outfit under EO 13224, was unconcerned with America. In post-Barre Somalia, Sheikh Aweys went toe-to-toe before losing to Gen. Aidid's militias in 1991, and again to SSDF militias of Abdullahi Yusuf Ahmed on June 19, 1992. For a time, during the operations of UNOSOM II, AIAI provided paid armed escorts for humanitarian reliefs from the West, earning cold cash thereby becoming financially stronger.[5] It was in the Gedo region in southwest Somalia, near the border with Ethiopia, that AIAI became a powerful force in the districts of Lugh, Balaad Hawo and Burdubo. Fearful of the growing influence of the group, the Ethiopian military attacked it between August 9, 1996 and September 18, 1996, driving it into Gedo mountains.[6]

Yet, completely ignoring the 1992-1994 experience that showed that Somali clan system tended to be suspicious of all outsiders,[7] US policymakers began pushing the false notion of Somalia as the next big attraction for al Qaeda terrorists. As far back as April 5, 2002, James Phillips, a senior policy researcher with clout inside the US Department of Homeland Security wrote,

> To prevent al-Qaeda from moving its base of operations to Somalia, the United States should place a top priority on intercepting its leaders in transit, before they can establish themselves there. Washington also needs to bolster U.S. intelligence gathering inside Somalia to determine the extent of al-Qaeda's presence. The United States then should calibrate its military and political commitment in Somalia to match the threat posed by al-Qaeda forces.[8]

In fact, prior to 9/11 and for five more years afterward, there was not a single evidence of an organized armed Somali group publicly or covertly targeting US citizens, facilities and interests. In a secret diplomatic cable dispatched on Monday, December 5, 2005 to his boss US Secretary of State Condoleezza Rice, US ambassador to Kenya William M. Bellamy conceded this point, writing,

> The Al-Qaida terrorist threat in Somalia is numerically small, with limited resources, but still poses a very significant danger to US interests...For the most part, these extremists are inwardly focused, i.e. their main concern is control over souls, territory and resources inside/inside Somalia.[9]

Bellamy was attempting to influence US policy in Somalia, as it were, nudging the State Department to adopt a new approach toward Somalia, one that did not try to pick the winning clan. Insightfully, Ambassador Bellamy was not concerned with terrorists in Somalia. Only three individuals, in fact, all suspected remnants of al-Qaeda East Africa from the 1998 deadly attacks on US embassies in Kenya and Tanzania, were believed to be hiding in Somalia. They were Saleh Ali Saleh Nabhan, Abu Talha al-Sudani and Fadil Harun aka Fazul Abdullah Mohammed.[10] Saleh Nabhan, a Kenyan citizen of Yemeni heritage and Fazul Mohammed, born in the Comoros Island, were listed on the Federal Bureau of Investigation's (FBI) ten most wanted individuals. Fazul had a $5 million bounty offered by the FBI for his head, dead or alive.[11] The two were suspects in the mid morning bombings of two US embassies on August 7, 1998. The bomb at the American Embassy in Nairobi, Kenya killed 224, of which 12 were Americans. Meanwhile the bomb in Dar es Salaam, Tanzania, killed 10 Tanzanians. Nabhan was also fingered as leading and directing the al-Qaeda operatives in the planning of the November 28, 2002 attacks in Kenya's coastal city of Mombasa. A powerful car bomb exploded at the front of Israeli-owned Paradise Hotel frequented by Israeli tourists, killing eleven Kenyans and three Israelis, two of them children. Minutes earlier before the car bomb went off, two (SA-7 Grail) Strela 2 shoulder-to-air missiles were fired at a Boeing 757 airliner belonging to Israeli-based Arkia Airline as it took off from Moi International Airport in Mombasa. The missiles missed their target. The plane flew safely to Israel, landing five hours later at Ben Gurion International Airport.

Still, in the immediate aftermath of 9/11, American policy toward Somalia was driven with laser-like intensity as if the country was swarming with frothing-in-the-mouth-anti-USA hardline Muslim terrorists. But al-Shabaab as a cohesive radical Islamist powerhouse with strong al-Qaeda ties, whose main goal was to wage terror against Western allies and America, was nonexistent. Suicide bombing, even for a country already soaked in decades of blood, was a distant rumour for most Somalia people in 2001. The ghosts Washington was chasing had no bearing with the reality unfolding on the ground in Somalia.

## The courts of Islamist Reformers

The inward-focused militant players in Somalia that Ambassador Bellamy mentioned in his secret cable to Washington were in fact not so new. They grew organically out of the chaos and discord that plagued the country for over a decade and half even as the era of the warlords dimmed. Following the death of Farah, the locus of power slowly shifted away from the clan warlords. In ascendancy, instead, were the local clerics serving shari'a Islamic courts, the first of which appeared in August 1996 in north Mogadishu in the enclave controlled by Ali Mahdi's Hawiye/Abgaal sub-clan, and from whom ordinary Somali sought justice in resolving neighbourhood disputes. The first Islamic court was established in south Mogadishu in May 1998 by the Saleban sub-clan of Habar Gidir, and was quickly emulated a year later by two other Habar Gidir sub clans, Ayr and Duduble. In time, the popularity of the Islamic court extended beyond Mogadishu to areas controlled by the Ayr including Lower Shabelle, and the town of Merka.

Exhausted by decades of war and chaos, Somali people were easily won over by the Islamic courts. Clan militias became the unofficial enforcers of law and order of court rulings. As the courts expanded their influence over Mogadishu so did the power of militias associated with them. One of the most powerful militias supporting the Islamic courts was the remnant of Sheikh Aweys's al-Ittihaad al-Islamiyya which returned to Mogadishu, guns and all, just in time to catch the growing success of the Islamic courts. Never one to miss an opportunity to be a powerbroker, Aweys quickly established the Ifka Halane Court which drew support from his Ayr sub clan of Hawiye/Habar Gidir, and employed the muscles of al-Itihaad al-Islamiyya to implement court rulings.[12]

In late 2002, with the backing of well-organised militias including AIAI, the Shari'a courts began consolidating. A mild mannered and gentle-spoken Hawiye/Abgaal schoolteacher named Sheikh Sharif Sheikh Ahmed became the chairman of the Islamic courts in north Mogadishu. A year later, the courts in north Mogadishu amalgamated with the major courts in south Mogadishu. "Our only focus at that time was bringing peace and stability to the neighbourhood that had experienced so much violence," said Sheikh Ahmed in a 2012 interview through an interpreter.[13] The Islamic Court Union (ICU) was formed in 2003, uniting the smaller courts under one umbrella.

The ICU was careful not to raise the spectre of a holy religious war in Somalia or anywhere else. In any case, ICU militias were mostly preoccupied with enforcing the law dictated by the courts. The alliance between the clerics and militias worked rather well, bringing together a conglomeration of disparate parties and clans with similar interests in supporting business entrepreneurs rather than the discredited warlords.[14]

But 9/11 happened, and the world had changed. Despite America's hands-off policy toward Somalia, the emerging grassroots Islamic justice system in Mogadishu with its focus on local stability, law and order soon drew the intense scrutiny from America's intelligence. Washington policymakers watched nervously as the Islamists gained strength in Somalia. In time, US officials began referring to the ICU leadership as jihadists.[15] But taking the ICU head on with American boots on the ground was not an option. The American public was still averse to any military involvement whatsoever in Somalia. Instead, the US military began building a robust presence in the Horn of Africa. A year earlier, on Saturday October 19, 2002, the Combined Joint Task Force—Horn of Africa (CJTF-HOA) was established at Camp Lejeune, North Carolina as an integral albeit specialized part of the US African Command (AFRICOM). Led at first by US Marine Corps, and later the US Navy, it comprised of troops from different sectors of the US military including US Marine Corps, US Air Forces, US Army, US Navy, and US Special Operation Forces.

Although its stated goal was to work with partner nations in the Horn of Africa to build capacity and strengthen regional stability, the core mission of CJTF-HOA was to counter extremists and counter-terrorism, hunting al Qaeda fugitives fleeing war elsewhere and neutralizing them. As one American writer put it, the mission was "Kill anyone still alive and leave no unidentified bodies behind."[16] The combined joint operating area (CJOA) was initially defined to include Ethiopia, Djibouti, Eritrea, Somalia, Kenya, Sudan and Seychelles. Elements of the task force would later expand to carry out training and support missions in Uganda, Liberia, Mauritius, Tanzania, Comoro Islands, Rwanda, Burundi, Madagascar, Mozambique, South Sudan and Chad.

On Thursday December 12, 2002, with an initial 400 troops and support personnel, after 28 days sailing aboard the US 6th fleet flagship, the USS Mount Whitney, CJTF-HOA set base dockside in Djibouti. Five months later, on Tuesday May 6, 2003, after operating from aboard the ship, the CJTF-HOA headquarters moved ashore to Camp Lemonnier, an ex-French military barracks leased from the Government of Djibouti for $38 million a year.[17] Camp Lemonnier quickly became the largest permanent US military base on continental Africa. Thus the US war on terror which initially focused on Afghanistan under the emblazoned banner Operation Enduring Freedom, expanded to Horn of Africa and beyond.

## CIA Covert Operations

The US war on terror in Somalia focused specifically on the Islamic clerics whose growing influence and clout in enforcing law and order was being felt in Mogadishu and elsewhere in Somalia. The CIA went into overdrive with different schemes to control the Islamists in Mogadishu, throwing money at warlords willing to do battle with the ICU. Early in 2005, from its various secret stations in Ethiopia and Djibouti, the CIA began targeting the ICU leadership. The agency collaborated with handpicked Somali warlords, elements within the TFG security forces and clan elders in coordinating subversive actions against officials within the ICU. Jeremy Scahill's article "Blowback in Somalia: How US proxy wars helped create a militant Islamist threat" published in September 2011 documents the skullduggery hatched by the CIA and executed by its Somali agents, including the kidnapping of leaders of the ICU which became commonplace in the late 2004 and early 2005.[18] Several commanders of militias associated with Islamic courts, mysteriously disappeared in Mogadishu, some kidnapped or assassinated.

In July 2005, in response to the unexplained disappearances and killings of certain of its leaders, the Islamic Courts elevated a ruthless little known Islamist militia leader named Hashi Aden Ayro as commander of an autonomous youth wing of AlAI that, with time, gained the epithet Hizbul Shabaab (HS), the youth movement. HS began targeted murders of its own, killing security officials and personalities associated with President Yusuf Ahmed's TFG.

The tension developed into open conflict. Early in 2006, the CIA upped the ante by financing and arming Somali factions and warlords to fight the ICU. In January and then again in February 2006, the CIA funneled several hundred thousand dollars in hard cash to Mogadishu Hawiye warlords. One of the recipients of Uncle Sam's largesse was Muhammad Qanyare, a militia businessman. The warlord boasted openly about receiving upward of $150000 that he considered "pocket money".[19] Some of the funds went to pay militias and buy weapons for Alliance for Restoration of Peace and Counter-Terrorism (ARPCT), a CIA supported group unveiled in early March 2006.[20] The unrepentant Qanyare lamented to Scahill that America gave up too soon on ARPCT just when victory was within reach.[21] In an interesting twist, Ethiopian intelligence reports later revealed that Qanyare eagerly sold at a profit to America's enemies weapons bought with American money and stashed the loot in bank accounts in Djibouti.

The flow of CIA seed money did little to dent the growing influence of the ICU. ARPCT lacked motivation and conviction to face the broadly supported Islamic courts. Moreover, having lost some financial edge to the growing clout of the ICU within the business community in Mogadishu, the warlords that made up ARPCT were eager for the free handout money from America. They reported what their CIA handlers wanted to hear, which was that they were winning on the ground when they were not.

## The Period of Paradise
Toward the end of March 2006, the CIA effort to derail the ICU eventually blew up spectacularly in America's face. The tinderbox that catapulted the ICU to power was ignited by an acrimonious business feud between Abukar Omar Adane and Bashir Rage, two Mogadishu Abgaal businessmen. Their bitter wrangle over control of the lucrative El Ma'an seaport soon became a skirmish with both sides to the dispute calling for back-up forces. Bashir Rage summoned the muscles of the US-funded ARPCT. Abukar Omar Adane, having earlier finessed his ICU connections with generous donations to various ICU causes, mobilized al-Itihaad militias, including the fearsome Hizbul Shabaab youth wing led by Hashi Aden Ayro.[22] Block-by-block battles raged for days, back and forth. Civilians scampered for dear life throughout Mogadishu. By the beginning of April, the Islamists were in control of a large swath of Mogadishu and, encouraged by a populace fed up with the insatiably greedy US funded warlords, pushed hard through the first week of May into June until the entire city fell under its control on Monday, June 5, 2006. Now, for the first time, America's worst nightmare scenario had actually played out. Former warlord allies were on the lam for their lives, leaving behind a victorious and stronger ICU in Mogadishu, scattering toward the borders of neighbouring states for refuge.

By the middle of June, the ICU militias had defeated all the warlords, and established a de facto control over much of Mogadishu and elsewhere in Somalia. The ascendancy to power of the ICU brought Mogadishu residents a much welcome peace. Under the ICU's tightfisted 90-member *shura* council headed by Sheikh Hassan Dahir Aweys, a new calm settled over Mogadishu. Gunfire that daily punctuated the rhythm of Mogadishu life fell silent. The looting and robbery that plagued the city for much of the previous fifteen years suddenly disappeared, perhaps because many of the same players were now in a position of authority, and were obligated to keep the peace.

In time Somali people began referring to the peaceful period between June and December 2006 as *lix bilood oo janaah* or *lixdii bilool ee janada ahayd*, the period of paradise.[23] Neighbours met neighbours, lingering a while under the verandas or street corners to gossip, sip hot tea or chew *qat*. Women wrapped in beautiful bright and colorful traditional Somali *guntiino* dresses could be seen on the streets on their way to and from the market again. Mogadishu was a city in convalescence.

The change atmosphere especially disadvantaged the free-wheelers and dealers who profited by engaging in *haram*, forbidden activities such as money changing at exorbitant profits and racketeering. As retold by a Mogadishu resident, the story popular in the streets of this period was about a war profiteer named Mahad "Dollar", so named because of his unrequited love for the American dollar.[24] Mahad's illegal enterprises included staging robbery and looting to get his hands on the dollar. When the ICU became the authority in town, most other warlords took off for their own safety. Mahad, however, hung around Mogadishu, motivated to make as much money as he could before everything was shut down. Soon, however, he found himself in hot water with the new sheriff in town. One day, he received a not-so-discreet phone call from none other than Hashi Aden Ayro. After Mahad identified himself to the caller, there was a pregnant pause on the other end of the line. Ayro finally spoke with menace hanging on every syllable, telling Mahad to pack his belongings and leave Mogadishu that very day. "Just so that you know I am serious, I have American dollars here for your transport out of town," Ayro added ominously. Choosing personal safety over the mighty dollar, Mahad skipped town immediately, never to come back.

The peace, however, did not last. The defeat of the CIA-backed warlords in Mogadishu sent shockwaves within the US intelligence and diplomatic communities whose best laid plan, not to mention the million of dollars poured into the counter-terrorism project, was in tatters. US military planners scrambled afresh to the drawing board, desperately seeking new options. With two wars already raging in Afghanistan and Iraq, sending American troops on the ground in Somalia was a non-starter in Washington. The Americans simply did not have the stomach for another tragedy similar to the Black Hawk debacle of 1993.

Stymied and desperate, American military strategists began rethinking the Somali problem. Whatever needed doing had to be done without getting the US hands dirty. The preferred option was to work with just one country, in this case, Ethiopia, to destroy the pesky ICU. As a neighbour and long time enemy of Somalia, Ethiopia had both the might and motivation to get inside Somalia to kick the ICU out of Mogadishu, so went the thinking. Top US official now gravitated toward the recommendations articulated by Homeland Security policy wonk James Phillips in 2002. "Officials of the CIA, the State Department, and the Pentagon also should consult with their counterparts in Ethiopia, Kenya, and Djibouti to get up to speed on Somalia.... Ethiopia, which has fought three wars with Somalia, is well-positioned to assist American efforts to combat al-Qaeda or its local Somali allies," wrote the senior researcher.[25]

Arguably, this was the biggest and most alarming turnaround for US position on Somalia. Until the turn of dramatic events in June 2006, the US had vehemently opposed the involvement of frontline states in Somalia. In fact, the US had worked hard to kill all initiatives to deploy African troops in Somalia. The story of that effort is worth telling on its own.

# 3

# To Deploy or Not

On the evening of Thursday, June 22, 2006, the US envoy to Djibouti Ambassador Marguerita Dianne Ragsdale, hosted a lavish cocktail dinner inside the heavily fortified US Embassy complex, perched on the lip of the opening to the Gulf of Tadjoura, along Boulevard du Maréchal Lyautey on the elevated Plateau du Serpent in Djibouti City.[1] After the day's temperature that soared to a sticky 95°F/35°C,[2] the cool evening breeze from the Arabian Sea was refreshing and welcome by the well-heeled guests in attendance.

The occasion was to honour visiting US Assistant Secretary of State for African Affairs Dr. Jendayi Frazer and Dr. Bashir Hamad Attalla. The latter a career diplomat from the Republic of Sudan was the Executive Secretary of the oddly named Intergovernmental Authority on Development (IGAD) based in Djibouti. The membership of the regional organisation included Djibouti, Eritrea, Ethiopia, Somalia, Sudan, Uganda and Kenya.[3]

The event also served as a farewell of sorts for Ambassador Ragsdale. With her two years up, only a couple of weeks remained before her appointment ended on July 6, 2006. For Ragsdale, it must have seemed only like yesterday when President George Bush nominated her in October 2003 for the ambassadorial post in the impoverished nation of Djibouti. She was an African American woman of distinction with a doctorate from the University of Virginia and a juris doctorate degree from Columbia University in New York. News of her nomination had brought cheers from the congregation at Big Bethel Baptist Church back home in Mckenney, Virginia, where she worshipped every Sunday whenever she was in town, and was fondly referred to as Sister Marguerita for her generous work in the church community.[4]

The Congressional Records of October 15, 2003 included a brief from the US Senate Committee on Foreign Relations acknowledging the executive nomination of Ragsdale. It read, "Marguerita Dianne Ragsdale, of Virginia, a career member of the senior foreign service, class counselor, to be ambassador extraordinary and plenipotentiary of the United States of America to the Republic of Djibouti."[5] Prior to the nomination to represent her country in Djibouti, Ragsdale had served in various diplomatic roles in Kuwait, Somalia, Tunisia, Sudan, South Africa and at the State Department in Washington. At the confirmation hearing before the committee chaired by Senator Richard "Dick" Lugar (R-Ind) on the morning of November 5, 2003, Ragsdale dazzled with her poise and knowledge of Africa in general and Djibouti in particular.[6] She was confirmed for the job on December 9, 2003, and immediately began preparation to take over from her predecessor in Djibouti, Japanese American Ambassador Donald Yamamoto who was called back to the State Department to serve as Deputy Assistant Secretary, African Bureau.

Ragsdale presented her credentials to Djibouti President Ismail Omar Guelleh on February 23, 2004. Soon after starting on the job, Ambassador Ragsdale requested a meeting with Dr. Attalla. The two met at the IGAD Secretariat, shortly after Attalla returned from Nairobi where he attended the March 12 Ministerial Facilitation Committee Meeting on

Somalia Reconciliation.[7] Attalla told Ragsdale he was not optimistic about the outcome of the Somali reconciliation process. Some of the key players like Djibouti and Ethiopia were "playing games" with their Somalia allies.[8] Moreover, the Somali participants were mostly former warlords, not politicians, who discussed peace only in terms of how much they got to keep for themselves. Nonetheless, Attalla was willing to wait and see how the follow-up meeting slated for March 22 would be any different. In any case, he promised to fully brief the ambassador on the outcome of that meeting.

Dr. Attalla had worked hard to cultivate the support of the US on Somalia, working closely with Ambassador Donald Yamamoto and, now, he was eager to impress Ambassador Ragsdale. Back in April 2000 as the new executive secretary of IGAD in Djibouti, Attalla found the organisation facing many challenges. Formed in January 1986 originally as an intergovernmental authority on drought and desertification (IGADD), the organisation overextended its reach in November 1996 to include food security and environmental protection, political and humanitarian affairs including conflict protection, and regional economic cooperation. The newly revitalized organisation shortened the moniker to intergovernmental authority on development (IGAD).

Attalla also discovered member states were in constant state of internal civil conflict or war with each other. Moreover, the secretariat in Djibouti operated on a shoestring budget totaling a meager three million dollars, that employed two dozens personnel doing diverse work from environmental protection to working on peace initiative. The organisation was content to issue mostly meaningless communiqué that were ignored. Attalla worked to change that, first, by making it a viable organisation with a vibrant ambition to be a forceful player on continental issues and, secondly, be heard on security issues in the Horn of Africa. Attalla saw the US as a natural ally.

The next meeting between Ambassador Ragsdale and Dr. Attalla took place on the morning of Thursday, March 25, 2004. The conversation focused on the IGAD ministerial meeting of March 22, 2004, three days earlier in Djibouti.[9] Attalla had a lot to say. Unprompted, he gave Ragsdale the inside scoop. He narrated how he survived a putsch by the Kenyan delegation determined to turf him out and replace him with a Kenyan at the helm of IGAD. Attalla also called out Uganda as the most delinquent member of IGAD. For several years in a row, Uganda had refused to pay its annual dues totaling over $3 million. Djibouti, the next villain, owed over $500,000 to IGAD in unpaid dues. Yet, Attala lamented, Djibouti citizens held more than half the posts in the IGAD secretariat. In Attala's good books under the column "very faithful" to IGAD were Sudan, Ethiopia, Kenya and Eritrea.[10]

Dr. Attalla then nudged the discussion to IGAD's plan for Somalia. Attalla painstakingly explained to Ragsdale why it mattered that the US support IGAD's plan to send regional forces to protect the TFG in Somalia. Ambassador Ragsdale listened patiently to what would soon become a very familiar pitch. IGAD could help the peace process in Somalia, was the refrain from Attalla. What Attalla could not appreciate was how very prickly the US was on the subject of security on the Horn of Africa. Specifically, American policymakers were alarmed by IGAD's plans to send regional troops into Somalia. Fearful that IGAD's meddling could embolden the Islamists in Mogadishu, the US began waging fierce closed-door diplomatic war against deployment of African troops. Unknown to Attalla, US diplomats in Europe and Africa were working overtime to shoot down IGAD's proposal for a Somalia peace force christened IGAD Peace Support Mission to Somalia

(IGASOM).

## IGASOM, Still-born

The idea of deploying African troops in Somalia was not new. It had been on the table for more than two years.

IGAD's push for the deployment of a regional force in Somalia had gained traction among African leaders when Uganda's President Yoweri Museveni took over as Chairman of IGAD on October 24, 2003. Museveni was keen to see the plan for deployment take shape early in 2004 to protect the Transitional National Government (TNG) formed in Djibouti in May 2000.[11] The Uganda leader had already ordered Uganda military commanders to start planning and training troops in preparation for deployment to Somalia.[12] A joint AU-IGAD technical fact-finding mission to Somalia in May and June 2003 had recommended an AU military observer mission comprising of 81 military observers. In July and August 2003 AU reconnaissance missions in Somalia determined that it was possible to deploy an AU Military Observer Mission in Somalia.

All that was abandoned, however, in favour of a robust troops presence in Somalia. Dictated by the changes on the ground, starting January 9, 2004 until January 29, 2004, as co-hosts, Museveni together with Kenya's President Mwai Kibaki invited Somali leaders to a conference at the Nairobi Safari Park Hotel on Thika Road. The retreat brought together a broad spectrum of Somali leaders and civil society including the TNG, the chairman of the SNSC Muse Suudi, the Chairman of Somali Restoration and Reconciliation Council (SRRC), Hussein Aidid, the Chairman of the Group of Eight (allied faction leaders), Mohamed Qanyare Afrah, and other Somali leaders. At the end of twenty days of non-stop haggling, discussions, blustering and posturing, Somali leaders agreed to have a Transitional Federal Charter, Transitional Federal Government of the Somali Republic (TFG) and 275 members of transitional federal parliament of which 12% would be women.[13]

On the urging of President Museveni, IGAD began thinking bigger, putting together a concept for a regional force that could, with time, be deployed in conflict situations like Somalia. On February 16 and 17, 2004, IGAD brought together East African chief of defense staff in Jinja, Uganda to explore the possibility of establishing an Eastern African Standby Brigade (EASBRIG).[14] The broad coalition went beyond IGAD membership to include Uganda, Kenya, Comoros, Djibouti, Eritrea, Madagascar, Mauritius, Seychelles, Rwanda, Burundi, Tanzania, Sudan and Somalia. A 13-person planning element (PLANELM) was established to draw out the specifics of the force, with countries pledging troops and equipment. The meeting proposed that EASBRIG be molded on the Chapter VI peacekeeping as outlined by the AU. It would have more robust troops than previous initiatives suggested. The idea of using EASBRIG in a complex conflict like Somalia, however, was overtaken by the dynamics on the ground. On October 10, 2004, the TFG elected as president Abdullahi Yusuf Ahmed whose administration, it was hoped, would rally the Somali people in the long process toward peace and institutional building. Ahmed and his cabinet were to move to Johwar or Baidoa inside Somalia, and wait on the sideline for the multinational African intervention force, IGASOM as it became known, to clear the path to the seat of power in Mogadishu.

Five days after Ahmed's election, at IGAD Special Summit in Nairobi on October 15, 2004, the Heads of State issued a directive calling for the training of a Somalia own security forces, but "Suggested that in the meantime, the African Union and IGAD should explore practical and more affordable ways to support and sustain a peace restoration and protection force for Somalia."[15] The idea of deploying troops in Somalia gathered steam when, during his visit to the AU Commission in Addis Ababa on October 25, 2004, TFG President Abdullahi Yusuf Ahmed addressed the Peace and Security Council, and asked for between 15,000 to 20,000 peacemaking troops from Frontline States (FLS), Africa at large, brotherly Arab States, and the rest of the world including Indian Ocean countries.[16] The Somalia leader also asked that 20 to 30 national police and troops be recruited and trained for joint operation with the AU troops.

Two weeks later, a seminar of experts on Somalia convened by the AU commission on November 4 and 5, 2004 in Addis Ababa agreed in principal that the TFG should work a peace agreement with other factions to give way for deployment of a protection and stabilization force. To get a grip on the fast evolving situation inside and outside Somalia, the AU Commission convened a two-day meeting of experts on peace and security in Nairobi, Kenya on December 15 to 16, 2004. Representations came from the AU, the TFG, IGAD Secretariat and Member States, the European Union (EU), League of Arab States (LAS), United Nations (UN), Italy, Sweden, and the Somalia Demilitarization Planning Unit (SDPU). The experts recommended a fact-finding mission to Somalia made up of representatives of all the key players to determine first hand the mood for deploying a peace support force in the country.

Because, at first, the US kept hidden from view its opposition to the creation and deployment of an IGAD regional force in Somalia, African leaders pushed ahead with planning for IGASOM. On January 5, 2005 the AU Peace and Security Council (PSC) agreed in principle on AU Peace Support Mission (AU PSM) to be carried in conjunction with IGAD. At the 6th Session of AU Summit in Abuja, Nigeria, on January 31, 2005, IGAD Heads of State took time away from the main session to draft a communiqué that essentially laid out the commitment for the deployment of IGASOM. It stated in part, "the commitment of Djibouti, Ethiopia, Kenya, Sudan and Uganda to provide troops and/or equipment for the deployment of a Peace Support Mission to provide security to the TFG of Somalia in order to ensure its relocation to Somalia and guarantee the sustenance of the outcome of the IGAD peace process."[17] Later the same day, the Assembly of AU Heads of State unanimously adopted Resolution Assembly/AU/ Dec. 65(lV) which "Welcomes the decision adopted by the 22nd Meeting of the Peace and Security Council (PSC) of January 5, 2005 in which the PSC accepted, in principle, the deployment of an AU Peace Support Mission in Somalia..."[18] The declaration further "Requests the Commission to expedite the preparations of the recommendations requested by the PSC to facilitate the speedy deployment of an AU Peace Support Mission, as part of the efforts to create propitious security conditions and to normalize the situation in order to assist in the effective functioning of the Transitional Federal Institutions." Essentially, with the blessing of the African heads of state, IGASOM got the green light for deployment. Left to be determined later was the size of the force, its structure, mandate and funding.

The PSC, at its next meeting on February 5, 2005, following quickly on the recommendation of the AU, authorized the deployment of IGASOM to Somalia. The PSC then planned to dispatch a fact-finding reconnaissance team to Somalia from February 11 to February 26, 2005. Representatives from IGAD Secretariat, the LAS, Uganda, Ethiopia, Kenya, the EU, UN, Italy and Sweden made the team.[19] The terms of reference for the mission included identifying strategic installations, key facilities for training police and army and finding suitable locations for deploying the force.

Originally scheduled to depart Nairobi for Mogadishu on February 11, 2005, the team was delayed ostensibly to assess the security situation on the ground, then the EU team bailed out altogether. The official reason for the last minute cancellation by the EU and UN was "security reasons for their own representatives."[20] In a letter to the AU Commissioner for Peace and Security, dated February 7, 2005, Jean-Marie Guéhenno, UN Under Secretary General for Peacekeeping Operations, wrote, "under the current security circumstances (in Somalia), the Department of Peace Keeping Operations (DPKO) was not able to send any of its staff to Somalia."[21] The European Commission chose to send two personnel to Nairobi to attend the pre-departure briefing only, and promptly returned to Brussels.

The mission subsequently departed on February 14, 2005, arriving in Somalia later that afternoon to the warm welcome from Ibrahim Omar Sabriye, the Mayor of Mogadishu. Over the next several days, the team held consultation with an array of civil and militia leaders, members of parliament, and the Governor of Lower Shabelle Yusuf Muhammad Siyaad "Indhacade". The governor clearly stated his opposition to the deployment of foreign troops, saying that Ethiopia and Djibouti had taken sides with different factions in Somalia and had become part of the problem. Although Kenya had done much to facilitate the peace process, it too was no longer neutral, the governor added.

The strongest opposition came from the Acting Chairman of the Somali National Alliance (SNA) Abukar Ganey. The SNA, he said, would oppose any foreign troops whether they were "African, European or Arab."[22] Still, despite the opposition, there was also support for deployment especially in Johwar in Middle Shabelle region where the fact-finding team was welcome by Governor Mohamed Dheere and TFG Minister of Education Ali Abdullahi Ossoble, and in Baidoa where Governor Ahmed Muqtar said his town was ready to receive the TFG, and provide security for it. Overall, the support for deployment was stronger outside of Mogadishu in outlying areas of Somalia.

With the IGAD mission literally on the runway ready for takeoff, an operational meeting of chief of defense staff from contributing countries met on March 7 to 11, 2005 in Entebbe, Uganda to hammer out the final details and lay ground for the deployment of IGASOM troops.[23] The ministers of defense of the contributing countries also met in Entebbe on March 12—14, 2005. At the conclusion of the meeting on Monday, March 14, President Museveni again reminded the ministers that the people of Somalia were suffering, and further delay was unacceptable. "What are we waiting for? You should work out the deployment programme as soon as possible," he berated the meeting.[24]

The ambitious plan that envisioned the first wave of African peacekeepers hitting the ground in Somalia by April 2005 was endorsed within the week, on March 18, 2005 by the IGAD Council of Ministers meeting in Nairobi.[25] IGAD Secretariat would manage the mission, overseeing coordination of all the elements of deployment. In Phase 1, Uganda and Sudan would contribute the troops, a battalion apiece of 850 fighting troops. Troops contributing countries would initially meet their own cost of operations for the first 90 days, and be reimbursed at a later date. IGASOM initial deployment would last nine months in five sectors of Somalia. Sector 1 comprised Bay and Bakool, Sector 2 spanned Central Region, Sector 3 focused mainly on Puntland, Sector 4 on Juba Valley and Sector 5, the Benadir Region. The total cost of deploying a battalion was pegged at $51,234,183 and twice that amount for the two initial battalions.

All that was left to do was for the United Nations Security Council to lift the arms embargo imposed on Somalia under UNSCR 733 on January 23 1992. The UN also needed to scrap UNSCR 751 (1992) that established a monitoring committee to ensure compliance. With both resolutions gone, the TFG would get the weapons it needed to train Somali troops.

Later the same day, however, the Council of Ministers put out a statement stating its dismay after learning of "the problem created by some members of the Federal Transitional Parliament of Somalia during their session held on 17th March, 2005 at the Grand Regency Hotel in Nairobi (Kenya)..."[26] The ugly story from the meeting at the Grand Regency was that the majority members of the Somalia Parliament voted against the deployment of an IGAD force and, in time, the already raucous meeting turned nasty as members traded blows and threw chairs at each other.[27]

The biggest pop in the IGAD's balloon was caused, however, not by fisticuffs from energised Somali parliamentarians, but by the statement that the US sent to the Council of Ministers on Thursday, part of which read, "We do not plan to fund the deployment of IGAD troops in Somalia and are not prepared to support a U.N. Security Council mandate for IGAD deployment in Somalia."[28]

## US Throws Monkey's Wrench

The plan for IGASOM, inconveniently, interfered with the CIA plan to sponsor Somali warlords promising to deliver Somalia under the control of America. IGAD's plans to send troops to the war-torn country was impudent and more than a minor irritant. Even before the council of ministers left the IGAD meeting in Nairobi, the plan for IGASOM was unraveling fast. The US publicly denounced the plan, threatening to veto any UN Security Council resolution that placed frontline states inside Somalia.[29]

In reality, the US public outburst and tantrums were a year in the making. From the moment the plan of an African mission was first floated in early 2004, the US was concerned it could interfere with its counter-terrorism goal of getting rid of the Islamic Courts Union (ICU) altogether. Such a regional effort could fail and, instead, legitimize the ICU's growing influence in Somalia. On orders from the State Department, US diplomats had jumped all over it. One month before staking a public opposition against IGASOM, for example, the behind the scene arm-twisting by the United States of America, was the cause of the last minute "flu" developed by the representatives from the UN, EU and Sweden that prevented them from joining the February 2005 fact-finding mission to Somalia. To the Americans, the EU had made a big mistake dangling 6 million Euros to support such an African intervention force, and by participating in the fact-finding delegation to Somalia. The secret campaign to sabotage IGASOM, therefore, targeted European partners and the United Nations. The US argument, the talking points of which were delivered as reference telegraphs (reftels) to US diplomats working in all EU partner nations, was that the inclusion of frontline states in any African mission in Somalia could trigger violence.[30]

On February 11, 2005, Marc J. Meznar the US Refugee and Migration Affairs Officer at the US Embassy in Brussels met with Mark Boucey, an officer at the European Commission's Directorate-General for International cooperation and Development (DG DEVCO).[31] Meznar made it clear the US was against the IGAD African mission involving frontline states (FLS). Boucey responded evenly that the EU shared American angst about the involvement of the so-called FLS in Somalia. Boucey also revealed that a EU team was already in Nairobi to join the fact-finding mission and, in fact, due to depart in two days for Mogadishu on February 13, 2005. As it were, the EU planners never made it to Mogadishu.

At a different meeting the same day, Christian Manahl, a member of the African Task Force within the General Secretariat of the Council of the EU told Todd Huizinga, US Political Officer (POLOFF) in Brussels, that the one thing Somalis were united on was their "hatred of Ethiopians."[32] It was what Americans wanted to hear. It gave credibility to US push to stop IGAD now. Three days later, on February 14, 2004, the IGASOM intervention force for Somalia was placed on death watch during a US-EU meeting attended by the Director for Defense Aspects of European security and defence policy (ESDP), Claude-France Arnould, EU Planner Matthew Reece and US Deputy Assistant Secretary of Defense for African Affairs Theresa Whelan. Reece who had just returned that morning from Nairobi referred dismissively to IGAD's idea of an African intervention force in Somalia as "wildcat plans".[33] IGAD, he narrated, had no capacity for planning and synchronizing a military operation in Somalia. The fact-finding mission, he added, was sent off to Mogadishu with no hope of success.

The main problem for the Europeans was that America did not provide an alternative plan. The general feeling in the EU, unlike the US, which opposed not only IGASOM but also the idea of an African mission itself, was that the AU plan at least be considered before allowing IGASOM to collapse under its own inept weight. In the absence of US leadership on Somalia, one by one, EU members began poking around the ashes of IGASOM to see if parts could be rekindled. The first indication that the Europeans were having second thoughts about killing IGASOM came on Friday, March 18, 2005 at a confidential meeting at the US Embassy in Vienna, Austria. The US Counselor for Economics and Political Affairs Gregory E. Phillips met with Dr. Caroline Gudenus, the head for Sub-Sahara Africa Unit at the Austrian Ministry for Foreign Affairs. Dr. Gudenus revealed that the EU shared the US concern that frontline states not be deployed in Somalia, especially Ethiopia that could provoke a "strong resentment."[34] However, Gudenus added that this position existed before a new plan had emerged that would ensure that in fact no frontline state was deployed in Somalia. Dr. Gudenus added that the EU agreed that any deployment to Somalia should occur as a result of a consensus among all the players in the region including African Union. Gudenus, without saying as much, was not ruling out the possibility that the EU could support a fresh, well-thought plan for deployment with or without US participation.

Gregory Phillips did not like what he was hearing. IGASOM was supposed to be dead already, except the Europeans never knew when to leave well enough alone. What's more, Gudenus was not acting alone. On the same day, 1,200 km to the southwest of Vienna, a different meeting in Rome between Italian diplomats and US left the latter sweaty and hot around the collar. The Italian bottled the stubborn mood of EU partners to defy the US and deploy African troops to Somalia. At the meeting, the Director General for Sub-Saharan Africa at Italy Ministry for Foreign Affairs Stefano Dejak told Tom Countryman, the US Counselor for Economic and Political Affairs at the US Embassy in Rome that Italy shared US concerns over possible IGAD troop deployment in Somalia.[35] Dejak added that the previous day, Thursday March 17, 2005 at an IGAD meeting in Nairobi Kenya, Italy's Ambassador to Kenya Enrico Gerardo de Maio expressed similar concerns over the deployment of troops from frontline states in Somalia. Dejak went on ominously, Italy would continue to consult on deploying troops to Somalia, though he personally did not see the value in speaking publicly in opposition of it.

Dejak promised to consult with his superiors on US concerns and the two agreed to meet again. The meeting occurred five days later on March 23, 2005. Stefano Dejak told Countryman that Italy was happy with the amended plan for IGASOM. In the plan, Dejak crowed, Uganda and Sudan would provide the troops for deployment in Somalia. The remaining IGAD countries, especially the frontline states (FLS) would provide logistics, equipment, emergency assistance and training. According to Dejak, the revised plan was viewed favourably by Somali groups, and would soon be endorsed by IGAD and the AU Peace and Security Council and, "sooner than expected", be tabled to the UN Security Council for approval.[36] Dejak made it clear that Italy and the core group working on the Somali issue wanted to make sure that they were on the same page as the US.

Countryman was dumbfounded. This was going from bad to worse. Not waiting for a response, Dejak pressed Countryman point-blank on what the US position was on the amended IGAD plan for deployment. Would the US support the plan when it came before the UN Security Council? Naturally, Countryman needed to consult with the US State Department on the emerging consensus among European nations. The meeting ended with Countryman promising to get back soon to Dejak.

For a while, at least, the EU appeared on course to revive IGASOM. Led by the free spirited Italians, a fierce full-fledged rebellion was afoot against continued US opposition to IGASOM. The pussyfooting by US officials on the deployment plan was not working. The showdown came a month later on April 20, 2005 in Brussels.[37] The meeting dubbed transatlantic consultations on Africa (COAFR) was, in fact, the diplomatic equivalent of the OK Corral. The EU brought the big guns in tow. The heavy weights included Alain de Muyser, Director for African Affairs at (MFA) Luxembourg, Nadia Ernzer, Senior Advisor for Africa and CIS Affairs (MFA) for the Luxembourg Presidency; Ambassador Aldo Ajello, EU Special Envoy for the Great Lakes and Koen Vervaeke, Head of the EU Council Secretariat Africa Task Force. Also present from the EU Secretariat were desk officers Peter Clausen, Jesper Tvevad, Genoveva Hernandez, Christian Manahl and Ran van Reedt Dortland, Anders Henriksson, Director for the Horn, East and Southern Africa (DG DEV), Elizabeth Pizon, Unit Head for Central Africa (DG DEV), Miriam Brewka-Pino, African, Caribbean and Pacific (ACP) Issues Unit for the European Commission (EC); and Tim Hitchens, Head of the Africa Department (Equatorial), UK Foreign and Commonwealth Office and Ruth Bradley-Jones, Deputy Permanent Representation for the UK at the EU.

Leading the much thinner and outgunned US government delegation was Ambassador Michael Ranneberger as Principal Deputy Assistant Secretary, African Affairs (AF). With him was Donald Heflin, Deputy Director, AF/Regional and Security Affairs, Patricia Lerner, Development Counselor USEU/USAID, and Marc Meznar Political Officer, US Mission to the EU. The first part of the agenda focused on the situation in the Great Lakes especially in the Democratic Republic of Congo (DRC). There was little to disagree about. No shots were fired.

Then the topic of Somalia came up. Alain de Muyser, at first, went soft at the Americans. He thanked the US for getting back on board with issues in Somalia. Then Anders Henriksson jabbed the Americans. He reminded them that the EU remained in Somalia throughout the 1990s even as everyone else fled. Tim Hitchens then pricked the sore point, asking the US delegation to spell out exactly where the US stood on the issue of deployment to Somalia. Ambassador Ranneberger stuck to the State Department talking point. The US, he said, opposed deployment that involved troops from frontline states. He added very vaguely that the US, in any case, could support deployment when the conditions were right.

Left dangling awkwardly in the air was the question of what those conditions might be. To fill the void, Ambassador Ranneberger added that the US was looking at specific benchmarks. Again, the ambassador did not spell out what those benchmarks were. The Europeans let him talk. As the Somali say, *Hal diideysaa geed ay ku xoqato wa weydo*, If a she-camel does not want to do something, she finds a tree against which to rub herself.[38] Clearly grasping at straws, Ranneberger pushed on, raising every thinkable excuse. There were also other obstacles to the IGAD deployment plan including costs and the concern that the AU might bite more than it could possibly chew, thereby over-extending itself and regional partners in peace operations. Ranneberger then asked rhetorically if there was unanimity among AU members for such an operation. He answered his own question. Alpha Oumar Konare, the Chairperson of the African Union Commission, for one, was "lukewarm at best", the ambassador noted.[39]

The Europeans had come prepared for just such obfuscation by the Americans. And they had had enough of the pompous Ranneberger. Henriksson countered Ranneberger's pessimistic tone, reminding the ambassador that while the deployment plan was not popular in Addis Ababa, the EU was extremely keen to see it through as the best hope for peace in Somalia. Summing it all up, Hitchens said the EU plan for Somalia was "yes, but..." whereas the US approach was "no, unless...". The US stance had already caused enough damage, he added. The Americans were missing out something crucial—the Africans were determined to carry their own weight this time around. With Yoweri Museveni leading the pack, Uganda's cooperation with the AU could make it possible to deploy in Somalia, argued the EU officer.

Across town, at that very moment as the EU-US drama was unfolding, the European Union High Representative for the Common Foreign and Security Policy Janvier Solana was meeting with Uganda's President Yoweri Museveni in Brussels. Museveni reconfirmed Uganda's commitment to contribute troops for the mission in Somalia. But at the EU-US meeting, the US delegation simply sat on their hands. The exchange ended with Ambassador Ranneberger proposing further dialogue on the issues via video teleconference. The teleconference took place on May 2, 2005. Nothing came of it.

The standoff with the EU remained, at least, for a year. The CIA, meanwhile, cooked up its own secret plan to sponsor warlords to take on the ICU in Mogadishu. The scattered, contrarian and ineffectual US approach to Somalia was what prompted US Ambassador to Kenya William Bellamy to send the now famous secret cable to Washington on Monday, December 5, 2005. Then, Bellamy had dire warning for the State Department, writing,

> Ethiopia, Italy, Yemen, Uganda and parts of the African Union have long been partisans of Yusuf. Kenya has recently joined this chorus. Now the EU, Sweden, Germany and World Bank are moving forward with larger-scale support for Yusuf and the TFG executive. If this campaign rolls on without any US involvement or mediation, it could embolden Yusuf to make the wrong choices, igniting conflict and possibly undermining our CT goals...We cannot remain neutral or on the sidelines if we want to position ourselves to influence the political and security dynamic in Somalia. Hence the need for a new strategy of engagement.[40]

In the spring of 2006, barely five months after Bellamy's warning, the CIA plan to arm Somali warlords went up in smokes. The ICU forces smashed the US-backed warlords, taking Mogadishu and then spreading its influence to other parts of Somalia. By then, IGASOM was dead. It had been dead long before Dr. Bashir Ahmed Attalla set foot inside the US Embassy in Djibouti for the cocktail party on that June evening in 2006. A perennial optimist, Attalla was still running his mouth about sending regional troops into Somalia. In the thick of the murky politics of the Horn of Africa, it fell on Ambassador Ragsdale to make sure that was all Attalla did, run his mouth and nothing else.

Jendayi Frazer was dispatched from Washington to turn things around in Somalia, while at the same time keep Attalla and IGAD at bay. As a graduate student, Frazer spent time in Kenya researching a dissertation topic on the relationship between Kenya Military and Government. After graduating from Stanford University she served as assistant professor at the Josef Korbel School of International Studies at the University of Denver, and at the Kennedy School of Government at Harvard University. Her meteoric rise to the Parthenon of power and influence in Washington, though, was due in no small measure to her mentor and former Stanford teacher Condoleezza Rice, at the time the US National Security Advisor to the fledgling administration of President George Bush.[41] Dr. Frazer was first appointed to government by President George Bush in 2001 as Special Assistant to the President and Senior Director for African Affairs. Blessed with a sharp intellect, keen and a quick study of world affairs generally and vast knowledge about matters pertaining to Africa, Frazer quickly became a leading voice in the State Department on African issues, helping set and promote US strategic agenda on the continent.[42]

To boost Frazer's razor-thin diplomatic experience, Rice lobbied President George Bush and had her appointed US Ambassador to South Africa on May 25, 2004. The first woman to serve as US envoy to the country that gave the world Nelson Mandela, Frazer presented her credentials to then South African President Thabo Mbeki on August 10, 2004, and threw herself into getting to know the host country, receiving an honourary degree from the University of Cape Town.[43]

Barely five months on the job in Pretoria, there were obvious signs of bigger things to come for Frazer. She was invited to the formal swearing-in ceremony of Condoleezza Rice as US Secretary of State on Friday, January 28, 2005. At 9:45 a.m. in the Benjamin Franklin Room at the U.S. Department of State, as Frazer looked on from a prominent seat among the dignitaries including President George W. Bush, U.S. Supreme Court Justice Ruth Bader Ginsburg administered the oath of office to Rice.[44] In the spring of 2005, Frazer was promoted by President Bush to Assistant Secretary of State for African Affairs and sworn on August 25, 2005.

Frazer, in short, had the confidence of the White House to act as she saw fit in shaping America's policy toward Somalia. Like a dog with a bone, she threw herself into the eye of the storm. The day before the dinner in Djibouti, Wednesday June 21, 2006, Frazer was in Nairobi, Kenya, in endless meetings with Somali leaders and groups discussing the Somali crisis. Much to the chagrin of the US diplomat, adding to the fast moving Somali dynamics was the meddlesome Dr. Attalla who refused to give up. At every opportunity, the Sudanese diplomat brought up the argument that the US was on the wrong path by shunning the regional initiative that had the blessing of the African Union.

Not surprisingly, at a press conference in Nairobi at the end of the day, Frazer parried questions from journalists wanting to know whether the US now supported IGAD's plan to send troops into Somalia. Frazer had given a long rambling answer that said little:

> On the issue of foreign force, that's the second time I am asked a question on foreign forces in Somalia. We haven't taken a position. As you know, America in the past has been very clear, that there needs to be an arms embargo and there shouldn't be external forces going into Somalia. We have taken note of the IGAD and the AU communications, once again asking for IGAD forces, not the front line states, but rather Sudan and Uganda to go in to support the Transitional Federal Government as well as the call for a relaxing or ending the arms-embargo to allow the Transitional Federal Government to get the resources to provide security and to establish authority. This is a very dynamic period and we don't want to exacerbate with external intervention that would prevent the dialogue within Somalia from taking place.[45]

Dodging media queries on African troop deployment to Somalia was one thing. Frazer, who jetted into Djibouti early the following morning, needed to get Attalla to back off from still talking about IGAD forces in Somalia. The plan was simple: give Attalla plenty of audience, stroke his ego by complimenting him on the fine job he was doing, tell him the US was with him, and then give him the boots. The glitzy cocktail dinner, and the red-carpet treatment worthy of a head of state were to shower Attalla with attention.

As the cocktail dinner got under way, Ambassador Ragsdale deftly divided her attention between her boss, the assorted guests of ranking US military officers from nearby Camp Lemonnier, friendly diplomatic missions, Djibouti government officials, guests from neighbouring Somalia, and Dr. Attalla. The man was not easily dissuaded from his core mission. His enthusiasm palpable, Attalla launched into the rationale for the immediate deployment of the all-African intervention force into Somalia, and the need for US support. Jendayi Frazer and Ambassador Ragsdale listened. "We want the United States to be part of the process," Dr. Attalla told Frazer.[46] He explained that when America dropped off and tuned out of Somalia, the action greatly discouraged those working to achieve peace in the country. America needed to take an active role, he admonished.

"Be assured we will be involved in Somalia," Frazer responded. "That is the reason for my visit here today," she added. Then she quickly moved in to damper the mood by inserting doubt about the IGAD planned deployment to Somalia. Frazer told Attalla that she had heard from members of IGAD and Somali leaders that there was lack of unanimity on the way forward. "There appears to be differing views within the TFG and among IGAD member states on how this involvement should occur," she told Attalla. Frazer who had met with President Museveni two days earlier in Kampala, observed coolly that the Ugandan leader might be unclear on how to proceed given the lack of clarity on the issue.

This was not true, of course. President Museveni had been bullish about the Somalia mission longer than any member of IGAD. He had pushed hard to get the peace mission underway. Frazer was being disingenuous by questioning Museveni's resolve. This, however, was her strategy to spell out to Attalla that America did not support IGAD's planned deployment or any other African intervention force by another name entering Somalia when the African leaders were confused about such deployment.

Undeterred by Frazer's cold response, Dr. Attalla pressed on anyway, arguing that Somalia had become a "safe haven" for terrorists from all over Asia and the Middle East. The way he saw it, the TFG led by President Abdullahi Yusuf Ahmed could succeed with robust support especially from America. IGAD would provide just such an intervention force. President Yoweri Museveni was eager to send in troops right away to rescue the situation, Attalla added confidently. What Attalla could not know at that moment was that the US was transitioning to a new position. Adamant in public pronouncements about not involving frontline states in Somalia, the US was swiftly courting a frontline state to go into Somalia. Ethiopia.

Frazer was done talking about IGAD's planned deployment to Somalia. Tactfully, as they do in Washington's diplomatic cocktail circuits, the American diplomat moved on to speak to the foreign minister of self-declared independent Somaliland Edna Adan Ismail. The question of whether or not to deploy regional forces into Somalia was soon buried in the clinking of elegant wine goblets and clanging of silver cutlery.

# 4

# Playing the Ethiopian Card

On Monday June 19, 2006, three days before the lavish cocktail dinner at the US Embassy in Djibouti, the Americans came knocking on doors in the corridor of power in Addis Ababa, Ethiopia.[1] Leading the US team to the secret meeting was the highly decorated Lebanese-American General John Philip Abizaid, Commander of US Central Command (USCENTCOM). Also at the meeting was Acting US Ambassador to Ethiopia Vicki Huddleston. None of them was smiling. The senior Ethiopian official the Americans had come to meet was the soft-spoken Lieutenant General Samora Yonus, Chief of General Staff of Ethiopian National Defense Forces (ENDF). Yonus was not a man easily intimidated, not even by a general from the most powerful nation on earth, but that did not stop General Abizaid from trying. His reception of the Americans was polite, but lukewarm.[2]

General Abizaid, a US Army veteran with 33 years under his belt that included service in the Persian Gulf Wars, Kosovo and Afghanistan, was testy and blunt that morning. The US general demanded to know what Ethiopia intended to do about the expanding ICU momentum in Somalia. Should Ethiopia not be thinking the unthinkable option—an Ethiopian invasion of Somalia? If not, why not?

From General Yonus's viewpoint, General Abizaid was downright nasty.[3] The Ethiopian General was not going be pushed around. He was calm, collected and looked Abizaid straight in the eye. American forces then ensconced in the Ogaden as part of CJTF-HOA needed to leave the area until Ethiopia had cleaned it up, said General Yonus.

On Somalia, the real reason for the meeting, General Yonus felt too much was being made about the ICU in Mogadishu. Mostly made of clerics and irregular militias instead of disciplined army, the ICU forces possessed 'technicals' and perhaps a few armoured personnel carriers. The leadership in Addis Ababa just did not see the urgency in waging war on their neighbour, and would only move into Somalia to protect its national security or on behalf of IGAD to protect the TFG government in Baidoa. Several times General Abizaid pressed the Ethiopian commander to provide a head count of the ICU forces in Mogadishu. The questions were ignored. General Yonus reiterated that Ethiopia would not allow the Mogadishu Islamists to attack the Somali Transitional Federal Government (TFG) in Baidoa.

Finally, having had enough, Gen. Yonus turned the heat on his visitors. He took the Americans to task for not supporting the IGAD peace initiative, even after the plan was revamped to keep out frontline states and, instead send Uganda and Sudan. The gist of the meeting was that Ethiopia was not eager to get into a brawl with the Somali Islamists at that moment. And no, Ethiopia did not need any equipment, maybe helicopters, but not much else. Empty-handed, the US General left disappointed.

The US needed urgently to change Ethiopia's calm approach to the ICU problem to red alert. On Friday, June 23, 2006, four days after the stormy meeting of the generals, Jendayi Frazer called on Meles Zenawi, the prime minister of Ethiopia.[4] Frazer was accompanied by

US Charge d'affaire to Ethiopia Vicki Huddleston, commander CJTF-HOA Admiral Rick Hunt, and Special Assistants Kendra Gaither and Lieutenant Commander Michael Sowa, and Somalia desk officer Nole Garey. Meles had with him acting MFA director general for Europe and America Almaz Ameha and special assistant Gebretensai Gebremichael. Frazer, a contrast to Gen. Abizaid, was friendly, bringing greetings to the Prime Minister from President George Bush. In measured tone, Frazer admitted upfront that the US was reconfiguring its policy toward Somalia, and told Zenawi that the US understood Ethiopia's policy of deterrence toward the ICU in Mogadishu. It was a good approach said Frazer, but warned, "Don't move preemptively."[5] Perhaps the US diplomat did not want to telegraph America's burning anxiety about the ICU in Mogadishu. Perhaps she wanted to give the impression of the US being in control of the situation. Whatever her motive, the warning was a step-back from the frenetic sky-is-falling approach of General Abizaid to get Ethiopia to do something about the ICU.

Zenawi, in any case, was not in a rush to get into Somalia. He would only do so if the ICU attacked Baidoa, he told Frazer. He wanted the US to support the IGAD initiative to send a peacekeeping force to protect the TFG government. Although it had crossed his mind to arm the TFG to defend itself, Zenawi said he was content to wait for the legal green light from UNSC to partially lift the ban on arms. The meeting concluded with Zenawi highlighting the need for America to be more forthcoming with information about what it was doing in Somalia. "We need to know what you are doing. We always let you know what we are doing," he said.[6] Frazer responded that she would let Washington know.

In the meantime, the calamitous debacle of the American-sponsored ARPCT counter-terrorism campaign in Mogadishu provided endless unconcealed glee among Ethiopia's senior officials. A giddy mood had settled over Addis Ababa at America's expense.[7] During the heated exchange with General Abizaid, for instance, the Ethiopian top general let fly the remark that warlord Qanyare was selling his arms and ammunition and depositing the funds in Djibouti. Although the meaning was clear as day, the Americans likely missed it. What Gen. Yonus meant was this: If Qanyare, the US backed warlord had used the weapons supplied by the CIA to fight the ICU instead of selling them for profit, the menace in Mogadishu could be long sorted out. The unsaid implication was that if Americans were dumb enough to trust a crook like Qanyare with such important mission then they deserved what was coming and, consequently, need not look to Ethiopia to bail them out.

At every turn, the Ethiopians delighted in reminding American officials of the mess they created in Mogadishu. The long-serving Ethiopia's Deputy Foreign Minister Dr. Tekeda Alemu best expressed the I-told-you-so attitude within Ethiopia's ruling class in a meeting on Saturday September 16, 2006 with Donald Y. Yamamoto, Principal Deputy Assistant Secretary in the US Bureau of African Affairs, and shortly to be appointed US ambassador to Ethiopia.[8] Alemu could not resist taking shots at America's spectacular crash in Somalia. Ambassador Yamamoto recalled later the same day in a confidential diplomatic cable to Jendayi Frazer that the irrepressibly loquacious Dr. Alemu let the cat out of the bag, saying that thanks to U.S. support for the warlord alliance against terrorism in Mogadishu, the ICU was now firmly "part of the landscape".[9]

Dr. Tekeda Alemu further rubbed more salt into America's wound a month later, on Wednesday October 18, 2006 at a meeting in Addis Ababa attended by UK Ambassador to Ethiopia Bob Dewar.[10] He told the US Acting Ambassador Vicki Huddleston, also at the meeting, that the government of Ethiopia (GOE) had invited ICU Chairman Sheikh

Sharif Ahmed for dialogue, but that the latter still had not responded. In any case, Dr. Alemu went on, GOE had an "open door policy" toward further entente with the ICU.[11]

The laissez faire attitude of GOE was beginning to get on the nerves of US officials. It was one thing for Ethiopia not to take action against the ICU in Mogadishu. It was, however, quite another to plan to talk to America's enemies in Mogadishu. As far as the US was concerned, giving the ICU such a platform could help the Islamists consolidate their grip over the Somalia landscape, legitimizing their presence. Most alarming for the Americans was the shrewd and pragmatic ICU Chairman Sheikh Sharif Sheikh Ahmed who had sent all the right international signals aimed at humanizing his organization as a friend and not foe of the West. Sheikh Ahmed had written a cordial letter to Washington saying he wanted to be a friend of the US.[12] To skeptical State Department officials, Ahmed's charmed offensive was nothing more than a charade meant to buy the militants time to consolidate their gains.

In a last ditch effort to cajole Ethiopia's warhorses for possible military action in Somalia, the US assembled a powerful delegation to confront the lackadaisical leadership in Addis Ababa, and bring it back to its senses. Attending the meeting held in the Prime Minister's office in Addis Ababa on October 26, 2006 were US Acting Ambassador to Ethiopia Vicki Huddleston, General Carl Fulford (ret.), Ambassador Peter Chaveas from the African Center for Strategic Studies (ACSS), Major General Robertus C.N. Remkes from US European Command (EUCOM J5), Michael Phelan, a Senate Foreign Relations Committee staffer, and a US political and economic staffer.[13]

The meeting started off on the wrong footing. Prime Minister Meles Zenawi quietly let drop that original plan to deploy Uganda and Sudan as part of IGAD's intervention force, IGASOM, was off the table. With the cover of an African multilateral force now blown, Ethiopia was having a tough time considering whether to act alone. Zenawi explained that Uganda was planning to host the Commonwealth Heads of Government Meeting (CHOGM) with Queen Elizabeth II scheduled to open the conference a year away on Saturday November 24, 2007. He had learned that Uganda had become gun shy following intense pressure from a prominent member of the Commonwealth that insisted that sending Uganda troops to Somalia would be "inconsistent" with serving as host of the upcoming Commonwealth Summit. US officials at once suspected that the "prominent member of the Commonwealth" that Prime Minister Zenawi was talking about was none other than the United Kingdom.[14]

Although a very close US ally on all matters of global security, the UK was doggedly opposed to intervention of frontline states (FLS) in Somalia. It had adopted exactly the same position that America had taken in killing IGASOM. After the ICU's rout of the warlords in June 2006, and Washington's abrupt U-turn on the question of involving FLS in Somalia, the British stood pat on their conviction that involving FLS in Somalia was flirting with disaster, a view it pushed among African members of the Commonwealth.

As the meeting progressed, the US delegation dangled some sweeteners to Zenawi. The Ethiopian Army could expect some robust logistical military support, theirs to keep after the big showdown with the Mogadishu Islamists. The Ethiopian leader softened his stance a bit. Despite the lack of an international cover for sending Ethiopian troops into Somalia, Zenawi told the gathering, not all was pessimistic about such a venture. Ethiopia had long considered going it alone in Somalia anyway.

Like hungry vultures anxious that the carrion might suddenly get up and walk away, the Americans quickly pounced on the statement. Gen. Fulford pointedly asked the Prime Minister whether IGAD countries and the African Union (AU) would rally behind a unilateral Ethiopian military action in Somalia to defend the TFG. "I am confident of the support from Uganda and Kenya," Zenawi replied. "As a matter of fact," he added conspiratorially, "President Museveni wants Ethiopia to move more quickly."[15] Zenawi reiterated that he was not at all concerned about the AU squawking too loudly about such an intervention. The GOE had already discussed with leaders in the AU Commission the very real possibility of an Ethiopian military intervention in Somalia. There was an understanding on the matter. Zenawi concluded that the AU "should at least not pose a problem."

The American delegation left, buoyant with a sense of accomplishment. There was now movement. Ethiopia would act. All that was left was working out the finer details, the logistics and international support for the military incursion to roll into Somalia.

## Blazing Shuttle Diplomacy

On the to-do list before Ethiopia's army could enter Somalia was the urgent need to reel in skeptical European allies. It was going to be a tough sell to Europeans who had long bought the US argument that disaster awaits FLS in Somalia. Jendayi Frazer was the person for the job. Her soft round face belied a steely woman with the tenacity of a pit bull.[16] Pleasant, agreeable and quick to laugh by nature, Frazer was unapologetically tough as nail when it came to pushing issues of US national interests. She was by turn aggressive without seeming to be in a hurry, quick thinking while giving the impression of being easy-going and laid-back. She knew precisely when to use her charms and when to deploy her needle-sharp influence.

Called upon to deliver by getting European and African support for an Ethiopian military incursion into Somalia, Dr. Frazer took to the diplomatic offensive like duck to water. Only a few months earlier, she had worked hard to head off the intervention of frontline African states in Somalia. Now, she seemed uniquely qualified to succeed in doing the opposite. With Ethiopia in the bag, the US diplomat worked to convince reluctant allies to back the plan. She crisscrossed the continent in a Gulfstream jet, her sole and only goal to provide effective cover for the ENDF to move into Somalia at the earliest possible opportunity. Her talking point was straight forward enough. Each passing day gave the ICU militants with ties to al Qaeda opportunity to entrench themselves in Mogadishu, a development the US wanted to nip in the bud. Top on Frazer's list of appointment on the continent was Uganda's President Yoweri Museveni. The two had an excellent working relationship. Museveni, an avowed Africanist, respected Frazer as a top American diplomat but, as an African-American, he welcomed her as a daughter of Africa.

His own man, and one to speak his mind with brutal clarity, President Museveni was far from being a stooge for American foreign policy or anyone else's. Instead his involvement in Somalia was a commitment born out of deep ideological conviction that pre-dated the American mess in Somalia.[17] The only African head of state to enter post-Barre Somalia, Museveni demonstrated a singular bravery by flying into war-torn Mogadishu on October 3, 1992. Huddled in a hot crowded room with no air conditioning at a private villa in south Mogadishu, Museveni addressed Somali leaders including General Farah. He was there to show solidarity with the Somali people, he told them. Fighting each other was not the answer, the Uganda leader counseled. Invoking the nationalism of the anti-colonial fighter

Mad Mullah who defied the British in the 1880s in order to free Somalia, the younger and fresh-faced Museveni appealed directly to General Aidid and other influential Somali leaders to unite behind a common peace solution.[18]

Years passed, and the warring in Somalia continued. More than a decade later, President Museveni retained his commitment and sense of obligation toward the suffering people of Somalia. The way he saw it, African nations needed to sort out crises in their own backyard. Museveni then took a principled position on intervention. To whoever cared to listen, he advocated doing whatever was necessary, including military intervention, to stop the country from descending into further violence. But he also insisted on the backing of the international community before sending Uganda troops in harm's way in Somalia

To make sure President Museveni was still onside for an intervention on Somalia, Frazer met the leader in London, UK on Tuesday, November 21, 2006.[19] Museveni reiterated the same point he had been making for several years, and from which he had never deviated. Uganda was ready to send a battalion to protect the TFG in Baidoa. What was needed was the UN mandate in hand to do so. Furthermore, Museveni added that the question of logistics for supporting the troops needed to be sorted out before boots hit the ground. To Frazer's relief, Museveni confirmed what Zenawi revealed to the US delegation a month earlier. Ugandan leader was fully aware that only Ethiopia's presence in the vicinity of Baidoa was preventing the ICU from overrunning the TFG. Still, Museveni was insistent that IGAD and not Ethiopia take on the mission, noting a battalion of Uganda soldiers with tanks was "ready and waiting."[20]

Frazer told Museveni that in order to maintain flexibility the US was talking to the UK to allow the tweaking of the Operative Paragraph 2 of the UNSC resolution that precluded the deployment of frontline states. Although she did not say it in so many words, the flexibility the US was seeking was the involvement of Ethiopia in the Somalia mission.

Reassured after meeting Museveni, Frazer huddled with her officials to prepare for a much harder conversation later the same day with cynical senior UK officials in charge of African affairs. She was well aware that involving frontline states in any military action inside Somalia was the line in the sand the British would not cross. With hardly any pushback from African nations around the idea of Ethiopia's intervention in Somalia, she could afford to crank up her diplomatic offensive to overcome the last hurdle created by UK's opposition.

Jendayi Frazer brought from the US Embassy in London the US Deputy Chief of Mission David T. Johnson and political affairs officer Richard M. Mills, Jr.[21] Accompanying the UK Parliamentary Under-Secretary of State, Foreign and Commonwealth Office (FCO) Lord Triesman were FCO Africa Director Andrew Lloyd, FCO Head of East Africa and Horn Section Ben Lyon, and a representative of Secretary of State for International Development Hilary Benn. As expected, with typical British bluntness, Lord Triesman did not bother to hide his deep displeasure over the development in Somalia. The sudden insistence by the US on an intervention force in Somalia that included frontline states was a non-starter for him. A bothered Lord Triesman wasted no time putting it to those around the table that he was least interested in the idea.

Moreover, Lord Triesman lamented, the previous day he spent "the gloomiest seven hours in a very long time" in the British House of Lords fending off spirited attacks from the Opposition that UK foreign policy played second fiddle to Washington.[22] Hansard, the official record of proceedings in the British Parliament, indeed, showed that on Monday

November 20, 2006, Lord Triesman endured sharp-tongued jabs in the Upper House from Lord David Howell of Guildford. Among the verbal grenades lobbed at Lord Triesman, Howell accused British foreign policy of lacking backbone, saying,

> United Kingdom foreign policy at present does not reach a very high level. It is in fact, as one kindly commentator put it the other day, a foreign policy in limbo. We are waiting on others. At the moment, we are all waiting to see what Mr. James Baker and Mr. Lee Hamilton have to say in their Iraq Study Group. When they say something, no doubt we will respond in some way or another.... In effect, we are chained to the chariot wheel of United States policy in Iraq and waiting for a change in the wind there, if one is coming.[23]

Lord Triesman had jumped to his feet at 10:00 p.m. to respond to Lord Howell's biting accusation, retorting, "The United States relationship is not shallow, as he knows, and I do not think that it would be right to describe our work with Europe as a flop."[24]

Obviously still smarting from the stinging attacks from peers in the British Upper House, Lord Triesman was in no mood to play ball on Somalia. Frazer, cool as a cucumber, ignored the glowering baron, instead asking for UK's support in getting a United Nations Security Council Resolution (UNSCR) on Somalia that was "flexible enough that frontline states could play a positive role."[25] She revealed that African Union members especially Uganda was ready to sign off on the idea, and that only the UK was holding matters up.

Lord Triesman had also met President Museveni the previous day and voiced his opposition to the idea of involving FLS in Somalia. Facing Frazer, he argued stridently that the whole idea made no sense to him. On the one hand, the UK was expected to support a UN Security Council resolution that allowed the Ethiopians to intervene in Somalia, yet "inevitably, we would be asked to denounce Ethiopia in the UN," he reasoned.[26]

Without conceding the point, Frazer countered that America had not yet given Ethiopia the green light to send troops into Somalia. This was not true, of course, but it did not matter. Frazer was happy to note that Ethiopia's intervention in Baidoa had saved the Somali Transitional Federal Government (TFG) led by Abdullahi Yusuf Ahmed. She also pointed out that the two countries were merely "five words apart" on the draft UNSC resolution. "It must not be worded so narrowly that we have to come back to the Council in two months," she argued forcefully.

Unable to conceal his impatience any longer, Lord Triesman shot back. While the US had a point for crafting a flexible UNSCR that took the long view of a stable Somalia, UK Secretary of State for International Development Hillary Benn was convinced that involving frontline states in Somalia would be "fatal".

Deadlocked, the meeting was adjourned for the following day Wednesday, November 22, 2006. The same faces from the previous day were at the table.[27] The only addition was Secretary Benn who chose to personally attend the meeting. Benn demanded that the Operative Paragraph 2 of the draft UNSCR include specific language excluding troops from frontline states in Somalia. Frazer, pulling the classic shell game of diplomacy, appeared to concede without really bending, pushed back hard. She argued that UK concerns were taken care of in the Preamble of the draft UNSCR. As it were, highlights for this section of the draft were lifted right out of the sub-regional organization IGAD's statement on keeping frontline states' troops out of Somalia. However, she went on, the US was intent on moving forward with a draft resolution that was flexible enough to allow frontline states to enter Somalia, if needed. What's more, the US had enough support from members of the UN Security Council to push through the draft Resolution.

Frazer's take it or leave it approach left little room for the UK politicians to say no to the draft resolution that could see Ethiopia cross into Somalia. Thankfully, Lord Howell was not in attendance to witness confirmation of his earlier argument in the House of Lords that on matters of foreign policy the UK held on to aprons of the Americans.

## Green light at Last

On December 6, 2006, as members of the UNSC prepared to debate the draft resolution 1725 at the United Nations in New York later in the day, the issue of Somalia came up in the British House of Commons. Susan Kramer, the Member of Parliament for Richmond Park asked UK Secretary of State Hilary Benn to assure the British people that troops from frontline states would not be deployed in Somalia. When Benn rose to respond to the question, he chose his words carefully. The exchange was recorded in the Hansard:

> Susan Kramer (MP for Richmond Park): The Secretary of State referred to the US draft resolution that would give the intergovernmental authority on development in Somalia the power to bring in peacekeeping troops, and which includes a partial lifting of the arms embargo. The Arab League is facilitating the peace talks but is concerned that the resolution could spark an expansion of serious civil war in Somalia and lead to a broader regional conflict. Will he do what he can to ensure that the focus is on making the peace talks effective and that military force is used to support a ceasefire instead of creating further conflict?

> Hilary Benn: I agree completely. The situation is very delicate and volatile. The Hon. Lady has set out precisely the matters that the UN Security Council will take into account when considering the US resolution. As IGAD itself has said, it is very important that front-line states are not involved in support and training missions.... When she gets an opportunity to read the resolution, she will see that it lays a heavy emphasis on the peace negotiations that have been taking place in Khartoum. As I said earlier, the peace process is the only way forward for Somalia.[28]

Despite Benn's assurance, UNSCR 1725 passed later the same day in New York. The fingerprints of the US were smudged all over it. Cleverly written to avoid the mention of frontline troops intervening in Somalia, Paragraph 1 of the resolution pointedly left a back door wide open for troops from frontline states to enter Somalia. It stated in part that it "affirms therefore that the following provision of the present resolution, based on the decisions of IGAD and the Peace and Security Council of the African Union, aim solely at supporting peace and stability in Somalia through an inclusive political process and creating the conditions for the withdrawal of all foreign forces from Somalia."[29]

Without appearing to do so, essentially, UNSCR 1725 not only authorised in Paragraph 3 of the Resolution under IGASOM, for AU troops to enter Somalia, it practically gave blessing for certain unspecified foreign troops to get into Somalia ahead of the AU deployment and to remain in Somalia until conditions were right for them to withdraw. In other words, with the UNSC blessings, a country (i.e. Ethiopia) keen to send its troops into Somalia could do so. The only condition was that such an action must be taken before IGAD forces were deployed on the ground. In a nutshell, UNSCR 1725 was the international green light Ethiopia was waiting for to invade Somalia with massive force.

The Ethiopian invasion of Somalia happened two and half weeks later on Wednesday December 20, 2006. Supported by American intelligence, the Ethiopian National Defense Forces (ENDF) first took Baidoa in the northwest of Somalia. Then, in a lightning move in tanks and armoured vehicles, the ENDF moved swiftly toward Mogadishu. As anticipated and planned by the US, the Islamists militias were no match against the mighty Ethiopian army. It crumpled and scattered, mostly retreating southward toward Afgooye and Kismaayo. The ICU leadership including chairman Sheikh Sharif Sheikh Ahmed fled Mogadishu, first settling in Kenya where he was briefly detained, and later travelling to Yemen where he stayed under virtual house arrest in Sana'a.[30] Within days, the invading force reached the outskirt of the city and, without much of a fight, Mogadishu fell on Thursday December 28, 2006. In early January 2007, Ethiopian Forces captured ICU's last stronghold of Kismaayo, and the TFG was able to enter Mogadishu.

In both the British House of Lords and House of Commons, the issue of Somalia was completely absent from the agenda for most part of early 2007. Interestingly, Lord Triesman devoted considerable time in the House of Lords on January 30, 2007 reporting on the escalating conflict in Darfur, Sudan, and the following day, January 31, 2007 on the controversial appointments of Kenya's electoral commissioners but, uncharacteristically, kept a stiff upper lip on events unfolding in Somalia.[31]

Ethiopian Prime Minister Meles Zenawi had no such reticence. The day after New Year's Day 2007 on the Gregorian calendar,[32] he triumphantly took to the podium in the Ethiopian Parliament and, in an upbeat speech, wowed parliamentarians with stories of the lightning success of the ENDF invasion of Somalia. The Somali people had turned out in throngs to welcome the ENDF with songs of praise and dances. "We have routed the forces that stuck to our back like a thorn, removing it in good time (before it caused significant damage) with a proportional response," Zenawi said to wild applauses and hoots.[33] "As far as Ethiopia is concerned, we have achieved our main objective," he added. "Our next focus will be the return of our forces and strengthening our ongoing struggle against poverty." This time the applause was thunderous. It was followed by a standing ovation.

# 5

# African Union Mission to Somalia (AMISOM)

On Thursday, January 4, 2007, barely forty-eight hours after his triumphant speech to the Ethiopian Parliament, Prime Minister Meles Zenawi, impeccably dressed in a tailored dark striped suit, sat brooding in his spacious office at the Grand Menelik Palace in Addis Ababa. His long-time loyal personal assistant Atto Gebretensai Gebremichael, sat nearby, silent. The prime minister was waiting for the US delegation. He was going to push for the withdrawal of Ethiopian troops from Somalia. He did not have to wait long. The Americans led by Jendayi Frazer were soon ushered in. With Frazer was US Ambassador to Ethiopia Donald Yamamoto, Charge d'affaire Vicki Huddleston, US Ambassador to Kenya Michael Ranneberger, US Special Envoy for Somalia John Yates, CJTF-HOA Commander Rear Admiral Richard Hunt, CJTF-HOA Foreign Policy Advisor (POLAD) Fred Cook, African Affairs Special Assistant Fatuma Sanneh, AF/E Somalia Desk Officer Nole Garey, and Eric Wong, the US deputy political and economic counselor in Addis Ababa. Wong was the designated note-taker.[1]

The Americans knew going in that this would be a bumpy meeting. The Ethiopians had done the US a big favour by getting rid of the ICU in Mogadishu. Now, the US needed to come up with plans for next steps. But the American team was ill prepared for what was to come in the meeting. At first, Zenawi listened attentively as Jendayi Frazer laid out a catalogue of itinerary of her travel to secure support for deployment of African troops in Somalia. The to-do list was impressive. The top US diplomat for Africa was scheduled to chair a meeting of the International Contact Group on Somalia the following day, Friday January 5, 2007 in Nairobi. She planned to follow that with a face-to-face conversation with Uganda's President Yoweri Museveni on the deployment of Ugandan troops to Somalia. She also planned to make quick trips to Djibouti and Yemen. Hopefully, accompanied by Kenyan Foreign Minister Raphael Tuju and UN Special Representative of the Secretary General (SRSG) to Somalia François Lounceny Fall, she planned to travel to Mogadishu. The focus of that trip was to consult with TFG Prime Minister Ali Mohamed Ghedi, civil society and clan leaders on the way forward. There, she planned to emphasize US commitment for Somalia.

When his turn came to speak, Zenawi politely reminded Frazer that the ENDF was stretched thin over vast territory of southern Somalia. Somali resistance was popping up everywhere, and growing fiercer by the hour. Ethiopian troops needed to withdraw to avoid becoming a lightning rod for Somali resistance. Asked about the timeline for troop withdrawal from Somalia, Zenawi shocked his US guests with his nonchalant response. The ENDF should begin withdrawing within two weeks, he said, with one week dedicated to "mopping" up operations. In that time, the PM hoped the international community would have gotten their act together to deploy a neutral force to step into the void left by withdrawing Ethiopian troops. The continental troops he hoped would come from Uganda,

Yemen and Rwanda.

The mood in the room abruptly changed. The announcement had sucked out the very air from within the room. Jendayi Frazer could barely breathe. Visibly upset, the US team exchanged quiet stunned glances. The timetable was downright impossible to meet. It was sheer lunacy. Even for a miracle worker, Frazer knew there was no way to beat the bushes and raise replacement troops within two weeks. The best bet was Uganda's offer of troops. But President Museveni needed at least three weeks to consult with his cabinet and parliament. Frazer promised to give it her best shot, before retreating to plot a new strategy. There was not much time to waste. The US team had to hit the ground running to get things moving.

The following day, Friday, January 5, 2007, clearly on a mission, Frazer co-chaired the meeting of the International Contact Group on Somalia in Nairobi, Kenya. The other co-chairs were Kenyan Foreign Minister Raphael Tuju and Norway's Deputy Foreign Minister Raymond Johansen.[2] In attendance were representatives from the European Union (Presidency and European Commission), Italy, Kenya, Norway, Sweden, Tanzania, United Kingdom, United States, African Union, and Intergovernmental Authority on Development (IGAD), League of Arab States, and the United Nations. Frazer wasted little time getting to the point. The U.S. Government would provide $40.5 million in new assistance for Somalia. She added that it was a "down payment" with further support to be expected down the road. She reminded the gathering that the US had already earmarked US$19 million to support the international peacekeeping in Somalia. She wanted quick action on this, with something on the table by the end of two weeks.

In marked contrast to the aloof US attitude of the previous year, there was a new sense of urgency in the communiqué issued at the end of the meeting.[3] The US now challenged the Contact Group to do more to facilitate the deployment of a stabilization force in Somalia based on UNSC Resolution 1725. Kenya promised to dispatch a high-powered delegation led by foreign minister Raphael Tuju to different African capitals to scour for troops. Uganda had already pledged troops and was working with US planners on the logistics for deployment in late January 2007. In all, the operation called for 8,000 peacekeeping troops.

To Frazer's irritation, previously keen on deployment, the EU now seemed to hold back; Italy led the pack putting on the brakes. The EU offered to fund the peacekeeping operations on condition that the TFG held discussions with all segments of the Somali society. Such a discussion could take months, even years in the making. The US had no time for discussion of that nature. Always the spoilers in the eyes of US diplomats, the Europeans had to either put up or shut up. The US was on the move and would brook no nonsense even from its own allies. Frazer wanted to see immediate action. She concluded the meeting on that note. Action now was the marching orders to all US diplomats on Continental Africa, Europe and at the UN.

## Preparation for Deployment

Frazer worked late into early Saturday morning before turning into bed for a couple of hours of sleep. She had talked with various EU diplomats, shoring support among the most recalcitrant of the lot, Italy. She also sat with African leaders. Those willing to consider, let alone commit, to providing troops were few. Uganda's offers of troops, thankfully, was still standing firm.

On Saturday, January 6, 2007, bug-eyed from lack of sleep, Frazer flew to the Yemeni port city of Aden. Here amidst the antiquity and tall white minarets, some dating centuries before Christ was born, Frazer met with Yemeni President Ali Abdullah Saleh and Foreign Minister Abu Bakr Abdullah al-Qirbi.[4] Four months back, on September 23, 2006, already in office for sixteen years since the unification of North and South Yemen in 1990, President Saleh was declared an overwhelming victor for another seven-year term. European Union election observers had declared the polls mostly free and fair. But opposition leader Faisal bin Shamlan accused Saleh of rigging the ballots. The continuing rumbling from disgruntled Yemeni was getting louder, with Iranian-backed al-Houthi rebels openly fighting government forces in Saada region, northwest of Sana'a, on the border of the Kingdom of Saudi Arabia.[5] Yemen could support the international effort in Somalia in other ways, perhaps by facilitating talks with exiled Somali leaders including the chairman of the ICU Sheikh Sharif Sheikh Ahmed who remained under house arrest in Kenya but planned to seek asylum in Sana'a. Troops contribution for an African-led mission in Somalia was out.

After two hours of discussion, Abu Bakr Abdullah al-Qirbi escorted Frazer to the hastily convened news conference. al-Qirbi, a short and balding man in designer gold-rimmed glasses that gave him the appearance of a cultured professor, was a graduate of the University of Edinburgh, Scotland where he studied internal medicine. Impeccable as he was effusive, the minister thanked Frazer for the visit. The two nations had agreed to continue to pursue common interests in peace, security and stability of Somalia, he said in perfect English. Frazer repeated the exact same phrase, saying, "I discussed with President Saleh and Foreign Minister Abu Bakr al Qirbi joint work to support Somali people and creating means to guarantee restoring security, peace and stability in Somalia."[6]

Frazer then flew out to Djibouti where she met briefly with President Ismail Omar Guelleh. Mindful of the hard currency the US was pumping into his coffers to pay for Camp Lemonnier, Guelleh listened with sympathetic ears to Frazer's pleas for troops for Somalia. He could not pledge outright the number he could commit on the ground. However, Guelleh promised to do something for friendship sake. Tired, frustrated with nothing concrete to show for the hard work, Frazer flew back to Nairobi later the same day, still scrambling for troops for Somalia, empty-handed.

The following day, Sunday January 7, 2007, did not bring better luck. Frazer's planned venture into Mogadishu was scrapped. Her itinerary had leaked and was now widely known. The hardline Islamists, more than likely, were waiting to give her a rousing Mogadishu-style welcome, complete with RPG, mortar shells and small arms fire. She would have been the highest ranking US official to set foot in Somalia since the hasty retreat of US troops in the spring 1994. Instead Frazer appeared at a news conference with UN Special Representative François Lounceny Fall. She called on the Somali government of Abdullahi Yusuf to start a dialogue with defeated members of the Islamic Courts Union (ICU) toward establishing peace in Somalia. More urgently, more troops were needed for the deployment of continental forces in Somalia.

## A Fool's Errand

Monday January 8, 2007, was a busy day for everyone. Dr. Jendayi Frazer was up before dawn. The big plan had Kenya's senior cabinet ministers divvy up travels to different African capital cities in search of troops for the Somalia mission. The list included South Africa, Rwanda, Angola, Algeria, Nigeria, Ghana, Benin and perhaps Senegal.[7] Quietly slipping out of Jomo Kenyatta International Airport, Kenya's Foreign Minister Raphael Tuju and his entourage flew to South Africa. It was the beginning of what proved to be a fool's errand, with nothing to show for it at the end. In Pretoria, Tuju was out of luck. South Africa's President Thabo Mbeki refused to bite the plan to send troops to Somalia. As explained by Deputy Foreign Minister Aziz Pahad, South Africa was committed elsewhere to other missions.[8] The real likely reason for rejecting the request was because South Africa did not want to be seen to be fighting a US war in Africa.

The hunt for troops came up empty elsewhere too. Kenya's Minister for Local Government Musikari Kombo, on January 11, 2007, presented Rwanda's President Paul Kagame with a formal request for troops for Somalia. Kagame did not come out with a flat no. Aware the US was behind the request, tactfully, the leader responded that Rwanda would find the appropriate role to play in Somalia.[9] Similar non-responses were given to Ethiopian Foreign Minister Seyoum Mesfin who was given a weak assurance of troop contribution by Nigeria and Libya, a support role by Algeria, and a flat refusal by Angola.[10] Nigeria was evasive and noncommittal when pressed for specifics. In any case, it could not meet the end of January 2007 deadline to deploy troops. Algeria, meanwhile, was willing to provide logistics, perhaps planes to ferry troops from committed countries. Meanwhile, a delegation to the Democratic Republic Congo and Angola led by Ethiopian Tourism Minister Mahmoud Dirir fared no better. Angola was emphatically clear about not sending troops to Somalia. Barely five years had gone by since the Angolan people emerged from a war that ravaged the country for almost two decades and half. Angola had enough trouble of its own without looking for more elsewhere in the deserts of Somalia.[11] In DRC, the delegation was provided with refreshments, best wishes and sent on its way.

Some African nations, however, saw in the invitation to send troops to Somalia an opportunity to beef up personal armies. That was the case with Government of The Gambia (GOTG). US Ambassador to Gambia Joseph Stafford was skeptical Gambia could raise the 500 requested by AU Commissioner Said Djinnit. In a confidential cable to Washington, Stafford concluded almost sarcastically, "Nonetheless, the GOTG doubtless remains keen to burnish its foreign peacekeeping credentials—and garner the attendant financial benefit for its forces—and hence might well be prepared to supply some troops for a Somalia mission, although probably less than 500."[12] Stafford who retained utter disdain for Gambia's President Yahya Jammeh whom he described in one confidential diplomatic cable as "an irascible president",[13] nonetheless, met with Gambia's foreign minister Bala Garba Jahumpa on Thursday, January 18, 2007 on the matters of troops to Somalia. Jahumpa repeated Gambia's request for foreign donors to equip troops going to Somalia. Ambassador Stafford responded that the US effort was focused on getting resources to support Ugandan troops already in theatre. At that moment, the US was not able to make promises to potential troops contributing countries. In the follow-up confidential cable to Washington, Stafford doubted Gambia could raise troops larger than the 196 men it already contributed to Darfur. Stafford did not rule out the possibility that Gambia could come through with the troops, but he did not push it hard either.

Six weeks later, on Friday March 2, 2007, Gambia's Chief of Defense Staff (CHOD) Colonel Lang Tombong Tamba met with Ambassador Stafford in Banjul.[14] Col. Tamba tipped the real motive of his government by asking that the US support include 10 armoured personnel carriers in order to increase the size of troops in Darfur. The American envoy shrewdly noted that the Gambian army was a puny 1000 troops. Col. Tamba calmly responded that additional personnel could be drawn from the Gambian national guards.

Ambassador Stafford said he would advise Washington of the request. There was no mention of Somalia this time.

On January 24, 2007, Rwanda's State Minister for Cooperation told US Ambassador Michael Arietti that Rwanda could support the AMISOM mission with training of troops or with civilian police (civpol).[15] But it was disinclined to send Rwandan Defense Forces (RDF) on the Somalia mission. She reminded the ambassador that Rwanda had already deployed troops in Darfur as part of African Union Mission in Sudan (AMIS). Behind the scene, US officials were aware of Rwanda's unhappiness with the level of AU logistical and medical support for its troops serving in Darfur. Salaries were often several months late. Rwanda was not interested in the Somalia mission.[16]

Rwanda's attitude mirrored what many African nations were thinking—this was clearly someone else's issue. On Saturday, January 27, 2007 African heads of states gathered in the Ethiopian capital for the Eighth Ordinary Session of the Assembly of the African Union (AU Summit). Somalia was at the top of the summit's agenda scheduled for January 29-30, 2007. Jendayi Frazer, accompanied by US Ambassador to Ethiopia Donald Yamamoto and US political-economic counselor Eric Wong, met with Prime Minister Meles Zenawi again in Addis Ababa. Things were looking desperate. The Ethiopian premier was not happy to see Frazer. The US had not helped matters by going after the few al-Qaeda operatives holed up in different parts of Somalia. Three days earlier, US warplanes bombed several places where suspected al-Qaeda fighters were operating. Frazer's explanation to Zenawi was that some of the ICU leaders were "devoted to chaos", and that it was preferable to work with Sheikh Sharif Sheikh Ahmed.[17] This would pre-empt hardliners from using him as a figurehead for their ends. US Ambassador to Kenya Ranneberger had met with the Somali Islamist leader in Nairobi, and urged him to renounce violence. She feared further talks would be futile if Sheikh Sharif left Kenya for Yemen.

Zenawi was sympathetic. Ethiopia was already doing all it could. The ENDF was training the TFG police and army. Weaponry was not a major issue. The problem was organisation and skills. The TFG forces had none. It was a disaster. The AU force was needed "to give space and time to the TFG to sort out its political and security problems," Meles said.[18] A minimum of two to four thousand troops was needed. Meles Zenawi said he was planning to personally ask Paul Kagame to send troops. Rwandese troops were excellent he said, and would make good contribution. Nigeria was a tough nut to crack. President Olusegun Obasanjo was for deployment. The Nigerian military brass was not. It was a wait and see game said Zenawi. Frazer did not tell the Ethiopian leader that the US had struck out in Rwanda, and although it was continuing with the lobbying in Nigeria, nothing concrete had come of it.

On the positive side, Zenawi said the Chief of Defense Forces of Uganda People's Defence Forces (UPDF) Gen. Aronda Nyakairima was already coordinating with the ENDF for the deployment of Uganda troops. Uganda was still keen to do what needed done. Not all was lost. Frazer added she learned Malawi could contribute troops. She had the $19 million dollars from the US government ready for supporting the deployment. She also revealed the US government was pushing the EU hard to release the African Peace Facility funds that were earmarked for Somalia. The United Kingdom, Norway and Sweden were on side in the effort to shake loose the money from the European purse. The perennial thorn in the bush was Italy, which was still not playing ball. The meeting ended politely. Zenawi left to meet other African heads of states coming to his town.

One thing was clear. Ethiopia wanted out of Somalia as quickly as AMISOM troops could be corralled to replace the ENDF. Already troops were fighting an increasingly confident insurgency. Not a good sign.

The following day, Sunday, January 28, 2007, Jendayi Frazer sought out President Yoweri Museveni who was in Addis Ababa on the eve of the African Union Summit. With Museveni was Uganda's ambassador to Ethiopia Edith Grace Ssempala. The latter had served as Uganda's ambassador to the US for many years. Frazer brought along US Permanent Representative to the AU (USAU) Ambassador Cindy Courville, USAU Military Advisor Colonel Timothy Rainey, AF/Sudan Program Groups Director Lauren Landis, AF Special Assistant Fatuma Sanneh, and deputy political-economic counselor Eric Wong.[19] Frazer wanted to know how preparations for deployment of Ugandan troops to Somalia were proceeding. Upbeat and in a jovial mood, President Museveni responded that things were looking up. Uganda's Parliament was debating the deployment plan before approving it. If all went according to plan, Ugandan troops could hit the ground in four to five days, in fact as early as February 1 or February 2. The primary mission would be to support the TFG and provide training for Somali forces. Ambassador Ssempala piped in that the AU, IGAD, TFG and potential troops contributing countries were planning to meet the following week in Addis Ababa, suggesting further delay of the mission. Museveni, clearly impatient with any further delay, brushed aside Ambassador Ssempala's unsolicited input. He hoped, by then, his troops would have deployed in Somalia. He added that Uganda troops were ready for anything short of a general insurgency. Uganda military had experience of Somalia, he expanded, giving Frazer a quick history lesson. Uganda troops fought in Somalia against the Italians during the Second World War and as part of colonial contingent known as the King's African Rifles (KAR).[20]

President Museveni was never shy to let the world know that his troops were very competent lot, not the hapless and feckless blunderers like others who went to Somalia before them. Earlier in the month, on Friday, January 5, 2007, while launching the planning for the Commonwealth Heads of Government in Kampala, President Museveni had declared to assembled Western diplomats, "Our peacekeeping is different from these Western countries. The Western countries do not listen carefully. They are full of themselves, they think they know everything. That's why they make mistakes."[21]

Obviously pleased with Museveni's unshakable commitment to Somalia, Frazer repeated her talking points. There was $19m for troops deployment. Italy was still playing games with funds from the European Union. EU Development Commissioner Louis Michel was in Italy's camp. He wanted the funds released on condition that political dialogue was restarted among Somali leaders and the restoration of impeached TFG Parliamentary Speaker Sharif Hassan Sheikh Adan. Even so, the US government was doing the heavy lifting and would do everything necessary to get Uganda's troops on the ground as soon as possible.

At that moment, seated with the one man in the world who was solidly committed to sending troops to Somalia, Frazer was extremely anxious not to say anything that could make Museveni change his mind. She listened carefully to Museveni, taking in every word, as if her life depended on it. One anxious moment came for the American when Museveni observed that AU Commission Chairperson Alpha Oumar Konare seemed to have some doubts about deployment. Frazer, alarmed, immediately read too much into the comment. Konare, the two-term former president of Mali was a respected elder in the AU, where his voice carried weight. The question was whether Konare's comments could cause president Museveni to have second thoughts about deployment. After all, so much work had already gone into the planning.

Leaving nothing to chance, Frazer and her team went all out to reassure Museveni. The Commissioner for AU Peace and Security, Ambassador Said Djinnit of Algeria was very much on side for deployment. Surely Djinnit had a better understanding of the situation on the ground than Konare. Frazer also told Museveni that despite attacks against Ethiopian forces by Somali insurgents, Somali community leaders, including the Hawiye/Habar-Gidir/Ayr sub-clan, had given their words that they would welcome peacekeepers. She added that Nigeria and Malawi were ready to deploy, and Burundi would provide a battalion.

Frazer should not have worried. Once decided on a course of action, Museveni was loath to change his mind. Still, Frazer threw in as much reassurance as she could, even when it meant stretching the truth somewhat. For example, with the exception of Burundi and a tentative indication from Djibouti, all the other African countries that had been approached about contributing troops had either refused outright or given verbal commitment they did not intend on keeping. Still, Frazer told Museveni that Nigeria and Malawi were on side to contribute troops immediately. South Africa would provide planners, but the US government was pushing for equipment as well. Mozambique could be a troop contributor. Tanzania still had not responded. Ambassador Courville added that Egypt and Algeria might provide funds for airlifting troops. The meeting ended with the Americans delegation looking much relieved. Museveni was a man of his word. He was not going to cut and run for the hills as others had.

The next day, Monday, January 29, 2007, the AU General Assembly took time to speak to the agenda to send troops to Somalia. Ten days earlier, at its 69th meeting on January 19, 2007, the AU Peace and Security Council had defined the mission to be called African Union Mission to Somalia (AMISOM). It would initially deploy for a period of six months. The troops were to provide support for the Transitional Federal Institutions of Somalia, facilitate the provision of humanitarian assistance, and create conducive conditions for long-term stabilization, reconstruction and development in Somalia. 9 infantry battalions of 850 troops apiece, supported by maritime and air components would constitute AMISOM.

With all the African heads of states assembled in one place, the AU General Assembly formally recognised AMISOM's role in Somalia. The declaration from the assembly read in part:

> Calls for an immediate deployment of the African Union Mission in Somalia (AMISOM) in accordance with the decision of the 69th meeting of the Peace and Security Council (PSC) and calls on member states to contribute troops in order to avoid a security vacuum following the withdrawal of Ethiopian troops from Somalia.
>
> Urges the international community to provide financial, logistical and technical support for the deployment of AMISOM.
>
> Expresses concern that many of the pledges by the donor Community have not been honoured and calls upon the international community to disburse the funds without delay and without political preconditions.[22]

The declaration was now mostly left to Uganda to bring into reality. Before coming to the Summit in Addis Ababa, Museveni carefully laid the groundwork for committing his troops. He briefed his cabinet on the progress to deploy Uganda troops to Somalia. The decision was then made to bring the issue to Uganda's parliament for formal debate on whether Uganda troops should be deployed at all into the volatile Horn of Africa. The debate, which began on Wednesday, January 31, 2007 in Uganda's Parliament, was not without drama, and some nail-biting moments for the Americans who could only sit and watch from the visitor's gallery.[23] The previous day, opposition members of parliament had walked out in protest for a completely different matter. The government was anxious to move straight to a vote, skipping the mandated three-day rule for the issue to be debated. Unexpectedly, some members of the ruling National Resistance Movement (NRM) party opposed suspending the rule. The surprising vote was 45 against suspending the rule, 43 for suspending it, and 4 abstained. The government, faced with a rebellion within its ranks, had no choice but to defer the bill for another day. Members were concerned about rushing the bill through without proper debate. There was also demand for more information about the deployment. There were many unanswered questions. Would troops from other African nations be joining Uganda? Was there robust support and equipment for Uganda troops? Could Somali insurgents overrun Uganda troops?

Later the same day, US Ambassador to Uganda Steven Alan Browning met Uganda's Minister for Internal Affairs Ruhakana Rugunda and State Minister for External Affairs Henry Okello Oryem to ruminate over what happened in Parliament. Okello Oryem quipped that what the ambassador saw was "democracy in action".[24] It was important to reassure the rebellious members of parliament and the opposition that Uganda troops would be adequately equipped and would be joined by other African troops. The unexpected opposition, in any case, delayed the vote to the following week, Tuesday, February 6, 2007.

There were further delays while Defense and Internal Affairs Parliamentary committee studied the bill.[25] The final bill went before Parliament on February 13, 2007 for final debate and was passed by majority vote; although members of the Opposition did not participate in the debate or vote, they supported the deployment of the UPDF to Somalia.[26]

Before Uganda troops could deploy to Somalia, there were flurries of last minute preparations to complete. There was the small bureaucratic matter of United Nations Security Council Resolution 1725 that had authorized IGAD forces to be deployed to Somalia. Since this was an AU mission backed by the United Nations, that resolution no longer applied. As well, the rules of engagement needed to be defined for AMISOM troops to act in Somalia. On the evening of February 20, 2007, the UN Security Council met to consider draft resolution 1744. The meeting started at 5:38 p.m. and was adjourned at 5:50 p.m. In a little less than twelve minutes, the Council unanimously passed the resolution. Acting under Chapter VII of the Charter, the Council authorized the African Union mission to take all measures, as appropriate, to carry out support for dialogue and reconciliation by assisting with the free movement, safe passage and protection of all those involved in a national reconciliation congress involving all stakeholders, including political leaders, clan leaders, religious leaders and representatives of civil society. Section 4 specifically spelled out the mandate of the mission:

(a)  To support dialogue and reconciliation in Somalia by assisting with the free movement, safe passage and protection of all those involved with the process referred to in paragraphs 1, 2 and 3;

(b) To provide, as appropriate, protection to the Transitional Federal Institutions to help them carry out their functions of government, and security for key infrastructure;

(c) To assist, within its capabilities, and in coordination with other parties, with implementation of the National Security and Stabilization Plan, in particular the effective re-establishment and training of all-inclusive Somali security forces;

(d) To contribute, as may be requested and within capabilities, to the creation of the necessary security conditions for the provision of humanitarian assistance;

(e) To protect its personnel, facilities, installations, equipment and mission, and to ensure the security and freedom of movement of its personnel.[27]

In the days ahead, the stipulations under Article 4 would be tested in real life. For now, Uganda military planners busied themselves with last minutes checking of logistics and contingency plans for the new troops that would replace the ENDF. To help coordinate logistics with Uganda's military planners, General William E. (Kip) Ward, Deputy Commander, Headquarters US European Command, Stuttgart Germany, spent two days in Uganda, between February 27 and 28.[28] Ward, a highly decorated black American who served in Korea, Egypt, Somalia, Bosnia, Israel, and two tours in Germany, paid a quick courtesy call on President Yoweri Museveni. The Uganda leader was looking forward to seeing his troops in the field in Somalia. Museveni was grateful for US support, and Gen. Ward was gracious in thanking the leader for the troops. Sometimes, it was better for the US to play a support role rather than the lead role as was in the case of Somalia, said Gen. Ward. Museveni agreed.

The next day, Gen. Ward met with his Uganda counterparts in the Uganda military. In the meeting was Uganda Minister for Defense Crispus Kiyonga, Chief of Defense Forces General Aronda Nyakairima, Commander of Uganda's Land Forces General Wamala Katumba and Defense Permanent Secretary Brigadier Noble Mayombo. The Uganda military made several requests. Gen. Aronda asked the US to carry out maritime patrol along Somalia's long undefended coasts. It would be pointless for Uganda to make all the effort, only to have leaky coastal entry points through which illegal weapons could be smuggled into Somalia. Gen. Ward promised to raise the issue with the US Central Command whose jurisdiction included patrolling the Indian Ocean along the Somali coast.

The Ugandans also wanted to see better flow of intelligence information. To date, they complained, the US had been fairly stingy with intelligence gathered inside Somalia. Brigadier Mayombo asked when the funds for supporting the troops would be forthcoming. Gen. Ward replied that it was being worked on even as he spoke. The Congressional notification had been made, and there would be a follow-up. Ugandans also wanted to know when the training of the next contingent of troops for deployment would begin under the African Contingency Operations and Training Assistance (ACOTA). The Defense Attaché at the US Embassy in Kampala answered that the coordinator for training was due to return to Uganda and begin working on the next set of training.[29]

Back home in the US, lawmakers were working flat-out to support the Somali mission. The US Congressional notification that Gen. Ward referred to was a critical piece of legislation that allowed the US to support African troops in Somalia. Two weeks earlier on February 6, 2007, Senator Russell Feingold (D-WI) introduced Bill 492, also known as the Somalia Stabilization and Reconstruction Act of 2007.[30] The importance of the bill was underscored by the bipartisan support it received across party lines, from both Democrats (D) and Republicans (R). The bill's co-sponsors included Senator Norm Coleman (R-MN), Senator Amy Klobuchar (D-MN), Senator John Sununu (R-NH), Senator Sherrod Brown (D-OH), Senator Susan Collins (R-ME), Senator Chuck Hagel (R-NE), Senator Christopher Dodd (D-CT), and Senator Richard Durbin (D-IL). The bill directed U.S. policy to "support efforts by the people of Somalia to achieve peace, economic growth, and democracy, and to eradicate extremism and terrorism from their country and region." It specifically directed US president George Bush to appoint a special envoy for Somalia to "coordinate U.S. involvement in the region and to ensure that the U.S. government remains informed of and engaged in efforts to resolve the instability in Somalia." Further, the bill also instructed the U.S. Permanent Representative to the United Nations, at the time Alejandro Daniel Wolff, later Zalmay Khalilzad, to work with the appropriate U.N. agencies, regional organizations, nongovernmental organizations, and the international community to "establish an International Donor Trust Fund for Somalia." Most importantly, the bill authorized Bush to support a regional or international peacekeeping force for Somalia; and to provide assistance to support efforts for a peaceful resolution of the conflict in Somalia as well as the establishment of a representative government in Somalia.

To further strengthen the case for the swift passage of the bill into law, Jendayi Frazer appeared before the US Senate sub-committee for Foreign Relations chaired by Sen. Feingold on the morning of February 6, 2007. In an eloquent testimony appropriately titled "Establishing a Comprehensive Stabilization, Reconstruction and Counter-terrorism strategy for Somalia," Frazer outlined the case for US support of intervention in Somalia.[31] "The most striking lesson I took away from my early January trip to the region is this: Somalis are ready. Somalis are ready for peace; they are tired of war."[32] Then, to drive home the urgency of the need for change in Somalia, Frazer told the committee, "Several AU member states have expressed their desire to contribute troops or provide logistical support for this effort. Uganda came forward first offering to deploy 1,500 troops based on United Nations Security Council Resolution 1725. Ugandan president Museveni's initial offer has since been followed by some other countries including Ghana, Nigeria, and Burundi expressing desire to provide troops for this effort."

Again, regarding Ghana and Nigeria, Frazer may have been stretching the truth to get ahead, but it did not matter. Bill 492 was not enacted into law. Instead it formed the basis of future US commitment to Somalia generally and specifically to the peace-making effort of African troops in Somalia. In essence, it established the new US approach to Somalia, one in which the US provided support while African nations, in this case Uganda and later Burundi, Djibouti, Kenya, Sierra Leone and Ethiopia, stepped forward to set Somalia back up after years of insecurity, some of it fueled by America's own meddling policy, and some of it brought on by the Somali themselves.

At long last, after so much wrangling, waiting, and negotiations, the first African led mission into Somalia was ready for early dawn takeoff from Entebbe International Airport on Monday, March 5, 2007. It was decidedly a low-key affair, to be witnessed by a few early risers. Late Sunday afternoon, March 4, 2007, an urgent succinct message came from Mogadishu to UPDF Commander of Land Forces Gen. Wamala Katumba. The Mission compromised, abort mission! Uganda's Civil Aviation Authority (CAA) at Entebbe Airport, it turned out, had inadvertently faxed to Mogadishu the entire flight manifest for the troop airlift the next morning. The potentially fatal security breach was discovered by UPDF Contingent Intelligence Officer Major Sserunjogi Ddamulira while doing a final sweep and check at Aden Abdulle Airport to make sure there were no last minute hiccups.[33] Part of a small advance team that landed the previous week in Mogadishu, Maj. Ddamulira was already aware of one thing—the Ethiopian commanders had carefully created the impression that all was calm, quiet and peaceful in Mogadishu so as not to spook the incoming Uganda forces. The situation on the ground, however, was anything but peaceful. Eagle-eyed and alert, Ddamulira's team began closely monitoring the Somali personnel at Aden Abdulle Airport. Extremely worrisome for the intelligence officer was a Somali-Kenyan personnel named Ali, in charge of air traffic control for aircraft landing and taking off. Ali, the team suspected, was communicating vital air traffic information to the insurgents. Since he was in possession of the closely guarded flight information for the airlift of Uganda troops from Entebbe, there was no knowing who else had it and, most importantly, what they could do with that information. The prudent action was to cancel the airlift altogether, and reschedule for the early morning of Tuesday, March 6, 2007.

# 6

# The Mission Begins

Just after 8:00 a.m. on Tuesday March 6, 2007, an unmarked Russian-made Ilyusin Il-76 military cargo aircraft landed on the tarmac at Aden Abdulle International Airport in Mogadishu. The plane taxied slowly to the terminal, rolling to a stop some distance. The cargo hatch opened, and the crew began quickly unloading two Russian made BMP-2 armoured personnel carriers (APC) mounted with 30 mm 2A42 auto cannon and PKT machineguns as secondary armament, followed by a Buffel (Afrikaans for buffalo) and Mamba, both South-African made mine-resistant APCs. AU logos in large black letters were clearly stenciled on the sides of all four vehicles dressed in white paint. It was as if the African Union was keen to broadcast a simple message to Somalia and the world—the Africans have arrived on a mission for Africans by Africans.

The ramp in place, the personnel door of the aircraft opened and, one by one, out came six officers of the Uganda People's Defence Forces (UPDF) in combat fatigues, resplendent in green berets and green armbands trimmed in white and gold colours of the African Union. First out was Contingent spokesperson Captain Paddy Ankunda. Young, handsome, and smartly dressed, Capt. Ankunda would become the face of AMISOM in the weeks to come as the force settled in its new role in Mogadishu. His role and that of over two battalions comprising 1605 Ugandan avant-garde troops would form the core of African Union Mission in Somalia (AMISOM).

Within the hour, one after the other, two brand new Lockheed Martin turboprop C-130 cargo planes belonging to the Algerian Air Force landed with 376 Uganda troops, and their gear. Inside the first Lockheed, troops were instructed to remain in their seats to allow Colonel Peter Elwelu, the overall contingent commander (CONTICO) of Ugandan troops, to exit first. Elwelu, a stocky man in his prime, rose to his feet, clasping tightly the Uganda flag. He waited for the door to open before emerging triumphantly. This was it, the mission had begun, Elwelu thought as the hot humid Mogadishu air hit his face.[1]

The commander descended the steps, marched smartly to the receiving line, stopped, saluted and ceremonially handed over the Ugandan flag to AMISOM's first Force Commander (FC), Major General Levi Karuhanga. On hand to witness the arrival of the first AU troops to Somalia was the Director of AU Peace and Security Department Geoffrey Mugumya, the chief of staff of Somali Armed Forces, General Abdullahi Omar Ali, Somalia Minister for Interior Muhamud Ahmed Guled, deputy defence minister Salad Ali Jelle, Mogadishu mayor Mohammed Omar Habib Dheere, and Ethiopian commanders of various ranks. A police band belted out Somali and Uganda national anthems.[2]

As the ceremony unfolded on the airport tarmac, Gen. Karuhanga stood at attention, inscrutable, never giving a hint of what his battle-tested sinews were telling him about this mission. It was not his character to show emotion, happy or sad, his face remained the same, a sphinx. Soft-spoken, unassuming and deliberate, the commander was known for taking time to consider all possible factors, traits he developed as a veteran of the National Resistance Army (NRA) war against the Milton Obote regime in 1981 that brought

Yoweri Museveni to power in January 1986. He was among the initial five dozen fighters who started the resistance, and was accustomed to doing more with less. Following the NRA victory, Karuhanga was appointed division commander in northern Uganda in 1987. His skills as a soldier diplomat were recognized a year later when he was reassigned as a military attaché to Dar es Salaam, Tanzania from 1988 to 1990. He resumed his position as commander of 4th Division between 1990 and 1992. Along the way, he commanded troops in the face off with the plucky Lord's Resistance Army (LRA) led by Joseph Kony. In 1994 Gen. Karuhanga was appointed the second in command of the Uganda contingent (UGACON) that supported the United Nations Observer Mission in Liberia (UNOMIL), and led a battalion of 731 soldiers to serve as part of the Economic Community of West African States Monitoring Group (ECOMOG).[3]

As force commander, Gen. Karuhanga took seriously his responsibility to welcome, coordinate and deploy the Ugandan contingent as well as troops from other contributing nations. To be effective as the first commander of the extremely dangerous mission that some media commentators already predicted was DOA, dead on arrival,[4] Karuhanga never spared a minute to educate himself about the Somali, and learn more about what made them tick. Five days earlier, on the morning of Thursday, March 1, 2007, accompanied by four UPDF officers including Major Ddamulira, General Karuhanga had clandestinely arrived in Baidoa. Although his presence was a closely guarded secret, a careless remark by Baidoa's police chief Adan Biid Ahmed nearly unmask him. In excitement, the police chief told the press that the Ugandans had landed. From Kampala, force spokesperson Capt. Ankunda issued a swift denial. "There are no Ugandan troops in Baidoa; there are no Ugandan troops in Somalia," Ankunda told a reporter.[5] The ruse was imperative to allow the general time to assess the situation in Somalia from the inside. On a similar reconnaissance trip in January, the general flew with a small team from Addis Ababa, landing inside Somalia then travelling by road to Baidoa where he met with President Abdullahi Yusuf Ahmed.

Over the weekend before the mission was set to begin, Gen. Karuhanga slipped into Mogadishu. He first stayed incognito at the Ambassador Hotel on Maka al-Mukarama Road before relocating to the Global Hotel, further east in Karaan district. Wasting little time, Gen. Karuhanga huddled with his commanders for last minute planning to balance the safety and security of the troops within the parameters defined by United Nations Security Council Resolution 1744 (2007).[6] The list of assignments outlined in Section 4 of the resolution was long. With a life-span of just six months, the mission was responsible for supporting dialogue and reconciliation, assisting the free movement of the parties, providing protection for the Transitional Federal Institutions and key infrastructures, coordinating the re-establishment and training of an all-inclusive Somali security forces, creating necessary security conditions for the provision of humanitarian assistance, and protecting its personnel, facilities, installations, equipment and mission.

This was asking a lot even under normal circumstances. Mogadishu was anything but normal. When force was needed, the UNSC crafted resolution 1744 to provide plenty of room for generous interpretation by the commanders. Drawn under Chapter VII of the UN Charter, Section 4 of resolution 1744 authorised AU mission "to take all necessary measures as appropriate to carry out the following mandate".[7] Along the way, however, the operational order from the AU headquarters was to keep the mission as low-key an affair as possible. Left unclear and undefined by the African Union was what the necessary measures looked like when bullets started flying. Gen. Karuhanga, in other words, was laced in the strait jacket of the classic peacekeeper, expected to be a good soldier, mostly play diplomat, and stay out of trouble. As Maj. Ddamulira recalled, "We were to go in there, dig our trenches, stay behind the wire and keep our heads down."[8]

The running joke among the Uganda soldiers was that AMISOM was operating under Chapter 6½, not Chapter 7 of the UN Charter, effectively relegating them to the role of bystanders on the sideline, watching violence unfold on the social and political landscape of Somalia, and only intervening with force when the dynamics and the rhythm of the conflict spilled into the operation of the mission. Gen. Karuhanga had to be inventive. To mitigate the potential for confrontation between AMISOM and Somalia insurgents, he instructed his commanders to exploit every opportunity to push to the Somali people the neutrality of AMISOM. The intent was to send the right signals to calm the nerves of former ICU leadership, and educate the insurgents that the AU troops were not replacing Ethiopians troops to carry the same policy of occupation of Somalia.

The oft-quoted metaphor was that Ugandan troops were coming to Somalia to mediate the feuds between two brothers rather than to pin down the arms of one brother while the other pummeled him. At a farewell parade in Jinja town in eastern Uganda for troops shortly deploying to Mogadishu, President Yoweri Museveni clearly stated that the mission was not a peacemaking one. "We will not go to Somalia to impose peace on the Somalis, because we shouldn't do that and we can't do it. What we are going to do in Somalia is to empower our Somali brothers to rebuild their state."[9] Echoing a similar message, Col. Peter Elwelu, the man in-charge of leading Ugandan troops on the ground, confirmed that his troops were being deployed in Somalia to "sympathize with our brothers in Somalia... and help them to bring peace and security."[10] Once on the ground, AMISOM spokesman, Capt. Paddy Ankunda stood before the small coterie of reporters inside the bullet-scarred airport terminal, and repeated the message of support for the Somalia people, saying, "We are very happy to be the first African Union peacekeepers to Somalia. We are not imposing anything on Somalis. We know our mandate; we will work toward restoring law and order in Somalia without targeting anybody."[11]

The AU Peace and Security Council in Addis Ababa, similarly, reinforced the image of a benign, neutral, pacifist force with no ill intentions toward any Somali faction or group. As Ugandan troops were landing in Mogadishu, AU Commissioner for Peace and Security, Said Djinnit, summed it neatly by stating that what Somalia needed was "political process and dialogue to bring peace and stability", and not confrontation.[12] To underscore the intent of the mission as dovish and non-aggressive, the AU ordered all military vehicles and troop carriers destined for Somalia including those ferried aboard the aircrafts that morning painted in the classic white colour scheme familiarized by UN peacekeeping missions in the world's hotspots.[13] For all concerned, AMISOM was about holding hands with the people of Somalia.

But avoiding trouble in Somalia was like being in the proverbial snake pit crawling with venomous critters. One was more likely to be bitten than not. The situation in Mogadishu especially had become bad. In various neighbourhood of the city, the insurgency was gaining momentum. For weeks before the AU troops arrived not a single day passed in the sky without reports of clashes and casualties involving Ethiopian troops and insurgents. These encounters were usually brief firefights that lasted a short time. By mid-February 2007, however, the frequency with which these attacks occurred had increased. Gun-incidents punctuated the very day the first AMISOM troops arrived in Mogadishu causing a catalogue of casualties of varying degrees.[14] Early that morning, an Ethiopian patrol was peppered with small arms and RPG fire in a Mogadishu neighbourhood. In the ensuing firefight, three civilians were killed and six wounded. A further 11 Somalis died in four separate incidents around town. In the afternoon, unidentified gunmen opened fire on a police colonel as he chatted with a friend. Two civilian bystanders died in the shooting. Early in the afternoon, at another location in Mogadishu, gunmen shot dead a senior cleric and three businessmen. The men were reportedly working to set up a neighbourhood watch to prevent insurgents from using the neighbourhood as launching ground for mortars. Unknown gunmen also killed three other men in two separate incidents in the city.

The violence did not spare the AMISOM welcome ceremony at Aden Abdulle Airport. At around one-thirty in the afternoon, shortly after the colourful flag-waving ceremony had showcased a small platoon of Somali soldiers in their finest green uniform marching down the runaway, Mogadishu mayor Mohammed Dheere began to speak. Suddenly the insurgents sent their calling card that demanded the complete attention of Gen. Karuhanga, the troops and all concerned. One after the other, more than eight mortar shells landed on the military side of the airport, interrupting the pomp and circumstance, and causing VIPs to scramble for cover. Acting quickly and calmly under fire, AMISOM Chief of Staff Ugandan Colonel Emmanuel Musinguzi took command of the situation, directing defence and providing sanctuary for the dignitaries. Luckily, the poorly aimed missiles caused little damage. Shrapnel lightly injured one Somali personnel. The ceremonies were relocated and completed elsewhere.

The insurgents later denied responsibility for the mortar attacks on the AU troops. A pre-recorded message broadcasted over Mogadishu Koran Radio instead blamed Ethiopian forces for the deed. Insurgent commander Aden Hashi Ayro, however, left no doubt about his feelings toward the new African troops. The African Union peacekeepers were not welcome in the city. "It is time for the Somali youth to fight the occupation by Ethiopia and others.... The Muslims shall not surrender to non-believers," he added darkly.[15] Not long after, Eritrean information minister Ali Abdu demanded that Uganda troops withdraw from Somalia, warning of dire consequences if the troops were not pulled out.[16] It was not entirely an empty threat. There was evidence that Eritrea was aiding and abetting the insurgents in Somalia.[17]

In late afternoon, for their first night in Mogadishu, the tired and hungry Ugandan troops were trucked to the grounds of Afisiyooni, formerly a marine training school, not too far from the airport. The perimeters of their new living quarters were unfenced and, all around, ringed by higher grounds accessible to intruders from all sides. Inside what felt like a naked fishbowl, the AU troops pitched their green tarp tents but kept alert for any sign of trouble. There was no shaking the brooding sense of foreboding that hung heavy over the AMISOM troops. The occasional barking of dogs, revving of truck engines and squealing of tires, pierced the hot night. Eerily absent were the episodic tao-tao of light automatic weapons that often added to the midnight chorus in Mogadishu. Mostly, the night was uneventful.

The next day, Wednesday, March 7, 2007, brought clarity to AMISOM's carefully nurtured peaceful deployment posture. The insurgents, unable or unwilling to distinguish between the ENDF and AMISOM troops, targeted the newly arrived Ugandan troops early in the morning. During security sweep of the perimeters at Afisiyooni, soldiers discovered freshly dug grounds at the entrance that showed signs of tampering. Upon careful investigation, ordnance engineers uncovered two buried anti-vehicle landmines. Luckily, no vehicle had left or come into the perimeter before the explosives were dismantled.

Col. Elwelu had spent a sweaty restless night with his troops at Afisiyooni. He woke up already unhappy with the poorly defended area that essentially exposed his troops to danger. The discovery of the mines was the final straw. The commander decided the force had to relocate to a new defence, ahead of the hundreds of more troops arriving by the end of the day. He phoned the head of the TFG Intelligence Service, Colonel Mohamed Warsame Farah, nicknamed "Darawiish", also acting as liaison personnel with the Ugandan contingent, and asked if there was another space to review for setting up base camp. Yes, the Colonel answered, there was Halaane, near the airport, the former training ground for the Siyaad Bare military. Then the Colonel added in a worried voice, the area was practically abandoned by everyone including the insurgents because it was infested with venomous snakes and prickly thorn bushes. Unappealing as it sounded, Col. Elwelu, Major Ddamulira and a few officers piled into the Mamba and headed to the site.

The new site was strewn with dilapidated long crumpled concrete structures, overrun by thick thorn bushes taller than a man's head, and almost impenetrable even in broad daylight. From a strategic defensive consideration, it was plainly obvious why this was the most secure staging ground for AMISOM, and before that the US Task Force Ranger on that hot afternoon in October 1993 when it took on Somali warlord Farah. To the south east of the area known as Halaane, the ocean provided a natural defense for the airport, always a quick escape route for the peacekeeping forces in the event of evacuation. Meanwhile, those foolhardy enough to sneak into the base from the city side would first tangle with thick natural thorn bushes that ringed the base, and whose sharp long needles could tear a chunk of flesh off a man's face. Somalis say the Americans planted the thorn bushes by spraying seeds from aircrafts, but none really knew how they got there. Thorn bushes, in any case, are everywhere in this semi-arid country. More likely than not, sixteen years earlier, the Americans made the thorns their best allies when all around them were murderous militias eager to spill American blood. The prospects of the thorn bushes often persuaded insurgents to resort to firing from great distance wildly inaccurate mortar rounds into the base, hoping to hit something.

"This is where I am going to set up my base and, if need be, where I will die," Col. Elwelu remarked to the officers. He barked the command on the radio for the troops camped at Afisiyooni to pack up their equipment, *fanya haraka!*, do it quickly and hurry to the new site.[18] The vast space was divvied up into sectors, each unit commander instructed to get his men to work, clearing the bushes with machetes and axes. Snakes were everywhere, though nobody was bitten.

At sunset, exhausted following a brutal day of cleaning of the bushes, and relocation of equipment to the new site, the troops settled for what was supposed to be a restful second night in Mogadishu. Around six o'clock, Maj. Ddamulira's intelligence team received a tip from a credible source. There could be an insurgent attack on the Global Hotel where General Karuhanga had returned for the night. Acting swiftly, a convoy of seven clearly marked white armoured AU vehicles and trucks carrying Ugandan troops left to reinforce the Global Hotel. At KM-4 intersection, the leading Mamba was hit by a powerful IED. The crew, never having experienced a remote-controlled IED attack, mistook the explosion for a RPG attack. The Ugandans punched right back with machinegun fires. Two Uganda soldiers were wounded. The hatch of the Mamba slammed on a third soldier, hurting his head. A soldier had serious ear pain caused by a piece of shrapnel. A mortar round fired by insurgents missed the convoy and slammed into a nearby crowded restaurant. When the dust settled, thirteen civilians were dead and as many as twenty wounded in the crossfire.[19] Private Robert Bamutaraki and Lieutenant Michael Wandera, hit by shrapnel in the leg and the arm, became AMISOM's first wounded.

Despite serious damage to a tire and the water-tank, the Mamba limbed to KM-0, in the Shanghai Old city neighbourhood before finally grinding to a halt, surrounded by the other vehicles. Ethiopian and TFG troops were dispatched to the rescue, one team reaching the stricken vehicle around eight at night, while another evacuated Gen. Karuhanga to the safety of the newly established Halaane base camp. The wounded soldiers were brought back to the newly established camp to be treated by the medical team led by Commanding Officer Level 2 Field Hospital Captain Dr. Ambrose Oiko. Born in 1971 in Serere in eastern Uganda, Oiko grew up with the ambition of following his father into medical practice. Bright and focused, he attended Makerere University Medical School, Mulago where he graduated with two medical degrees. He joined the army in 1998, and was not concerned when selected to lead the first contingent medical team to Somalia. Calm under pressure, Dr. Oiko used dim light from candles to carry out emergency procedures to stabilize the wounded men. Both soldiers were flown back to Uganda on Thursday morning, March 8, 2007.[20] Wounded Somali civilians, meanwhile, piled for treatment at nearby Medina Hospital.[21]

Whether AMISOM troops intended to fight or not, was a moot point. The insurgents clearly saw AMISOM troops as legitimate targets and further pushed the commanders of the AU force toward the difficult choice of using force. The insurgents struck again earlier on Friday, March 9, 2007. The target was a TransAVIAexports Airlines IL-76TD four-engine cargo plane, registration EW-78826, rented by Jubba Airlines to airlift military equipment including six BMP-2 tanks, nine Belarus crews and six UPDF tank-drivers for the African Union peacekeeping force in Somalia.[22] The plane caught fire as it came for landing at Aden Abdulle International Airport in Mogadishu. The pilot of the plane believed his craft was hit by some kind of projectile, fired from the direction of the ocean. Some witnesses claimed that it was shot while landing, and initially AMISOM officials denied the claims.[23] Later an AMISOM signal officer who had climbed a tall structure at the time to establish a communication connection reported seeing a Jeep appearing from the direction of Medina, stopping between an oil refinery and a training school. Then as the IL-76 plane came for a landing, there was an explosion and, shortly afterward, the Jeep was seen speeding away.[24]

When the plane landed, the nine crews escaped through the emergency hatch in the flight deck and the six soldiers jumped to safety through the starboard door, unharmed. Suspiciously, the only fire truck at the airport was inoperable because the driver reportedly had gone to town, and nobody knew how to operate the vehicle. Captain Byanyima, commander of fighting vehicles organized concerted effort to put out the fire. Every available man grabbed a bucket, filled it with sand and threw it into the searing flame. The soldiers won after an hour, finally tamping down the fire. The equipment in the cargo hull was safely removed. One vehicle was slightly damaged by fire. The aircraft was beyond repair.[25]

Fortuitously, the weekend gave the AU troops the opportunity to define itself in the minds of Somalis as an army for the people, different from the Ethiopian troops accused of killing civilians. Saturday had dawned badly enough. More than sixty soldiers developed serious cases of diarrhea, keeping Dr. Oiko and his team extremely busy. The outbreak could not immediately be traced to a specific source. The medical team suspected that the illness had something to do with drinking water. Soldiers feeding on dry rations while working outdoor under humid conditions had used up allotted clean water ration, causing a drinking water crisis. The clean water purification system was still to be installed. With no extra fresh water forthcoming the thirsty troops could no longer wait. In sheer desperation some soldiers had rushed to the ocean to collect water, but retreated just as quickly after finding seawater intolerably salty and undrinkable.

Mysteriously, on Friday afternoon some soldiers seemed less intense on finding water. Someone had discovered a hidden source of sweet water that was a closely guarded secret of the few in the know. These were the lot now seriously sick. After questioning the sick soldiers, the medical team finally uncovered the truth. Indeed, the soldiers who became sick had found what they believed was clean spring water in a ravine nearby, kept the discovery secret, and had been drinking it. Sample water collected looked clean to the naked eye, but when tested was found teeming with millions of deadly microbes. The team knew they had serious cases of cholera on their hands. The sick were isolated from the main body of soldiers, treated with antibiotics and rehydrated with intravenous drips.[26] Armed sentry, meanwhile, was posted around the clock to guard the water in the ravine with strict instructions to arrest anyone attempting to collect the water.

In the midst of the cholera crisis at Halaane base, an event occurred involving the cure of a young Somali boy that some AMISOM commanders would later describe as a 'game-changer' for the direction and future of the mission.[27] Over time, it gained a mythical status. The troops had not yet put fences around the base, and Somali civilians freely walked through, some on their way to the ocean to fish, a few to spy on the new arrivals. On Saturday afternoon, March 10, 2007, a Somali man named Omar and his wife walked into Halaane Base, desperately seeking medical help for their sick 11-year old son, Hassan.[28] The bedraggled couple half-dragged and half carried Hassan. The boy was suffering from terrible diarrhea similar to what the troops were experiencing. Skeletal, Hassan was brought by his loving parents to AMISOM doctors as a last resort, the alternative being death and burial. There was a serious debate among the commanders whether to treat the boy or acquiesced to AU/UN army regulations that forbade the use of medicine meant for troops to treat civilians. When the issue reached Col. Elwelu, he turned to the one thing he knew very well—the UPDF doctrine drilled into soldiers during training and in the field by UPDF civil military cooperation (CIMIC) officers who sang the same song everyday: A jerry can of clean water, tablets of good medicine and a mug of rice are more powerful than machinegun bullets in winning the hearts and minds of the thirsty, the sick and hungry. The people's army helped people in need, AU/UN regulations be damned.

Hassan was admitted into the sickbay that afternoon, provided a bed in an army tent and given antibiotic treatment by Dr. Oiko and his medical team. When not busy with work, Uganda soldiers dropped by the sickbay to get the medical status on Hassan. This was their adopted little Somali brother, a son. Everyone prayed for the boy's recovery. A week after he came in more dead than alive, Hassan walked on his own two steady legs, his large round smiling eyes lighting up Halaane camp.[29] Ugandan soldiers cheered in happy jubilation. Hassan's parents left with a living son and, that very evening, spread the word of the miraculous cure by the AMISOM doctors. The following morning, Halaane camp was a 'sea of people'. The old, sick, dying and everyone else in between, came from all of Mogadishu neighbourhoods including Medina, which had the only functioning hospital in the city.[30] Overwhelmed by the humanity, a call was made to General Wamala Katumba, asking for direction on what to do with the multitude of sick Somali looking for medical care. At first unhappy with the development, Gen. Wamala revisited the UPDF doctrine that said, "Reach for the hearts and minds of the people, be a human first before you are a soldier." He knew then what to do to counsel the commanders in Mogadishu. If the Somali people needed medical treatment, it was a duty of the UPDF to provide it. With that, the AMISOM Outpatient Department (OPD) was born and, in years to come, turned into a cardinal feature of the peace mission in every town reclaimed by AMISOM troops. The public service was expanded to include provision of clean water and, later, food given to some women in return for cleaning Mogadishu streets with brooms. Meanwhile, assisting the army doctors as the language interpreter at that initial OPD that later became known as Gate of Hope was none other than Hassan's father, Omar.[31]

## The Curse of the Ethiopians

The real trouble, however, was the deep nationalistic passion and hatred the Ethiopian invasion had stirred in Somali people. A proud warrior stock, the Somali people seemed to bury previous clan feuds to focus solely on getting Ethiopians forces out of their land. Insurgents stepped up attacks on ENDF troops. Somali deemed collaborators of the Ethiopian forces were also targeted for assassination.[32] At the beginning of the following week, AMISOM commanders assessed the immediate predicament of the mission. Being close ally of the ENDF had some advantages and obvious drawbacks. The ENDF had the troops, the equipment needed to support the fledgling mission in difficult times. One of the first tasks for which AMISOM needed Ethiopian support was the arrival and protection of President Abdullahi Ahmed Yusuf and his cabinet expected from Baidoa. Mercifully, the polarizing Prime Minister Ali Mohamed Ghedi was already in town after riding on the wings of Ethiopian invasion, and reaching Mogadishu on Thursday, December 28, 2006.[33] Among others challenges, playing baby-sitter for the senior TFG officials against the uncertain and violent backdrops of Mogadishu, required military equipment to do the job. On its way by ship was a tank battalion that included several dozen T-55 tanks, several Buffel and Mambas, fuel tankers, and troop transport vehicles. The equipment had left Kampala by rail on Thursday, March 1, 2007,[34] arrived in the port city of Mombasa on Saturday, March 3, 2007,[35] and from there, went on a DynCorp chartered ship for the ten-day trip on Indian Ocean to the port of Mogadishu. If all went according to plan, the load should be delivered by March 20, 2007.

In the meantime, guilty by association with ENDF, AMISOM could end up in pitch battles with the insurgents, something Gen. Karuhanga wanted to avoid. Equal caution was needed in working too closely with an assortment of Somali security forces and militias, some of them former nationalists and businessmen who could well be working with the insurgents.[36]

Presented with potentially catastrophic consequences, especially for the safety of troops, the dilemma of associating or not with Ethiopian troops was easy to resolve. If the artillery of the Ethiopians could keep the AU troops alive, so be it. This was the case on Monday, March 19, 2007, when TFG forces, ENDF and Ugandan troops moved firmly to secure Mogadishu seaport in preparation for the arrival of military hardware from

Mombasa. Captain Paddy Ankunda explained to the press that there would be limited access to the seaport because the AU was receiving a delivery of equipment for their peacekeepers.[37] Later in the day, as anticipated, the insurgents unleashed a wave of mortar fire, pounding the seaport. AMISOM troops supported by Ethiopians fought back. When it was over, at least two people were killed when a mortar hit their home in the Hamar Jajab neighbourhood, near the seaport.[38]

As the bombardment rocked the seaport, President Museveni called intelligence chief Major Ddamulira to get updates. "What is going on?" asked Museveni. "Your Excellency, we are being bombarded by the insurgents, but we are continuing with unloading of our equipment," Ddamulira reported. President Museveni asked if there was anything he could do to ensure the safety of the troops. Major Ddamulira responded that there was little to be done except continue the work. The president signed off with instructions to be kept informed on the progress.

After it was all over, Capt. Paddy Ankunda was especially careful to note what did not happen. "Six mortars landed inside the port but none of our soldiers was wounded since we had taken the necessary precautions," he said. Ankunda added that the military equipment the AU troops had been expecting had arrived. What the spokesperson left out was the intensity of the pitch battle that played out at Mogadishu Seaport that afternoon, and the calm courage Uganda troops displayed under fire. No sooner had the DynCorp chartered ship carrying AMISOM's equipment arrived, and being unloaded, than the bombardment began. Frantic tank crew dodged mortars as they dashed into the ship, pulled out each tank, and drove it to safety. The same manouver was repeated again. Through it all the insurgents never let up, shelling the port again and again. Some thought it was a miracle there were no casualties among the soldiers.

The risk was worth it. On Tuesday, March 20, 2007, better equipped with the freshly arrived weaponry it needed, AMISOM troops reinforced positions around the presidential palace. On that day, it also provided security for AU Peace and Security commissioner Said Djinnit who came to town to see the progress made in two weeks since Ugandan troops landed, and to hold talks with President Abdullahi Yusuf Ahmed at Villa Somalia. There was some progress, but the insurgents were bolder, AMISOM commanders briefed Djinnit.

Just how determined the insurgents were became apparent in the dying days of March, extending through April into May. To counter the growth of insurgent activities, TFG security chief Mohamed Warsame Farah and deputy defense minister Salad Ali Jelle proposed a massive sweep for weapons in Mogadishu neighbourhoods. Jelle bombastically promised to "have Mogadishu under control within thirty days," beginning the middle of March 2007.[39] This would be a joint operation involving TFG, Ethiopian troops and AMISOM. On conferring with AMISOM commanders, Gen. Karuhanga heeded the consensus to stay out of the operation. Thousands of weapons were hoarded in Mogadishu since the times of the US intervention in 1992, not to mention the utter stupidity and futility of the exercise. Collecting weapons from Somalis was outside the mandate of AMISOM. The porous Somali borders, in any case, ensured steady smuggling of fresh supplies of new weapons. Tactfully, Gen. Karuhanga informed Jelle that AMISOM troops would focus on securing key infrastructures including the airport, seaport and Villa Somalia, the presidential palace.

The wisdom of AMISOM troops sitting out the disarmament operation was soon apparent. At early dawn of Wednesday, March 21, 2007, TFG and Ethiopian troops finally launched the weapons cleanup effort. The answer was swift and fierce from the insurgents who responded with massive force of their own. At around ten in the morning, TFG and Ethiopian forces were ambushed near the Ethiopian base at the former Ministry of defense headquarters. The fighting escalated to several neighbourhoods including the Bakaara Market.[40] By mid-afternoon, the fighting had claimed casualties including Ethiopian soldiers, TFG and civilians and some TFG troops captured by the insurgents.[41] Some of the prisoners were summarily executed and, amidst much jubilation reminiscent of Black Hawk Down in October 1993, their burnt bodies dragged through the streets of Mogadishu, and subjected to indecent humiliation.[42]

AMISOM troops watched from the sidelines as the fighting ping-ponged, back and forth, through the night into the morning of Thursday March 22, 2007. Ethiopian troops regrouped with support of the artillery battalion on the outskirt of the city. Thousands of city residents, meanwhile, fled for safety elsewhere. At the heart of the insurgency was the Hawiye/Habar Gidir/Sa'ad and Dudluble sub-clans. Support came from the Hawiye/Abgaal/Warsangeli, the sub-clan to which the prime minister belonged.[43] At a truce meeting to allow the sides to bury their dead, Hawiye leaders gave Ethiopians three options—stay in Somalia but remain neutral, continue to support President Abdullahi Yusuf Ahmed, a Darood that the Hawiye viewed as an enemy or simply pick up and leave.[44] On February 23, 2007, around five-thirty in the evening, insurgents staged a surprised attack against Ethiopian forces based at *Wasiirka Wasaaradda Gashandiga*, the former Defense Ministry headquarters. The Ethiopians retaliated with artillery fire, killing ten civilians including four children, and wounding as many as fifteen.[45]

The US meanwhile worked furiously from the shadows to calm down the escalating violence. Having set into motions events that sparked the insurgency in the first place, the least the Americans could do was help put out the fire. On the evening of Thursday, March 22, 2007, Ambassador Ranneberger put a call to President Abdullahi Yusuf Ahmed to gauge the situation. Yusuf was in a fighting mood, telling the Ambassador, "We have to clean out the city and break the backbone of those causing violence."[46] Ambassador Ranneberger pointed to the president that the violence could become an all-out war pitting clan against clan, sub-clan against sub-clan and everyone else. The ambassador was reassured that the operation would only last three to four days. That evening, not entirely sold that the Somali leader was in a mood for compromise, Ambassador Ranneberger gave an interview on Mogadishu-based Horn Afrik Radio.[47] On the broadcast, Ranneberger counseled that the best way forward for Somalia was an inclusive national reconciliation process. Violence, he argued, only pushed back the prospects for peace.

Nobody, least of all the insurgents, paid Ambassador Ranneberger any attention. The next day, Friday March 23, 2007, at around 2:00 p.m., another Ilyusin 76TD, registration number EW-78849, belonging to TransAVIAexports Airlines was likely brought down by a missile of unknown kind as it left Mogadishu International Airport.[48] The plane had brought equipment to cannibalize for reusable parts the previous IL-76 that crash-landed at the airport on March 9, 2007. The eleven-crew members including 45-year old aviation unit commander Igor Vashkevic died when the aircraft ploughed into a farmer's field near Mogadishu.[49] All the bodies of the dead were recovered, brought to Halaane Base, and evacuated by land to Baledogle National Airport, northwest of Afgooye, where they were flown back to Belarus on March 30, 2007.

The daily body count was piling up fast for ENDF troops. On Monday March 26, an electronic and watch salesman named Adam Salad Adam drove his Toyota inside the Ethiopian base, getting as close as possible to the canteen where troops were milling about, before detonating the bomb-laden car, killing 63 Ethiopian soldiers and wounding another 50.[50] Whatever restraint the Ethiopians had was thrown out the window as ENDF troops shelled many neighbourhoods using BM-21 multiple rocket launchers and mortars. Meanwhile, Ethiopian use of helicopters in the fight seemed to drive the insurgents to frenzied abandon on the belief that Americans were now in the war.[51] A rocket-propelled grenade fired by insurgents brought down an Ethiopian Mi-24 helicopter on March 30, 2007. The following day, March 31, 2007, as ENDF troops traded artillery with the insurgents, a mortar aimed toward Villa Somalia where AMISOM troops were monitoring the fight claimed the life of Wilber Muhwezi, the first AMISOM fatality and wounded five Ugandan soldiers. All told, more than 400 people died in the intense fighting before it petered out in the first week of April.

Interestingly, on Monday April 2, 2007, AMISOM troops carried out the first patrol of Mogadishu reaching into the heart of Bakaara market, the first time an international force entered the area since the Americans were driven out after Black Hawk Down. Col. Elwelu worked with his unit commanders to draw a plan for the patrol. The overwhelming sentiments were to leave the security of Halaane base, and meet ordinary Somali people. "The time has come for us to show a friendly face to the Somali people, we cannot hide behind the wire forever," Col. Elwelu told his unit commanders.[52] The commander hastened to add that the patrol was not a show of force, rather it was a "show of presence." The timing was also right. There was a lull in the fighting between the ENDF and the insurgents. Also, except on Friday, the insurgents tended to be less active during the rest of the week. After prayers on Friday, the young Somali fighters were usually spoiling for a fight. From Halaane, the long convoy of white AU vehicles that included five technicals belonging to the TFG snaked its way down Maka al-Mukarama Road to KM-4, turned left on Janaral Daud Road, another left on Wadnaha Road, passing through Fiorensa Junction, onto the Tarabunka area and, eventually reaching Bakaara Market. The Somali people, the old and children, came to the street corners to watch or greet the AU force, many with big friendly smiles, waving. Troops gave out water bottles that were scooped up by happy residents.

There was not a single shot fired at the AU force to and from the patrol that lasted more than two hours. In some neighbourhoods, especially in Wardhigleey district where there was considerable concentration of Hawiye Habar Gidir clan, the African Union troops were met with stone-cold hostile stares and, in some dramatic moments, the men and women on the streets simulated the open hand motion across the neck, the near universally understood gesture for "We will slit your throats." The message was clear to Col. Elwelu who made a mental note that there were hostile as well as friendly pockets of Somali in Mogadishu. AMISOM needed to know how to navigate the two solitudes.

The political process of reconciliation between Somali factions, meanwhile, dragged on. The ceasefire hastily arranged between the Habar Gidir and the Ethiopians held barely. Often in fits and starts, fresh firefights shattered the peace. For the most part, after throwing bellyful of punches at the opposite sides, a cooling off period ensued. On the morning of Tuesday May 15, 2007, US Ambassador Ranneberger met with President Abdullahi Yusuf Ahmed in Nairobi. The Somali leader was on his way to meet with Uganda's President Yoweri Museveni in Kampala. In the meeting, President Yusuf assured Ambassador Ranneberger that things were moving in the right direction. The Hawiye were splintered with the Abgaal declaring support for the TFG government. Further talks was planned to bring on board the more recalcitrant leaders of the Ayr, Suleiman and Duduble sub-clans.[53] Upbeat, President Yusuf revealed the TFG was close to concluding agreements with the three Hawiye sub-clans. For his part, Ambassador Ranneberger reminded President Yusuf of the urgency of convening the National Reconciliation Congress. Somali leaders and civil society needed to agree on the way forward including power sharing.

After the meeting, Ambassador Ranneberger thought President Yusuf was a tad too optimistic, and had painted a rosy picture of the TFG and the Hawiye working together. American sources within the Ayr sub-clan gave a different version on what was happening.[54] On one thing, however, the ambassador agreed with the president. There was need to expedite the deployment of more AMISOM troops in Somalia. It so happened that the day before, Monday May 14, 2007, Ambassador Ranneberger met with Jean-Christophe Belliard, the Personal Envoy for Somalia of EU Secretary General, Janvier Solana.[55] Belliard who had a stopover in Addis Ababa before flying to Nairobi, reported that he met Alpha Oumar Konare, the Chairperson of the Commission of the African Union (AU). According to Belliard, Konare was "focused on building up AMISOM and he does not appear interested in transitioning AMISOM to a UN operation."[56] Konare was working to raise 1700 troops from Burundi and a battalion from Nigeria. More importantly, according to Belliard, Konare told him that "The Ugandans are doing very well, but they need additional financial and troop support."[57]

The AU Chairperson's optimism for AMISOM was well placed. The uneasy truce between the TFG and the Hawiye in mid-2007 provided the Ugandan troops the window they needed to settle into routine within the new environment. The unwritten rules for navigating the deadly streets of Mogadishu were simple. The bulk of the troops kept mostly within the main base at Aden Abdulle International Airport. From there, regular rotations relieved the 100 personnel stationed at Seaport, and similar numbers deployed at the presidential residence at Villa Somalia and the strategic KM-4 junction. AMISOM troops also provided armoured escorts for government officials and visitors to Mogadishu. Usually, three or four armoured vehicles transported the VIPs from the Aden Abdulle Airport to Villa Somalia and back.

Troops stationed at the Seaport supervised the loading and unloading of goods, as well as the inspection carried out by TFG security. There was no interference with the flow of traffic at the port. To avoid predictability that could be exploited by the insurgents, daily patrols were irregularly scheduled along the routes connecting the four deployment areas. Troops in bunkers fortified with sandbags atop tall buildings overlooked the routes to ensure that AU patrols did not come under ambush. Soldiers were forbidden from moving on foot in exposed areas without the support of armoured personnel carriers. AMISOM soldiers monitored the occasional clashes between TFG soldiers, Ethiopians and the insurgents from a distance, but stayed out of the scraps. In return, the insurgents appeared to hold their twitchy trigger-fingers when Ugandan troops happened by.

Inside AMISOM headquarters, meanwhile, AMISOM's OPD became the go-to medical treatment center for all manners of ailments including gunshot trauma, burns and, much later, fistula treatment.[58] The medical-surgical unit staffed by three doctors—Dr. Ambrose Oiko, Captain Dr. Joseph Mwesigye, Captain Dr. Daaki, clinical officer Joseph Sabila and about 40 nurses and medical assistants, cared for troop casualties, and also ran the outpatient department (OPD) for Somali civilians just outside the gate to the airport.

Three times weekly between 100 and 120 civilians lined at the gate for treatment from the facility. Once or twice a week, Dr. Oiko assembled a small armoured convoy to travel the short distance to Medina Hospital to collect drugs for civilians use in the OPD. Somehow, for the Somali patients, drugs from AMISOM was stronger than those from Medina and other medical facilities—it did not matter that some of the drugs came from the hospitals they were avoiding in the first place. So long as an AMISOM doctor dispensed it, it was good medicine. The AU Peace and Security Secretariat did not sanction the practice of treating civilians. It could do nothing to stop it.

Disaster struck on Wednesday May 16, 2007, the day after President Abdullahi Ahmed Yusuf and President Museveni met in Kampala. The IED attack occurred in the afternoon as the convoy of AU armoured vehicles escorted the Force Commander Gen. Karuhanga to Villa Somalia where he was scheduled to meet President Yusuf. As the convoy neared the Ministry of Finance building in Mogadishu seaport area, a remote-controlled roadside IED hidden beneath a pile of garbage exploded under an AU truck. The powerful explosion ripped up the vehicle, killing four Ugandan soldiers and wounding six others. Civilian casualties included a man who was killed while urinating nearby, and two children wounded while playing in the area.[59] The wounded soldiers—commander Lt. Fred Ssentongo, Boaz Kasswala, Peter Mucunguzi, Simon Tumusiime, Sulait Labu and Odong Okoth—were rushed to Halaane base to be stabilized by Dr. Oiko's medical team, before being flown to Nairobi for further treatment.[60]

The team of three doctors and several nurses worked flat out for several hours under inhumanly humid conditions. Sweat poured from their bodies as they battled to save the soldiers. At one point, Captain Dr. Joseph Mwesigye lost so much body fluid he became dehydrated, disoriented, eventually collapsing from sheer exhaustion. He retired to rest, get rehydrated before he could return to the job.

The following day, Somali Prime Minister Ali Mohamed Ghedi narrowly escaped death while on his way to attend the repatriation ceremony for the dead Uganda soldiers at Aden Abdulle Airport. A wire-detonated IED exploded, leaving a crater in the road just in front of the second vehicle. Ghedi, riding in the fourth or fifth vehicle in the convoy, was unhurt and continued to the airport where he bade goodbye to the dead Ugandans.[61]

The four dead soldiers, Private Fredrick Wanda, Private Osbert Tugume, Private Julius Peter Ongu and Private Ojok Kilama Lagule, were flown back to Uganda for burial in their ancestral homes.[62] Their violent deaths in Mogadishu created a firestorm back home with cries to bring back the troops. At the burial of Ojok Kilama Lagule on May 20, 2007, mourners in his village blamed the Uganda government for deploying Ugandans to die in foreign lands. "Our children were recruited to defend and serve Uganda and not anywhere else," a local leader said.[63]

In Kampala, the incident caused a dumfounded disbelief in top government leadership. The question everyone was asking was how a peacekeeping force patrolling in white clearly marked AU vehicles could be so violently targeted. At a meeting of top military officials, some suggested immediately bringing back the Contingent Commander Col. Peter Elwelu to face charges before a military court martial for negligence of duty.[64] President Museveni, as Commander in Chief, and never one to spare his commanders from high expectations, asked many tough questions about the situation on the ground, and what was needed to ensure the safety of the troops. At last, the calm voice of Gen. Katumba Wamala carried the day. He had already visited the troops on numerous occasions. The situation in Mogadishu was extremely volatile, Wamala explained. While the majority of Somali people were welcoming to Uganda peacekeepers, there was a decidedly violent section for which peace meant the loss of influence, power and even wealth. In short, there was no peace to keep in Mogadishu, Gen. Katumba said. The sooner everyone adjusted to this reality, the better it was for the troops on the ground.

In Mogadishu, meanwhile, the AU troops carried on with their mandate. Spokesman Captain Ankunda without pointing fingers confirmed that the blast was a roadside bomb and its intention was to hit peacekeepers.[65] However, there was a small possibility that the bomb-makers had intended it for TFG and Ethiopian forces, and not Ugandan troops. Such thinking suggested the Ugandans were at the wrong place at the wrong time. The opportunistic bombers simply seized the moment to make a hit. If, as Captain Ankunda explained, the Ugandan troops were the real target of the bombing, then the incident signaled the start of a new phase in the deployment of AMISOM. The insurgency had metamorphosed into something more virulent, potent and extremely deadly. This was no cakewalk for the seasoned Ugandan forces.

As far as Gen. Karuhanga was concerned, more boots were urgently needed on the ground. Uganda could not go it alone. The hunt for more troops was on. Nations that promised troops needed to stand up to be counted.

# Beating the Bushes for Troops for Somalia

The deaths of the four Ugandan soldiers brought further clarity to the mission. Though experienced and upbeat, Ugandan troops could not sustain the mission without additional troops coming into theatre as reinforcement. With Ethiopia continually threatening to withdraw its troops from Somalia, AMISOM was facing imminent danger of collapsing. President Museveni had obtained a promise from Prime Minister Zenawi that in the event the AU ordered the withdrawal of AMISOM troops from Mogadishu, the ENDF would watch UPDF's back. Hopefully, it would not come to that.

To make sure AU troops withdrawal did not become a reality, the US government went into diplomatic overdrive, hunting all over continental Africa for more troops to deploy in Somalia. The responses were mixed from various African nations. Angola had given an unqualified no in January 2007 to send troops to Somalia. President Eduardo Dos Santos said his troops were needed for internal reconstruction.[1] Still, Jendayi Frazer chose to give it another go, jetting into Luanda on May 31, 2007 to a very warm welcome by the Government of Angola.[2] Frazer brought along US Ambassador to Angola Cynthia Grissom Efird for the meeting that included Angola's Minister of Foreign Relations Joao Bernardo Miranda, Vice Minister of Defense General Agostinho Nelumba Sanjar and Admiral Andre Mendes de Carvalho 'Miau'. There were the usual diplomatic pleasantries. Miranda was grateful for Frazer's congratulatory message on Angola Day on May 9. The discussion then turned to regional issues involving Southern African Development Community (SADC), of which Angola was a member. Zimbabwe's aging and out-of-touch President Robert Mugabe was spiraling out of control, again. SADC needed to act more forcefully to prevent Zimbabwe from complete and chaotic collapse, Frazer counseled.

Frazer then zeroed in on the real purpose of her visit. Angola had a sizable and strong military, she observed, hopeful. Angola needed to volunteer troops for peacekeeping in Sudan and Somalia, she added. Miranda neither missed a beat nor minced his words when responding. There was no reason to send Angolan troops far from its borders, he said. The Angolan people were not "psychologically prepared" to see troops return from dangerous missions in flag-draped coffins.[3] With that, the discussion politely turned to more palatable topics. Frazer left as she had come, with nothing.

To the northeast of Angola, meanwhile, the Government of Tanzania (GOT) seemed especially skittish when peacekeeping and Somalia were mentioned in the same conversation. The American diplomats in Dar es Salaam suspected that President Jakaya Mrisho Kikwete was in a cat and mouse game where Kikwete was the mouse and the Chief of Tanzanian Peoples Defense Forces (TPDF) General George Marwa Waitara, the cat. Described by US Ambassador to Tanzania Michael L. Retzer as "a carry-over from the Mkapa era", a reference to the socialist leaning third president of Tanzania Benjamin William Mkapa who led Tanzania from 1995 to 2005, General Waitara seemed immovable on the issue of peacekeeping, let alone in Somalia.[4]

Most puzzling for the Americans, back in December 2006, the government of Tanzania appeared eager to train a battalion for deployment in Darfur, Western Sudan. In preparation for the start of troops training, senior TPDF commanders including a major general, six-brigadier generals and sixteen colonels and lieutenant colonels attended a five-day seminar in Dar-es-Salaam from December 11, 2006 to December 15, 2006.[5] The seminar was organised by the US under the African Contingency Operations and Training Assistance (ACOTA), which first began in 1997 as African Crisis Response Initiative (ACRI) with the goal of building the capacity of regional forces to respond to regional security crises. The US Government funded program was managed by the US Department of State. On the third day of the workshop, December 13, 2006, the Chief of Staff of the TPDF Lieutenant General Davis Adolph Mwamunyange met privately with ACOTA Program Manager Paul Nell. General Mwamunyange told Nell to relay to ACOTA organisers that the TPDF was eager to train peacekeepers as soon as possible. A day earlier, on December 12, 2006, at a breakfast meeting in Accra, Ghana where he was visiting to inspect peacekeeping facilities belonging to Economic Community of West African States (ECOWAS), Tanzania's Minister of Defense, Dr. Juma Kapuya met separately with ACOTA Coordinator Chip Beck. Kapuya told Beck that President Kikwete was clearly behind the ACOTA initiative in Tanzania. According to the minister, Kikwete wanted to promote democracy and "avoid future conflicts in Africa."[6]

Then things changed. Less than two weeks after the ACOTA seminar in Tanzania, Ethiopia invaded Somalia. The US priorities abruptly shifted from training troops for Darfur to finding troops to deploy in Somalia. Tanzania was formally requested for troops during the meeting on January 5, 2007 of the International Contact Group in Nairobi co-chaired by Jendayi Frazer. As a follow-up, Kenya dispatched a minister to Tanzania to request for troops for Somalia. By the third week of January 2007, all that the Tanzanian Head of the Security Council Unit of the Multilateral Division of the Ministry of Foreign Affairs, Vitus Njiku could tell US Embassy staffer Mary B. Johnson was that President Kikwete had consulted with General Waitara.[7] A decision was forthcoming. Njiku also intimated that the TPDF wanted logistical support similar to what was pledged to Uganda. In any case, Njiku promised Johnson that the US would be the first to be notified when President Kikwete reached a decision.

On February 1, 2007 at a meeting with his Minister for Foreign Affairs Bernard Membe, and deputy permanent secretary in the Ministry of Foreign Affairs, Charles Sanga, President Kikwete did get around to making his intentions known about deploying troops to Somalia.[8] Tanzania had no intention of deploying to Somalia, the president told the two men. Instead, Tanzania planned to take a lead in training as many as 1000 entry-level army officers of the Somali TFG. Tanzania was still committed to Darfur, but not to Somalia.

The US clearly did not anticipate the bad news. Rather than fold up and play dead, Ambassador Retzer cabled Washington with a confidential memo for Jendayi Frazer who was due in Tanzania on February 9, 2007, for another meeting of the International Contact Group.[9] "With countries like Nigeria and Rwanda so actively engaged in peacekeeping deployments, we think Kikwete will be looking for opportunities to establish Tanzania's own peacekeeping credentials in some way," Retzer wrote. The ambassador further suggested that Frazer dangle in front of Kikwete a sweetener the Tanzanian leader could not possibly resist. "Point out that any commitment to Darfur (or Somalia) would trigger USD 1 million in equipment assistance for each battalion deployed," he wrote. Retzer concluded the memo on an optimistic note, "If the training gets underway on schedule in mid-March, the TPDF would have three battalions fully trained in peacekeeping by March 28, 2008."

On arrival in Dar es Salaam on February 9, 2007, Jendayi Frazer made a beeline for *Ikulu ya Rais*, the State House for the meeting with President Jakaya Kikwete. The American delegation included Ambassador Michael Retzer, Ambassador John Yates (Head of Somalia unit, US Embassy Nairobi), Deputy Chief of Mission Daniel Purnell Delly, Nole Garey (Somalia Desk Officer), Special Assistant to Frazer, Fatuma Sanneh and Political Counselor Mary Johnson who doubled as note taker for the meeting.[10] Tanzania's Permanent Representative to the UN Ambassador Augustine Mahiga, Tanzania's Ambassador to the US Andrew Daraja, Head of Americas and Europe Division at the Tanzanian Ministry of Foreign Affairs Ambassador Pastor Ngaiza, and Vitus Njiku flanked President Kikwete. Somalia was at the top of the agenda. Frazer wasted little time coming straight to the point. Tanzania's support was direly needed to help stabilize Somalia. Kikwete listened then repeated what the Americans already knew. Tanzania would train up to 1000 entry-level Somali army officers. To underscore the commitment, Kikwete added, "We will do the training in Tanzania, where it is calm, utilizing several of the camps that were used to train freedom fighters like the ANC and FRELIMO." Frazer probed to see whether Kikwete could consider sending Tanzanian troops to Somalia if the mission transformed to a blue-hatted UN mission. Kikwete was unequivocal in his answer. "To Darfur, yes, but not to Somalia; our major contribution will be this training program." The meeting drifted to other items on the agenda including the new African Command (AFRICOM), AU chairmanship, Sudan, Eritrea-Ethiopian relations, and Zanzibar. As in Angola, Tanzania handed Frazer an empty gourd.

Three months later, the US confirmed what it suspected all along was behind Tanzania's reticence to sign up for ACOTA training to prepare troops for deployment in Darfur or Somalia. On May 2, 2007, Ambassador Michael Retzer met Tanzania's Minister for Defense Dr. Juma Kapuya, at the latter's request.[11] Dr. Kapuya wanted to apologize for the delay in starting the ACOTA training of Tanzanian troops. For good reasons, said the minister, the new date was now August 1, 2007. The minister revealed that by choosing that date, President Kikwete was "trying to avoid open confrontation and buying time" until the retirement in July of Chief of Defense Forces Gen. George Waitara.[12] Dr. Kapuya provided proof to the Ambassador—a letter the minister wrote to the CDF in April to inquire when ACOTA training could begin. The Minister never heard back from Gen. Waitara. Given the sensitive nature of what Retzer referred to as a "temporary obstacle", Dr. Kapuya was dispatched by President Kikwete to brief the ambassador in person. Ambassador Retzer responded that he understood Kikwete's dilemma. In a follow-up cable to Washington to report the secret information provided by Dr. Kapuya, Retzer commented, "The cost of waiting 12 weeks until General Waitara retires appears a small price to pay compared to open confrontation with Tanzania's most senior military officer whose attitude is, 'ACOTA over my dead body.'"[13]

Gen. Waitara eventually retired on Thursday September 13, 2007. On the same day, President Kikwete appointed Lt. Gen. Davis Mwamunyange to full general, and elevated him to position of CDF.[14] Ten days later, on September 24, 2007, Tanzania indicated to the US that it was ready to start ACOTA training. Deploying TPDF to Somalia, however, was a long forgotten footnote in the annals of the Kikwete-Waitara cat and mouse saga.

## Nigeria: Tomorrow We Deploy to Somalia

The drama surrounding the non-deployment of Tanzanian troops to Somalia paled in comparison to the tragi-comedy of the Government of Nigeria on the same issue. When the AU made the initial request for Nigerian troops for Somalia in February 2007, President Olusegun Obasanjo who had only two more months in office promptly promised a battalion.[15] Against the backdrop of an impending regional and national elections slated for April 14 and 21, President Obasanjo had more pressing issues to deal with at home. A former military general who ran for office as a civilian, Obasanjo was set to hand over power to another civilian. This was a first in Nigeria's post-colonial politics. As expected, with political parties angling for power, the campaign reached fever pitch. There were widespread accusations and counter accusations of vote buying, corruption and rigging. At one point in the campaign, Obasanjo's handpicked candidate and the flag-bearer for the Peoples Democratic Party (PDP) Umaru Musa Yar'Adua collapsed, was evacuated to Germany for medical treatment. The rumour mill went into stratospheric production. The news within the foreign diplomatic corps was that Yar'Adua had died.[16] Yar'Adua, it turned out, was very much alive. He went on to win the election on April 21, 2007, although his victory was hotly disputed, dismissively described as a charade and taken to court.[17]

Against the election noise in Nigeria, the question of Nigerian troops for Somalia was resuscitated on Monday May 28, 2007 when Jendayi Frazer flew to Abuja to attend both the inauguration ceremony for President-elect Umaru Musa Yar'Adua and the inaugural dinner at the Presidential Villa slated for next day Tuesday May 29, 2007. Arguably the hottest ticket in town, the event was the appropriate setting for the highest ranking US official in Africa to make connection with the incoming regime, and lobby for troops for Somalia. The US Embassy in Abuja dutifully requested for Jendayi Frazer to meet President Yar'Adua after the inauguration ceremony.[18]

Arranging the meeting was not a problem. As it turned out, with strong ongoing court challenge of the election results, President-elect Yar'Adua was anxious for the world to know that the US government saw him as the legitimately elected leader of Africa's most populous nation. US Ambassador John Campbell put it bluntly in a cable to Frazer, noting, "You should expect that the Nigerian media will be interested in your visit and that the pro-government press will attempt to portray your presence as the U.S. government's endorsement of the new Yar'Adua administration."[19] The loud post-election noise about Nigeria's stolen votes, in fact, forced Frazer's meeting with President Yar'Adua shortly after the inauguration on May 29, 2007 to focus on US concerns about election irregularities. The status of AFRICOM and troops for Somalia were discussed in passing.

On the job barely a few hours, Yar'Adua could not respond with any clarity or assurance other than that he would review the issue and hoped to keep the promise his predecessor made.[20] Nigeria was willing to work with the US " to invest in peace", he added as an afterthought. In the weeks and months following Frazer's initial meeting with President Yar'Adua on Nigeria's commitment of troops to Somalia, a drawn out US versus Nigeria diplomatic chess game ensued. The issue of troops for Somalia was discussed at virtually every meeting at all levels between Government of Nigeria (GON) and US Embassy officials in Abuja. The intense US lobbying also used almost every US official visiting Nigeria to raise the issue of troops for Somalia.

Like the *ikorikori* dotted catfish found in some of the country's fresh water, Nigerian officials proved slippery, and unbeatable players in the game of diplomatic make-believe.

Aware the US desperately needed troops for Somalia, Nigerian top government and military officials played the game to their benefits. On May 31, 2007, just two days after Yar'Adua's inauguration, US Ambassador to Nigeria John Campbell met at Transcorp Hilton Hotel with Nigeria's Ambassador to the US George Obiozor and Special Advisor to President Yar'Adua, Harvard-trained Benjamin Ademola "Danny" Adebiyi.[21] The Nigerians had a small request to make to Ambassador Campbell. The 33rd G-8 meeting was less than a week away, on June 6—8, 2007 at the Kempinski Grand Hotel in Heiligendamm, Germany. US President George Bush was expected at the summit, as was the newly installed President Yar'Adua. The Nigerian officials begged "even for two minutes" to allow the two leaders to meet.[22] Ambassador Campbell said he would relay the message to Washington. In the meantime, Campbell reminded the two officials about Nigeria's promised troops for Somalia, telling them that the US expected GON to fulfill the commitment. The promise would be kept, the men earnestly assured Campbell.

Two days later, on June 2, 2007, US Senator Clarence William "Bill" Nelson (D-Fla), a member of the Senate Intelligence Committee, met with President Yar'Adua at the Presidential Villa in Abuja.[23] Also present was Ambassador Campbell, Mrs. Grace Nelson, and the Chief of Staff for Senator Nelson, Pete Mitchell. Sen. Nelson congratulated Yar'Adua on his inauguration. The two mostly discussed issues around Nigeria State Security Service. The unspoken reminder, however, was that the Americans were still waiting for Yar'Adua's response on AMISOM.

Yar'Adua, meanwhile, eager to show the world that he was firmly in control, flew to Germany for the G-8. Once there, he met with German host Angela Merkel. He was unable to meet President George Bush who came down with a stomach ailment. The delay of promised troops for Somalia was becoming a sore point for the US-Nigeria relations. In a confidential cable to the US Secretary of Defense, Robert Gates, copied to the CIA and Defense Intelligence Agency (DIA), Ambassador Campbell pulled no punches in relaying the assessment of the status of Nigeria's readiness to deploy troops.[24] The Nigerian military battalion designated to serve in the African Union Mission in Somalia (AMISOM), he wrote on June 21, 2007, was "undermanned, under-equipped, and under-trained."[25] The Defense Attaché (DATT) at the Embassy made the conclusion following a meeting in early June with Nigeria's Chief of Defense Staff (CDS), General Andrew Owoye Azazi. The CDS admitted that Nigerian peacekeeping units were grossly undersupplied. Units serving with the African Union Mission to Sudan (AMIS), for example, did not have sufficient arms for all the troops, forcing some soldiers to use uncalibrated weapons left by troops who have exited theatre. Ambassador Campbell further noted that the US government continued to offer help to build Nigeria's troops capacity, however acceptance "has been erratic".[26] In any case, Campbell suggested, Washington should offer one million dollars for equipment, provide additional funds for ACOTA training and give transport and logistical support for Nigerian AMISOM units for a minimum of six months on deployment.

With his tenure as envoy ending in July 2007, Ambassador Campbell pushed one more time for the promised troops for Somalia. At a farewell meeting with President Yar'Adua on July 18, 2007, Campbell raised the issue of troops for Darfur and Somalia.[27] Nigeria was an indispensable country in Africa in peacekeeping, the ambassador told the president. Yar'Adua responded that Nigeria would "shoulder its responsibilities for peace in the region and on the continent." The vague response was not reassuring for the American diplomat, who could only do so much and hope his successor would have better luck following up with officials in Abuja.

While waiting for the arrival of ambassador-designate Robin Renee Sanders only just nominated by President Bush on July 11, 2007 and, once confirmed by the Senate, due to take her post in early December 2007, US Embassy staff in Abuja used every opportunity to aggressively pursue the issue of troops for Somalia.[28] Visiting US officials, regardless of the purpose of their trips to Nigeria, were pressed into service to discuss the matter with Nigerian government officials. On August 20, 2007 US Congressman Donald M. Payne, as member of US Committee on Foreign Affairs, and chair of subcommittee on Africa, met with President Umaru Yar'Adua, the new Minister for Foreign Affairs Ojo Maduekwe and officials of the Nigerian Ministry of Foreign Affairs.[29] Congressman Payne wasted little time doing what other Americans before him had done—he reminded President Yar'Adua of Nigeria's strong role in regional peace and security. He pointedly asked Yar'Adua to stand by Nigeria's commitment to peacekeeping troops for Darfur and Somalia. Yar'Adua, by now two months on the job, picked his words more carefully. Nigeria was very committed to peacekeeping, he said, pointing to the assignment of General Martin Luther Agwai as overall commander of the United Nations-African Union Mission in Darfur (UNAMID). But on Somalia, there was no specific mention of troops. Instead, the president vaguely promised to "work within the African Union to find a solution."[30] Sensing that the American delegation expected to hear more, the permanent secretary to the Nigerian Ministry of Foreign Affairs, Hakeem Baba Ahmed, quickly added that there was a need for sound security on the ground before troops could be deployed to Somalia. This, of course, required more funding.

If money was the only hurdle between Nigerian troops and Somalia, then Washington needed to know. On August 22, 2007, two days following the Yar'Adua-Payne meeting, Charge D'Affaires at the US Embassy Robert E. Gribbin cabled Washington urgently. The subject-line read, "A Strategy for getting Nigerian troops to Somalia."[31] Gribbin argued that lack of information from Mogadishu was hindering Nigerian officials from making informed decision. The remedy was to share information with Nigeria's foreign minister, minister for defense and the general in charge of peacekeeping operations. To that end, an initial report needed to describe in detail the Uganda deployment, their quarters and daily activities. The report needed to include the reception that Ugandan troops received from the Somali Transitional Government, local community and relations with the Ethiopian troops. Gribbin added, "We believe that sharing information will help Nigerians to come to informed decision about AMISOM and Somalia. While there is a risk that the reality of the situation will scare Nigeria away, we hold out little hope of moving from the current limbo in the absence of better information."[32]

A steady stream of officials from Washington, meanwhile, continued with the high level lobbying of the Nigerian government. On November 12, 2007, US Deputy Secretary of State John Dimitri Negroponte accompanied by Jendayi Frazer held an hour-long meeting with President Yar'Adua at the Presidential Villa at Aso Rock.[33] Present at the meeting was Nigeria's vice president Goodluck Jonathan, Secretary to the Government of the Federation Babagana Kingibe, Chief of Staff in the President's Office Gen. Abdullahi Mohammed, National Security Advisor Gen. Abdullahi Mukhtar and Foreign Minister Ojo Maduekwe. Yar'Adua was clearly in poor health. Between bouts of incessant coughing, he confirmed that Nigeria would meet its commitment. He however added that the military was "overstretched", causing delay and problems in training of troops. Frazer chipped in by saying that the US was ready to provide $3 million to help equip and deploy the battalion pledged. Yar'Adua promised to instruct his minister of defense and chief of defense staff to get the Somalia battalion ready "as soon as possible."[34] The president was confident that Nigerian troops would be deployed to Somalia no later than the end of December 2007.

At a side meeting the same day, Ojo Maduekwe and PS Hakeem Baba-Ahmed seemed to contradict President Yar'Adua on Somalia. Maduekwe told Negroponte and Frazer that the government of Nigeria wanted more information about the deployment. Most surprising of all, Nigeria suddenly wanted a discussion involving all parties to the Somalia conflict including the representatives of the defunct Islamic Courts. Frazer, again, reminded the foreign minister that the US had $3m on the table. The meeting suggested by Maduekwe was not only difficult to organise, it would drag out the promised deployment of troops. Both sides agreed to continue the dialogue.

In the meantime, with the end of the year fast approaching, US African Command (AFRICOM) top officials descended on Abuja to discuss AFRICOM with Nigerian government officials.[35] Deputy to the Commander for Civil and Military Affairs Mary Carlin Yates accompanied by the Deputy Commander for Military Operations, Vice Admiral Robert Moeller, met with the Chief of Defense Staff Andrew Owoye Azazi and National Security Advisor Abdullahi Mukhtar. Also present was Ojo Maduekwe and ECOWAS Commission President Mohammed Ibn Chambas. Yates explained to the Nigerian officials that AFRICOM was not a militarization of US diplomacy in Africa. AFRICOM did not pose a threat to the sovereignty of African nations. Maduekwe responded that he was relieved to hear from the horse's mouth what AFRICOM really was. At the end of the discussion, the Nigerians mentioned that the issue of troops to Somalia was being handled. There was no additional information.

Still, US officials clung to the hope that Nigeria, given the commitment at the highest level, eventually, would come through with troops for Somalia. Anything less would be a major diplomatic embarrassment for Nigeria. On December 4, 2007, the new US Ambassador to Nigeria Robin Renee Sanders took her post in Abuja. An African American from New York, Sanders was previously US Ambassador to the Democratic Republic of Congo from 2002 to 2005. She was appointed twice as the Director for Africa at the National Security Council at the White House. In Nigeria, the top priority for Ambassador Sanders was following up on the deployment of troops to Somalia. From the onset of her new job, she asked government of Nigeria for a definitive answer on when troops would be ready. On January 9, 2008 the Nigerian Chief of Army Staff sent to the US Embassy a list of equipment for the designated battalion to be deployed to Somalia, 231 Infantry Battalion located in Jos, Plateau State.[36] Listed were 20 APCs, cargo trucks, assault boats, mortars and anti-aircraft guns, ammunitions, communication gear, office equipment, clothing, medical supplies, tools and mess facilities. It was not clear why the Nigerian military felt troops bound for Somalia needed anti-aircraft guns, given that the insurgents had no aircraft to speak of, and the only viable airport in Somalia was already occupied by Uganda troops. Even without the said weapons, the price tag for the listed items far exceeded the funds the US had set aside for the troops.

Money worries aside, US officials in Abuja were growing increasingly leery that GON could deliver troops in good time. The concern was raised in the confidential cable accompanying the Nigerian wish list to Washington. Ambassador Sanders wrote, "In the wake of the Haskanita debacle,[37] however, and with the prospect of confronting an ideologically motivated enemy in an urban setting, Post doubts that Nigeria is up to the task."[38] The US growing doubt on whether GON intended to send troops to Somalia formally found voice in US Deputy Assistant Secretary in the Bureau of African Affairs Todd Moss at a meeting with Nigeria's top military brass on January 24, 2008.[39] The US was becoming deeply concerned about peacekeeping delays Moss told the meeting attended by Nigeria's Minister of Defense Alhaji Mahmud Yayale Ahmed, Gen. Owoye Andrew Azazi, Gen. Kefre Ekwo representing the Chief of Army Staff, Admiral K. Ibrahim representing Chief of Naval Staff, Air Marshall Eche Agwungwu representing Chief of Air Staff. Alhaji Ahmed reassured the American officials that "there were no hitches with the African Union save the Memorandum of Understanding, which he expected to be resolved shortly." According to Ahmed, the troops for Somalia "had been ready for the past year, and only required the equipment that the USG offered...."

Ambassador Sanders was still concerned about Nigeria's promise of troops for Somalia. In an assessment of the Yar'Adua's government after eight months in office, she had written in a confidential cable, "The GON remains committed to its peacekeeping in Sudan and Somalia (although slow here in delivering), but its lofty statements of support are often contradicted by military's financial and equipment limitation."[40] Moreover, a general consensus was emerging in Nigeria that President Yar'Adua, a former regional governor not used to the fast-paced life as head of state, was taking an unusually long time making a decision on any substantive issue. Various aides to the president who discussed the problem with US Embassy staff reported that, typically, when President Yar'Adua was briefed on various subjects, he then asked for more time to think about them.

A whole year slipped by without Nigeria making a firm decision to send troops to Somalia. On February 26, 2008 the Nigeria Election Tribunal dashed the hopes of opposition parties by upholding the election of President Yar'Adua and Vice President Goodluck Jonathan.[41] Despite the clear backing from the courts on the mandate to rule, President Yar'Adua seemed to vacillate on committing troops to Somalia. On June 25, 2008, the Nigerian Army took the unusual step of confirming for the first time in the media the status of the Somalia bound troops. According to Reuters News Agency, Nigerian Army Spokesman Brigadier General Emeka Onwuamaegbu said that the 800-strong battalion was ready to deploy to Somalia.[42] The spokesperson claimed Nigeria had the capacity to send more than one battalion if the government wanted to do so. It would take at least two months for the US to deliver the military equipment that Nigeria requested. Ambassador Sanders wrote to Washington, "...the earliest that Nigerian peacekeepers would be ready to deploy to Somalia is November or December."

Three days later news surfaced of more delays. On June 28, 2008, Vice President Goodluck Jonathan met a US delegation led by Congressman and Chairman of Foreign Affairs Committee Howard Berman, accompanied by Representatives George Miller, Ed Royce, Tom Davis, Donald Payne and Linda Sanchez.[43] The issue of troops for Somalia came up, naturally. Jonathan sounded positive about the commitment. All that remained was "infrastructure support, training and other support in order for Nigerian troops to go to Somalia."

Already a year and half had gone by. Things could not get any worse. Yet, on August 20, 2008, presidential spokesman Olusegun Adeniyi announced that President Yar'Adua had made changes in the army leadership.[44] Air Marshall Paul Dike replaced Gen. Owoye Andrew Azazi as Chief of Defense Forces. Air Vice Marshall Oluseyi Petinrin took over as

Chief of Air Staff. Meanwhile Maj. Gen. Abdulrahman Bello Dambazau took over from Lt. Gen. Luka Yusuf as Chief of Army Staff. Finally, Rear Admiral Ishaya Iko Ibrahim became the new Chief of Naval Staff, replacing Vice Admiral Ganiyu Adekeye who was implicated in stealing Nigerian crude oil in what was known as "bunkering".[45]

Further exacerbating the situation was the firing on September 8, 2008 of the Secretary to the Government of the Federation Babagana Kingibe, and his replacement by the Minister for Defense Mahmud Yayale Ahmed.[46] The sweeping changes in the leadership of Nigeria military created turmoil for the pending deployment of troops to Somalia. Effectively, the US needed to start from scratch the entire process of building confidence with top Nigeria military leadership about the plans for Somalia. It was no easy task given the resources already invested in the project with very little, if anything, to show for it. Still, rather than give up, the US continued the hunt for troops anyway. On September 11, 2008, the US Assistant Secretary of State for Democracy, Human Rights and Labour (DRL) David Kramer, and DAS Jeffrey Krilla met Foreign Minister Ojo Maduekwe to further discuss the issue of peacekeeping. Maduekwe restated Nigeria's commitment to peacekeeping, especially pointing to the upcoming deployment to Somalia.[47] Maduekwe sounded confident that Nigerian peacekeepers "Should deploy by next month" to bolster AMISOM's severely undermanned forces. Maduekwe also added that he recently met with Nigeria's new UN Military Advisor to Ban Ki-Moon, General Chikadibia Isaac Obiakor to discuss peacekeeping operations. Maduekwe reported that he and the general agreed that US support was critical to Somalia deployment as it was "not a typical peacekeeping operation." Added Maduekwe, "I don't want our troops to be sitting ducks."

With the date of the Somalia deployment fast approaching, the Defense Attaché (DATT) and Political Officer (Poloff) at the US Embassy Abuja met on October 21, 2008, with Nigeria's Director of Peacekeeping Operations Maj. Gen. F.N. Osokogu to discuss the finer details of the mission, and get updates. Gen. Osokogu reported that the Somalia bound units were "identified, trained, and have been on standby for some time." Osokogu observed that the recent heavy urban fighting experienced by Uganda troops in Mogadishu had convinced Nigeria to acquire some essential items including light tanks, possibly Scorpions. These were already available in the inventory of the army, but needed to be sent at the earliest opportunity to support deployment of Nigerian troops.

Later the Defense Attaché commented that Osokogu was very open and informative. The only drawback was that the general did not appear well briefed about the status of AMISOM, and was unaware that this was an African Union initiative. Osokogu also did not know that Nigeria had dispatched a scouting mission to Mogadishu to check out things on the ground. In any event, as the year ended, Nigeria was still promising troops which so far were not deployed. On December 30, the US Deputy Chief of Mission (DCM) in Abuja, Lisa Piascik met with Nigeria's Minister of State for Foreign Affairs Ambassador Bagudu Hirse.[48] Bagudu repeated for the benefit of the US official that his country was still committed to sending troops to Somalia, and asked for a written note outlining US points to take up with "higher authorities." Ambassador Sanders noted later in a confidential cable to Washington, her frustration boiling to the surface, that this had become a game for Nigerian officials. She wrote, "Given Nigeria's track record to date on responding to this issue as well as the pending $3 million the USG has promised Nigeria for military equipment, we doubt that GON will move in a timely manner on this demarche, but we will continue to push the issue."[49]

Fed up, frustrated and continually strung along by Nigerian government officials, Ambassador Sanders had had enough. On March 7, 2009, fully two years after the initial request was made for Nigerian troops for Somalia, Sanders confronted Foreign Minister Ojo Maduekwe at his house in Abuja.[50] The time had come for Nigeria to put up a specific date for deployment of troops for AMISOM or the US would start talking to other friends about the issue, she told Maduekwe. The minister claimed that around the cabinet table, he was one of a few still pushing for deployment of troops to Somalia. The Minister of Defense Shettima Mustapha who was barely three months on the job, and the military chiefs were reluctant to deploy troops to Somalia. Maduekwe also complained that $5 million the US was offering was hardly enough to put Nigerian troops in peace enforcement capacity. Ambassador Sanders was having none of the previous dancing around, so she asked point-blank whether or not GON would deploy troops to Somalia. She later reported in the cable to Washington, "Still reluctant to give a straight yes or no answer, the foreign minister further explained that if he had a little more time he may be able to sway the president, but added that the Bashir indictment had added to the GON internal review of the AMISOM issue."[51]

At best, the Omar el-Bashir issue was a red herring. The indictment of the president of Sudan by the International Criminal Court (ICC) at The Hague on March 4, 2009 had nothing to do with the deployment of AU troops in Somalia. Instead, looking for every excuse to wiggle out of its commitment to send troops to Mogadishu, Nigeria latched onto it. Increasingly, Ojo Maduekwe seemed to exploit discussion about AMISOM to ask for a favour from the US Embassy staff in Abuja. Toward the end of the meeting with Ambassador Sanders, Maduekwe expressed the desire to meet with newly appointed US Secretary of State Hillary Rodham Clinton during his upcoming trip to Washington. The ambassador acted on the request, and confirmation came back within fifteen minutes— Maduekwe could meet with Clinton in Washington. America was still holding its side of the bargain, but was Nigeria?

Obviously, the central theme of Maduekwe's meeting with Secretary of State Clinton would be AMISOM, the minister promised. But Ambassador Sanders was no longer fooled by Nigeria's self-serving game of promises without delivering troops for Somalia. Her concluding assessment in the cable to Washington was candid. She wrote, "The MOD and Service Chiefs are not impressed with the 5 million dollar USG equipment offer as they seem to want a lot more and for us to pay to revamp their entire armed forces. We would recommend seeing if the Foreign Minister can deliver by the time he meets with the Secretary on AMISOM, and if he cannot, then we should move on to other partners because in order to save face the GON will continue to drag this out."[52]

The final straw for Ambassador Sanders came a week later. Ojo Maduekwe called her late Saturday, March 14, 2009. The minister requested to meet for lunch the following day Sunday, March 15, 2009.[53] Maduekwe told the American envoy that he wanted to talk about AMISOM following his meeting with President Yar'Adua on the issue. A corollary discussion was on his scheduled meeting with Secretary of State Hillary Clinton. As agreed, Ambassador Sanders made the lunch appointment on time. When she entered the private parlor, Sanders noticed a woman in dark glasses sitting in the corner. Maduekwe told Sanders that he had someone whom he wanted the Ambassador to talk to, an arrangement he thought about at the very last minute. Once the mystery woman removed her glasses, she was revealed to be none other than the Chairwoman of the Economic and Financial

Uganda troops during early boarding at Entebbe Air Base, March 6, 2007. (Photo credit: UPDF Archives)

UGABAG 1 Contingent Commander Col. Peter Elwelu, left, presents Uganda's flag to AMISOM Force Commander Maj. Gen. Levi Karuhanga, right, at Aden Abdulleh Airport, March 6, 2007. (Photo credit: UPDF Archives)

Ugandan troops in a convoy of white AU Armoured Personnel Carriers (APCs) return to Halaane Base, Mogadishu, March 12, 2007. (Photo credit: UPDF Archives)

Clinical Officer WO II Kabuye (with stethoscope) of a UPDF medical team treats a Somali civilian in the Outpatient Department inside Halaane Base, May 2007. (Photo credit: UPDF Archives)

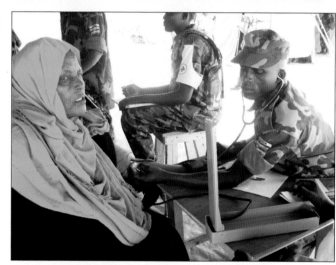

Uganda troops and Somali officials at a repatriation ceremony on May 17, 2007 at Aden Abdulleh Airport for Pte. Fredrick Wanda, Pte. Osbert Tugume, Pte. Julius Peter Ongu and Pte. Ojok Kilama Lagule, killed the previous day by IED. (Photo credit: UPDF Archives)

Uganda AMISOM soldiers, left to right, Lt. JM Mukhwana, a UPDF officer and Capt. Sande Mugema, at Halaane Base, Mogadishu on May 17, 2007, read Ugandan papers with headlines about the casualties from the IED blast the previous day. (Photo credit: UPDF Archives)

UPDF engineers constructing a new hospital clinic at Halaane Base, Mogadishu, August 28, 2007. (Photo credit: UPDF Archives)

Left to right, ENDF Colonel
Gebre-Egzabher Alemseged
(in civilian clothes), AMISOM
Spokesman Capt. Paddy
Ankunda, ENDF Brigadier
Gebre-Medhin Fecadu,
unidentified Ethiopian major
general, and Col. Peter Elwelu
at Aden Abdulleh Airport,
September 29, 2007. (Photo
credit: UPDF Archives)

UPDF Commander of Land
Forces (CLF), Maj. Gen.
Katumba Wamala speaks to a
Uganda soldier at Halaane gate,
Mogadishu, September 29, 2007.
(Photo credit: UPDF Archives)

CLF Maj. Gen. Katumba
Wamala chows down ugali
na maragwe, corn-meal and
beans with rank and file of
Ugandan soldiers serving in
the AU mission in Mogadishu,
September 29, 2007. (Photo
credit: UPDF Archives)

iv

Front left, Chief of Strategic Planning and Management Unit of Peace and Security Commission Maj. Gen. Buta Benon Biraro leads an AU Technical team on a visit to AMISOM, Mogadishu, October 5, 2007. (Photo credit: UPDF Archives)

Contingent Commander of Burundi National Defence Forces Brig. Gen. Juvenal Niyoyunguruza (red beret) with, left to right, a Somali guard, Col. Peter Elwelu and a senior Somali commander during walkabout in Halaane upon the arrival in Mogadishu of the Burundi contingent on Sunday, December 23, 2007. (Photo credit: UPDF Archives)

Front, left to right, Gen. Levi Karuhanga, Brig. Gen. Juvenal Niyoyunguruza, Col. Peter Elwelu; back left, Col. Rurayi and Brig. Gen. Jérémie Ntiranyibagira (half hidden behind Karuhanga) at a joint meeting of senior officers of Uganda and Burundi contingents in Mogadishu December 2007. (Photo credit: UPDF Archives)

Uganda Minister of Defence Crispus Kiyonga (with flag) on Friday, January 18, 2008, accompanied by, left to right, Gen. Katumba Wamala, Maj. Gen. Geoffrey Muheesi, Col. Muwuma, Gen. Ivan Koreta and other UPDF officers after a welcome ceremony for returning UGABAG 1 troops at Entebbe Airport, Uganda. (Photo credit: UPDF Archives)

Right, Transitional Federal Government of Somalia (TFG) President Yusuf Ahmed Abdullahi meeting in his office in Villa Somalia, with AU Special Representative of the Chairperson of the Commission (SRCC) Nicolas Bwakira on February 22, 2008. (Photo credit: UPDF Archives)

Newly elected Somalia President Sheikh Sharif Sheikh Ahmed (white shirt) on arrival at Aden Abdulleh Airport on February 7, 2009, is flanked by Somali leaders while AMISOM Force Commander Maj. Gen. Francis Okello salutes during the playing of the national anthem of Somalia. (Photo credit: UPDF Archives)

Far right, A South-African made Casspir burns after the direct impact of a VBIED bomb that hurled it 30 m away at AMISOM HQ, Halaane Base. After stepping out of the vehicle moments earlier, former deputy AMISOM Force Commander Maj. Gen. Niyoyunguruza of Burundi was killed, along with 16 other AMISOM peacekeepers. (Photo credit: UPDF Archives)

Left to right, Dead young al-Shabaab suicide attacker was killed by the deadly bomb blast before he detonated the suicide body-pack fashioned out of a blue UN flak vest, visible under his white shirt, with yellow and blue wires taped to the left wrist and a Nokia phone nearby. His companion fared much worse from the blast, with head flattened like a bun and lower bottom blown off. September 17, 2009. (Photo credit: UPDF Archives)

A Somali officer and an AMISOM soldier, lucky enough to walk away from the bomb blast with superficial wounds, wait at the AMISOM clinic for treatment by Uganda doctors dealing with more critical cases. Those with extreme injuries were evacuated by air to Nairobi, Kenya. (Photo credit: UPDF Archives)

Left, Col. Dr. Kiyengo drenched in sweat, is assisted by other medics, as he stitches the head wound of AMISOM Force Commander, Maj. Gen. Nathan Mugisha who was able to walk away from the massive car-bomb blast at Halaane base. (Photo credit: UPDF Archives)

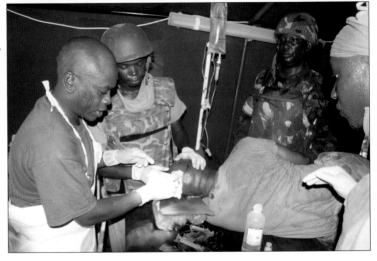

The day after the bomb, Center block, which housed the Office of the Force Commander, sits abandoned, with empty flagpoles and a destroyed Toyota double-cabin belonging to the commander; foreground, a deep crater left in the ground at the spot where the suicide vehicle exploded. (Photo credit: UPDF Archives)

Battle for Mogadishu: Lt. Col. John Mugarura commander of Uganda's 69th Bn in the El Hindi area of Mogadishu recently captured from insurgents, leads soldiers on August 2, 2010 to inspect a long resupply tunnel constructed by al-Shabaab to move munitions and fighters to battlefront. (Photo credit: UPDF Archives)

CLF Gen. Katumba Wamala peers through the scope of a Romanian-made PSL semi-automatic sniper rifle propped against sandbags at Jubba Hotel, Mogadishu, waiting for an insurgent target holed up 300 m away at the former Italian Embassy on August 18, 2010. Looking on, left to right, UGABAG 5 Commander Lt. Col. Francis Chemo, Gen. Nathan Mugisha, Col. Michael Ondoga and, far right, Maj. Sahad Katemba. (Photo credit: Author)

Battle for Mogadishu: Ugandan AMISOM troops manouver tanks past a front line position in Mogadishu, Somalia on September 23, 2010. (Photo credit: Stuart Price)

President Yoweri Museveni, front centre, on a surprise visit to Mogadishu to support the AMISOM war effort against al-Shabaab, after inspecting a guard of honour at 'White House' in Halaane Base Camp, accompanied by Col. Michael Ondoga (left) and Maj. Gen. Nathan Mugisha (right), followed by Lt. Col. James Birungi (red beret), aide de camp to the president Col. Wilson Mbadi, and Col. Innocent Oula (behind Mbadi), on November 28, 2010. (Photo credit: UPDF Archives)

Battle for Mogadishu: Burundi Contingent operations at Gashandiga, former
Ministry of Defence, northern Mogadishu, Somalia on March 7, 2011. A
commander showing a target to a soldier. (Photo credit: Stuart Price)

Battle for Mogadishu: Chief of Defense Forces of UPDF, the late Gen. Aronda
Nyakairima is met by happy soldiers on arrival at Aden Abdulleh Airport in Mogadishu
for a visit of troops on March 22, 2011. Aronda was instrumental in building
AMISOM into a viable peacemaking force. (Photo credit: UPDF Archives)

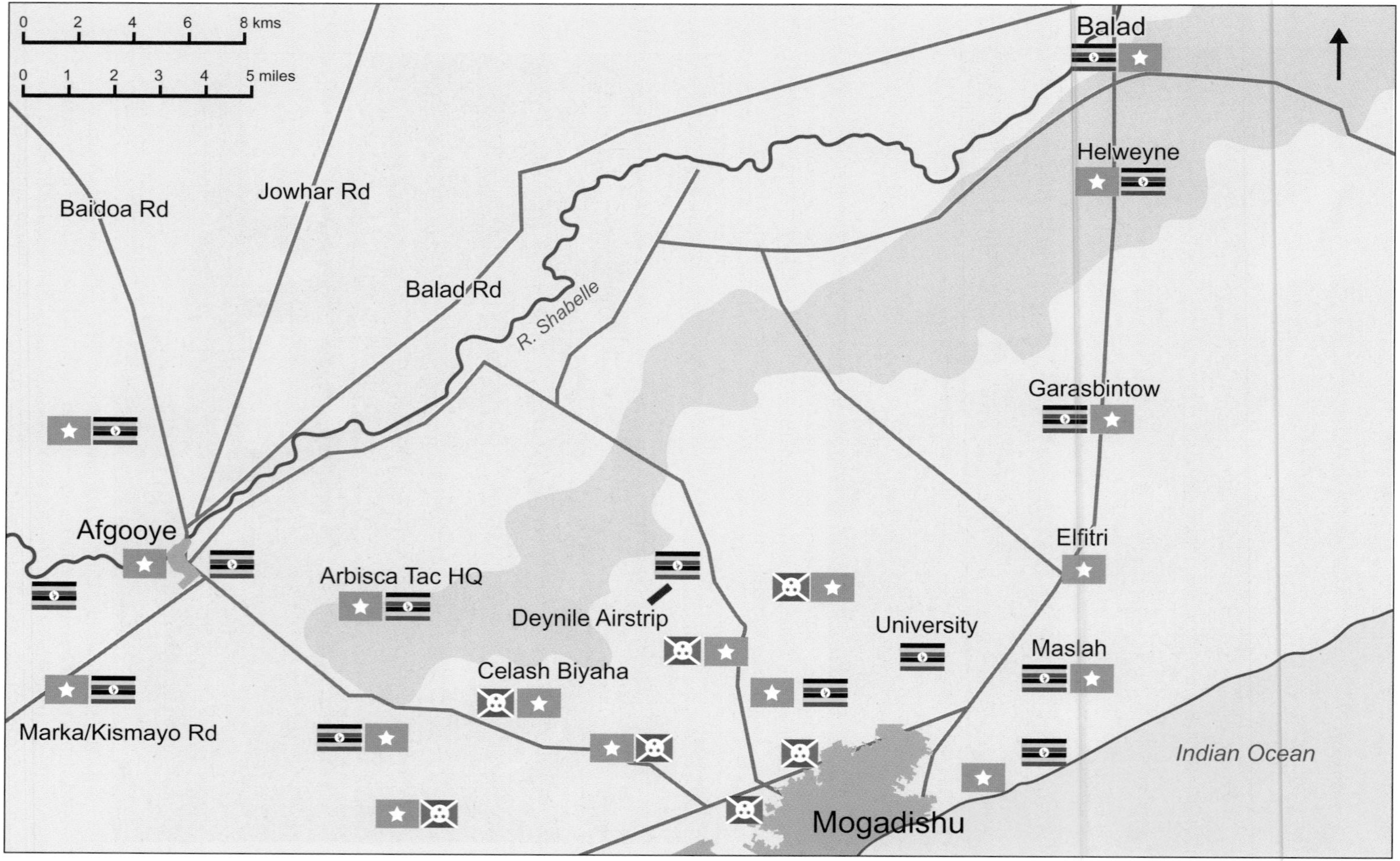

Amisom Troop Positions. (George Anderson)

Indian Ocean

Balad

Helweyne

Garasbintow

Elfitri

Maslah

University

Mogadishu

Deynile Airstrip

Celash Biyaha

Arbisca Tac HQ

R. Shabelle

Balad Rd

Jowhar Rd

Baidoa Rd

Afgooye

Marka/Kismayo Rd

8 kms
5 miles

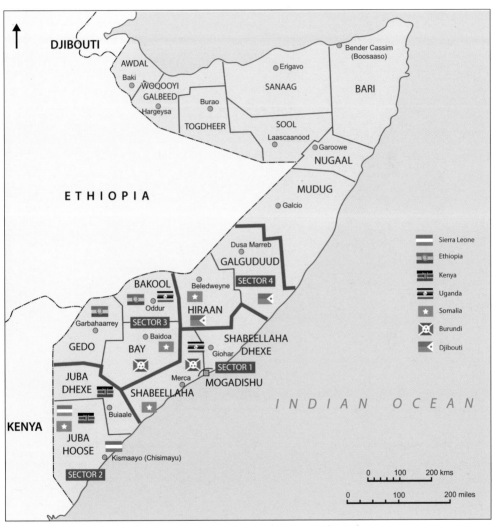

Amisom Operation Sectors. (George Anderson)

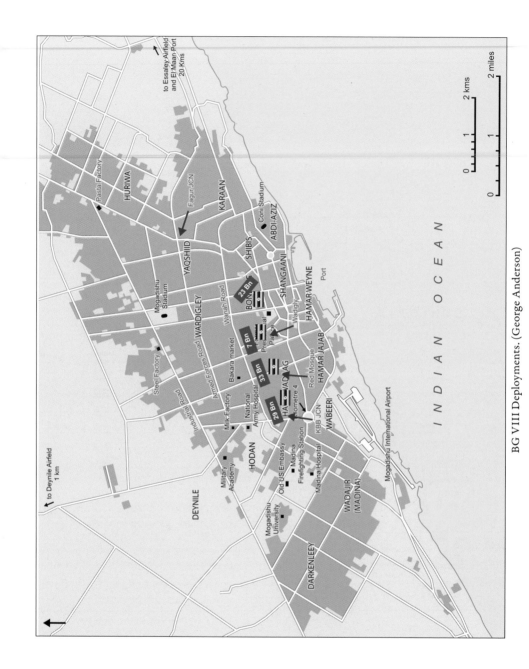

BG VIII Deployments. (George Anderson)

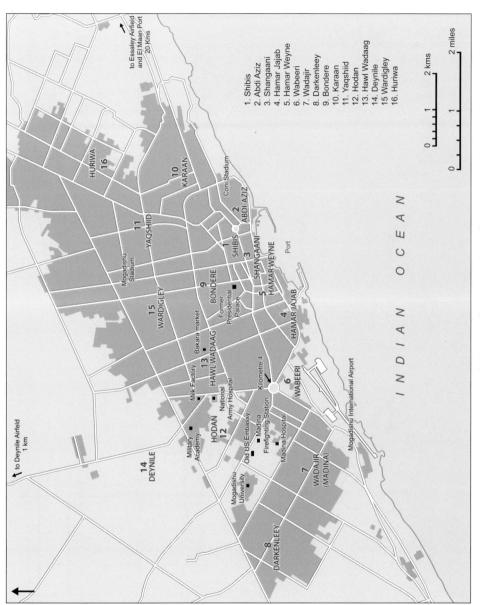

Mogadishu City. (George Anderson)

1. Shibis
2. Abdi Aziz
3. Shangaani
4. Hamar Jajab
5. Hamar Weyne
6. Wabeeri
7. Wadajir
8. Darkenleey
9. Bondere
10. Karaan
11. Yaqshiid
12. Hodan
13. Hawl Wadaag
14. Deynile
15. Wardigley
16. Huriwa

OFS Secret Plan. (George Anderson)

Crimes Commission (EFCC), Farida Waziri. Ambassador Sanders was taken aback by the revelation. The strictest order from Washington was for US Embassy staff to have absolutely no contact with Waziri. The order was based on the US perception that the EFCC, established by former President Obasanjo in 2002 as an anti-corruption agency that successfully prosecuted extremely powerful Nigerian personalities for corruption under its former chairman Nuhu Ribadu, had become toothless after Yar'Adua appointed Waziri in June 2008.[54] In US eyes, Waziri was damaged goods.

Ambassador Sanders was furious with Maduekwe for making the duplicitous arrangement. Never one to mince words, she said exactly how she felt about the trickery. She could not stay for lunch so long as Waziri was in the room. She would have flatly refused to come had she known Waziri was also invited for lunch. The Ambassador let Maduekwe know in clear language that she was extremely unhappy with his "little play", and that she would let Washington know about what just happened. Embarrassed with his own childish prank, Maduekwe apologized profusely and took responsibility for being a "rascal". Maduekwe then asked his wife, Mrs. Ucha Maduekwe, to escort Waziri out. The drama concluded, the two sat down to a one-on-one lunch on AMISOM and other issues. The damage was done and, from this point onward, the US government did not pursue vigorously the issue of deploying Nigerian troops to Somalia. Instead, the US effort switched to finding other African nations to contribute troops for Somalia.

Following a lackluster response from African nations initially approached by the US to provide troops for Somalia in early 2007, tiny Burundi stepped forward. Burundi was not on the US top list of potential African troops contributing countries for the Somalia mission. President Pierre Nkurunziza, elected by Burundi's two houses of parliament on August 19, 2005, was at that very moment engaged in protracted negotiations with various political forces to end the long-running civil strife, and form a unity government. The work of the president was complicated by the focus to integrate several thousand former rebels into the Burundi National Army.

The return to democracy was painfully slow following four decades of devastating ethnic conflicts that pitted the majority Hutu against the minority, but politically and militarily dominant Tutsi. An estimated half a million Burundians died in back and forth ethnic inspired killings, with Tutsi killing Hutu, and Hutu killing Tutsi. There were several flashpoints, the first being the October 1965 massacre of about 500 Tutsi in the Province of Muramvya and several thousand Hutu in the province of Bururi.[55] The April 1972 massacre started with a Hutu uprising along Lake Tanganyika that killed several thousands Tutsi, but was followed by a genocidal repression in which between 150,000 and 300,000 mostly ethnic Hutus were killed by rampaging Tutsi dominated army and civilians.[56] Hundreds of thousands fled into exile in neighboring countries including Tanzania, Rwanda and the Democratic Republic of Congo (DRC).[57] In 1988 ethnic Hutu massacred several hundred ethnic Tutsi in Ntega and Marangara, two northern communes along the Rwanda border, precipitating a now familiar response from the Tutsi-dominated army that indiscriminately killed several thousand ethnic Hutu, while tens of thousands fled to Rwanda.[58] Following the assassination of popularly elected President Melchior Ndadaye, a Hutu, on Thursday October 21, 1993, Burundi descended into a bloody period of indiscriminate ethnic killings of Hutu and Tutsi civilians, with the death toll placed between 50,000 and 100,000.[59]

To underscore Burundi's fragile progress toward peace, 1100 peacekeeping troops from the South African National Defense Forces (SNDF) deployed in October 2001 under

African Mission in Burundi (AMIB), that eventually transitioned to United Nations Mission in Burundi (ONUB), and were still at their post in Bujumbura almost six years later.[60] The US, a strong supporter of the Burundi peace process, meanwhile, was concerned about the rampant abuses of human rights by the army and the police force, raising the issue in private meetings with Burundi leadership,[61] and at the United Nations General Assembly.[62] The latest was the Muyinga Massacre in July and August 2006, in which 31 civilians detained by the army in Muyinga province either died in mysterious circumstances or simply disappeared without a trace.[63] The US Ambassador to Burundi Patricia Moller also let Washington know that she was wary of the powerful high-level 'military quartet' who wielded enormous power, known to have the ears of President Nkurunziza, and for giving the leader bad advice.[64] The well-connected men included the Burundi minister of interior Evariste Ndayishimiye, the head of National Intelligence Services (SNR) Adolphe Nshimirimana, Deputy Army Chief of Staff Godefroid Niyombare, and the Director General of National Police Alaine Guillaume Bunyoni.

Yet, against its own background of political instability, Burundi insisted on contributing troops for the Somalia mission. This was an opportunity to show the world that Burundi had turned a page on many of its problems, and was willing to help the Somalia people solve theirs. At the very least, the government of Nkurunziza wanted to project to the home crowd a new confidence in its ability to play at the continental level alongside more stabled countries like Uganda. On March 12, 2007, six days after Uganda troops landed in Mogadishu, US Deputy Assistant Secretary for African Affairs, James Swan met Burundi's Minister for Defense, Lt. Gen. Germain Niyoyankana in Bujumbura.[65] Swan was on a three-day working visit to Burundi. In contrast to the disinterested attitude of the Nigerian Army toward the Somalia mission, Gen. Niyoyankana expressed the urgent need to include Burundi on the mission. His motivation was to buff Burundi's image on the regional and international stage by raising the profile of the army. He reiterated the offer of two battalions for Somalia. Swan thanked Gen. Niyoyankana for the generous offer of 1700 troops. Swan told the general that as the Ethiopians pulled out of Somalia, AU troops were expected to do the heavy lifting to protect the TFG government of Abdullahi Ahmed Yusuf. He was aware that Burundi forces needed help getting ready for deployment. Swan suggested that the government of Burundi consult with the African Union planning team in Addis Ababa to assess the needs of their peacekeeping force.

Gen. Niyoyankana's tad optimistic and over-enthusiastic demeanor was meant to impress the Americans. He told Swan that Burundi was extremely keen to share with Somalia its experiences in conflict resolution. He estimated that Burundi could deploy to Mogadishu within two months. He, however, forcefully underscored the need for US support with the logistics of moving troops and equipment to Somalia. A more detailed draft listing the needs of Burundi troops would be forwarded to the US by the following day, added the general. Swan strongly suggested that Burundi seek the help of South Africa with training the troops before deployment. The meeting ended on an upbeat note.

Burundi's priority, however, was to secure the backing of the international donor community. On March 23, 2007, Gen. Niyoyankana and Burundi's Minister for External Relations, Antoinette Batumubwira convened a meeting of potential donors with representatives of the US, European Union, Russia and the African Union.[66] Niyoyankana went straight to the reason for the meeting. He told the gathering that the Burundi parliament had not yet approved the contribution of troops to Somalia. The Burundi Army, however, was moving forward with all the requisite plans for deployment. To that end, Niyoyankana presented a long list of needs requiring immediate attention for deployment to proceed. The list ranged from pedestrian items such as office supplies, cooking utensils, water cisterns, and personal equipment like sleeping bags, to big equipment like aircraft, helicopters, bulldozers and trucks. Burundi also wanted assurance that for the three months that the troops were in Somalia, each soldier would get paid a monthly salary of $500 and a per diem of $750 per capita. To underscore the dire need of the Burundi forces, Niyoyankana revealed that a 30-person reconnaissance team did not travel to Somalia in February because of lack of resources.

Gen. Niyoyankana pressed hard for US support for the deployment in a private meeting with the US chargé d'affaires to Burundi Ann Breiter three days later, on March 26, 2007.[67] Niyoyankana told Breiter that the US had demonstrated active commitment to Ugandan troops already deployed to Somalia, and Burundi wanted to get compatible equipment so that the two forces, Uganda and Burundi, work together seamlessly. Niyoyankana also told the Charge that Burundi had grossly underestimated the number of troops it could field. Instead Burundi would contribute two battalions of 850 men each, and additional 300 personnel to serve as command staff and military advisors. Altogether, Burundi was looking at putting 2,000 personnel in Somalia in short order. Breiter responded that she had faxed the entire list of Burundi forces needs to Washington, and that the USG would carefully consider the request.

Later, the same day, in a confidential cable to Washington, Breiter wrote, "It is clear that, although Burundi is willing to deploy forces to Somalia, it cannot do so without significant donor assistance. The Embassy will continue to coordinate with potential donors here to determine what type of assistance other countries may be willing to provide."[68] But Burundi was impatient. During a stopover in Addis Ababa where she met with US envoy to the AU, Ambassador Cindy Courville accompanied by Ambassador Donald Yamamoto, on April 2, 2007, Burundi Foreign Minister Antoinette Batumubwira pressed for a quicker response from the US.[69] On her way to Accra, Ghana, Batumubwira told the American diplomats that Burundi was committed to deploying the troops. But there were many challenges, she said, not the least of which was strategic lift for the troops. Burundi also wanted to survey the area where the troops were to be deployed, get additional equipment for the mission, and provide additional training. Batumubwira further argued that the mission would be successful with an outreach to the people to explain what the mission was all about. Clearly, throughout the discussion, the minister was anxious to portray her country as moving in the right direction. The political situation was getting better, and President Nkurunziza was in control. Courville responded by describing the situation on the ground, making no promise on what the US was willing or able to provide for the Burundi troops.

Despite flatly saying no to deploying its own forces to Somalia, meanwhile, South Africa was open to training Burundi troops. At a meeting with US Deputy Chief of Mission (DCM) to South Africa Donald "Don" Teitelbaum on April 13, 2007, South Africa's envoy to the Great Lakes and DFA Deputy Director General, Ambassador Kingsley Mamabolo observed that his government would support the training of Burundi troops.[70] The request for training needed to come from the AU itself rather than from Burundi. South Africa Department of Defense would take the lead in the technical discussion. Before all this could happen, Mamabolo suggested, Burundi needed equipment for the troops.

To assess the needs of the Burundi troops, AU military leaders flew to Burundi on a four-day working trip from June 10 to 13, 2007.[71] Led by Uganda's Major General Benon Buta Biraaro, the eight-person team included representatives from the US, UK and French forces. The team inspected two Burundi battalions on June 12, 2007. It also held a lengthy discussion with Burundi's Ministry of Defense officials led by Gen. Germain Niyoyankana. Biraaro and his team were at pain to describe in plain details the expectations on the ground in Somalia. The mission was a difficult one, and Burundi needed to be prepared to avoid a disaster. Niyoyankana was not deterred.

Later, in a private discussion with US Ambassador to Burundi, Patricia N. Moller, Gen. Biraaro provided his candid assessment of the capabilities of the Burundi forces designated to serve in Somalia.[72] Burundi was determined to send no less than a battalion to Somalia, said Biraaro. Gen. Niyoyankana had made that very clear to the AU technical team. Niyoyankana had also insisted that the force have the capability to defend itself if the situation arose. The AU team, however, was not convinced that Burundi was ready. If all went well, and training started the week of June 18, 2007, the deployment of troops could begin toward the end of July 2007. Burundi direly needed equipment. Gen. Biraaro suggested that the long list of requirements could be shortened somewhat, especially since Burundi troops were slated to provide force protection units for military installations, the airport, and seaport. This arrangement would free up Uganda troops already familiar with the situation in Somalia to engage in more complex mission. At a minimum, according to Gen. Biraaro, Burundi troops needed additional training, body armor, water capabilities, transportation and communication equipment as conditions for deployment. On the positive side, Biraaro saw Burundi's deployment to Somalia as the push other African countries needed to contribute troops toward the Somalia mission. If tiny Burundi could do it, surely other more established African nations could do the same.

Despite the reservations of the AU team, Burundi Army released a press statement saying that the AU Team had confirmed Burundi's troops technical competence. The "first battalion could leave in July for Somalia", the announcement said.[73] This was all dependent, of course, on the provision of equipment for the troops. In a follow-up meeting on June 14, 2007 in Bujumbura, Gen. Niyoyankana insisted to Ann Breiter and the Embassy Acting Defense Attaché (A/DATT) that Burundi must send a battalion, nothing less. He repeated his argument that the larger number would allow the troops to defend themselves in a hostile environment. Breiter responded that the US could not provide weapons and ammunitions, but could provide equipment and other services.

In mid-July, Belgium's Minister for Defense Andre Flahaut met General Niyoyankana in Bujumbura to discuss what, if anything, Belgium could do to support Burundi's impending deployment to Somalia.[74] The Burundi general told Flahaut that Burundi needed tanks for the protection of Burundi troops. Since the US had already assured Burundi on equipment for one battalion, Niyoyankana asked that Belgium match the US contribution with a similar pledge of equipment. As narrated later to US Embassy officials in Brussels by Belgium's Senior Envoy to the Great Lakes Josef Smets, Flahaut's blunt assessment was that Burundi was not capable of fielding a single unit, let alone a battalion.[75] Belgium would help, likely with training of officers, logistics, administration, management, and medical staff.

There was further bad news for Burundi's planned deployment to Somalia. At a Paris meeting with US Embassy Deputy Chief of Mission Mark A. Pekala on August 8, 2007, the Desk Officer for Somalia at the French Ministry for Foreign Affairs, Thierry Caboche told the American that France would not provide additional resources for Burundi Forces deploying under AMISOM.[76] Caboche said the Government of France was already doing more than its share in other African-related projects including the coming deployment of EU peacekeeping mission to Eastern Chad and part of Central African Republic (CAR). France might work toward eliminating piracy along the coast of Somalia, but direct contribution toward AMISOM would not happen.

On September 18, 2007, while meeting Burundi's government officials to discuss ongoing political deadlock between Burundi's ruling party and opposition parties, DAS James Swan reassured Gen. Niyoyankana that the Americans were doing everything to ensure the delivery of equipment for troops bound for Somalia.[77] According to Swan, the US was doing everything feasible to ensure that DynCorp delivered the equipment as soon as possible. Despite the delays, the first 100 Burundi troops landed in Mogadishu on Sunday, December 23, 2007. At the head of the Burundi troops was the contingent commander Brigadier General Juvenal Niyoyunguruza. Tall, lean and with a certain noble bearing, General Niyoyunguruza cut a very exacting figure of a leader. Captain Paddy Ankunda, the AMISOM spokesperson, could not keep the excitement out of his voice when he announced to the media, "One hundred peacekeepers from Burundi have just landed here."[78] The following day, Monday, December 24, 2007, a further 92 Burundi troops were flown into Mogadishu in a Uganda cargo plane.[79] Armed with AK-47 automatic weapons, the new arrival marched off with a swagger toward their temporary quarters within the AU base near the airport. They were the avant-gardes sent to prepare the way for the rest of Burundi's two battalions whose arrivals were expected within two weeks in January 2008.

General Karuhanga, having weathered the first nine months of the mission hunkered down in one place, took the arrival of Burundi troops in stride. Addressing the media, he said appreciatively, "We are privileged to have Burundian troops deploying here." Then, he added as he always did, "We appeal to other African peacekeepers that pledged peacekeepers to emulate and deploy their troops to Somalia."[80]

By the time the bulk of Burundi troops arrived, unpacked and settled in their new dig at Mogadishu University, the reality on the ground had changed drastically. Gen. Karuhanga, Col. Elwelu and AMISOM spokesperson Capt. Ankunda had ended their tour of duty in Somalia in February 2008, and expected back home on February 20, 2008. Maj. Gen. Francis Okello, the new force commander, had a new team to work with including the new contingent commander for Ugandan forces Colonel Godfrey Golooba and AMISOM spokesperson Major Barigye Ba-Hoku. The new team worked hard to maintain the status quo established by their predecessors, staying out of trouble with the insurgents. As in the early months of deployment, self-defense was interpreted in the narrowest terms possible. The political bosses at the AU Secretariat in Addis Ababa clung stubbornly to the outgunned notion that this was a peacekeeping mission. Maj. Barigye Ba-Hoku summed up neatly the stay-out-of-trouble policy. The unwritten rules of engagement, he explained to the media, meant that "insurgents could have a party in front of our gate and we couldn't do anything unless they attacked us first."[81]

The insurgency, too, had matured into a movement with a big following, structure, and war plan. Almost daily now, the insurgents were trading artillery and gunfire with the Ethiopians and the TFG forces. Moreover, the bulk of insurgents had begun consolidating under one fighting group. It was known as Harakat al-Shabaab al-Mujahideen (HSM).

# HSM — Harakat al-Shabaab al-Mujahideen

The invasion of Somalia by Ethiopia with US military involvement galvanized and united the fractious Somali people as no other previous event had since the overthrow of Siyaad Barre. By the beginning of January 2007 as many as 30,000 Ethiopian troops were in Somalia to support the weak TFG militia propping the Transitional Federal Government (TFG) of President Abdullahi Yusuf Ahmed.[1] Drawn mostly from the president's area of Puntland, the TFG conscripts were hastily trained by Ethiopia in the early months of 2007, and numbered around 5,000.[2] The US military, while keeping well into the background, was just as involved in the war with Islamists. In early 2007, the CIA ramped up the hunt for Saleh Nabhan and Harun Fazul, and senior members of the Somali militants. On January 7, 2007, in an assault coordinated with Ethiopian forces in Somalia, a Lockheed AC-130 ground attack aircraft flew out of a base in eastern Ethiopia and attacked a militant camp near the isolated fishing village of Ras Kamboni in southern Somalia, killing as many as 20 people. Barely two weeks later, on January 23, 2007, the AC-130 gunship struck a second time. The target this time was Sheikh Ahmed Madobe, a senior member of the Islamic Courts Union (ICU). Madobe survived. On June 1, 2007, a US Navy destroyer from the 5th fleet operating in the Red Sea fired cruise missiles at the hideout of Somali militants with ties to Al Qaeda near a mountainous village in semi-autonomous Puntland.

In the early morning of May 1, 2008, after three missiles fired from a US navy ship slammed into a house in Dusamareeb district in Galguudud region of central Somalia, the Americans scored a big coup. Somali militant leader Aden Hashi Ayro, and several of his aides were killed. In the excellently researched book *al-Shabaab in Somalia*, Stig Jarle Hansen writes that Ayro was an important military trainer and one of the early leaders of young militia fighters known as Hizbul Shabaab who formed the nucleus of the resistance against the Ethiopian troops.[3] The others were Muktar Robow aka Abu Mansoor as overall military commander, and Ismael Mahmoud Muhammad leading the political wing. Shabaab was instrumental in the ICU victory six months earlier over the warlords, and had aggressively recruited among the youth. Beginning June 15, 2006, the militant youth enjoyed an immense influence within the Islamic Courts Union. Under Ayro's command, the youth fighters were rewarded and replenished with huge quantities of arms flown aboard four Eritrean military planes that landed at an airport near Dhusamareeb.[4] AK-47 assault rifles, PKM machine guns, Russian-made RPG-7VR, ammunition and military uniforms were delivered, loaded onto trucks which then drove away toward Mogadishu, trailed by 12 technicals. More arms were shipped from the port of Assad in Eritrea, arriving on June 19, 2006 at the El Ade seaport near Mogadishu, all of it distributed to militant fighters in Mogadishu, Marka, Baraawe and Kongo training camp, near Johwar.[5] The militants' biggest show of strength came on September 24, 2006 when the combined forces led by

Aden Hashi Ayro and Hassan Turki entered the port city of Kismaayo without as much as firing a shot.

Under Aden Hashi Ayro, the young militants quickly gained prominence within the rapidly evolving resistance that, in the early days of Ethiopia's invasion, operated as disparate militias with names such as al-Harakah al-Muqawaamah al-Sha'biyah fi al-Bilad al-Hijratayn (The Popular Resistance Movement in the Land of the Two Migrations, PRMLTM), Tawhid wa'l-Jihad Brigades, even Young Mujahideen Movement in Somalia.[6] Collectively known by the general population as the "Muqawaamah", the resistance soon became synonymous with the mostly underground urban warfare directed by al-Shabaab at Ethiopian and TFG forces.[7] Using mortars, small arms and improvised explosive devices (IEDs) the resistance fighters began engaging Ethiopian troops, targeting their bases at the former Ministry of Defence building at Ganshandiga, Digfer, New Seaport, Villa Somalia, around the center of the city at Kilometer Four (KM-4) and convoys traversing Industrial Road. Although mostly ineffective against the superior Ethiopian armour and well-armed troops, nevertheless, these attacks gave a sense of resilience and pride to many Somali people. The Ethiopian invasion was not being taken lying down.

Early in 2007 reports began emerging of Islamic militants recruiting young Somali men for training by jihadists in various camps around the country. The recruitment was mostly by word of mouth, carried out at night at specific locations, targeting mostly Hawiye youth in Mogadishu.[8] The trend soon emerged for young men with guns to grow big beards. At first derisively referred to as *mooryan gerley*, bearded militias, a dismissive description of some of the young city layabouts who began growing beards after the Ethiopian invasion to impress and bother ordinary Somali on city streets, the militias grew in number and strength.[9] They also began talking to people about matters of morality, piety, and jihad. As one Mogadishu resident familiar with the group in the early days of the resistance put it, "They throw a few words in Arabic and quote from the Quran as if they are muftis."[10]

By the middle of 2007, however, young men who previously disappeared from Mogadishu neighbourhoods and other big towns across Somalia began reappearing as Islamist fighters opposed to the Ethiopian occupation of their country. The youthful militants increasingly referred to as al-Shabaab toward the beginning of 2008 fashionably put around their necks red or black *cimaamad* scarves, and wore headdresses similar to those worn by radical Islamists in Pakistan, Afghanistan and the Middle East. Depending on the specialization, recruits were trained at various camps throughout southern Somalia. Those slated for suicide operations were trained with the Al Faruq Brigades at Elberde in the Bakool region in Hiraan province, and the Salaaxudhin unit in the Huriwa district of Mogadishu. Recruits at the al Faruq Muaskar base in Ras Kamboni, fashioned by al-Qaeda operatives Saleh Ali Nabhan and Abu Talha al Sudani to resemble the al Faruq training camp near Kandahar, Afghanistan, were taught to handle automatic weapons and hand-to-hand combat. At the Eel Aarfid training camp, recruits specialized in reconnaissance and kidnapping for ransom as well as to bargain for the release of al-Shabaab members in government prisons. In addition to weapons training and martial combat, the recruits spent part of the day learning about the Jihad against people who hate Islam, the invaders coming to take over all Muslim lands. It was the duty of every good Muslim to fight the "crusaders" and, if need be, die a martyr for the cause of liberating Muslim people, not only in Somalia but elsewhere around the world.

By early 2008, al-Shabaab emerged as the focal point for the resistance against

Ethiopia and later African Union and TFG forces. According to researcher Stig Jarle Hansen, al-Shabaab offered a clear leadership structure and organizational discipline after the ICU leadership fled Mogadishu ahead of advancing Ethiopian forces.[11] A new *shura* council inclusive of different clans and foreign elements was established with leadership that included an executive committee, a military council and lower level commanders and regional representatives. At the top of the political and military structure was Ahmed Aw Abdi Mahamoud Godane. Known also as Mukhtar Abu Zubeyr, from the Arab subclan of the Isaaq clan, Godane attended an Islamic school in Hargeisa in Somaliland, and travelled to post-Soviet Afghanistan for an unknown number of years until 2001. Godane was appointed to the post of secretary general of the Islamic Courts Union when it ascended to power in June 2006. He would fashion himself the overall emir of the organisation, seeking counsel from the shura, yet not beholden to it for decisions and direction of al-Shabaab.

The inner circle of power and influence included Fu'ad Mahamed Khalaf 'Shongole', from the Awrtabe subclan of the Darood clan, first appointed to lead the education committee by the ICU shura, and later used his lived experiences in Sweden where he acquired citizenship to formalize financial, law and order structures within al-Shabaab. An equally forceful thinker in the upper leadership of the organisation is Mukhtar Abdullahi Ali Robow who spent some years in Afghanistan, where he likely picked up the *nom de guerre* Abu Mansur. From Leysan subclan of Rahanweyn clan, he demonstrated his military leadership during the ICU campaigns in mid-2006 and was instrumental in setting up the military structure of al-Shabaab in 2007. He also later became the spokesperson for the organisation. Especially crucial in giving mature guidance toward consolidating the al-Shabaab structure was veteran militia leader Hassan Dahir Aweys who, although from the Ayr sub clan of the Hawiye/Habar Gidir, was focused on the larger mission of establishing Somalia as an Islamic state.[12]

By the middle of 2009, the top echelon of al-Shabaab transcended clan politics to include powerful leaders like political chief Hussein Ali Fidow (Hawiye/Murusade), spokesman and commander Ali Mohamed 'Raghe' also known as Ali Dheere (Hawiye Murusade), military spokesman Abdi Aziz 'Abu Mus'ab' (Darood/Marehan), co-heads of Maktabatu Amniyaat, the intelligence and internal security organ, Muktar Abu Seyla'i (Isaaq) and Mahad Mohamed Ali also known as Mahad Karate (Hawiye/Habar Gidir), head of al fatwa Mukhtar Mohamed Osman (Mirifle/Rahanweyn) and regional commander in Puntland Mohamed Sa'id Atom (Darood/Warsangeli). While each personality brought his own vision of what the organisation needed to focus on, there was unanimity on expelling the foreign troops from Somalia.

At the height of its strength, from mid-2009 to July 2010, al-Shabaab was a lean, structured and very well funded organisation pulling in as much as $15 million per month from an array of revenue sources including port taxations and trade in charcoal and sugar, 'zakat' or jihad contributions from individual citizens as war contribution, diaspora remittances from its supporters in Europe, the Americas and elsewhere in the Middle East, and external assistance mainly from Eritrea. The funds were used to buy weapons and to pay the militias and for specific contributions during battle against the Ethiopian forces, the TFG, and AMISOM.[13]

Five months prior to the invasion of Somalia by Ethiopia, Osama bin Laden called on Muslims everywhere to support the fledgling Islamic Courts Union (ICU) after its sweeping victory over the warlords. The message sent from hiding said in part, "We warn all the world not to agree to America's request to send international forces to Somalia. We swear to Allah that we will fight its soldiers on Somali soil, and we reserve the right to punish on their own soil, or anywhere else, at the appropriate time and in the appropriate manner."[14] The message was meant to boost the morale of the Islamists in Mogadishu. After all, the militant leadership of the Somali Islamists had sheltered elements of al-Qaeda East Africa—Abu Talha al Sudani, Fazul Harun and Saleh Ali Saleh Nabhan— who supported the ICU's push for control over Somalia in early 2006. al Sudani, a Sudanese citizen who first travelled to Somalia in the fall of 1993 to fight the Americans, and later trained in various al-Qaeda international camps including Bekaa Valley in Lebanon, featured prominently as a commander in the battle for Kismaayo in September 2006. After the ICU established its authority over Somalia, the three al-Qaeda operatives were responsible for global recruitment, organising weapons and explosive trainings, and arranging logistics including weapons from Eritrea. They were especially effective in early 2007 in securing human expertise from Afghanistan and Pakistan in the making and deployment of improvised explosive devices (IEDs) used with devastating results by al-Shabaab.

In working with al-Qaeda operatives, the leaders of the Somali militant deliberately ignored any contradiction between the ideology of global jihad and the nationalistic resistance focused primarily on dislodging Ethiopian forces and the TFG largely seen as a puppet government for Ethiopia. Stig Jarle Hansen succinctly encapsulates the group's strategic exploitation of the al-Qaeda connection. Hansen writes, "The exact border between pan-Islamism and a form of patriotism becomes blurred, and this confusion, combined with a lack of knowledge of the organisation, probably helped al-Shabaab to gain local acceptance, as did its heavy emphasis on bringing justice to Somalia, to prevent crime."[15]

By framing the Somali resistance as a global struggle to protect Muslims from attacks from non-Muslims, a fight between Islam and imperialism, no less, the resistance leaders captured the imagination of young foreign Muslims after the Ethiopian invasion. From a trickle, young Muslim recruits started arriving in Somalia using well-established underground network of contacts in North America, Europe, Middle East, Kenya and Somalia. By mid-2007, alarmed US law enforcement began receiving reports from concerned family members of dozens of young Americans of Somali heritage disappearing from their relatively comfortable suburbia homes in Seattle, Minneapolis, and Detroit, to return to a country they hardly knew.[16] Similar trends were noted in Canada where socially isolated young Somali men left Toronto, Calgary and Edmonton to travel to Somalia.[17] These youth, radicalized in mosques across North America with the belief that it was their moral duty as good Muslims to answer Allah's call, were turning up in Somalia to join the war against the occupying Ethiopian army. Fighting the Ethiopian "Crusaders" was a good war, a jihad. Carrying American, Canadian and European passports and cash rustled from mostly sympathetic relatives and friends, the youth easily travelled to Kenya before slipping into Somalia. Once in Somalia, they were given guns to begin training in camps dispersed throughout Somalia, especially in Mogadishu, Merka, Kismaayo and Afgooye.

Information on the al-Qaeda link to the disappearing American youth got a boost in July 2009 when a US federal grand jury in Minneapolis, MN indicted two Somali Americans Salah Osman Ahmed and Abdifatah Yusuf Isse on one count apiece for providing material support to terrorists and conspiracy to kill, kidnap, maim or injure people overseas.[18] Ahmed was in Somalia the previous year, and provided officials with an inside look of the militants' training camps. Less than a month later, a Minnesota man Kamal Said Hassan pleaded guilty in a Minneapolis court to travelling to Somalia "to fight the Ethiopians".[19] From the information provided by Hassan and the other Somali men in custody, the CIA created detailed intelligence on the violent militants operating inside Somalia. Most crucially, the agency finally had a finger on the habits and movements of Saleh Nabhan and Fazul Harun, the two most wanted al-Qaeda operatives actively involved in recruiting, training and fielding youth from overseas.

Among the first North American youths to enter Somalia was Omar Hammami, later to become famous as al-Shabaab publicist known by the *nom de guerre* Abu-Mansoor al-Amriki. A central figure in the propaganda war waged by al-Shabaab through social media to both to win sympathy and new recruits from Europe and North America, Hammami helped give a face to the insurgents. Among the global recruits who answered the call were Muslim convert Troy Kastigar, known by his Somali peers as Mohamad Abdurahman, 27, and American-Somali Mohamoud Hassan, 23, both from the Twin City of Minneapolis, Minnesota.[20] Sometime between Nov. 1, 2008 and Nov. 3, 2008, both men left Minneapolis for Somalia. Three other young American men of Somali descent accompanied them on the trip. Hassan, an engineering student at the University of Minnesota, loved poetry, and could recite quotes from the Quran by heart.

Troy Kastigar was different. Not a Somali by birth but Muslim by choice, he was part Native American and part white. Before leaving for Somalia, he was a delinquent American kid involved in petty crimes. He wrote bad cheques, and drove without permit on the streets of Minneapolis. At some point in 2004, he began hanging out with Somali youth in Minneapolis who, like him, felt like outsiders, left behind by the promise of the American Dream of the good life. Troy began frequenting mosques where he felt welcome and "at home" among the Somali people. He grew a small goatee. Then he took on the Muslim name Abdurahman, servant of the Most Merciful.[21]

According to those familiar with the story of the two American in Somalia, both trained at various camps including at Laanta-Buro in Afgooye where other American youths, mostly of Somali descent trained to fight the Ethiopian invaders, and later AU forces.[22] They were easily among the most active recruits in camps. Hassan was the storyteller. Exceedingly intelligent and a confident fighter, he was well liked by the commanders. They said he was a born leader. He was prepared to die for al-Shabaab, something many American youth his age could never quite fathom, they said.

Unlike the outgoing Hassan, Kastigar was mostly a loner. When not in training, he was often seen sheltering under a tree away from the hot Somali sun, brooding or writing something in a small black notebook. During operations in Mogadishu in early 2009, Kastigar walked with a swagger, a bristle of beards on his chin, looking the part of a jihadist. A 40 minutes al-Shabaab recruitment video made sometime in early 2009, featured Dahir Gure also called Mu'sab, Mohammed Hassan and Troy Kastigar. The latter, thin, gaunt and missing an upper front tooth excoriated American youth for their soft purposeless life. "This is the best place to be, honestly," Kastigar had said in the video recorded during training. "If you guys only knew how much fun we have, this is the real Disneyland. You need to come here and join us, take pleasure in this fun."[23]

It was no fun at all in the battlefield. News of casualties among American youth fighting in Somalia grew more common in 2009. Burhan Hassan, 17 from Minnesota was reported killed in a battle in Mogadishu in the first week of June 2009.[24] Dahir Gure died around the same time while commanding an al-Shabaab unit against TFG and African Union forces. Then there were the deaths of Hassan and Kastigar. For the benefit of young foreign and domestic recruits, al-Shabaab elevated to mythical proportion the story of the deaths of Troy Kastigar and Hassan Mohammed. According to the propaganda released by al-Kataib, the al-Shabaab media production team, the two were killed during a gun battle with AMISOM and TFG forces in north Mogadishu in the early morning of September 6, 2009. The storyline in the video titled *The Path to Paradise: From the Twin City to the Land of Two Migrations* was that the two Americans died on the Seventeenth day of Ramadan, a most holy period for Muslims.[25] As dusk gathered the previous evening, and Mogadishu residents were preparing for *iftar*, dinner to break the day long fast, the two young Americans joined the frontline attack on the Burundian troops based at Jalle Siyad Academy in Mogadishu.[26] The fight lasted the night, and extended for several days, with many casualties including five civilian deaths. At some point in the battle, as they fought the Burundi troops, both Hassan and Kastigar were fatally injured. Videos taken from the frontline showed Hassan and Kastigar laid side by side on their death mats while another militant intoned the Muslim prayers for the soul of the departed.[27]

Such videos of young foreign fighters killed in action were especially valued as al-Shabaab's teaching tool for those recruited for suicide missions in which the attackers perish alongside the targeted victims. The potent tactic of killing oneself in the course of inflicting mass casualties was foreign to Somalia, but quickly adopted as a weapon of choice by al-Shabaab. It was borrowed from al-Qaeda in Pakistan and Afghanistan, and used strategically to telegraph how committed al-Shabaab youth fighters were to the cause.[28] Youth recruited by al-Shabaab for suicide operations spoke about *shahada*, martyrdom as the true path, and dying a *shahid*, a martyr, as more noble than being blown up in inter-clan feuds. Those willing to die as martyrs were held as models for recruits to emulate, and in whose footsteps the chosen few should walk proudly.

The earliest confirmed incident of suicide attack was on September 18, 2006.[29] A car bomb targeted the convoy of the president of the Transitional Federal Government Abdullahi Ahmed Yusuf while on his way to address members of his parliament in Baidoa town. The president was not hurt, but the attack killed his brother and eight others, and destroyed all the cars in the convoy, forcing the president to walk back home on foot. The second suicide attack was on November 30, 2006.[30] It targeted an Ethiopian control post on one of the roads entering Baidoa in northwestern Somalia, killing eight people. As many as four suicide attacks took place in 2007 including the suicide car bomb attack on the Mogadishu home of Somalia transitional Prime Minister Ali Mohamed Ghedi on the afternoon of Sunday, June 4, 2007. The New York Times reported that the attacker sped through a roadblock outside the prime minister's home and rammed through a set of gate before exploding in "a fireball that flattened several buildings and scattered debris for blocks."[31] Six bodyguards and a student of a Koranic school across the street were killed. The multiple suicides attacks on October 29, 2008 on the semi autonomous regions of Somaliland and Puntland were significant, first, because of the sheer scale of the coordination. In the city of Hargeisa in Somaliland, three car bombs exploded at the Presidential Palace, the United Nations Development Program compound and Ethiopian consulate. Twenty people died at the Ethiopian consulate and at least five others in the other two facilities. At about the same time in Bosasso, the capital of Puntland, two suicide attackers drove their bomb-laden vehicles into the intelligence building, killing three people inside.[32]

More importantly, in that attack, an American Somali, Shirwa Ahmed, 26, was confirmed as one of the four suicide bombers.[33] The news provided conclusive information to US security services on how deeply committed and active radicalized American youth were in the war in Somalia. It also confirmed to relatives of some of the disappeared Somali youth the rumours of casualties in Somalia.

From a rag-tag militia army, al-Shabaab had grown into a powerful force that could field well-armed fighters into battle against equally well-armed Ethiopian army. The addition of training for suicide operations made al-Shabaab all the more deadly, especially against the African Union troops whose handlers in Addis Ababa clung to the outmoded notion of neutrality in the Somali conflict. To al-Shabaab, AMISOM was now a legitimate target, and it intended to pull the trigger.

The gathering strength of al-Shabaab worried US policymakers. More worrisome for America, Ethiopia was not being subtle about pulling out its troops and leaving the TFG government on its own. On February 27, 2008 during a visit to Baidoa, Ethiopian Foreign Minister Seyoum Mesfin met with President Abdullahi Ahmed Yusuf, Prime Minister Nur "Adde," and the Speaker of Parliament Sheikh Adan Mohamed Madobe together and separately to convey a tough message from his government. The TFG "shouldn't expect the Ethiopian umbrella to be cast for long unless they sat down to serious business" of building national institutions of governance and promoting reconciliation and stability.[34] Faced with an Ethiopian withdrawal, the US policy pirouetted toward finding a political solution to the crisis by engaging the very same people the US-supported Ethiopian invasion threw out of Mogadishu in December 2006. To get the reconciliation process in gear, the US put pressure on the TFG and at the UN. In a memo to US Ambassador to the United Nations Zalmay Khalilzad, Secretary of State Condoleezza Rice instructed the envoy to talk about Somalia reconciliation to the UN Security Council. Rice wrote, "We stress the need for all Somali stakeholders to not allow the efforts of extremist elements or the setback of recent clashes around Bakaara Market to deter from the overriding objective of achieving lasting peace and stability in Somalia."[35]

On the ground, the US forcefully nudged President Yusuf to accept the reconciliation process. In the evening of March 10, 2008 while in Nairobi on an overnight transit from Mogadishu to Dakar to attend the Organisation of Islamic Cooperation (OIC) summit slated for March 13-14, 2008, President Abdullahi Yusuf met with US Special Envoy for Somalia John Yates and Ambassador Michael Ranneberger briefly. The President revealed that the TFG cabinet had prepared a draft document for reconciliation of all the stakeholders, and he endorsed it. Yusuf, however, was not sure the extremists would join the process, and added, "Personally I do not want them to come."[36]

The draft reconciliation document in hand, the US, Somali Prime Minister Nur "Adde" Hassan Hussein and UN Special Representative of the Secretary General Ahmedou Ould Abdallah began reaching out to members of the opposition, especially the Eritrean-based Alliance for the Re-Liberation of Somalia (ARS) led by former ICU Chairman Sheikh Sharif Sheikh Ahmed. At the request of US Ambassador to Eritrea Ronald McMullen, a meeting was held on March 19, 2008 in Asmara with seven senior members of the group led by former Speaker of Parliament Sharif Hassan Sheikh Adan.[37] The ARS delegation included Puntland president Jama Ali Jama, former U.S. Marine Hussein Mohamed Farah, former Minister of Finance Colonel Omar Hashi Adan, and former Prime Minister of the Transitional National Government, Mohamed Abdi Yusuf. Former Somali Minister of Gender and Family Affairs, Fowsiya Mohamed Sheikh Hassan walked in with the group but quickly bowed out, leaving only the men to discuss the issues. The group let Ambassador McMullen know it was open to working with the US and engage in reconciliation talks. The problem was the continuing occupation of Somalia by Ethiopia. It had elevated al-Shabaab gunmen in the eyes of Somali people, now hailing the insurgents as heroes and freedom fighters. So long as Ethiopian forces were in Somalia, ARS could not talk to the TFG government. "There can be no solution while Ethiopia occupies Somalia," was the unanimous sentiment within the group.[38] In a follow-up meeting with Ambassador Michael Ranneberger and Special Envoy Yates in Nairobi the week of March 31 through April 4, ARS leaders, this time led by Sheikh Sharif Sheikh Ahmed, reiterated the same talking point—ARS was committed to the reconciliation process but, first, Ethiopia needed to get out of Somalia.[39] Ranneberger urged the group to legitimize itself by openly issuing a public statement calling for a neutral UN force to be deployed in Somalia.

The US, having abandoned President Abdullahi Ahmed Yusuf because the leader on principles opposed talks with ARS, discreetly arranged for the president to be away in Washington from mid-April to the second week of May 2008 while Somalia Prime Minister Nur Adde pushed the reconciliation process. Ranneberger wrote in a secret cable to Washington of the opportunity Yusuf's visit to the US presented, observing "With President Yusuf in the United States, he will be unable to influence directly day-to-day events in Somalia during a critical moment where reconciliation is gaining momentum."[40] With Yusuf neutered, SRSG Ahmedou Ould Abdallah spearheaded a meeting between ARS and TFG delegates in Djibouti on May 10, 2008. Incidentally, President Yusuf returned the same day from his three-weeks long trip to America. This time, Yusuf quietly admitted to Ambassador Ranneberger and Special Representative Yates that he was in support of talks with ARS.[41]

Further talks between the ARS and TFG started on the last day of May, and concluded ten days later with the initialing of an agreement between the parties on June 9, 2008. The agreement called for a UN force within 120 days, the re-deployment of Ethiopian troops out of Somalia, and cessation of violence.[42] Ethiopia began withdrawing some troops at the end of July 2008, and this accelerated toward the end of the year.

By mid-October, Ethiopia secretly began discussions to boot out of power Abdullahi Ahmed Yusuf. Ethiopian State Minister for Foreign Affairs Dr. Tekeda Alemu never one to speak softly, put it straight to Ambassador Donald Yamamoto during a meeting in Addis Ababa on October 14, 2008, saying, "Yusuf used to be our friend," but that he had become incorrigible.[43]

By the end of October 2008 US policy makers had completed the U-turn. Fully transitioning behind Sheikh Sharif Sheikh Ahmed, the very man previously called an Islamist against whom Washington supported an Ethiopian invasion of Somalia, it now regarded the former ICU chairman as a friendly moderate. With encouragement from Jendayi Frazer to show leadership on the ground, Sheikh Sharif led an eight-person delegation to Somalia on November 1, 2008, starting his trip in Johwar to rally the population to support the Djibouti Peace Agreement.[44] Four days later, on the night of November 5, 2008, the US elected Barack Hussein Obama, the first African-American President. The time was ripe for the US to act out more forcefully before the new Obama administration took over in January 2009. The first casualty of the new policy of reaching out to former foes was President Yusuf. During a private chat with Jendayi Frazer on December 22, 2008 at Nairobi Kenyatta International Airport, the envoy told Yusuf that the US government planned to openly support Prime Minister Hassan Hussein Nur Adde in the ongoing epic struggle within the TFG leadership. Plain as daylight, America had finally thrown Yusuf overboard, put the dagger in his back. A week later on December 29, 2008 at 10:00 a.m. in Baidoa President Abdullahi Ahmed Yusuf tendered his resignation.[45] Standing before 120 or so lawmakers, Yusuf said, "Most of the country is not in our hands and the international community has failed to help us."[46] Shortly afterward, Yusuf flew out to his home in Puntland.

At one time the enemy of America, the fortune of former chairman of the ICU was in ascendancy. On January 25, 2009, from different corners of the Horn of Africa, over 240 Somali members of parliament gathered at Djibouti's Peoples Palace to tweak the Somali constitution, and to elect a new president following the resignation of Yusuf. In the early morning of January 31, 2009, in second round of voting by an enlarged parliament, ARS Chairman Sheikh Sharif Sheikh Ahmed beat ten other candidates to become the new President of TFG. US Ambassador Ranneberger, in a cable to Washington two days later, with no trace of irony, wrote, "Ambassador Yates congratulated Sharif on his victory and recalled that his good working relationship with Sharif had begun in early 2007."[47]

The hardliners inside Somalia, however, were winning. Baidoa was added to the control of the insurgents. The carnage kept growing. Despite Zenawi's earlier promise to President Museveni that the ENDF would provide support should Uganda wish to withdraw its forces from Mogadishu, Ethiopia continued to plan to leave by the end of January 2009.[48] Uganda, in any case, chose to stick it out in Somalia. AMISOM forces under Force Commander Major General Francis Okello had been hamstrung by restrictive rules of engagement to be effective in stopping the territorial expansion by al-Shabaab, which had increasingly become bold and confident. More disturbing, the situation seemed to affect the morale of Uganda troops, forcing President Museveni to recall General Okello back to Uganda in early July 2009.[49] The replacement Force Commander Major General Nathan Mugisha who took over in July 2009 was different— he was a fighter not afraid to take the fight to the insurgents, and win. War between AMISOM and the insurgents was inevitable. The only question left was when it would happen. al-Shabaab provided the answer by taking the fight to AMISOM on September 17, 2009, the day suicide bombers attacked AMISOM base.

### Preparation for a Suicide Operation

An al-Shabaab commander told Omar Mohamud, 18, on September 7, 2009 that he had been chosen for a mission to be carried out in a few days in Mogadishu. Omar was one of several young Somali-American recruits who arrived in Somalia between the fall of 2007 and the fall of 2008. According to a source, the youth had not been happy with his life in America where he never felt he belonged.[50] His exit from Seattle, Washington, where his father ran a small shop to support the family, was uneventful. He was just another immigrant youth travelling to Africa for a short visit with relatives. From Seattle-Tacoma International Airport, Omar flew to Europe, and took a flight to Nairobi, Kenya. There he stayed with strangers in a house in Eastleigh, a suburb of Nairobi with many Somali residents. The contacts eventually arranged for him and a half dozen other young men to travel to a coastal town north of Mombasa where a small boat ferried them to Somalia.

In Somalia, Omar passed through Muaskar Faruq base in areas controlled by Ras Kamboni militias, before moving to the Laanta-Buro camp, 40 kilometers southwest of Mogadishu, near the village of Hawo-Tako in Afgooye district in Lower Shabelle. There he joined recruits from America and other countries undergoing weapons training. At Lanta-Buru camp, some of his Somali peers nicknamed him Omar al-Amriki, the American. The local recruits used the nomenclature "al-Amriki" with just about any recruit who came from America and Canada. To the Somali-born recruits who grew inside Somalia, Omar was a black Somali kid on the outside but white on the inside. American Somalis often sprinkled their English conversations with phrases of Arabic and Somali. They also retained American mannerisms such as hi-fiving each other, drinking bottled water because they feared the local water was contaminated and were favoured by the senior al-Shabaab commanders, who gave them better treatment.

Omar felt he was black like the other Somali youth, and could not understand why his Somali peers could not accept him as a Somali first, not a foreigner from America. In training, Omar learned to fire machineguns, the use of suicide belts, surveillance of targets, blending with the local population, and staying undetected until the last moment of attack.

On the morning of Wednesday, September 8, 2009, Omar and a dozen other fighters packed their meager belongings for the 40 minutes journey on the back of a pick-up truck to Maslah training camp, located just north of Mogadishu. There, he joined young fighters from other camps also assembled, many meeting each other for the first time. Altogether the group numbered about fifty young fighters between the ages of 17 and 24. Over the weekend of September 12-13, 2009, Omar met four other young men—Mohamed Abdullahi, 25, also known as 'Ato', Ahmed, Ali, and Abdi.[51] All five young men were specially selected for *istishhad*, martyrdom.[52] None other than Saleh Ali Nabhan whom they knew only as *Moalim Saleh*, the teacher, carefully nurtured the five youths for suicide missions. Nabhan and top al-Shabaab commanders had drawn up a detailed plan for the suicide attack inside the African Union forces base in Mogadishu.

The operational leader of the group was Mohamed Abdullahi. A Galjeceel of the Hawiye clan, Abdullahi was selected for his confident leadership. Before joining al-Shabaab a year and half earlier, Abdullahi was often seen around Suuqa Holaha livestock market in north Mogadishu.[53] He earned money as a gifted negotiator with a silver tongue. He played both sides of the livestock commerce, something he was very good at. Many a goat seller got good money for his goats and sheep and, for the right price, Abdullahi also got the best price for a buyer. When the call came for young recruits to join al-Shabaab, Abdullahi gave up his lucrative trade, and joined the insurgents. He was a natural born leader, eloquent, confident and always eager to do well.

Two months earlier around midday on July 20, 2009 the insurgents had commandeered two white Toyota Land Cruiser 100 series vehicles from the walled compound of the UN World Food Programme (WFP) headquarter in Wajid. A UN bulletin released in Nairobi later the same day said simply, "al Shabab members visited the WFP compound in Wajid for a meeting. They took away two cars and some furniture that were not WFP property."[54] The cars were then brought to Mogadishu where they were carefully modified by mechanics to carry the massive bombs put together by expert bomb-makers. The bomb-makers, from Algeria, Pakistan and Afghanistan had put the final touches to the elaborately constructed bombs at an al-Shabaab base at the former steel factory in North Mogadishu, located a scant 800 meters from Mogadishu Stadium. The bomb components included several mortar shells strung together by fuses and other parts smuggled into Mogadishu. The payloads to be delivered in the two vehicles were powerful enough to spew death for several meters from the point of detonation.

al-Shabaab commanders had discussed at great length the order in which the bomb-laden vehicles were to arrive at the gate of AMISOM base. The commanders decided that the lead car should carry the bigger bomb targeting AMISOM headquarters. The two Toyota trucks would drive the massive vehicle-borne improvised explosive devices (VBIED) through the gates leading to AMISOM base in Halaane. The lead Toyota carrying a front seat passenger and two others in the cabin seats was to turn right to use an alternate gate to enter AMISOM Forces Headquarters. The second vehicle driven by a lone driver would turn left, enter through Medina gate and head for the DynCorp warehouses at the foot of Aden Abdulle Airport. The warehouses served as a clearing point for logistics serving the continental troops from Uganda and Burundi. That way, should the first Toyota truck make it inside the fenced base, the driver of the lead vehicle was to drive on to AMISOM headquarters and detonate the bomb. If entry was denied to both vehicles, both vehicles were to rendezvous near the alternate gate, use one bomb to open way for the other to go through onto the base to deliver the bomb. AMISOM headquarters was the main target, hitting it was the prime goal of the attack.

Omar's role was crucial for the success of the mission. Omar grew up in America and, therefore, spoke excellent English with the carefree attitude of a Somali exposed to American culture. Since Abdullahi, the operational leader and the other three youth spoke little or no English, Omar Mohamud was to do the talking at the Halaane gate. al-Shabaab commanders agreed that Omar Mohamud would ride with Abdullahi in the front seat of the lead Toyota. Ahmed and Ali, the two passengers in the back seats of the lead vehicle, were to be passed off as UN Somali contract workers. Abdi, the lone driver heading for the DynCorp warehouses, though not fluent, spoke enough English to gain him entry into the base. A young Hawiye with a prominent forehead, and narrow face dusted with scraggly hints of beard, Abdi was an easy-going young man. In school, he had a good head for numbers, and his parents wanted him to become a doctor. When the war came in December 2006, he was drawn into the insurgency.

Over the next few days, the youth trained, prepared and shot videos of their last testimonials. On the early afternoon of Sunday, September 13, 2009, Mohamed Abdullahi took the four youth to Mogadishu Stadium to unveil the mission. In its heyday, the stadium constructed with the help of Chinese engineering in 1978 during the era of Siyaad Barre, could hold as many as 35,000 spectators. Athletes from across the continent competed in various sporting events. The long civil war mostly reduced the venue to a dilapidated skeletal concrete that served as a live fire training facility for al-Shabaab militants. Here militants tested the effectiveness of armour piercing .50 calibre bullets against slabs of metal of varying thickness that simulated AMISOM's armored personnel carriers and battle tanks. Fired at close range, the powerful bullets left telltale holes drilled clean through steel. It was enough evidence of the firepower that al-Shabaab had amassed. AMISOM's armored vehicles were vulnerable.

At the stadium Mohamed Abdullahi gathered his charges at the center of the pitch. He arranged pieces of broken white concrete blocks to represent the targets. Using a stick, he pointed out the triangular block that stood apart from the others representing the DynCorp warehouses at Aden Abdulle Airport. The plan was to get as close as possible to the warehouse before unleashing the bomb that would obliterate it. Abdullahi then turned his attention to the three small blocks set side by side. They represented the three buildings that made up AMISOM Forces headquarters inside the Halaane Base. The first car bomb was to be detonated in front of the middle block that housed the office of AMISOM Force Commander. From outside, as chaos ensued following the detonations of the twin bombs, assault units would attack the base with small arms fire and mortar to wreak maximum casualties. As Abdullahi spoke, Abdi seemed a bit distracted. He pulled absentmindedly on bits and pieces of grass on the ground, lost in his own thoughts. But then to cheer everyone up, a live-round rehearsal was conducted inside the stadium to simulate the auxiliary forces storming of AMISOM headquarters.

The five young men were ready for martyrdom.

# Operation Celestial Balance

On Monday, September 14, 2009, at 12:31 p.m., three days before the twin suicide bombing at AMISOM Forces base in Halaane, Mogadishu, a pair of AH-6 Little Bird gunships and two MH-60M Black Hawk helicopters revved up their engines for take off from the open wind-swept deck of the USS Bataan (LHD5), the 844 feet long US Navy Wasp-class amphibious assault warship nicknamed "Dirty Nickel", homeport Norfolk, Virginia. Moored in the Indian Ocean, just off the coast of Somalia, the naval vessel was part of the US 5th Fleet patrol in the Gulf and Horn of Africa. On board the choppers were two dozens US Special Forces of the Red Squadron from the Naval Special Warfare Development Group (NSWDG or DEVGRU), recognized worldwide as SEAL Team Six (ST6). These were the elite in the US secret arsenal for fighting terrorism around the globe. The SEAL never announces its entrance or exit from a mission. Not given to much display of emotion, these tough men of action trained hard for dangerous undertakings such as the one they were about to engage in inside Somalia.

With the midday sun biting down on their heads, a few of the ship's crews assembled on the deck of the warship to see the boys off on the daring daylight mission. On hand was commanding officer of the USS Bataan Captain Samuel Charles-Henry Howard. At over six-foot tall, the African American sailor born in Fort Dix, New Jersey, towered over most of the men. With him was Colonel Gareth Brandl, the commanding officer of the 22nd Marine Expeditionary Unit (MEU), ranking officers, petty officers and a bunch of SEAL not on this mission.[1] Flight deck crewmen in bright orange vests and fat earmuffs covering their ears from the deafening roar of engines and whirring blades directed the choppers in preparation for takeoff.

With the signal for takeoff given, one after the other, the Little Birds, then the Black Hawks lifted lazily into the air. The four choppers banked sharply right, then skimming just above the blue waters of the Indian Ocean, headed west toward the white sandy coastline of Somalia. They were piloted by experienced members of the First Battalion of the US 160th Special Operations Aviation Regiment (SOAR), based in Fort Campbell, Kentucky. Also known as Night Stalkers for their specialty in night flying, these were easily the best helicopter pilots in the world, their skills especially called for on this mission.

The SEAL's mid-afternoon foray inside Somalia was codenamed Operation Celestial Balance. The order for the mission came directly from the White House in Washington. It was to take out a high value target (HVT), an al-Qaeda affiliate. Information from the CIA and Intelligence Support Activity (ISA) indicated that the HVT and seven militants were travelling in a two-vehicle convoy from the Somali coastal town of Merka to the port-city of Kismaayo, located about 500 kilometers southwest of Mogadishu. The HVT and four other foreign fighters were in a beige all-terrain UAZ-469 truck. Providing escort were three young Somali militias riding in a red Toyota Hilux "technical" mounted with a Soviet-made DSHKM heavy machine-gun. All the militants were considered armed and deadly.

The movement of the HVT that morning was confirmed through human intelligence

(HUMINT), provided by a former Somali warlord with trusted contacts inside the insurgency but also on the CIA's payroll. Riding the tail of Ethiopian invasion of Somalia in late December 2006, the CIA opened a base in Mogadishu in early 2007 where, up close, the agency could monitor events inside Somalia, and also gather valuable information on a dozen or so senior members of the militants in Somalia. Then there was the three al-Qaeda operatives rumoured to be in Somalia, especially Saleh Nabhan and Harun Fazul. The CIA tried unsuccessfully to buy information that could lead to both, but their trails had gone cold. The hunt for the pair got a boost in 2009 when President Barack Obama assumed office and sustained the war on terror initiated by George Bush after the events of 9/11. Under Obama, the CIA perfected to an art the tracking and elimination of foreign terrorists seen as threats to America and America's interests around the globe. With more money, the CIA ramped up its global effort to identify emerging terror outfits including inside Somalia. Once their identities were unmasked, the Islamic radicals were dispatched off with little fanfare, usually by silent cruise missiles fired from beyond the clouds by killer RQ-4 Global Hawk HALE Version operated remotely from Fort Myers.

In Somalia, Nabhan and Fazul had become the CIA's top priorities. All hands were on deck to track and eliminate the al-Qaeda operatives before something else bad happened to American citizens. Piece by piece, the intelligence team peeled back the shroud surrounding the two. By the end of July 2009, the FBI and CIA simultaneously working the domestic and foreign fronts had enough information to place the men as valuable and resourceful members of the emerging Somali Islamist militants that were still not well known outside Somalia. Both were experienced weapons instructors, jihadist propagandists, and ideological mentors to youth recruited from East Africa, North Africa, the Middle East, Europe and North America. Nabhan also headed a group, the *al-Mujahirun*, made of battle-tested al-Qaeda fighters from Pakistan and Afghanistan, and possibly Iraq, now fighting alongside Somali militias.[2] There was a high possibility the SEALS were hot on the trail of one or both men.

Three unmanned aerial vehicles (UAV) flying 10,000 feet in the sky above southern Somalia beamed real-time action of Operation Celestial Balance half a world away to the headquarters of the US Joint Special Operations Command (JSOC) at Fort Bragg, North Carolina, where early dawn was just cracking. JSOC commander Vice Admiral William H. McCraven and his senior officers watched Celestial Balance unfold from a large television screen in the secure operations room. Since assuming command of the secretive special-ops outfit on June 13, 2008, Adm. McCraven, himself a former SEAL, maintained the aggressive hunt for al-Qaeda terrorists established by his predecessor US Army Gen. Stanley A. McChrystal. It was McChrystal's team that doggedly hunted down and killed in a US airstrike on June 7, 2006 the notoriously famous leader of al-Qaeda in Iraq, the Jordanian Ahmad Fadhil Nazzal al-Khalaylah, better known by his *nom de guerre* Abu Musab al-Zarqawi. Established in 1980 to answer directly to the President in the White House, the sharp tip of the US spear in the war on terrorism was always on the hunt for the next target.

President Obama had signed off on the executive kill order giving the green light for Operation Celestial Balance to proceed. Obama was too aware of the political risks of permitting US Special Forces to set foot on Somali soil in order to verify the kill. During the bruising presidential campaign of 2007-2008, first against Hillary Clinton and later Republican opponents especially Vice Presidential nominee Sarah Palin, Obama had made it clear that as president, America would brook borders of sovereign states in pursuit of terror threats. "It was a terrible mistake to fail to act when we had a chance to take out an al-Qaeda leadership meeting in 2005. If we have actionable intelligence about high-value terrorist targets and President Musharraf won't act, we will," Obama had said during one of the campaign stops in August 2007.[3] Later, he was accused of being naïve on foreign policy and soft on terrorists. Palin coined the famous phrase "palling around with terrorists" to underscore what she perceived as Obama's weakness.[4]

The presidential campaign sharpened Obama's conviction to follow the trails of the bigger fish to fry in the war against terror believed to be hiding in the border region between Pakistan and Afghanistan. His name was Osama bin Laden. For now Somalia stood as an example of his resolute resolve to pursue terrorists to every corner of the world. The hands-on tactic by the Special Forces who needed to land their helicopters on Somali soil long enough to scoop the dead and wounded in the raid that afternoon could give Obama the opportunity for a not so subtle reminder to his critics that he was not the weak-kneed bleeding heart liberal the far right had caricatured. For Obama's fledgling nine months old administration the success of the mission could be a dress rehearsal for future special operations by the US Special Forces.

Success was what Admiral McCraven, a man aversed to failure, was also rooting for. McCraven had a particular reason not to screw up Operation Celestial Balance. For sixteen long years, the US avoided overt military actions that placed American boots on Somali soil, however briefly. Still too fresh for the American public who did not want anything to do with Somalia was the spectacle of dead Americans being dragged in the dirt by gleeful Somali mobs in the streets of Mogadishu during the October 1993 Battle of Mogadishu. Celestial Balance was the first daylight mission inside Somalia involving a large number of US Special Forces since President Bill Clinton yanked American forces out of Somalia in the spring of 1994. The mission needed to be done right, neat and tidy.

Of course, none of that mattered to the Navy SEALs seated silently aboard the choppers now cluttering inside Somalia's airspace. And in fairness to the men, it was not in their job description to figure out who made what mess in Somalia. Their razor sharp warrior skills, honed by long experience and constant training, were focused on executing with deadly precision the kill orders from above. In typical American fashion for quick fixes, their job was done and over once the prize was stowed away in one of the US Department of Defense (DOD) specification black body bags brought for just that purpose, and the choppers were safely back to base on USS Bataan. The only objective that mattered was the HVT. Hit him, grab the body and get the hell out. This lesson, America had learned the hard way from previous engagements in Somalia.

With information that the HVT was on the move, US military planners had two options. One, use a cruise missile to take out the target like all preceding al-Qaeda targets killed before him—Nek Muhammad Wazir, June 18, 2004, Haitham al-Yemeni, May 14, 2005, Abu Laith al-Libi, January 29, 2008, Abu Ubaydah al Tunisi, September 17, 2008, Usama al-Kini and Sheikh Ahmed Salim Swedan, January 1, 2009, among many others. This option apparently fell through when at the last moment the cruise missile malfunctioned.[5] Instead JSOC commanders went with the riskier second option that put American boots on Somalia soil, ensuring the collection of bodies for positive identification of the HVT, dead or alive. The men often referred to as the silent professionals were to use stealth and secrecy in plain daylight to execute the mission.

Meanwhile, completely oblivious of electronic eyes watching from high in the sky, and the momentous violence about to befall them, the doomed militants in the two target trucks stopped briefly to refuel and buy snacks outside the coastal town of Baraawe. Looking relaxed and unconcerned, the HVT bought a half a dozen warm *qamdi* from a young Somali woman vending from the side of the road.[6] The sweet triangular Somali fried bread had the familiar taste and texture of the *mahamri*, popular along the east coast of Kenya, especially in his hometown of Mombasa which he left many years earlier, and had avoided visiting for fear of being discovered by the American hunters hot on his trail. The Somali woman put the purchase in a small polythene bag, tied the top in a quick knot before handing him the package with a smile.[7] The HVT paid in Somali shillings, waved his hand to indicate that the woman could keep the loose change, and walked back to the vehicle.

Soon the trucks were on the move again. The convoy did not get far. Minutes later, just before 1:00 p.m., flying in formation, the two Black Hawks and the pair of AH-6 Little Birds burst over the town of Baraawe. Then, moving in a tight circle like hungry buzzards waiting to alight on carrion, the choppers intercepted the convoy near the coastal village of Roobow in Baraawe district. The two Little Bird gunships strafed the trucks with M-134 7.62mm miniguns and .50cal GAU-19 machine guns, disabling them instantly. An explosive rocket hit the Hilux technical, setting it on fire. Three or four militants jumped out from the all-terrain vehicle, haplessly opening up with light automatic weapons at the angry helicopters buzzing overhead. These were swiftly silenced with burst of automatic weapons from the Little Birds. The encounter was brief but devastating. The occupants of the trucks did not have a chance. Some of the militias lay dead inside or beside the pockmarked and still smoking vehicles. Two others were wounded but still alive. Seeing no further hostile fires, the two Black Hawks landed nearby. The SEALs calmly set up defensive chalk perimeters around the fresh kills. The dead men were wearing the checkered head wraps popular with Islamic radicals. The HVT was easy to locate. His face matched the picture on the handheld computer carried by the SEALS. His small body was a crumpled rag of dripping blood inside the bullet-riddled truck. One of the SOF men called in to Operation Center, "HVT KIA (High Value Target killed in action)."

The bodies, still warm and oozing blood, were shoved into black body bags with six handles, standard equipment for this kind of operations. Zipped close, the bags holding the dead HVT and his colleagues were quickly bundled onto one of the Black Hawks. The two wounded men, hands cuffed, were placed on the other helicopter. Left by the roadside beside the burning trucks, were two of the dead militias. Radioing the code for 'mission accomplished' to the forward command post on USS Bataan, the Black Hawks were soon airborne again. Just as quickly as it started, Operation Celestial Balance was over in minutes.

In the White House, President Barack Obama was briefed shortly after breakfast by the United States Director of National Intelligence Admiral Dennis Blair on the successful Baraawe raid. Obama was preparing to board Marine One for the short flight to Andrews Air Force Base where Air Force One was on standby to take him for a daylong engagement in Manhattan, New York. He asked to be kept informed on the progress of the investigation.

Later that afternoon, as President Obama and his predecessor, former US President Bill Clinton sat down for lunch of fish, pasta and salad at Il Mulino Italian restaurant located in Greenwich Village at 86 West Third Street in New York,[8] the CIA confirmed the identity of the Baraawe kill. The HVT was Saleh Ali Saleh Nabhan. The British Broadcasting Corporation (BBC) was the first to break the news of the Baraawe raid.[9] By then Saleh Ali Saleh Nabhan and his dead associates had been photographed, fingerprinted and buried in the Indian Ocean. But the White House remained tight-lipped about the raid. Aboard Air Force One on the return flight to Andrews Air Force Base in Washington, White House Press Secretary Robert Gibbs was evasive when reporters travelling with the President asked about the Somalia raid earlier in the day.[10]

"Another topic, what was the U.S. involvement in the attack on the suspected terrorists in Somalia?" A reporter asked Robert Gibbs.

"I'm not going to get into that," Gibbs shot back.

"Was there any U.S. involvement?" the reporter persisted.

"I'm not going to get into that. I would point you to the Department of Defense if you have any questions," Gibbs responded and the subject moved on to trade with China.

Secretly though, the CIA and the American intelligence community were ecstatic about Nabhan's death. After years of hunting for the elusive terrorist, the CIA felt vindicated. It was worth the effort and hundreds of thousands of dollars spent hunting down the terrorist. It was justification enough for continuing the covert war on terror in Somalia and elsewhere around the globe. But without a clear vision in the Horn of Africa dating back to the independence of the impoverished African nation from colonial rulers in 1960, US policies amounted to a mixed bag of missed opportunity, poor timing and downright failure. Everywhere one looked, the fingerprints of US policymakers were clearly visible in the twists, deadly turns and labyrinths that preceded and followed two decades of despotic rule of former Somalia President Siyaad Barre, and the anarchic decades after his exit in January 1991. As the Somali say, *Arrinxumo abaar ka daran*, a bad decision is worse than a drought.[11] Long after ignorantly planting the seed for the rise of radical Islamists and jihadists with deep antipathy toward the West, America was now chasing its own tail in Somalia.

The Somali problem, as it was referred to at the Pentagon was much bigger than a single commando raid, even a dozen, could solve in one fell swoop. The targeted killing of Saleh Ali Nabhan that afternoon could only further stir the pot of chaos in Somalia, egging on those radical young Somali men to strap bomb-packed suicide vests to return the favour by blowing themselves and everyone else associated with America into thousands of bloody body bits. Like the *qori-ismaris*,[12] the form shifting man in the popular Somali folklore with the ability to transform into a hyena at nightfall by rubbing himself with a stick, some of the actors previously encouraged and supported by cold CIA cash had now morphed into a militant movement of young Somali fighters carrying Kalashnikov in one hand, and the Qu'ran in the other.

Moreover, unlike the US-led wars on terror in Afghanistan and Iraq where allied forces routinely share critical intelligence and information on important operations, the US did not inform the Force Commander of the African Mission in Somalia (AMISOM) of the plan to kill Saleh Nabhan Saleh.[13] Leaving General Mugisha in the dark was a deliberate oversight that could put in danger the lives of troops with the AU force. Part of the reason was that American military strategists never had confidence in the capabilities, abilities and experience of the AU troops from Uganda and Burundi that made up AMISOM to deal with the Islamist militants in Somalia. To them, AMISOM was a mere interim force invited into Somalia to hold the fort, so to speak, while Americans considered better options for dealing with the emerging terror threat in the Horn of Africa. But Gen. Mugisha was not thinking of his force as an interim stop measure. AMISOM was the real deal.

The news of Nabhan's killing reached al-Shabaab leadership shortly following *dhuhr* afternoon prayers. There was frantic bustling as senior commanders huddled for a crisis meeting in Maslah. The question on everybody's mind was whether the US had struck first after finding out about the suicide mission scheduled to take place within the week at AMISOM base. If so, it meant postponing the mission. After all, Nabhan had been the instrumental architect of the plan. As it turned out, the suicide mission was not compromised. After the killing of Saleh Ali Nabhan, nothing had changed. A senior TFG official working for al-Shabaab had monitored the activities inside the AMISOM base. AMISOM did not get advance warning of the Baraawe operations by US Special Forces.

On Tuesday, September 15, 2009, the day after the US helicopter raid killed Saleh Ali Saleh Nabhan, a spokesperson for the Somali militants Sheikh Bare Mohamed Farah Khoje, vowed that it would seek revenge for the killing. "Al-Shabaab will continue targeting western countries, especially America ...we are killing them and they are hunting us."[14] Sheikh Khoje's pronouncement left the impression that al-Shabaab combatants were facing off along a defined warfront with US forces. For Khoje, painting the picture of the Somali militias standing up to the world's superpower and actually inflicting casualties served to inflate al-Shabaab's image. It did not matter that unlike in Iraq and Afghanistan where American boots were on the ground, there were no American troops in Somalia. The few Americans in Mogadishu were either CIA operatives or civilian contractors working with DynCorp. All kept very low profile, making sure they were not publicly visible, let alone shot at. Sheikh Khoje understood this well. AMISOM was the only force that now stood between the angry young Somali men baying for revenge and the Americans.

# 10

# Twin Suicide Bombs

**September 17, 2009, AMISOM Forces Base, Mogadishu, Somalia**
**The warning**

Twenty minutes before the deadly twin suicide bomb blasts inside the AMISOM Forces Base in Halaane, Mogadishu, the high-level security meeting already underway in the Operations Room was abruptly interrupted by the noisy arrival of Somalia National Police Commissioner, General Abdi Hasan Awale Qeybdiid. The time was 11:11 a.m. AMISOM Force Commander Major General Nathan Mugisha stood up to welcome Gen. Qeybdiid. Other officials also rose to their feet including AMISOM Deputy Force Commander Major General Cyprien Hakiza from Burundi National Defense Forces (BNDF), a dozen AMISOM officers including the chief intelligence officer Major Abdu Rugumayo,[1] Chief of Staff Col. Innocent Oula and Major David Matua. Also in the room were a dozen or more senior security officials from the Somalia Transitional Federal Government (TFG) including Chief of Army Staff, General Hussein Yussuf Dhumal, Deputy Police Commissioner General Mohamed Nur, and TFG Infantry Commander Gamudule.

Qeybdiid, the wily veteran of many Somali wars with more lives than a cat, was uncharacteristically late to the meeting that started almost two hours earlier. The man was a walking encyclopedia on all things Mogadishu. The running Somali joke was that if a goat was slaughtered somewhere in the city Qeybdiid would have been briefed before the poor animal stopped kicking. In the early 1990s, Gen. Qeybdiid was interior and finance minister in the self-declared government of General Mohammed Farah when the Somali warlord stared down the US military. On July 12, 1993, US Task Force Ranger attacked a gathering in Qeybdiid's house known as Abdi House attended by around eighty elites of the Hawiye Habar Gidir sub-clan. Six Bell AH-1 SuperCobra gunships fired sixteen tube-launched, optically tracked, wire-guided (TOW) antitank missiles and hundreds of rounds from Boeing M230 30-millimeter chain guns into the building.[2] The devastating midmorning assault lasted no more than five minutes. When it was over, US Army sources said thirteen Somali were killed and seven wounded, but the Hawiye Habar Gidir counted fifty-four people killed including the clan's spiritual leader, 90-year old Sheik Haji Mohamed Iman Aden.

When the smoke cleared, standing in the middle of the rubble of the smoldering house, face blackened with soot and blood-soaked white shirt shredded, was Abdi Hasan Awale Qeybdiid.[3] Barely seven weeks later, on October 3, 1993, he was again the target of US Delta Force mid afternoon raid codenamed Operation Gothic Serpent near Bakaara Market that started what became known as Black Hawk Down. In the movie Black Hawk Down, Hollywood's depiction of the Battle of Mogadishu, Gen. Qeybdiid's character nicknamed "Mad Abdi" was in the thick of the battle that pitted US and UN forces against Somalia militia.[4]

In the decades that followed, Gen. Qeybdiid survived by changing sides often, sometimes fighting for Hawiye Habar Gidir militias, sometimes against them. A suave survivor, he became Somalia's police chief in 2001, working for the Western-backed Transitional Federal Government (TFG). Along the way, he built a formidable militia with a vast network of informers in every café in Mogadishu, mostly paid for with cash from Western donor countries.

Gen. Qeybdiid had walked into the room as final touches to the plan to engage the insurgents were being discussed. There was no mistaking the tense atmosphere in the room. This was the second high-level joint security meeting in three days involving Somali security agencies and AMISOM. The urgency was palpable for the allied TFG and AU forces to do something soon about the deteriorating security situation in Mogadishu. The intelligence gathered in the previous two days indicated that the insurgents were planning to attack the continental peace keeping mission to Somalia. Bluntly, Gen. Mugisha had put it to the two dozens or so attendees that AMISOM needed breathing room in the badly scarred city. Although the Islamist insurgents were entrenched into the very fabric of the Somali society, Gen. Mugisha made it plain that he did not like it one bit that AMISOM was playing defense. A soccer enthusiast, he gave the analogy that scoring required some daring moves. He was eager to work with TFG forces to neutralize the pesky insurgency cells around Mogadishu. Everyone in the room nodded in agreement with the emerging operational plan to take on the insurgents.

Gen. Qeybdiid had just plunked himself into a blue plastic chair when Gen. Mugisha's mobile phone buzzed. The commander took the call, nodding occasionally as he listened intently. The person at the other end of the line was a highly reliable Somali informant with vital intelligence from deep inside the insurgency. The message was unmistakable. The very building they were meeting in was about to be hit by a powerful bomb. It would be big, the informant emphasized, raising his voice to illustrate the magnitude of the impending catastrophe. Sure as day follows night, the attack could go off any minute now, the informant added breathlessly.

Gen. Mugisha suggested that the insurgents could be planning a mortar attack on the base, something they did often anyway with little effect. The informant was insistent and confident that the intelligence he received was from an impeccable source about the impending attack on AMISOM Force Headquarters. Soon after concluding the urgent conversation, Gen. Mugisha informed the gathering about the bomb threat. Always prepared to expect the unexpected, Gen. Mugisha immediately adjourned the meeting, and rose from the black high-back executive leather chair. He ordered his intelligence chief Maj. Rugumayo and a handful of soldiers to conduct a swift sweep from top to bottom of the entire building and adjacent ones. The searchers split up into three teams, and went to work.

AMISOM Forces Headquarters consisted of three white buildings on a rising ridge overlooking the Indian Ocean. On three tall white metal poles in front of the main building, the flags of the AU, Uganda and Burundi fluttered in the gentle wind from the ocean. A thick concrete walls rising four and half meters surrounded the three buildings. The only gate into the inner compound was barely large enough for a small truck to drive through. It was closed to all traffic except the brand new white double-cabin Toyota Land Cruiser belonging to Gen. Mugisha. It was always parked at the same spot just inside the gate, like a guard dog, its shining metal grills facing out. Two armed soldiers guarded the gate. On the ground outside, security was tight.

The methodical search for the bomb began right away, starting with the Operations Room located in the main center building. The house once belonged to a wealthy Somali family. Arranged in neat foursomes to create ornamental circles on the floor, the fading imported Italian-made sandy-coloured square ceramic tiles bore silent testimonies to happier years gone by, and the expensive taste of the owner. Now it served as the command post for the all-important peace mission. Only senior officers had offices on both floors.

The morning heat was already prohibitive in the poorly ventilated space measuring just a scant 25 by 32 feet. Two small windows grudgingly allowed some light into the crammed interior and nothing else. The security officials, many sweating freely, eagerly exploited the lull in the meeting to escape the oppressive humidity of the room. Some sought the relative comfort of the second floor balcony, with its breathtakingly spectacular view of the Indian Ocean, located barely five hundred meters away. From that vantage point, the blue ocean appeared glued to the side of a giant tray gently sloping to spill its content onto the runaway of Aden Abdulle International Airport. On the far horizon, as if to cool down the hot sun beating down on the white sandy beaches, the vast water reached up to the clear blue sky above. One of the officers shot the scene on his mobile phone video. Two seagulls lazily dived in and around each other, the tips of their wings briefly touching. All seemed so peaceful, nary a hint of foreboding. Beyond the walls, Uganda and Burundi soldiers in full combat gear and armed with machineguns patrolled the areas of the main building and the two adjacent ones.

While the bomb searchers went from building to building, Gen. Mugisha waited in his office. He was extremely concerned that some of the SNA personnel who attended the high-level security briefing the previous day, September 16, 2009, had the physical appearance of insurgents than Somali government security officials on official duty. It was possible that the news of the security briefing had leaked to the enemy. This was the al-Shabaab's way of demonstrating its far reaches by scooping military information on what the general was planning. The question was what the insurgents were planning to do.

Lean and physically fit, Gen. Mugisha was a man of action with sharp penetrating intellect of the warrior-philosopher. His no-nonsense leadership style distinguished him as a soldier's soldier in Uganda's bush war that brought Yoweri Museveni to power in January 1986. A rising commander in the Uganda People's Defence Forces (UPDF), he lead the hunt in northern Uganda for the notorious leader of the Lord's Resistance Army (LRA), Joseph Kony. He was experienced in the tough and tumble of bush war craft. During the period 1994-2001 and 2003-2006, as the 4th Division Commander of the UPDF, Mugisha actively participated in resolving the Lords Resistance conflict. When The LRA insurgency was successfully defeated in northern Uganda, many ex-combatants were integrated back into the community and the people of the north won over using the strategy of reaching the 'hearts and minds' that required the army to work closely with communities. The lessons learnt during Mugisha's tenure as commander in Uganda greatly influenced his preparedness for the unique and complex task of leading AMISOM.

Now leading the continental force, he was ready to meet the Somali insurgency head on. In fact, the new mood among the AU troops was buoyant since the changeover on Wednesday, August 12, 2009, at which Gen. Mugisha took command from countryman Maj. Gen. Francis Okello. Under him, no longer a sitting peace dove ready for plucking by Somali Islamist militias, AMISOM was willing to push the weight of UN Security Council Resolution 1744 adopted on February 20, 2007 that authorized the continental force to "take all necessary measures as appropriate to carry out the following mandate." In the meeting, Gen. Mugisha acknowledged to his deputy Gen. Hakiza that a lot had been accomplished in the more than two hours since the meeting began at 9:00 a.m. Troop commanders now needed to put into action the agreed plans.

After about fifteen minutes, the search for the mystery bomb ended. Maj. Rugumayo reported back to his commander, saying nothing suspicious was found on the premises. By then, as fast as their legs could carry them, some senior security officials from the Somalia police and Somalia National Army had scrambled altogether out of the building. They jumped into their waiting cars and sped away toward the main entrance leading out of the base camp. Left behind were a few officers from Somali police force, officers from the Burundi and Uganda contingents, who lingered on the second floor balcony, some making phone calls.

Less than a kilometer away from their targets, the two white Toyota Land Cruisers separated, one approaching the Medina gates. The other drove around to the alternate gate mostly used by AMISOM vehicles, and closest to the force headquarters. That morning, an hour before the suicide bombings, the two Toyota vehicles left a compound near the Medina neighbourhood. In the lead was the Right Hand Drive Toyota Land Cruiser driven by Abdullahi. Following closely behind was the second white Land Cruiser, a Left Hand Drive, driven by Abdi. In addition to overseeing the operations, Abdullahi was tasked with keeping an eye on Omar Mohamud. Seated in the rear cabin of Abdullahi's vehicle were Ahmed and Ali.

As he approached the secondary gate, Abdullahi slowed down, careful not to attract the attention of the guards by seeming to be in a hurry. Heavily fortified with hundreds of green sand bags on the outer perimeter of the base to protect troops against incoming mortar attacks, the gates were manned by alert soldiers from Uganda contingent.[5] The soldiers at that moment were focused on the two white armoured Casspir Mk III with big AU logos painted in black on them. The South-African built Mine Resistant Vehicle (MRV) was the preferred troop transport when navigating the dangerous streets of Mogadishu. Sixty-eight of the hardy vehicles were originally ordered by the African Union in 2007, and were quickly modified for combat before delivery in 2008.[6] A few harsh barks from its top-mounted 20mm cannon gun often quickly and efficiently silenced the most determined attackers. The unique V-shaped hull protected two crews and twelve passengers against machinegun fire, powerful landmines and military grade improvised explosive devices (IED). Weighing ten tons apiece, the vehicles raised plenty of smoke and dust in their wake as they rumbled and rattled toward their mission. The sentry guard waved the big battle vehicles into the base. Inside the two vehicles were Burundi troops moving from their main base camp at the former National University in Mogadishu to the Forces Headquarters. The ranking officer in the lead Casspir was a Burundi general.

With his left hand, meanwhile, the guard motioned to the waiting white Toyota to approach slowly. The guard kept the finger of his right hand on the trigger of his assault rifle. As the vehicle drew beside the machine-gun toting AMISOM guards, there was nothing unusual about the white UN Toyota truck. UN vehicles came through the guarded gates of the base camp all the time. The UN was closely involved with coordinating logistics and supplies for the AU mission in Somalia. Locally recruited staff made up part of the UN personnel, often as drivers and porters.

The young Somali passenger in the front seat of the vehicle flashed his beautiful white teeth. It was Omar. He greeted the guards cheerily in English. "Hi guys, we are UN staff, part of the convoy just ahead of us," the handsome young man said in perfect American accent as he pointed to the Casspir that had just cleared the guarded gates, and were now some 150 meters inside the base.[7]

The soldier peered closely inside the Toyota. The four occupants were all very neatly dressed young Somali men. The driver, and the two young men in the back seat left the talking to the front seat passenger. To the casual observer, the three passengers in the vehicle wore ordinary civilian clothes. They did look the part of UN Somali staff. Earlier on, the men had used a hand-held camcorder to chronicle their last earthly hours. The camcorder was dropped off in town before the young men drove toward their certain deaths inside AMISOM base camp.

Underneath their shirts, each passenger wore stolen modified blue UN flak jackets. These had been skillfully converted into suicide vests packed with shiny steel ball bearings. Two thin wires, one blue and the other yellow, carefully secured with black masking tapes ran along the left arm of each man before emerging from underneath the shirt and jacket sleeves to connect to the bomb triggers taped to the wrists. The Somali insurgent bomb-makers much preferred to use as triggers the Bodyguard BM-518 model manufactured for use as motorcycle alarms by China-based Zhejiang Bodyguard Electronic Technology Company. In skilled hands, the compact square plastic devices with short antennas that come in blue and brown shades were easily converted into deadly suicide bomb components. This was no exception for the bombs now strapped on the chests of the three young passengers seated in the lead Toyota.

The AMISOM sentry asked the driver whether there were weapons in the two vehicles. "No weapons, sir, we are UN," the cheery young man answered with a quick give-me-a-break laugh. The guard signaled to the soldiers manning the steel barricades to raise them up, then waved the Toyota vehicle into the base. A scant eight hundred meters away at the Medina gate, the second Toyota vehicle also gained entry into the base, heading straight for DynCorp warehouses.

By now the two white armoured Casspir had travelled the short distance to the Forces Headquarters, the lead battlewagon screeching to a halt right in front of the two soldiers standing guard at the gate of the walled compound. The vehicle's cavernous body partly blocked the entrance. Barely ten meters behind, the second Casspir also grinded to a stop, the nose of its 20mm cannon pointing directly at the white building. Both drivers slowly released the hydraulic system that operated the thick armoured rear doors of their vehicles, letting out Burundi troops.

Out of the back of the lead Casspir, jumped Burundi's Major General Juvenal Niyoyunguruza, a tall man who cut a trimmed stately bearing in his olive green military camouflage and green AU beret. The former deputy force commander for the continental force had relinquished command the previous month, in August 2009, to the new deputy force commander, countryman Major General Cyprien Hakiza.[8]

After his tour of duty ended in July, Gen. Niyoyunguruza had stayed in Mogadishu while waiting for his bosses in Bujumbura to sort out his next assignment. Five months earlier in April 2009, aware that the general's mission to Somalia was soon ending, the Burundi Senate briefly considered but rejected the general for the post of Chief of Defense and Security Corps. A seasoned career soldier who rose through the ranks of Force de Défense Nationale de la République du Burundi (FDNB), Niyoyunguruza witnessed first hand some of the worst civil strife in the tiny East African country in the 1980s and 1990s. Some Burundi senators were bitter that Gen. Niyoyunguruza failed to control troops under his command during the army coup in which Burundi president Melchior Ndadaye was assassinated on the night of Thursday, October 21, 1993.[9] An international commission looking into the events leading to and following that fateful night concluded that Burundi's First Airborne Battalion from Camp Para in Bujumbura surrounded the presidential palace in Bujumbura. Barely five months in office after being democratically elected, President Ndadaye, a Hutu, was taken away in an armored car to the barracks under the ruse that it was for his protection, and shortly after bayoneted to death.[10] Summoned to testify before the commission as battalion commander, Niyoyunguruza did not take responsibility, saying that junior officers under his command forced him to stay in a garage through the night while the coup was unfolding.[11]

The Burundi Senate instead appointed Major General Godefroid Niyombare as army chief. But whatever troubles Gen. Niyoyunguruza experienced a decade and half in the past did not hinder his upward career as a soldier. From the rank of Major, he rose to become a two-star general. Well respected by the peacekeeping troops in Mogadishu, he served as AMISOM's second in command to Maj. Gen. Francis Okello who preceded Maj. Gen. Mugisha. He also served as the first commander of the Burundi contingent, and was trusted as the man who could be counted on to be on hand to support his troops in difficult times as when they suffered brutality from the insurgency. Such was the case on February 22, 2009, when a Somali employee working inside the base of the Burundi contingent at the former National University turned suicide bomber, drove his car through the gates and detonated it, killing eleven Burundi AMISOM soldiers and wounding 20 others. Gen. Niyoyunguruza helped in the evacuation of the wounded and transfer to medical treatment facilities. He also coordinated the repatriation of the dead soldiers back to Bujumbura. There were many other attacks on the peacekeeping mission, but they only strengthened the general's conviction that the mission was worth the sacrifice.

On this morning, General Niyoyunguruza hitched a ride in the Casspir from the Burundi base to the force headquarters. His final destination was the AMISOM medical clinic, less than a kilometer away. Some sort of cold or flu virus had lingered longer than usual, and he planned to have the army doctors check it out. The general paused for a moment to witness the ritual greetings between the Burundi and Uganda soldiers stationed at the Forces Headquarters. The soldiers gave each other hi-fives. The Burundi troops spoke French, and the Ugandans English, and the two contingents lived in different camps. But using Kiswahili as the common lingua franca, the armies had jelled well together. They had great respect and camaraderie for each other, getting along so well that it was sometimes difficult to tell whether a soldier belonged to one nation or the other. This was the case at that moment before the bombs.

Once inside the sprawling base, there were no more checkpoints. Everyone within the large enclosure was considered friend rather than foe. Both white Toyota vehicles sped up immediately toward their objectives. The lead truck veered sharply to the right, following the route taken by the Casspir toward the AU Forces Headquarters. The second vehicle turned slightly left. The lone driver gunned the engine toward the DynCorp warehouses. Less than a minute stood between the soon to be dead, dying and walking wounded.

The vehicle-laden bomb at DynCorp went off first, its powerful blast shaking buildings at the airport, rattling windows, and setting off car alarms. At forces headquarters, momentarily, all eyes turned to see black smoke billowing half a kilometer away from the building that housed DynCorp. At the precise moment when attention was focused toward the airport, the lead stolen white Toyota truck sped aggressively up the short sandy drive toward the entrance of the walled compound of the forces headquarters. The young Somali driver seemed intent on driving right through the gate into the headquarters compound. But, like a bull elephant, the first Casspir stood in the way. Furiously, the driver tried to maneuver the Toyota around the armoured vehicle. That effort, too, was wasted. The protective bullbar at the front of the Toyota was hopelessly tangled with the back of the Casspir. The heavy troop carrier and the thick brick wall had completely blocked off the Toyota from access to the inner compound of the headquarters.

As if choreographed by invisible hands, the three young passengers in the Toyota truck jumped out. They tried to get inside the gate, but the Casspir and the White Land Cruiser blocked their paths. Omar, Ali and Ahmed dashed frantically away from the vehicles. In the confusion, one of the young men dashed back inside the Land Cruiser.

Insurgents! Someone shouted

The whole thing was over in fifteen seconds, may be less. Maj. Gen. Niyoyunguruza and the soldiers around him never had time to react. With a shout of Allahu Akbar! Abdullahi pushed the hot-button connected to the bomb detonator. WHOOSH! The bomb went off.

Moments earlier, after the first bomb went off at DynCorp, Gen. Mugisha took to the stairs to find out what was going on outside. Directly behind him was his deputy Maj. Gen. Hakiza. Immediately behind the generals was Maj. David Matua, a smart and confident young unit commander from Uganda Battle Group 5 (UGABAG 5). Daring in the face of danger, Major Matua never wore the mandatory protective body armour and bulletproof helmet to battle. The green AU wool beret unfailingly donned at a rakish angle, Matua was the face of the new generation of young highly educated Uganda army officers leading the transformation of the UPDF into one of the best-trained professional armies on continental Africa. Quick and efficient, he was at the heart of the planning of the offensive against the insurgents.

As the three men reached the stairs, Somali Deputy Police Commissioner Mohamed Nur who had remained in the meeting room ran past Gen. Mugisha on his way out. Nur, taking two stairs at a time, raced for the door leading to the main gate in order to get out of the building. No one paid him much attention. On reaching the doorway leading to the courtyard within the walled compound, Gen. Mugisha stepped smartly into the narrow corridor and peeked outside. Cool under fire, Gen. Mugisha first noticed the White Casspir at the gate. Then he caught sight of the front of the white Toyota Land Cruiser as it tried desperately to push its way into the gate.

It was the precise moment when the three young Somali suicide fighters jumped out of the vehicle, wielding automatic weapons. As two of the youths raced away from the vehicle, and a third jumped back toward the Toyota, General Mugisha called out a quick warning. Lookout, those guys are insurgents![12] At the same time, Gen. Mugisha took three quick steps back inside the door, backpedalling toward the stairs. Maj. Gen. Hakiza and Maj. Matua still stood on the stairs.

Then everything exploded. A giant hot fist punched through the wall, lifting Gen. Mugisha clean off his feet before smacking his body like a rag doll against the hard cement floor in the stairwell. Huge chunks of concrete, pulverized debris and dust rained on him, smothering his entire body in white chalk. Stunned, dazed, almost naked, but conscious, Gen. Mugisha lay still for a moment, not sure what had just happened. All he could hear was the sound of nothing, simply deathly silence. At the time, he did not know the explosion was so powerful and loud it rattled windows several kilometers away.

Gen. Mugisha, choking and temporarily blinded, could feel only the searing heat coming from outside. Dense black smoke and swirling dust swallowed the block of buildings. Major Matua and Maj. Gen. Hakiza had simply disappeared. One moment, they were standing there. The next moment, they were gone.

His military trainings and instincts kicking in, Gen. Mugisha staggered to his wobbly legs. He had to move away from the gaping hole in the wall to the backroom on the ground floor in case there was a secondary explosion. Moments later, Gen. Hakiza also covered in white dust, joined his boss. Together, the two generals broke open a small back window, crawled through the narrow opening, and landed in the alleyway just behind the general's now damaged Toyota truck. Crouching as they staggered to the back of the adjacent building, each man dashed into the bush, and took cover. Alert, watching, they waited to see what would happen next.

Gen. Mugisha was in rough shape. He could see blood on his dust-covered body. In the delirious state he was in, he could not tell whether it was his own blood or someone else's. All he could sense was a creeping numbness spreading all over his body, making him feel like falling asleep. With incredible will, he pushed himself to stay awake, just long enough for help to arrive. There was smoke everywhere, even in the bushes where he hid. The Forces Headquarters had been hit, and hit big.

Miraculously, despite flying glasses and concrete, Maj. Matua had survived the violent explosion without the smallest scratch to his body.[13] The ringing in his ears, however, made it impossible to hear a thing. Covered in a thick coat of white dust and missing his beloved green AU beret, Maj. Matua scrambled back to his feet, and raced into the damaged building, desperately searching the debris for his commander. Not finding General Mugisha, Matua carefully made his way toward the spot where the gate used to be. In the hazy dark smoke, he stumbled over a body lying on the ground. It was the Somali Deputy Police Commissioner Nur. He was still alive, but bleeding badly from wounds to his head. Major Matua was focused on finding his commander. Everything was happening so fast.

Instinctively, Matua raced to his left away from the raging inferno that engulfed what remained of the suicide vehicle and the Casspir, into the narrow alleyway that ran between the main building and another to the right. Half crawling, half walking, he reached a spot behind a wall where he squatted down, taking stock of the situation around him. It was as if the entire concrete perimeter wall never existed. Completely pulverized, the concrete columns that once stood proud guard at the gate were now a pile of cinder blocks. The three white flag poles still stood defiantly at the front, their flags blown away, leaving not a shred. Huge gaping holes were blasted into the wall of the main building next to the stairs where minutes earlier the three men stood. The protective wall took the direct impact of the blast, likely saving his life.

Maj. Matua left his temporary refuge and rushed to the front of the building where the enormity of the bomb blast was immediately apparent. The force of the powerful bomb had ripped the ground where the doomed Toyota stood just minutes earlier, leaving behind a crater deep enough to half bury a standing man. Strewn on the ground as if a killer giant's hands had wreaked havoc, were debris of bloodied concrete and burning human flesh. Everywhere Matua looked, a most heinous scene of death and devastation met his eyes. Men lay dead or dying. There were too many bodies to count, almost all missing limbs and heads. All that remained were burnt-out torsos that did not resemble the persons they were minutes earlier. For a moment, Matua thought they more resembled half-completed bronze art projects than human bodies. The thick sharp smell of burning fresh blood mingled with smoke and burning tires, however, pervaded the entire smoky scene.

The force of the blast had hurled some thirty meters away the heavy Casspir that earlier blocked the path of the Toyota Land Cruiser. The armoured vehicle had landed on all four wheels, its hull pushed into the thick thorn bushes. It was on fire. The South African technology had proven a worthy match for the big bomb, thereby confirming the manufacturer's bragging about the toughness of the vehicle. Except for a few fender benders, and deflated rear-tires, it was left mostly intact. But the extreme heat from the flame raging inside the hull was causing ammunitions stored in the vehicle to pop off like large angry firecrackers.

The second Casspir had suffered heavy blows to the front end that peeled back the steel plate covering the radiator, and cracked the bulletproof glasses. Otherwise, with the backdoor flung open, it appeared to be waiting to load passengers except that its former occupants were now all casualties strewn around the yard.

Some distance from the chaos, on the gravel pathway, Matua saw two bodies, mostly intact. He quickly determined these were two young Somali suicide bombers that Gen. Mugisha had seen jump out of the Toyota Land cruiser moments before the huge explosion. The car bomb blast was so powerful that shrapnel killed them before their bodies even hit the ground.[14] The youth in the white striped shirt died kneeling down, his left hand stretched as if reaching for the black Nokia mobile phone that lay half a meter away in the sand. Someone's intestinal remains were splattered rudely across his extended legs, soiling his clean khaki cargo pants. His younger protégé had fared worse. The blast tore clean half of his buttocks, and flattened his head like a bun. His left foot was missing a sneaker, which came to rest on the sand nearby. The other foot wearing neat black sock with purple ring was still inside the shoe. The dead youth were still wearing their unexploded suicide vests.

Everywhere one looked, the carnage was complete. Soldiers were now running around, helping the wounded, leaving the dead where they fell. The ammunitions were still exploding inside the crippled Casspir, forcing back any attempt to rescue those trapped near the vehicle. Taking charge of the chaotic scene, Major Matua yelled for water to be brought to put out the fires. For some, it was clearly too late. Those not killed outright, were breathing their last. But there were survivors too, and these needed to be evacuated to the medical clinics at the edge of the airport runaway. Trucks raced to the scene to load the wounded. Someone handed him a bucket of water. He poured it on the burning corpses. Someone identified the remains of General Niyoyunguruza by the boots he was wearing. There was not much else left.

By coincidence Col. Dr. James Kiyengo, the Director of Army Clinic and Chief of Emergency was not required to attend the ill-fated meeting that morning, and had hung back to prepare for the first surgery of the day.[15] The Somali civilian patient had a pituitary gland defect that needed an operation to correct. After prepping the surgical equipment, Dr. Kiyengo settled down to wait for the rest of the team. He soon became engrossed in *The Bourne Ultimatum* by John Grisham, a book he found fast-paced, fascinating, and a load of fun to while away little moments like this.

Trained as a doctor at Makerere University Medical School at Mulago in Kampala, Uganda, Dr. Kiyengo's eclectic taste for knowledge included expansive interests in astronomy, geology and life of insects. Nothing was dull to his infinitely curious mind.

The steeper the challenge, the more he was engaged and alive. In Mogadishu, he had quickly taken on the cases of Somali women with advance cases of fistula, and pioneered medical treatment for the condition that afflict many young girls who become pregnant too early before the pelvic was fully developed. Plagued afterwards with incontinence, these young women were shunned by family members and the community, often chased away to live apart because of the overwhelming stench they carried on their bodies. After a few successful operations, Kiyengo and his team began scheduling regular surgeries. He required each patient to give several pints of blood ahead of the surgery to be stored in the blood bank. It was a precaution against the possibility of blood shortage.

When the rest of the surgical team assembled that morning, the surgery on the civilian started off well. There was nothing exceptional about it, and Dr. Kiyengo was relaxed as he performed the surgery. He was about to make an incision when the building was shaken by the first blast. "The light shook violently," Kiyengo recalled.[16] Incoming! Someone shouted, but Dr. Kiyengo carried on. Like many who had lived through Mogadishu shelling by insurgents, he thought the base was under mortar fire, often not a big deal since most of the rounds never hit anything, falling harmlessly in the bushes. "You get to hear buzz from the locals that on such and such a day, you are going to get shelled, but we take it in stride, never really stopping to worry about it, and so when the first explosion went off, I did not think much of it," he said. The second explosion, however, was of such magnitude that the entire medical tent shook, causing the fluorescent bulb hanging in the ceiling to fall down on the anaesthetized patient.

Everyone on the surgical team dived for cover. Except Dr. Kiyengo who realized he could not leave the patient on the table. Dr. Kiyengo could hear people yelling and running outside. Someone shouted that there was thick black smoke rising from the Forces Headquarters. From experience, he knew immediately that casualties were soon coming to his clinic, so he directed the other medics to get surgical equipment ready, even as some of the medics began running toward the scene of the explosion. Dr. Kiyengo also ordered his assistant to call immediately all medical teams whose day it was to take a break to return for duty.

In a prefabricated structure a few yards away, Major Dr. Ibrahim Kimuli, another Mulago-trained Ugandan surgeon, was putting the final touches to a skin graft surgery on a female Somali patient whose right leg was shattered during mortar shelling a few days earlier.[17] It was his third surgery of the day, and all had gone well so far which, as a war doctor, he knew meant four or five more surgeries before he called it a day in the evening. Since arriving in Mogadishu on July 22, 2009, the young Ugandan surgeon had quickly adapted to the rhythm of life inside the base, getting up early for a quick jog within the secure perimeter of the base, a body wash, donning on his battle helmet and body armour, breakfast and then the clinic where he showed his exceptional skills, treating mostly Somali civilians brought to the forces clinic with grievous gun wounds and various traumas. Soon he became used to the shelling and shootings by insurgents who, on some morning, appeared to wake up with nothing else on their minds except pummel with mortar fire the AMISOM base.

When the first bomb went off that morning Dr. Kimuli, too, thought the base was under another routine mortar attacks. "The lights in the ceiling fell down, and we thought, what is this, this sounds different from mortar."[18] Shortly, a frantic Burundi soldier came running on foot to the clinic, bleeding profusely from a head injury. Breathless, the injured man blurted that a big bomb had just gone off at the Forces Headquarters, and that there were likely many casualties because he was much further away from the blast scene, may be 70 meters or more, but was blown off his feet by the sheer force of the blast, so there were bound to be casualties from the immediate area of the explosion. The soldier had sustained a superficial scalp wound that Dr. Kimuli quickly patched up with a bandage, stemming the flow of blood.

The first serious casualties arrived at the clinic in the back of pick-up trucks and, in no time, the bodies began piling up fast. There was no question of sending the casualties to another hospital in Mogadishu since the few that were opened barely functioned at the best of times, the rest lay abandoned, looted and dilapidated. Captain Dr. Ronald Mukuye, another young Uganda doctor, working with a team of medics set up a triage in an open tent just outside the surgical theatres, quickly determining the nature of the injuries, tying a black band on the wrist to indicate the patient was dead or dying shortly, red for injuries requiring immediate surgery, yellow for those under observation to be treated later, green for the walking injured with superficial wounds requiring quick bandage, and white for those that needed mostly first aid, but otherwise fine.[19]

The number of casualties needing immediate medical attention was staggering. Many of the casualties, in addition to suffering penetrating, even gaping wounds from shrapnel, sustained severe third and fourth degree burns that caused their skins to peel off like tree barks, leaving flesh hanging out. In some cases, the military fatigues burned and fused to the flesh in a peculiar manner that made it impossible to distinguish cloth from human flesh. The conscious survivors lay, sat or walked about in stupefied silence under the open tent, uttering neither a word nor a cry of pain.

A TFG soldier, the front of his military fatigue soaked with blood had taken a direct hit in the middle of his forehead which now protruded out like a third eye, but he was deemed a walking wounded to be treated later. Tim (last named omitted), an American citizen (AMCIT) working for DynCorp was brought on a stretcher. Wearing short khaki pants soaked with sweat, his right ankle was grotesquely twisted after the wall at DynCorp warehouse fell on him. He needed surgery too, but could wait to be evacuated to Nairobi. So was General Nur who was caught in the blast of the bomb that destroyed the outer perimeter wall of the Forces Headquarters. He was not fully outside the perimeter wall when the explosion occurred, but was hit with such force that it left him coming in and out of consciousness.

In the midst of the frantic efforts going all around him, Dr. Kiyengo placed an SOS call to AMREF Flying Doctors in Nairobi. The message was simple: Send all the planes you could round up to ferry those in critical state, and in need of advanced medical care to Nairobi. It would take a few hours before the first flight arrived from Nairobi, he was told, and so the doctor went back to work on the casualties. Inside the surgical tent where Dr. Kiyengo and his team were working, and in the prefab where Dr. Kimuli and team were set up, it was forbiddingly hot, causing the medical team to soak in their own perspiration. Yet, without pause, they pushed on, working furiously on every casualty, stabilizing the patient, and starting all over again with the next one, on and on.

The clinic ran flat out of blood supplies for transfusion. Luckily, there was a large stockpile of IV drips donated by Nuur Foundation Somalia, a UK and US based non-profit organization that regularly sent medical supplies to the war-torn nation for treating civilians. "On that day, these were worth every penny," said Dr. Kimuli.[20] At some point, the administrative assistant brought Maj. Gen. Mugisha to the medical clinic. He wore only an army-supplied olive green undershirt that was soaked in blood. Except for the two black spots where his eyes were located in his head he was completely covered in white dust. Without complaining, the general waited patiently by the door of the tent where Dr. Kiyengo was still working frantically on the critically injured casualties. When at last the doctor noticed the general seated in the operation tent, he ordered him brought to the operating table.

Dr. Mukuye and Dr. Kimuli helped clean up the cake of dust off the general's head and prepared him for treatment. The two doctors stemmed the bleeding on the general's head, and sent him on to Dr. Kiyengo to be stitched up. The general had lost a lot of blood, but he was conscious. When asked whether he should be evacuated to Nairobi when the planes finally arrived, the general balked. He needed to stay in Mogadishu with his troops and, damn it, he would walk out of the tent on his own two feet.

But when he tried to walk, the general collapsed to the ground. Temper flared in the hot crowded tent. Dr. Kiyengo finally snapped, delivering a kick at the leg of the poor anesthetist for not following orders. "I ordered the anesthetist to give the general IV treatment, but she got busy with something else, and I was furious with her," recalled Dr. Kiyengo. Gen. Mugisha intervened, explaining to Dr. Kiyengo that he had refused to have the IV sticking out of him. He did not want to give satisfaction to the insurgents that they sent him, Gen. Mugisha, to the hospital with serious injuries. He was finally persuaded to take the intravenous drip, although he remained inside a tent away from lurking eyes and cameras.

At around 5:00 p.m., the first plane arrived from Nairobi, a small jet engine taking three of the seriously wounded casualties, two sitting up and the other one lying on a stretcher. The injured AMCIT went on the first plane. Two more planes arrived shortly after, and the rest of the casualties including deputy Police Commissioner Gen. Nur were flown to Nairobi, and taken to Aga Khan hospital.[21] All told, there were as many as forty or fifty casualties from the bombing at the Forces Headquarters alone. Seventeen AMISOM soldiers, twelve from Burundi including Maj. Gen. Niyoyunguruza and five from Uganda died as a result of that bomb. The DynCorp warehouse bombing killed a Somali employee of the company, and wounded three others. Three more Uganda soldiers died the same day around 4:10 p.m. in a separate incident when a mortar round fired by the insurgents landed inside the base. The irony was not lost on the shell-shocked medical personnel. "Their errand was to fetch additional food from the army kitchen within the base to feed all the people now clustered around the clinic, unfortunately the shelling started, killing two soldiers outright and the third died on a stretcher where he lay waiting for treatment at the clinic. That day, a Burundi soldier was the only patient who died after receiving care from the heroic medical team led by Col. Dr. Kiyengo and his team. A double amputee, the soldier succumbed to his wounds because it took too long to evacuate him for specialized care in Nairobi.

In the evening, around 6:00 p.m., to the cheers of the troops and medical staff, General Mugisha emerged from the tent where he had been receiving care. Cleaned up and dressed in a clean smart army fatigue, he walked on his own two legs. "Today's event does not shake our resolve in fulfilling this mission. If anything, we are more determined to fight this enemy of peace in Somalia," he said and, instead of getting into the armoured truck waiting to whisk him away, the general chose to walk back to his quarters to rest for the night.

Shortly after 10:00 p.m. that night, Uganda's President Yoweri Museveni called. Never one to waste time in small talk, Museveni immediately asked for an update. "How bad is it?" the president asked General Mugisha.

"Bad enough Mr. President. We lost seventeen soldiers. Twelve Burundi and five Ugandans. And of course former deputy force Commander General Niyongoruza."

How many were injured?

"We have many casualties, almost 40 wounded. Our fine army doctors have handled most of the casualties. The serious cases we put on planes and sent to Nairobi."

"What about you General, how are you doing?"

"I am fine Mr. President. I sustained some cuts that our medical people have stitched up. I am good to go."

There was a long pause on the line. Then President Museveni spoke again. "This is an extreme provocation," he said. "We cannot accept it. Now, they have kicked the hornet's nest. Soon, they will know that Uganda troops are forged from steel."

"Take care General," the President said.

"Thank you Mr. President."

The conversation ended.

# Rethinking Rules of Engagement (ROE)

They buried Brig. Gen. Juvenal Niyoyunguruza on Sunday, September 20, 2009 in Bujumbura, Burundi. His coffin, draped in the red, white and green colours of Burundi national flag with three red stars in the middle, was laid alongside eleven similar coffins of his junior compatriots who also perished in the twin bombing in Mogadishu three days earlier. Prominent among mourners by his tall spare frame and receding silver-hairline was US Chargé d'affaires to Burundi Ambassador Charles H. Twining. Completely at ease in Africa, having previously served as interim ambassador to Benin, Ghana and Togo and, in 1996 to 1998, ambassador to Cameroon and Equatorial Guinea, Twining took careful catalogue of who was in attendance at the funeral.[1] The mourners in the VIP tent included Burundi's Vice President Yves Sahinguvu, Special Representative of the Chairperson of the African Union Commission for Somalia Nicolas Bwakira, the Secretary-General's Deputy Special Representative for Somalia, Charles Petrie, the Somalia TFG Minister of Interior Affairs and National Security, Abdisamad Mallin Mahamud Sheikh Hasan, representatives of the UN, EU, US and military officers from Rwanda and Uganda. Niyoyunguruza's boss, former AMISOM Force Commander Gen. Okello, also flew in from Uganda.

Earlier, the media had reported that the Burundi opposition was calling on the government to withdraw its troops from Somalia.[2] As the somber ceremonies unfolded, Ambassador Twining's immediate concern was how the people of Burundi were taking the deaths of the AU peacekeepers. The Government of Burundi had made a big deal of the event, declaring five days of mourning for the men beginning September 18, 2009. Burundi media all seemed supportive of the mission. The speakers at the funeral were equally determined that the Burundi mission to Somalia should continue. The Somali representative appealed directly to the people of Burundi, "Please, don't give up; we need your help."[3] The Special Representative of the AU Chairperson Nicolas Bwakira, a native of Burundi, put it more bluntly. "The time has come to re-examine AMISOM's mandate so that we can have the power to act when and as necessary," he told mourners. "We call today for more equipment, more financial means, reinforcements, and a stronger mandate which gives our troops the right to pursue if necessary," he added.[4]

Much to Twining's relief, Burundi leaders at the funeral seemed more determined than ever to see through the AU mission in Somalia. The military establishment and politicians alike had closed ranks in support of AMISOM. Burundi Vice President Sahinguvu quietly asked Ambassador Twining to tell Washington to push hard at the UN Security Council for more countries to contribute troops for the Somalia mission. Better equipment was also needed by the troops. Twining responded he would push for both. Burundi's Minister of Defense Gen. Niyoyankana, meanwhile, confided to Twining that he planned to fly to Kampala Wednesday, September 23, 2009, for a military meeting to discuss the need for more troops for AMISOM.

Thousands of kilometers away in New York world leaders were gathered on the eve of the 64th Session of the United Nations General Assembly. The future of AMISOM was the main topic for many. At a bilateral meeting later the same day, AMISOM dominated the discussion between Uganda's President Yoweri Museveni and US Ambassador to the United Nations Susan Rice. Museveni, scheduled to address the General Assembly on Wednesday, September 23, 2009, provided Rice with a candid appraisal of the AU mission to Somalia. AMISOM needed to be more proactive, robust and aggressive to take the fight to al-Shabaab, the Ugandan leader said. Uganda was contemplating sending more battalions to Somalia to clean out the terrorists, he told Rice. Then, instead of shying away from the hard assessment of the September 17 attack on AMISOM, Museveni owned the tragedy as "our fault".[5] Given the high threat level, Museveni argued, the security measures at the AMISOM base were insufficient at the time of the incident. The soldiers at the gate did not follow the strict training on security procedures they received in Uganda before they were deployed to Somalia. He trained them himself, and they had failed. There was also failure to deploy enough armament at the gate. Tanks or armoured trucks should have been guarding the entrance to the AMISOM headquarters. The incident had taught troops a lesson, Museveni concluded. Sitting there in front of Rice, President Museveni made the commitment that Uganda would not cut and run. Two days earlier, on Friday September 18, 2009, the spokesperson for Uganda People's Defence Forces (UPDF) Lieutenant Colonel Felix Kulayigye made the same commitment on BBC News, saying, "We do not run away when the situation worsens."[6]

The following day, Monday, September 21, 2009, Ambassador Rice and Assistant Secretary for African Affairs Johnnie Carson met Ethiopia's Prime Minister Meles Zenawi, also in New York to attend the UN General Assembly. Negash Kebret Botora, Ethiopia's Charge d'Affaires to the United Nations, accompanied Zenawi. The prime minister painted a much grimmer prognosis for AMISOM. He told Rice that Uganda and Burundi troops were poorly trained and were not prepared for the September 17 suicide bombing.[7] But, all things considered, Zenawi felt the TFG government of Sheikh Sharif Ahmed could hang on for as long as Uganda stayed in Somalia.

The focus was clearly no longer on AMISOM staying or leaving Somalia. The AU force was staying put. Rather, high-level discussions on both sides of the Atlantic centered on the next step for AMISOM in dealing with the Somali insurgents. Earlier that day, Gen. Niyoyankana met Ambassador Twining in Bujumbura to continue the dialogue started the previous day at the funeral of the peacekeepers. Niyoyankana felt strongly that AMISOM needed to change tactics and go on the offensive against the insurgents.[8] Ambassador Twining agreed. In a cable he dispatched to Washington later the same afternoon, Twining highlighted the growing consensus that change was needed in AMISOM. "If there is a consensus here on something," Twining wrote, "it is that the peacekeeping operation's mission needs to be expanded from that of static defense to a Chapter 7 type operation and, while we cannot figure out from here whether the ball is in the court of the AU or the UNSC, it would appear that it is time to pick up that ball."[9]

Twining's assessment was shared by AMISOM Force Commander Major General Nathan Mugisha. The man in charge of the Somalia mission did not care whose responsibility it ultimately was to make things happen for AMISOM. Not suffering from Zenawi's pessimism about AMISOM, Gen. Mugisha was barreling through bureaucracy and red tapes to get more boots and better equipment on the ground. He talked to anyone who would listen. On Tuesday, September 22, 2009, at a meeting in Kampala, Gen. Mugisha discussed his vision of AMISOM after the twin bombing with US Ambassador to Uganda Jerry P. Lanier, Deputy Chief of Mission John F. Hoover, Political/Economic Chief Aaron Sampson and the defence attaché (DATT).[10] Gen. Mugisha told the US officials that morale was high among the AU troops protecting key installations, providing medical services, clean water and food to 300,000 civilians in Mogadishu. But many AMISOM vehicles were worn out and degraded by IEDs. TFG forces mostly lacked education, and a six months training was needed for platoon level officers. The commander was convinced that with the right equipment and adequate resources including more troops, AMISOM was up to the task. He listed armoured personnel carriers, IED detection capability, boats and training for TFG militias. With extra 5,000 troops, AMISOM could take Mogadishu in two days, Gen. Mugisha said.

Gen. Mugisha may have been a tad too optimistic. But he clearly made a huge impact on Ambassador Lanier. In a cable marked "Secret" to Washington that afternoon, Ambassador Lanier wrote that Gen. Mugisha was "intelligent, dedicated and professional, his appeal for help was dignified and logical.[11] Lanier made clear that Uganda would not cut and run and appreciated the assistance AMISOM had already received. "One gets the sense that assistance with his very reasonable request could make the difference between success and failure in Somalia," wrote the ambassador.

Lanier's cable was shared with senior State Department officials including Assistant Secretary Johnnie Carson who was scheduled to attend the meeting of the International Contact Group (ICG) called for the next day, Wednesday, September 23, 2009 in New York. The afternoon gathering assembled under one roof at the United Nations all the major players on Somalia, fifteen countries and four organisations.[12] UN Special Representative of the Secretary-General (SRSG) for Somalia Ahmedou Ould-Abdullah chaired the meeting. At times heated and candid, the discussion for more resources for AMISOM dominated the agenda. In his opening remarks, the UN Under Secretary-General (USYG) for the Department of Political Affairs B. Lynn Pascoe told the gathering that the TFG presented the best chance in two decades for stability in Somalia. Pascoe called on more countries to shoulder the burden of supporting the TFG and AMISOM. Representing the US, Assistant Secretary Johnnie Carson responded that the US was committed to providing support for the TFG and AMISOM, and also asked other countries to do the same. More concretely, UN Under Secretary General for the Department of Field Support (DFS) Susana Malcorra told the gathering that the UN Support Office for AMISOM (UNSOA) was working to lift AMISOM up to UN peacekeeping operation standards. Already, UNSOA was providing to AMISOM full food ration, set up a medical evacuation system, and dispatched three shipments of equipment to Mogadishu. UNSOA was set to begin supplying fuel to AMISOM by the week of October 11, 2009. Still, to the disappointment of Italy's Foreign Minister Franco Frattini, the funds pledged in Brussels in April 2009 were not fully paid up. Yemen's Foreign Minister Dr. Abu Bakr Al-Qirbi captured the prevailing mood of the meeting that more needed to be done. He told the delegates that Yemen's representative at previous ICG meeting always reported, "The Meeting went very well."[13] In reality, argued Dr. Al-Qirbi, the ICG was not realizing concrete results toward implementing the Djibouti Peace process.

Interestingly, around the same time the ICG meeting was in progress, following his address of the General Assembly, President Barack Obama held a meeting down the hall with the heads of state and foreign ministers of the top contributors of troops and police to United Nations peacekeeping operations. The attendees included Bangladesh, Ghana, Nepal, Pakistan, Rwanda, Senegal and Uruguay. Uganda and Burundi were not invited to the meeting. Obama told the group, "If we do not help build local capacity to deliver basic services, repair infrastructure, jump-start the economy, secure territory and uphold the rule of law, we cannot expect international peacekeepers to depart without having to return."[14] Obama did not mention Somalia.

By the beginning of October 2009, AMISOM's mission had taken on a new urgency for the US, UN, AU and donor nations. Beefing the capacity of the mission was the new rallying point for the international community. On October 8, 2009, Under Secretary General Lynn Pascoe and UNSOA Director Craig Boyd briefed the UN Security Council on the situation in Somalia. Similar to his plea to the ICG group two weeks earlier, Pascoe made a passionate argument for more support for AMISOM and TFG. To underscore the immediacy of the situation, he told the UNSC members, "...money received today in Somalia will have a far greater impact on stability than that which arrives in three months time."[15] Craig Boyd hammered the point home when he told the Security Council that the funds pledged in Brussels were not coming quickly enough. Only ten million dollars had been placed in the AMISOM trust funds since July.

In response, both the permanent and temporary members of the Security Council were sympathetic to the TFG and AMISOM. France, United Kingdom, China, US, Costa Rica, Mexico, Croatia, and Libya all said the same thing. The international community needed to step up support for TFG and AMISOM. Vitaly Ivanovich Churkin, Russia's permanent representative to the United Nations, focused on the essentials of security, arguing that without first stabilizing the country it would be impossible to rebuild Somalia. The Russian envoy added that the scope of AMISOM's mandate as defined by UNSCR 1744 was sufficient to assist the TFG. AMISOM, in other words, did not require additional mandate to take the fight to al-Shabaab. What was needed was the will and the resources to transform the authority AMISOM already possessed to make it more assertive, pointed and lethal to the Islamist insurgency.

## Hitting the Snake Among its Eggs
Through October and early November 2009 discussions intensified among the stakeholders on refining AMISOM's rules of engagement. The prevailing sentiment was that the pacifist peacekeeping force had absorbed inordinate punishing body blows from al-Shabaab, and now needed to adopt an aggressive peacemaking role in Somalia. At a Joint Security Committee (JSC) meeting convened by the United Nations Political Office for Somalia (UNPOS) in Nairobi on Tuesday, October 13, 2009, TFG officials, AMISOM and donor representatives assessed the security landscape in Somalia and how AMISOM and TFG forces could move forward. Somalia Defence Minister Abdulla Boss Ahmed, accompanied by Interior Minister Abdulkadir Ali Omar and National Security Agency chief Mohammed Sheikh, told the gathering that the Islamists were splintering with al-Shabaab battling it out with Hizbul Islam in Kismaayo. AMISOM and TFG needed to take advantage of the infighting to further weaken the insurgents. AMISOM Force Commander Gen. Nathan Mugisha, also in attendance, told the meeting that a weakening insurgency could resort to unconventional warfare including hit-and-run, assassinations, bombing, for-cash kidnapping. As such, argued Gen. Mugisha, urgently needed was a two-pronged approach using the military to further degrade the enemy while, at the same time, engaging the civil

population through quick impact-projects. The latter would show the local population that the TFG was delivering services.

The lingering concern among US officials was that AMISOM going on the offensive against al-Shabaab could increase the risk for higher casualties for Uganda and Burundi troops. Increased casualties could cause Uganda and Burundi to consider pulling out prematurely from the mission. The US needed to know that Uganda understood what the reshaping of the AU mission meant for its troops. On Saturday October 24, 2009 US officials met with President Yoweri Museveni at State House in Entebbe.[16] Led by Assistant Secretary of State Johnnie Carson, the US delegation included Commander of African Command General William Ward, Deputy Assistant Secretary for Defense Vicki Huddleston, Ambassador Lanier and USAID Uganda Director David Eckerson. Uganda Defence Minister Crispus Kiyonga, Minister of Foreign Affairs Sam Kutesa, acting Minister of Finance Ruth Nankabira, Chief of Defense Forces General Aronda Nyakairima, and Permanent Secretary at the Ministry of Foreign Affairs Ambassador James Mugume flanked Museveni. Carson delivered a letter from President Barack Obama expressing his condolences for Uganda soldiers killed during the September 17 attack in Mogadishu. The US was firm in the commitment to AMISOM, and to the Somali government. Somalia President Sheikh Sharif needed to create an inclusive political environment that brought more Somali people to the table, Carson added.

For his part, President Museveni was fired up to take on al-Shabaab. Uganda clearly understood the risks, he told the American delegation. He would not have it any other way. The time had come for AMISOM to "either move forward or get out" of Somalia, he said.[17] What was strategically needed was more funding and equipment for both the TFG and AMISOM to push extremists out of Mogadishu, Kismaayo, Baidoa and any Somalia town with an airstrip or seaport. The last bit was important because access to landing strips and seaports allowed the extremists to bring in reinforcement, weapons and logistics. Uganda was prepared to send additional battalion to AMISOM. With the added muscles, Museveni was confident the AU troops could "push the extremists into bush."

Museveni's hawkish go-get-them stance against the Somali insurgents was echoed later the same day in Kampala when Carson, Lanier and Huddleston met Somalia President Sheikh Sharif Ahmed. The Somali leader was in town for the AU Special Summit for Refugees, Returnees and Internally Displaced Persons that concluded the previous day. Somalia Foreign Minister Ali Jama Jangali, State Minister for presidential affairs Hasan Moalin Mohamud Ali, and Somali Ambassador to Uganda Sayid Ahmed Sheikh Dahir, accompanied President Sharif Ahmed. Laid back and soft spoken as usual, Sharif Ahmed appeared to speak from the same talking point as President Museveni. The infighting between the Somali extremists had demonstrated to the world that they had no agenda beyond killing and slaughtering civilians, Sharif Ahmed told the Americans. The upside was that AMISOM had the support of the Somali public.

Sheikh Sharif Ahmed then revealed a recent conversation he had with the AU Commissioner for Peace and Security Ambassador Ramtane Lamamra. When the topic of AMISOM came up, Lamamra told President Sheikh Sharif Ahmed that AMISOM's mandate allowed the AU troops to attack enemy enclaves and, lately, AMISOM had begun doing just that, retaliating against the insurgents. Ahmed told Lanier that the TFG completely supported the new aggressive approach AMISOM had adopted. In any case, argued the Somali leader, when AMISOM failed to hit back, the insurgents used that as propaganda that AMISOM could not protect civilians. The local population would welcome an offensive by AMISOM, concluded President Ahmed. But AMISOM needed the resources to take on the insurgents, the Somali leader had emphasized.

The question of the resources for AMISOM came up again two days later, on Monday October 26, 2009, during a heated open debate at the 6206th meeting of the UN Security Council on how to finance AU peacekeeping operations authorized by the Security Council. The top UN body was responding to a report from the UN panel chaired by former Italian Prime Minister Romano Prodi. The report had recommended that African Union peacekeeping mission authorized by the United Nations be backed with stable funding from UN members instead of voluntary bilateral contributions. Assured, steady and robust, assessed contributions raised AU operations to the same level as UN peacekeeping operations, the report concluded. The African representatives for Uganda, Burkina Faso and Libya supported the Prodi recommendations for UN assessed contributions to finance AU operations. Ambassador Michel Kafando speaking for Burkina Faso reiterated the need for a "predictable, sustainable and flexible...financing mechanisms for United Nations-authorized African Union peacekeeping operations, with the ultimate aim of creating a standing African Union peacekeeping capacity and of providing African Union missions with operational resources."[18] The same argument was made by Libya's Deputy Permanent Representative Ibrahim Omar Dabbashi, saying, "...we remain convinced that funding from the United Nations regular budget is the best option, at least with regard to AMISOM." Uganda's Permanent Representative Ruhakana Rugunda pressed harder, arguing that voluntary contribution does not work for peacekeeping operations in Africa. Of the $230 millions pledged in Brussels in April 2009, only a fraction had been realized, argued Rugunda. "It is time that the Council took decisive action and committed itself to practical ways to provide effective support for the African Union when it undertakes peacekeeping operations authorized by the United Nations," the Ugandan envoy concluded.[19]

While representatives for the UK, Austria, China and Croatia edged toward supporting the position of the Africans, Russia, France and the US favoured the multi-donor trust fund model that relied on the largesse of the donors, and which could not be enforced by the UN.[20] Russia, US and Japan balked at the idea of becoming perennial cash cows for peacekeeping operations in Africa. Reassured that AMISOM was in it for the long haul, the US walked a thin line. US Ambassador Susan Rice rejected the idea of blanket contributions to all future UN-authorized AU missions. But America would buck the rule for just one case, and Rice was not shy to mention which one. "We have also supported, on an exceptional basis, the use of assessed contributions to support the African Union Mission in Somalia."[21]

At the end of the debate, it was left to the President of the Security Council, Vietnam's Permanent Representative Lê Lương Minh, to read out what members agreed on. While recognizing the increasing role that the AU played in peacekeeping on continental Africa, the Security Council effectively told the AU to clean up its act on how to "effectively plan, manage and deploy peacekeeping operations."[22] There, however, was one concession the Security Council was prepared to make. The UN support for AMISOM was firm. It would be used as a case study for future AU peacekeeping missions.

Although funding for AMISOM seemed assured at the UN, it remained a big concern for those on the ground working to reshape AMISOM into a peacemaking force. A week and half later after the Security Council debate, on Friday November 6, 2009, AU

Commissioner Ramtane Lamamra convened a meeting at AU headquarters in Addis Ababa. The attendees included defence ministers and military commanders from AMISOM troop contributing countries and donor partners.[23] Operationalizing the concept of an offensive rather than a purely defensive AMISOM was the theme that guided the daylong meeting. Commissioner Lamamra gave his blunt assessment of the security situation in Mogadishu, which he characterized as "more mediocre than before" with "ping-pong control of Mogadishu between TFG/AMISOM and insurgent forces."[24] Lamamra was critical of the lack of cohesion within the TFG, but also blamed donors for not coming through with support for critical military equipment that AMISOM and TFG needed. UNSOA Director Craig Boyd reported that of the $198.7 million pledged in Brussels, $70.2 million was received. UNSOA's budget for the July 1, 2009 to June 30, 2010 was a whopping $225 million. Moreover, some of the donors had strings attached to the funds donated that could be used only for certain items and not others. No lethal weapons, for example, could be purchased from AMISOM trust funds.

There were other woes as well. AU Representative to Somalia Nicolas Bwakira who formally announced his resignation at the meeting complained that the allowances for troops had not been paid. Yet, there was $25 million languishing in the UN bank account. Uganda's defence minister Crispus Kiyonga piled on the heap of things to be done the complaint that Uganda had not been compensated for using its own military equipment in Somalia. When the mission was authorized by parliament, the understanding was that it would not incur cost to Uganda. Added to that, there were problems with payment of death benefits to the families of those killed in action.

During break in the meeting, UN Special Representative for the Secretary General Ould-Abdallah privately told US Representative to the African Union (USAU) Ambassador Michael Anthony Battle that money meant for Somalia always got stuck in the UN system. He suggested that donors skip the cumbersome UN system altogether, and instead funnel money through PricewaterhouseCoopers mechanism. Battle promised to pass that information back to Washington.

When the meeting resumed, there were many issues to consider. Overall, there appeared to be progress. Lamamra neatly summed up the upbeat mood of the meeting. AMISOM was beginning to move in the right direction. The force's existing mandate was robust and flexible, he said. Tweaking the rules of engagement (ROE) would allow what he called friendly forces to take preemptive military action in certain cases. Improved equipment and resources would allow AMISOM to be proactive, "striking the snake among its eggs."[25] The attendees left the meeting feeling motivated, focused and optimistic.

## AMISOM Unchained

Unshackled from the moribund concept of peacekeeping that required sheltering in place when fired upon by the enemy, AMISOM commanders were no longer waiting for such provocations to occur. Instead, from a dovish peacekeeping role, AMISOM was slowly blossoming into a warrior peacemaking mission with the capability to make pre-emptive strikes at the insurgents, pursue psychological operations and engage in nimble media campaigns. Infighting within the militants gave AMISOM and TFG the opening they needed. The two largest Somali insurgent groups, al-Shabaab and Hizbul Islam were fiercely battling for supremacy. Throughout October to December 2009, Hizbul Islam was locked in a bitter three-way fight with al-Shabaab, Ahlu Sunna Waljama'a and TFG forces. On

November 18, 2009, Hizbul Islam declared war on al-Shabaab. "There is no more relations between us Hizbul Islam and the so-called al-Shabaab, and from now onwards the only thing they should expect from our side is battle, nothing else," said Hizbul Islam official Sheikh Abdi Nasser Serar.[26] This was welcome development for the AU forces already working on new strategies of dealing with the militants. General Mugisha gave the go-ahead to begin to inch forward to occupy more spaces in Mogadishu. At sunset on Sunday, November 22, 2009, backed by robust support fire, Uganda battle troops moved on Hizbul fighters in Hodan and Hawl Wadaag districts of Mogadishu. By early Monday morning, November 23, 2009, after inflicting heavy casualty on the insurgents who then retreated further west and north of Mogadishu, Uganda troops took complete control of Jidka Maka al-Mukarama Road east of KM-4, connecting the airport to the presidential palace, Villa Somalia. To the west of KM-4, meanwhile, Uganda troops now had control of the Jidka Afgooye up to the junction with Digfer Road, leading to Digfer Hospital. By noon the same day, in addition to KM-4, the airport, seaport and presidential palace, AMISOM troops added a new completely fortified base at the former Digfer Hospital.

The small success by AMISOM had immediate impact on the dynamics of the conflict. Surprised by AMISOM's assertive deployment, and perhaps seeking to minimize the damage done to the carefully nurtured image as the new power in Mogadishu, Hizbul Islam's spokesperson Sheikh Mohamed Osman Arus claimed that the insurgents carried out the offensive against AMISOM, and not the other way around. Later that same day, sitting in a plush brown leather chair at Villa Somalia and looking completely at ease in a navy-blue suit without a tie, President Sheikh Sharif Sheikh Ahmed told the media that the chances of survival for his government was greater than when he came to power in January. "There was a plan to defeat this government, and given the circumstances, the fact that the government is still in place is a success."[27] A week later, on Tuesday, December 1, 2009, cladded in a military fatigue, and walking with a newfound confidence, President Sharif Ahmed made his first foray into south Mogadishu, visiting several TFG militia bases in Wadajir and Dharkenleey districts.[28]

On the same day, the slightly shifting military equation that favoured AMISOM and TFG caused Hizbul Islam to announce more attacks targeting the AU troops. Most desperate to demonstrate that AMISOM and TFG forces were impotent to protect the population, the rebels also targeted civilians. On Thursday, December 3, 2009, a Danish Somali named Abdi, pretending to be a journalist, took advantage of lax security at Hotel Shamo in Mogadishu where a group of medical students from Benadir Medical School were gathered for a celebratory graduation ceremony.[29] The occasion was a very happy one for many Somali who saw the event as a triumph against all the senseless slaughter that the country had experienced. The hall was buzzing with expectation as the graduating students, wearing black graduating robes with gold trimmings, sat proudly at the front of the room while relatives and friends sat neatly in rows at the back, listening to the guest speakers. The TFG Minister of Health Qamar Aden Ali, also wearing a black dress with gold trims, dignified in her gray and dark blue headscarf sat at the front. Presumably preparing the speech she would never give, Ali used a blue ballpoint pen to scribble notes on the page of a journal. Suddenly, all went black as the bomber detonated a most powerful bomb, spewing deadly shards of metal and ball bearings in all directions. Moments later, a camera captured scattered body parts, mangled flesh, the dead lying in growing pool of blood while some survivors, stunned and grievously wounded lay all around, waiting for help. A critically injured man, barefoot, his clothes shredded by the bomb that tore into his flesh, fell face down, rolled on his back, before willing himself to sit up again to await help. He did not cry. Nobody cried, nobody said anything. It was eerily silent and final for many. Mohamed Olad Hassan, a reporter for the BBC and Associated Press who survived the bomb, recalled two weeks later that survivors began running, and screaming at the same time, all asking the same question, "Is it a bomb? Is it a bomb?"[30]

The tally from the attack was 23 dead, including three TFG ministers; Minister of Higher Education Prof. Ibrahim Hassan Addow, Minister of Education Ahmed Abdullahi Waayeel and Minister of Health Qamar Aden Ali. Among the fallen were Mohamed Amin, 24, a reporter for the local FM Radio Shabelle, Hassan Zubeyr, 29, a cameraman for Dubai-based Al-Arabiya and Abdulkhafar Abdulkadir, 28, a freelance photographer who three months earlier was instrumental in documenting the carnage left by the twin bombing at AMISOM base.[31] Over forty people were wounded including Sport Minister Saleban Olad Roble who, in critical condition, was airlifted to Aga Khan Hospital in Nairobi and, subsequently, to Riyadh in Saudi Arabia where he died two months later on Friday, February 12, 2010.

Although no one claimed responsibility for the bomb attack at Hotel Shamo, the insurgents were suspected behind the carnage. The swift backlash from angry Somali from around the world forced al-Shabaab out of its way to deny any responsibility for the bombing, saying through its spokesman Sheikh Ali Mohammed Rage that "it is not in our nature to target innocent Muslims."[32] Whoever was behind the bombing clearly wanted to discredit the TFG backed by AMISOM as incapable of protecting civilians. To AMISOM commanders, the bombing bore telltale signs of the insurgents making panicky decisions under pressure. There were no more pretenses on all sides that this was anything other than war, and that the insurgents were clearly in it to destroy AMISOM and the TFG.

The intensity and ferocity of attacks against AMISOM increased as insurgent leaders now called openly for war against the AU force. Overnight on December 3, 2009, while Mogadishu mourned the victims of the devastating attack at Shamo Hotel, al-Shabaab attacked the Burundi contingent based at the Jalle Siyad Military Academy. The attack lasted several hours, but was beaten back. On Saturday December 5, 2009 Hizbul Islam leader Sheikh Dahir Aweys called for fresh attacks on AMISOM. "The people can reach peace and progress if they fight against foreign troops in Somalia," he said.[33] In the dying days of December 2009, as the New Year approached, from their bases along Warshaddaha Street, north of Bakaara Market, insurgents aimed daily mortar attacks at AMISOM, including on Sunday, December 13, 2009 at Uganda troops based at KM-4, and the following day at Burundi troops at the Jalle Siyad Military Academy.

To instill confidence in the civil population, and cause psychological anxiety in the insurgency, the TFG government worked closely with AMISOM to show normalcy in Mogadishu. On Sunday December 20, 2009, the beleaguered city celebrated the 66th anniversary of the founding of Somali National Police, complete with a parade by hundreds of khaki-uniformed police personnel. The images were of a city rising back to its feet rather than cowering in a corner. As expected, to challenge the assertion of peace, the insurgents lobbed mortars at the event, killing thirteen including one policeman and wounding three others.[34] AMISOM troops returned fire, hitting insurgent areas around Bakaara. For the remaining days of 2009 including on Christmas Day Friday, December 25, the insurgents pressed the fight against the AU troops, but, increasingly, these attacks were met with ferocious firepower from AMISOM, causing the insurgents to retreat, and regroup elsewhere.

The sustained campaign by AU troops forced the insurgents to call temporary truce to ongoing infighting among the splinter rebel forces, and attempt to unite under one command. After three days of talks starting December 15 through December 18, al-Shabaab and Hizbul Islam failed to reach a compromise on truce.[35] Shortly, al-Shabaab leaders began making pronouncements seemed calculated to demonstrate to AMISOM, TFG, rival insurgents and Somali public that al-Shabaab was now firmly entrenched in Somalia, with the administrative capabilities to create and enforce Islamic laws. Pushing a dress code in Kismaayo, it ordered men to grow long beards, shave moustaches and wear trousers above the ankle.[36] On Wednesday, December 30, 2009, al-Shabaab official Mahad Omar Abdikarim from the Bay and Bakool region reaffirmed the group's link to al-Qaeda. While addressing demonstrators supporting al-Shabaab in Ufurow district in southwestern Somalia, he said, "We are not hiding the brotherhood relations with al Qaeda and our aim is to set up an Islamic caliphate."[37] The same day, spokesman Sheikh Ali Mohammed Rage banned Somalis from listening to Radio Mogadishu. "Radio influences people to accept almost everything that is on air, this is against the religion and anyone caught violating this directive will be punished the same way as the owners of the stations," Rage warned.[38] Then on New Year's Day, while officiating at the passing-out ceremony for young rebel fighters in Huriwa district in north Mogadishu, al-Shabaab commander Sheikh Muktar Robow Abu Mansour, made a grand gesture. He announced that al-Shabaab would soon send fighters to support al Qaeda in Yemen battling the government of President Ali Abdullah Saleh. "We tell our Muslim brothers in Yemen that we will cross the water between us and reach your place to assist you fight the enemy of Allah," Mansour said.[39] As for AMISOM, Mansour was confident that the young fighters could take on and defeat the AU troops. Adding that if they died in battle, "they are martyrs and will be rewarded in the hereafter. If they survive, they will live in blissful life."[40]

The reality, however, was much different. Like the Greek's mythical phoenix bird that rose from its ashes, backed by AMISOM, the TFG forces were not the pushover forces they previously were. Increasingly confident, the TFG took to the airwaves to announce the imminent retaking of Mogadishu from the insurgents. On December 29, 2009, perhaps prematurely, the Somali Minister of Internal Affairs Abdirashid Mohamed Hiddig announced the TFG would retake the entire capital in the New Year. "We hope to retake the entire city from opposition groups and we will hold our meetings in those places," he said while addressing a workshop for Benadir regional administration.[41] Somali Prime Minister Omar Abdirashid Ali Sharmarke while in Nairobi for the New Year was equally keen to highlight the plan to take the war to the insurgents, saying, "Our troops are prepared to act, and flush these terrorists out of the capital before the end of January, and continue taking over the control of territories from these fighters."[42] On Sunday, January 10, 2010, a joint force comprising TFG soldiers and militias from Ahlu Sunna Waljama'a attacked and dislodged Hizbul Islam fighters from the eastern part of Beledweyn. The fierce fighting continued through to mid-week, stalling into stalemate with neither side capable of pushing the other from the town.

Unlike in the past when TFG forces crumbled under attacks by insurgents, this time the force stood its ground. The stiffening of the back of TFG forces was mostly due to AMISOM's new approach. The AU forces would no longer be the punching bag for al-

Shabaab or anybody else's. The new optimism for Somalia was captured in the Report of the Chairperson submitted at the 214th meeting of the AU Peace and Security Commission on January 8, 2010 in Addis Ababa.[43] The report noted that AMISOM's strength was boosted by the deployment of additional battalion from Burundi in August 2009. The AU boots on the ground stood at 5268 troops, made of three battalions apiece from Uganda and Burundi. While this fell short of the required 8000 troops, gains were being made as AMISOM expanded its hold in Mogadishu. On January 28, 2010, the UN Security Council renewed AMISOM's mandate for another 12 months to January 31, 2011. Of course, there was serious work ahead of AMISOM that needed doing.

In the first week of February 2010, General Mugisha, working closely with the commander of Ugandan contingent Colonel Tumusiime Katsigazi, the commander of Burundian contingent Major General Prime Niyongabo and TFG commanders began coordinating plans for taking more ground. With fresh troops provided by Uganda Battle Group Five (UGABAG 5), Gen. Mugisha saw the feasibility of expanding the area under the control of AMISOM beyond the confines of the airport, Villa Somalia and Mogadishu Port. Plans for pre-emptive engagement of the insurgents began in earnest with the deployment of better-trained and equipped TFG forces in strategic areas of Mogadishu. Starting early dawn on Saturday, February 6 through Tuesday, February 9, around 2,000 TFG forces were deployed in various neighbourhoods. The movement of TFG soldiers did not go unnoticed by the insurgents whose vast network of informers were buried in every corner of Mogadishu society and even within the government of Sheikh Sharif itself.[44] On Tuesday, February 9, 2010, Hizbul Islam spokesman Mohamed Osman Arus spoke out about the gathering of TFG forces for an imminent attack. "We have information of this offensive planned by the apostate government against our position in Mogadishu and other parts of the country."[45] al-Shabaab, meanwhile, began ferrying young fighters into the city in preparation to counter the TFG planned offensive. The spokesman for the group Sheikh Ali Mohammed Rage claimed the fighters, part of a battalion, were recent graduates eager for the fight against AMISOM. "They are called Khalid bin Walid Brigade and will complete the war against the enemy," he warned.[46] On Friday, February 12, 2010, the TFG engaged the insurgents in several eastern districts of Mogadishu including Yaaqshiid, Bondheere, and Shibiis. Rounds of mortar landed around Towfiq Hotel in Yaaqshiid, killing five. The fighting spilled into the following week with truckload of insurgents being brought to the besieged city.

As the battle intensified, so did the media war. The insurgents were adept at using the media to promote a particular narrative and, when necessary, use the boots on the ground to translate the narrative into concrete action. On Sunday, February 14, 2010, for example, Somali State Minister for Defense Yusuf Mohamed "Indha Adde" Siyad told the media that the TFG was not overly concerned with the new built-up of insurgents around Mogadishu. "These deployments will not affect our operations; we are ready to defeat them."[47] Obviously paying attention, the insurgents wanted to prove that they were still very lethal. The following day, Monday, February 15, 2010, as he drove around Mogadishu, Siyad narrowly escaped assassination when a suicide bomber drove his bomb-laden vehicle toward the convoy and detonated it, injuring two of the minister's security detail. Two days later, on Wednesday February 17, 2010, a workshop planned at the Ambassador Hotel in Mogadishu to be attended by several government ministers was called off. An informer tipped TFG security that al-Shabaab organized the event in order to assassinate top government officials.[48]

AMISOM also learned to create its own narrative. The increased attacks from insurgents only strengthened the resolve of AMISOM's commanders to be seen and heard. In a departure from the past when AMISOM troops minimized exposure during daylight, on Saturday, February 20, 2010, Burundi troops fanned out along Warshaddaha Road leading to the Jalle Siyad Military Academy. Ostensibly, the troops were searching for mines planted by al-Shabaab. The real message to the insurgents that day was very simple. AU troops would not hide anymore. The AU troops still rattled around in battlewagons dressed in the white colours of peacekeeping, but increasingly their guns barked the harsh language of war. Eager to show AMISOM's muscles, Spokesperson Major Barigye Ba-Hoku, once the very model of a peacekeeper at the start of his deployment on Saturday March 1, 2008, now sounded like a rehabilitated former peacenik. He became adept at monitoring the airwaves for propaganda from the insurgents, quickly refuting their outlandish claims. "They know they don't have enough forces to engage us and move us back one foot," Maj. Ba-Hoku told the media on December 2, 2009, adding with a boast, "Our major achievement is that we have been able to demystify the idea that Somalia is a no-go area." [49]

The allied TFG and AMISOM forces seized every piece of good news to show movement and strength. On the same day that the Burundians were showing troop colours, there was good news to share. After two weeks of negotiations in Addis Ababa, the TFG government and moderate Islamists group Ahlu Sunna Waljama'a (ASWJ) signed a memorandum of understanding effectively ending ASWJ's war against the government of Sheikh Sharif Ahmed.[50] The power sharing deal negotiated with the blessing of the US gave some government posts to ASWJ officials. Most importantly, the deal brought thousands of ASWJ fighters into the fold of TFG.[51] It was a big win for the government, and for AMISOM.

General Mugisha moved quickly to capitalize on the good news. The AU troops kept pressure on the insurgents. On Saturday, March 6, 2010, AMISOM senior commanders and the rank and file celebrated three years in Somalia. Not one to linger too long at ceremonies, Gen. Mugisha used the occasion to coordinate operations against the insurgents with senior TFG commanders gathered for the occasion. The TFG was doing marginally better, but needed the discipline to get more aggressive, Gen. Mugisha told the Somali commanders. Indeed, bolstered by the AU forces, the Somali government forces were pressing on with planned offensive against the insurgents. From their base along Tarabunka Road, TFG soldiers began staging neighbourhood operations starting Tuesday, March 2, 2010, clashing almost daily with insurgents in Dayniile, Hawl Wadaag, and Hodan districts. On Saturday, April 3, 2010, both al-Shabaab and TFG claimed victory in the fierce gun clash the day before in Hodan district where as many as 13 people were killed. Clashes continued the following day Sunday, spreading to Rage Ele district in Middle Shabelle in southern Somalia.

With ASWJ, a former ally, now turning its gun on them, the stakes were much higher for al-Shabaab and Hizbul Islam. Increasingly al-Shabaab and Hizbul Islam vied to be seen as the dominant force in Somalia, each taking actions to help attain that goal. Their public pronouncements urgently telegraphed to potential recruits from around the world to join the war in Somalia. Meanwhile leaders of the two groups also sought to unify. One such unity meeting was organized at Celaasha Biyaha along the Afgooye Highway, on the outskirt of Mogadishu on Wednesday, March 10, 2010. The meeting was to bridge the

Battle for Mogadishu: A Ugandan soldier looks on as AO2 Musisi, trained by Bancroft engineers, uses an armoured front-end loader to fill anti-tank ditches dug by al-Shabaab in the el Hindi area, Mogadishu, May 11, 2011. (Photo credit: Rocky van Blerk (Bancroft))

Battle for Mogadishu: The commander of Uganda's 19th Bn, Lt. Col. Anthony Lukwago Mbuusi, works the frontline in Hodan District, Mogadishu on July 15, 2011. (Photo credit: Stuart Price)

Battle for Mogadishu: A Ugandan soldier framed by a 'mousehole' in Hodan district, Mogadishu on July 15, 2011. (Photo credit: Stuart Price)

Battle for Mogadishu: UPDF Public Information Officer Capt. Ronald Kakurungu, second left, on August 9, 2011, chats with Ugandan soldiers from UGABAG VII, Capt. Stephen Tayebwa (pointing) and Lt. Stephen Mugisha (right) while patrolling the deserted streets of Bakaara Market, near the scene of Black Hawk Down, which three days earlier was a strategic stronghold of al-Shabaab until their sudden withdrawal from Mogadishu on August 5, 2011. (Photo credit: Stuart Price/AMISOM)

Battle for Mogadishu: Change of the guard. Incoming AMISOM Force Commander Maj. Gen. Fred Mugisha and his predecessor Gen. Nathan Mugisha pose for a picture with Burundi and Uganda officers in August 2011. Left to right, Maj. Fred Wemba, Capt. Edy Germain Nkenshimana, Col. Pascal Bizimungu, Brig. Gen. Audace Nduwumusi, Maj. Gen. Fred Mugisha, Maj. Gen. Nathan Mugisha, Col. Oscar Nzohabonayo and Lt. Col. Paddy Ankunda. (Photo credit: Stuart Price)

Operation Free Shabelle: Uganda contingent commander Brig. Paul Lokech, nearside at front table, and his Burundi counterpart Col. Oscar Nzohabonayo during joint contingent planning for Operation Free Shabelle (OFS) on May 4, 2012, listen as Uganda Deputy Contingent Commander Col. Kayanja Muhanga, at podium, briefs Uganda and Burundi commanders. (Photo credit: UPDF Archives)

Operation Free Shabelle: Col. Kayanja Muhanga conducts rehearsals for OFS on May 16, 2012, north of Mogadishu. (Photo credit: UPDF Archives)

Operation Free Shabelle: Burundian commander Col. Oscar Nzohabonayo, center, draws a battle map on ground as Brig. Paul Lokech, left, and Col. Kayanja Muhanga, right, look on, during rehearsals for the OFS offensive, May 16, 2012. (Photo credit: UPDF archives)

Operation Free Shabelle: Private Martin Okwalinga, a Ugandan soldier, prepares to launch an RQ-11 Raven unmanned aerial reconnaissance vehicle, on loan from the US Army, during the OFS march to Afgooye for real-time intelligence on the movement of insurgents, May 23, 2012. (Photo credit: UPDF Archives)

Operation Free Shabelle: A welcome tea at Lafole, prepared by Bancroft team, on May 23, 2012. Left to right, Chief military Intelligence Officer Col. Henry Isoke, Bancroft trainer Brett Fredericks, TFG Gen. Abdikarim Yusuf 'Dhaga-badan', Brig. Lokech, Bancroft engineer Rocky van Blerk, and two Somali commanders. Fredericks was killed on Christmas Day, 2014 inside Halaane Base while trying to neutralize insurgents that had infiltrated the base. Gen. Abdikarim Yusuf Dhaga-badan was killed during a suicide attack on November 1, 2015 in Mogadishu. (Photo credit: UPDF Archives)

Operation Free Shabelle: A determined Commander of UGABAG 9, Lt. Col. Frederick Akiiki Rugadya, leads the final march toward Afgooye; back right, is Brig. Lokech and far behind is L/Cpl. Robert Amia (in dark glasses), aide de camp to Col. Muhanga, May 24, 2012. (Photo credit: UPDF archives)

Operation Free Shabelle: Brig. Paul Lokech crosses the River Shabelle Bridge into Afgooye at dawn on May 25, 2012, meeting no resistance as residents welcomed AMISOM troops into town. (Photo credit: UPDF Archives)

Operation Free Shabelle: Left, The author shares a light moment with AMISOM Force Commander Lt. Gen. Andrew Gutti at his office at Halaane Base, Mogadishu, July 18, 2012. Gutti oversaw OFS and the extension of the liberation of Somalia beyond Mogadishu, including the taking of Afgooye three weeks after he took command of AMISOM. (Photo credit: UPDF Archives)

Surrender for 218 al-Shabaab militants, in the background, is a firm handshake between the commander of UGABAG 9 Col. Stephen Mugerwa, left, and al-Shabaab commander Segu Abdu Yusuf (with headband), as Lt. Col. John Katongole Commander of 342Bn looks on, on Saturday September 22, 2012 in the town of Garsale, approximately 10 km from Jowhar and some 80km from the Capital Mogadishu. As a sign of goodwill, commander Yusuf was allowed to keep his gun, but 83 weapons were recovered by AMISOM troops. (Photo credit: UPDF Archives)

KDF Brigadier Anthony Ngere, centre, AMISOM Sector Two Commander and head of the Kenyan Contingent serving with AMISOM, greets field commanders at Saa'moja, 7 km outside the port city of Kismayo, October 1, 2012, a day before joint allied forces of AMISOM, the Somali National Army (SNA) and the pro-government Ras Kamboni Brigade advanced on and took over the last remaining urban bastion of the Al-Qaeda-affiliated extremist group Al Shabaab. (Photo credit: Stuart Price)

Soldiers of the Kenyan Contingent serving with the African Union Mission in Somalia (AMISOM), sit on a flat-bed truck as a convoy makes its way between the port of Kismayo and the city's airport. On 2 October 2012, Kenyan AMISOM troops supporting forces of the Somali National Army and the pro-government Ras Kamboni Brigade moved into Kismayo. (Photo credit: Stuart Price)

The commander of UPDF 4th Division Maj. Gen. Wilson Mbadi, speaking about service to the people to UPDF officers on February 6, 2013 at Gulu Barracks, before he was appointed in May 2013 as the Joint Chiefs of Staff (JCOS). The occasion was the annual celebration of Tarehe Sita, commemorating the UPDF launch of the bush struggle on February 6, 1981. UPDF's ideology of people first is credited with its huge success in Somalia. (Photo credit: UPDF Archives)

Ugandan Contingent commander Brig. Dick Olum on February 5, 2014, directs an operation from the top of his Gila armoured vehicle near the town of Gendershe on the coast of Somalia, on his march to capture Quoroleey in March, Buulo Marer in September and Baraawe on October 6, 2014. (Photo credit: UPDF archives)

Somalia President Hassan Sheikh Mohamud, left, shakes hands with AMISOM force Commander Lt. Gen. Silas Ntigurirwa, while welcoming Burundian President Pierre Nkuruziza, center, at Mogadishu Airport on 22 April, 2014 (Photo credit: Ilyas Abukar/AMISOM)

United Nation's Special Representative of the Secretary General, Ambassador Nicholas Kay, left, shakes hands with UPDF commander of land forces (CLF) Maj. Gen. David Muhoozi after delivering a speech during the Inauguration of the United Nations Guard Unit in Somalia on May 18, 2014. Standing behind the CLF is Aide de camp Lt. Daniel Kyatuuka. (Photo credit: David Mutua/ UN-AU IST)

Ambassador Maman Sidikou, at front, the Special Representative of the Chairperson of the African Union Commission (SRCC) for Somalia is taken on a tour of the Kismaayo seaport on Friday, February 13, 2015 by AMISOM Force Commander Maj. Gen. Jonathan Kipkemoi Rono (dark glasses). (Photo credit: Mohamed Barut/ AMISOM)

differences between the two insurgent groups.[52] Nothing came of it. Sheikh Hassan Dahir Aweys wanted more than al-Shabaab was willing to give him. The two remained bitter enemies. On Friday, March 19, 2010, unidentified gunmen assassinated Sheikh Daud Ali Hassan, a senior al-Shabaab commander in Dhoobley town in Lower Juba region. Though nobody claimed responsibility, Hizbul Islam was likely behind the killing. The two groups renewed their rivalry in southern Somalia especially in the Kismaayo area.

The rabid race by the two insurgent groups to assert control sometime took on a bizarre twist. On Tuesday, March 23, 2010, for instance, al-Shabaab commanders ordered the destruction of the tomb of renowned Somali cleric Sheikh Mohidin Eli located in Karaan district.[53] Sheikh Eli was a most influential leader of Somalia's main Sufi movement, Ahlu Sunna Waljama'a (The Companions of the Prophet), and whose son Sheikh Sharif Sheikh Muhieddin became the chairman of Ahlu Sunna Waljama'a.[54] For al-Shabaab commanders who mostly followed the Wahhabi sect, the Sufis were not true Muslims. Two weeks later, on Friday, April 9 2010, the group banned both the British Broadcasting Corporation (BBC) and Voice of America (VOA), claiming that both news organizations were fronts for the Zionist war against Islam.[55] Not to be outdone, Hizbul Islam tried to project itself as the heir apparent to al-Qaeda in the Horn of Africa. At a media event on Saturday, April 3, 2010, Hizbul Islam governor in the Benadir region, Moallim Hashi Mohamed Farah told journalists that Hizbul Islam leader Sheikh Hassan Dahir Aweys invited al-Qaeda leader Osama bin Laden to Somalia. "We are calling on all jihadists around the world to arrive in Somalia and help us defeat the puppet government and the Christian soldiers of African Union who are killing the Muslim Somalis ... . The arrival of Bin Laden will encourage Jihad in Somalia so we say [to] him welcome to Somalia," Moallim Farah added.[56] The governor also ordered locals radios to stop playing music and songs within ten days or face punishment.

Propaganda aside, both al-Shabaab and Hizbul Islam appreciated the threat posed by AMISOM troops no longer fettered by impractical rules of engagement. Starting Monday, April 12, 2010 through to Sunday, April 18, 2010, fighting rocked various Mogadishu neighbourhoods. That same day, a remote bomb targeting TFG officers exploded in Wabeeri district killing at least 8 people, and wounding many others. Insurgents also fired mortars at AMISOM base at Aden Abdulle Airport. AMISOM troops responded with heavy guns of their own, always working to avoid civilian casualties. On Friday, April 23, 2010, al-Shabaab scored some easy victory against ASWJ forces in Galguudud region, seizing the towns of El Der, Masagaway and Galad. A senior al-Shabaab official, Sheikh Yusuf Kabokudukade crowed about the wins, saying, "We have overrun those who tried to stop the efforts to spread Islam in Somalia. With the power of Allah, we have taken control of three districts in Galguudud region."[57]

AMISOM, meanwhile, continued expanding its footprints in Mogadishu. On Thursday, April 22, 2010, backed by strong support fire, Uganda Battle Group V under the command of the tough and combative Lt. Col. Francis Chemo moved under the cover of darkness toward the historic al-Urubah Hotel. For too long the insurgents had used the former playground to wealthy tourists, diplomats and their children, to shell AMISOM bases in Hamar Jajaab and Hamar Weyne districts. This once proud Italian settlement area was mostly ruins, the exquisitely crafted buildings scarred by war. Chemo's troops, fighting pitched battles with insurgents, moved east along Corso Primo Lugio and Via Egitto, first overrunning the Mogadishu Cathedral, before moving on to formerly Parco San Francesco di Assisi and, finally, massing at the junction of Via Corso Vittorio Emmanuele III and Via Egitto for the finishing assault on al-Urubah. al-Shabaab fighters put up a spirited fight, fritting between buildings and doubling back to create traps for Ugandan troops. By nightfall on Friday, Chemo's forces had taken over al-Urubah Hotel and, before daylight was out, had reinforced the position with hundreds of green sandbags.

The following day, al-Urubah Hotel became the new headquarters of UGABAG V. Never quitting without one more fight, al-Shabaab fighters made several attempts to dislodge AMISOM troops using mortar shelling, sniper fire and, when these proved ineffective against the well-entrenched Ugandan troops, deployed suicide bombers. On Tuesday, April 27, 2010, three young suicide bombers in a desperate quixotic run used a truck laden with petro fuel, explosives and bombs, to attack the newly established headquarters.[58] When the suicide truck crashed through the barrier, Ugandan troops immediately engaged it with RPG and small arms fire. The young Somali men still managed to detonate their deadly cargo, sending shards of metal flying in every direction. Three AMISOM soldiers were seriously injured in the blast, but the only dead were the bombers. The five AMISOM soldiers injured in the battle that day were airlifted to Nairobi for further treatment.[59] AMISOM troops, meanwhile, quickly devised an innovative approach to security by placing an armoured truck at the gate, moving it only to give way to vehicles identified as friendly.

Through May, June and July 2010, the situation in Mogadishu grew extremely tense. Fighting was a daily reality of life for residents as the insurgent groups jockeyed for firmer toehold in the city. AMISOM and TFG, meanwhile, seized every opportunity to expand deeper into the city. al-Shabaab countered by increasingly relying on suicide bombs and improvised explosive devices (IEDs). These were planted along roadside to target and, hopefully, slow down the progress of the continental force, and to thwart progress from rival insurgents forces. Assassination of senior officials within the TFG and the insurgency was rife. On Saturday, May 1, 2010, one of the group's senior leaders Fuad Mohamed Qalaf Shongole was targeted for assassination as he attended *dhuhur* midday prayers at the Abdalla Shideeye Mosque in Bakaara Market area. A twin bomb, one planted at the front and another at the back of the mosque exploded killing at least 30 and wounding as many as 55 people. al-Shabaab spokesman Sheikh Ali Mohammed Rage immediately blamed "foreign security companies" whose sole aim was to massacre Muslims.[60] The following day, Sunday, May 2, 2010, the slightly wounded but otherwise very much alive Sheikh Fuad Shongole called on Somali Muslims to fight against AMISOM. "The Muslim people of Somalia must fight the African Union troops of the occupying force using the means at their disposal, including suicide attacks," he urged in a broadcast on al-Shabaab's owned Mogadishu Somali Weyn radio.[61] In apparent retaliation, al-Shabaab executed three young men early Sunday, claiming they were traitors for Ahlu Sunna Waljama'a. Two days later on Tuesday, May 4, 2010, the group killed popular Mogadishu journalist Sheikh Noor Maxamed Abkey, working for the Somali Ministry of Information. The next day, Abdiwahid Hussein Hassan, a senior commander for Hizbul Islam, was gunned down as he left a mosque in Hawo-Abdi village between Mogadishu and Afgooye in Lower Shabelle.[62] On the same afternoon of Wednesday, May 5, 2010, AMISOM spokesman Major Ba-Hoku Barigye held a news conference to warn about suicide attacks planned by al-Shabaab. Major Barigye revealed very precise details about the attack, saying that the attacker was a man named Mohyaddin Yusuf. "They are going to use different cars for the attack including a

Toyota pick-up truck, land cruisers and minibuses," he said.[63]

In the age when the media played greater role in the war in Mogadishu, it did not take long for al-Shabaab to respond to Maj. Barigye. On Sunday, May 9, 2010, spokesman Sheikh Ali Mohammed Rage (Ali Dheere) shot back, saying Maj. Barigye's claims were baseless. Not concerned with how ridiculous it might sound to the world outside Somalia, Rage said it was AMISOM that was planning suicide attacks against civilians.[64] Sheikh Rage's intended audience, after all, were the Somali people within Somalia who, given the scale of violence, no longer knew whom to trust or to believe. This was war, and al-Shabaab matched its rhetoric with firepower on the ground.

At early dawn on Sunday, May 23, 2010, fresh fighting erupted as al-Shabaab militias attacked TFG bases in Hodan, Hawl Wadaag and Wardigley districts. When it moved closer to Villa Somalia, the intense firefight drew in AMISOM. President Sharif Ahmed was away on state visit to Turkey, but AMISOM decided enough was enough. Uganda units based at KM-4 and at the Seaport rushed in to support the units at the presidential palace. By day's end on Sunday, the insurgents were pushed back along West Hawl Wadaag Road toward Bakaara, leaving 14 dead and as many as 25 wounded. Despite the losses, al-Shabaab seemed pleased with the effort of their militias, and as part of its media campaign to recruit more fighters, used the occasion to discuss its goal. A senior al-Shabaab official in Benadir region urged fighters to prepare to seize Villa Somalia. "You know recently, the mujahideen took over more areas that were in north Mogadishu. The fighters attacked and seized new zones. The next attack would be Villa Somalia," said Sheikh Ali Mohamed Hussein, al-Shabaab appointed governor of Benadir region.[65] As expected an unnamed government spokesman denied reports that Villa Somalia was under siege, dismissing them as "pure fantasy".[66]

There was no denying the gathering strength of al-Shabaab. The end of May and the beginning of June 2010 wore hard on AMISOM and TFG. Despite the gains, the insurgents often returned much stronger, better organized and larger than the last time, causing some setbacks. On Thursday, May 27, 2010, for the second time, a roadside bomb targeted State Minister for Defense Sheikh Yusuf "Indha Adde" Siyad as he drove along Maka al-Mukarama Road in Mogadishu. The blast along the block between Deeqa Electronics and Weheliye Hotel killed three civilians and wounded three of his security detail, but as before, Siyad emerged unscathed.[67] At a news conference the following day, without offering proof, Sheikh Yusuf Siyad pointed fingers at insiders within the Presidential Palace as authors of the attempt on his life.[68] Siyad's drama was overshadowed by the intense firefight that began in Wardhigleey's district on the evening of Monday, May 31, 2010. The TFG working to recover grounds it lost to al-Shabaab in previous fights, soon needed supporting fire from AMISOM. On Thursday, June 3, 2010 as the battle raged along Sinai Road, a T-55 tank with a Ugandan crew fell in a thinly camouflaged ditch dug expressively for that purpose, and became stuck. Despite heavy supporting fire at the enemy to allow for the rescue of the crew, multiple rocket propelled grenades (RPGs) launched at close range by insurgents hit the tank causing it to burst into flames, trapping the doomed crew. On Friday, June 4, 2010, al-Shabaab displayed the charred remains to Mogadishu resident. Spokesperson Sheikh Ali Mohammed Rage spoke to the media about the displayed bodies, saying, "Today, we can all see the casualties we inflicted on them. We destroyed an armored vehicle, killing all on board. We also seized a bulldozer belonging to AMISOM."[69]

The loss of the front-end loading bulldozer was no small matter for Ugandan troops supported by the best team of engineers from Bancroft Global Development, "a not-for-profit nongovernment organization that implements stabilization initiatives in conflict zones."[70] Based in Washington, DC, the multinational organisation was sometimes unfairly lumped with multinationals that supply mercenaries to conflict zones.[71] In fact Bancroft's top-notched professionals whose ideological orientation was not making money from war, ensured that every AMISOM soldier deployed in the peace mission got to keep their limbs and lives. The Bancroft team in Somalia took its job extremely seriously and would drop everything to rush to a suspected IED site, often using their professional experience to safely defuse the menacing device, saving lives. Long after the last casualty is evacuated from an IED explosion site, the team continue working to gather crucial evidence for later analysis, the type of material used by the attackers, the sophistication of the bombs, what it was intended to do, and whether such a device was seen before. The information helped plan for deployment, movement of troops and when to suspect the insurgents were planning something else. Saving lives was the focus of the team, and the happiest day was when everyone returned safely to base camp to reminisce about the day's undertakings, and plan for the next.

The Bancroft engineers had become adept at using the two front-end loaders, sometimes under withering enemy fire, to help soldiers fill up green bags with sand for added fortification and protection against insurgents fire. Both loading machines pockmarked with battle scars from enemy bullets were guarded zealously as if they were living and breathing members of the fighting units. In areas that fell under AU control, green sandbags were immediately ubiquitous. With one of the machine in the hands of al-Shabaab, troops now had to improvise to make for the loss.

The following day Saturday, June 5, 2010, the deputy spokesperson for AMISOM, Lt. Col. Adolphe Manirakiza, reluctantly confirmed the deaths of the two soldiers and wounding of five others.[72] The day also brought some bit of good news for AMISOM. Information emerged of the death of the Algerian Abu Zainab Muhsin, also known as Binu Muhsin, killed two days earlier on Thursday, June 3, 2010 during fighting in Karaan district, north of Mogadishu. The 48-year old Muhsin was the main bomb-maker for al-Shabaab and his death was considered a blow to the group that had perfected the use of bombs and IEDs in the war.[73]

al-Shabaab and Hizbul Islam, meanwhile, continued the efforts to unite. The latter wanted unity more than the former. At a workshop organized for teachers, scholars and religious leaders, on Thursday May 27, 2010, Hizbul Islam leader Sheikh Hassan Dahir Aweys spoke in favour of unity with al-Shabaab. "It is important to unite the mujahideen and accept this idea as brotherly," he preached.[74] It soon became apparent why Aweys wanted unity as soon as possible. His organization was starting to bleed away fighters to al-Shabaab. On Thursday, June 17, 2010, Sheikh Abdulkadir Haji Ahmed, a commander of Hizbul Islam in Beledweyne defected to al-Shabaab with a sizable number of fighters. Although Aweys dismissed the group as a small faction, a trend was set. The following week on Monday, June 21, 2010, Aweys was forced to defend the news that his remaining fighters in Beledweyne vacated town without putting a fight against the incoming al-Shabaab forces. "The thing that forced us to peacefully vacate Hiraan region were to avoid clash with al-Shabaab and also to avert possible shedding of blood," he argued.[75] In effect, the admission completed the transformation of al-Shabaab from one of many insurgent groups vying for vacuum left by the ICU to becoming the main insurgent group in Somalia. While Hizbul

Islam would continue to fight another day, its stars were dimming rapidly.

With its main competitor effectively put down, al-Shabaab now focused sharply on AMISOM. For the group, this had become a no-holds barred war. All associated with AMISOM were considered targets. Its ruthless campaign of terror was about to get very dirty and very bloody. On the last day of June 2010, Gen. Mugisha, huddled to talk strategies with Uganda's new contingent commander Col. Michael Ondoga and Burundi's contingent commander Brigadier Maurice Gateretse. Barely two weeks earlier, on Friday, June 18, 2010, Col. Ondoga had boarded the early dawn flight from Entebbe Air force base to Mogadishu. On arrival at Aden Abdulle Airport, Col. Ondoga was warmly received on the tarmac by his predecessor, contingent commander Col. Geoffrey Katsigazi. The two had exchanged a hearty handshake.

Now, Col. Ondoga sat, waiting for his boss to speak. The situation was dire, began Gen. Mugisha. There was urgent need to focus on al-Shabaab as the main foe. The frequent attacks on AMISOM placed the continental troops in the difficult position of defending themselves. Still, Gen. Mugisha emphasized to the new commander that regardless of al-Shabaab's provocations, hospitals, schools, markets, places of worship and residential areas were uncompromisingly fire-free zones. AMISOM troops would continue the policy it adopted from the start of the mission to use maximum care when confronting al-Shabaab to avoid civilian casualties. Col. Ondoga listened attentively to Gen. Mugisha. He nodded to signal that he understood. Then nodded again to acknowledge the challenges for his troops. Fighting under the most inhospitable circumstances was not new to the Ugandan commander. Known for his jolly and quick laughs, Ondoga's friendly demeanor belied a quick mind of a battle tactician. Indefatigable, he was always looking for new ways to solve a battle problem. He cut his teeth perfecting jungle warfare against the Lord's Resistance Army (LRA) in northern Uganda in the 1990s. The LRA was a wily, hard-to-pin down enemy. Ondoga learned to adapt to its fighting style, walking for kilometers at a stretch and, laying in wait for days in one spot for the enemy to show up.

In Mogadishu, Col. Ondoga turned his mind to unraveling the al-Shabaab riddle. He had observed that insurgent fighters navigated with complete ease the densely populated urban landscape, forcing troops to fight running battles as happened with the US Rangers in October 1993 and Ethiopians soldiers from 2007 to 2008. It was exactly the kind of battle Somali militias excelled at because of intimate knowledge of the city terrain and alleyways. That knowledge translated into a huge tactical advantage that few regular troops could possibly match. At the height of the battle with US Rangers on October 3, 1993, for example, militias came from all direction, constantly pinning down the Americans who had to fight their way out, but often got lost in the mazes of narrow streets and dead-end alleyways.

Col. Ondoga was convinced very early on that the key to defeating the insurgents on their own home turf was to adjust to block-by-block fighting. Employing deliberate tortoise-like movement to inch one block at a time, sometimes pausing for days to secure the grounds recovered from al-Shabaab then moving again, AMISOM troops would follow retreating al-Shabaab fighters deeper into Hodan, Wardhigleey and Wadajir districts. As he sat there, Col. Ondoga told Gen. Mugisha that he was already working with his unit commanders on the new strategy. The risky move required AMISOM soldiers to move closer to insurgents, perhaps a mere twenty to fifty meters away and, with the targets clearly identified, open up with full force. He likened the concept to "hugging the enemy", something akin to hand to hand combat. This likely meant more casualties for AMISOM troops. It also greatly reduced unintended civilian casualties. It was worth a try.

The discussion over, Col. Ondoga organised a convoy of armoured personnel carriers. It would be nightfall in an hour, but the commander's work was far from finished for the day. Soon, leaving a wake of thick dust, the armoured convoy headed out toward the frontline in Karaan district where, for the third day, Uganda troops were battling al-Shabaab.

Without preamble, July 2010 arrived like Mogadishu's sudden midafternoon downpour that comes without warning and ends just as abruptly. The rest of the world was gripped by soccer fever as favourite teams fought for top honour in the World Cup game underway in South Africa. In Mogadishu, daily violence engulfed the whole city. The first sunrise of the month found President Sheikh Sharif Ahmed in battle fatigue at the war front clutching an AK-47. The Somali leader had spent the last night of June with the troops, getting up close and personal with the action at the frontline. A mortar fired by the insurgents landed a mere 300 meters from where the president was huddled behind sandbagged barricades.[76] He was unhurt.

Sheikh Sharif Ahmed was no longer safe anywhere. He was still at the frontline when an explosion occurred inside the presidential palace in a theatre where the celebration for Somalia 50th independence anniversary was planned. A bomb hidden in a bouquet of flowers apparently went off prematurely. AMISOM troops immediately sealed off all the entrance and exits to the Villa Somalia.[77] The fierce battle claimed at least 17 lives on Thursday, July 1, 2010, mostly insurgents. AMISOM also sustained casualties. Maj. Ba-Hoku Barigye revealed to the media that AMISOM lost two men and three were injured while on patrol in the battle zone.[78] As before, al-Shabaab displayed the body of one of the dead soldiers later on the Friday, July 2, 2010. A furious Maj. Barigye could no longer hide his utter disgust and contempt for al-Shabaab. "It is inhuman to put in the streets the dead body of an African who came for peacekeeping," he spat out.[79]

The intense fighting continued to Monday, July 5, 2010. Thousands of Mogadishu residents in Abdul Aziz, Bondere, Yaqshiid and Karaan districts stayed indoors for fear of being caught in the crossfire. President Sharif Sheikh Ahmed, meanwhile, flew out of his besieged city to Addis Ababa for a meeting with IGAD heads of states from Uganda, Sudan, Djibouti, Kenya and Ethiopia. There was no mistaking the SOS in the simple message he brought to Addis Ababa. The situation in Somalia was at a critical point. International intervention was needed immediately to shore up the TFG and AMISOM. For their part, IGAD leaders agreed to recommend to the forthcoming African Union head of states summit in Kampala in two weeks the immediate deployment of additional 2,000 troops to Somalia. As the host of the AU summit, President Museveni made it clear that if other nations would not contribute troops, he was willing to send the additional troops from Uganda. There was no turning back for Uganda.

Ever media savvy with ready response, al-Shabaab quickly pounced on the Addis Ababa recommendations for more AU troops. Mass rallies were organized in Independent Park in Kismaayo and in Dr. Ayub Stadium in Baidoa. Toyota trucks rigged with outdoor loudspeakers traversed neighbourhoods in the two towns, calling on residents to come out to show disapproval for IGAD's decision.[80] In Mogadishu's Suuqa Holaha, livestock market in Huriwa district, women dressed in black *burqa* clutched AK-47 machineguns. Some crouched on the ground to show off their combat skills, while others joined hundreds of protesters to denounce President Sharif Ahmed, AMISOM, and IGAD for authorizing additional troops for Somalia.[81] On July 5, 2010, al-Shabaab's leader Sheikh Muqtar Abdirahman Abu Zubeyr, in a ten-minute long audio message broadcasted on a local Mogadishu radio, claimed victory in the fighting in Mogadishu. He then concluded with a dark threat against Uganda and Burundi:

> You should know that the massacres against the children, women and the elderly of Mogadishu will be revenged against you. Keep in mind that the aggressions being committed by your leaders and soldiers is awaiting you.... We have to carry all-out Jihad campaign against the enemy and everyone should take part both young and old. That is the only way to end the massacres being carried out by the infidels in our country against the weak among us.[82]

Zubeyr's threat was not much different from those that al-Shabaab was accustomed to uttering whenever the fighting in Mogadishu got tougher or al-Shabaab lost a valuable commander. It had become routine for the insurgents to threaten to expand the war to other countries including Uganda, Burundi and the USA. This threat was different. On Friday, July 9, 2010, al-Shabaab spokesperson Sheikh Muktar Ali Abu Mansur Robow made the threat more specific. He called on jihadists everywhere to attack Uganda and Burundi diplomats. "We urge our brothers from Chechnya, Pakistan, Afghanistan, and from anywhere around the world to attack diplomatic missions of Uganda and Burundi," said the spokesman.[83]

Sunday July 11, 2010 was special for soccer fans around the world. Millions stopped to watch live television coverage as Spain and The Netherlands battled for the 19th FIFA World Cup final at Soccer City in Johannesburg, South Africa. In the semi-final matches played a few days earlier, The Netherlands had nudged out Uruguay 3-2, and Spain had bested Germany 1-0. Though it was now a European affair to settle world championship, soccer fans in Uganda's capital, Kampala, packed city's bars, watering holes and sports venues to watch the game. At the Kyadondo Rugby club in the city's east end, white plastic chairs were placed on the lawns for hundreds of patrons to sit on while watching the giant white screen erected to project the game. Intermittently, the revelers filled the festive air with cacophonic sounds of the *vuvuzela*, the noisy South-African inspired snorting plastic horn that became the rage during the World Cup. This was a joyous occasion for everyone. Ugandans are soccer crazy.

Barely five kilometers away, a distance that takes about half hour in traffic jam during Kampala rush-hour, a smaller but no less enthusiastic crowd sat in the courtyard of Ethiopian Village Restaurant and Bar located in Kabalagala, the Kampala suburb better known as Tank-Hill. All eyes were watching the live-telecast game on a large television screen set high above the crowd. At both venues, beer flowed freely as fans cheered on the Spanish goalkeeper Iker Cassilas who, time and again, frustrated the fierce Dutch offensive led by Number Eleven striker Arjen Robben. The cheers rose and died as the soccer battle continued three thousand kilometers away at Soccer City Stadium in South Africa.

At 10:25 p.m. local time in Uganda, English referee Howard Webb blew the whistle to signal half time in the soccer game.[84] As the sweaty exhausted men hustled off the soccer pitch in South Africa for half-time break, the scores nil and nil, a loud boom went off at the back of the crowd at the Ethiopian Village Restaurant. Some patrons thought the projector had exploded, almost all were showered with wet slimy blood and bits and pieces of human flesh.[85] Some realized a bomb had gone off, immediately seeking shelter from further explosion. Soon, dazed and shocked survivors were picking the pieces, trying to save the wounded.

Unaware of the tragedy unfolding at the Ethiopian Village Restaurant and Bar, the patrons at Kyadondo Rugby Club cheered on at the huge television screen at the resumption of the intense rivalry between the Dutch and the plucky Spaniards. Despite the valiant efforts by the Dutch, the game remained scoreless at three minutes to the end of regular playtime. The local time in Kampala was 11:18 p.m. Dutch Number Eleven, Robben, fought for the ball against Spanish Number Eleven, Capdevila, the latter winning the throw-in. At about this moment, a huge explosion went off in the middle of the Kampala crowd watching the game at Kyadondo Rugby Club. Moments later, maybe fifteen seconds or twenty seconds after the first blast, there was a second explosion. Many scrambled to get away. Some could not, and would never walk away. An unspeakable terror-filled carnage was all that was left. Bodies were shredded to the bones, other were missing limbs or were too critically wounded to move. The dead, some killed instantly where they sat, others disfigured beyond recognition, littered the ground amidst the bloodied upturned white plastic chairs.[86] It did not matter any more that the Spanish midfielder Number Six, Andres Iniesta, scored the only goal at the finals, lifting his team to sweet World Cup victory.[87] At Ethiopian Village and Kyadondo Rugby Club, nobody was watching the game.

After Uganda police carted away the last body the following day, the dead stood at 74, the wounded at over 70, and thousands shocked by the sheer barbarity of the terror action. Condemnation poured from around world. US President Barack Obama condemned the "deplorable and cowardly attacks",[88] Secretary of State Hillary Clinton called it "tragic moment",[89] and British Foreign Secretary William Hague called it "brutal acts of violence and terror."[90] African Union Commissioner for Peace and Security Ramtane Lamamra was outraged too. "We condemn this act that was directed at an African country that is active in promoting the goals of the African Union. The attack prove that terrorists can hit anywhere, including Africa," he said.[91] Late Monday evening, July 12, 2010, al-Shabaab claimed responsibility for the Kampala attacks. Spokesman Sheikh Ali Mohammed Rage (Ali Dheere) gloated, "We thank the mujahideens that carried out the attacks. We are sending a message to Uganda and Burundi, if they do not take out their AMISOM troops from Somalia, blasts will continue and it will happen in Bujumbura."[92]

President Yoweri Museveni declared seven days of mourning for the victims before retreating to his country home in Ntungamo in western Uganda to consider his next move. Three days later, on the evening of Thursday, July 15, 2010, Museveni had made up his mind. Near midnight, he spoke to the media. He declared war on al-Shabaab. "We are going to go for all who did this, in all areas, starting here. We were just in Mogadishu to guard the airport and the presidential palace that was all. Now, they have mobilized us to look for them. We were just doing our small mandate....now we are taking interest. It was a very big mistake on their side."[93] "It was a big mistake on the part of al-Shabaab to attack Uganda," he repeated. This was vintage Museveni. When angry, he spoke as if having a casual conversation with a neighbour. Those who knew him understood that he meant every single word he said. In plain English, Museveni was going to throw everything at the Somalia insurgents. And nobody was going to get in his way while he was at it.

He needed the AU behind him. When the Fifteenth Ordinary Assembly of the African Union got under way in the week of Sunday, July 25, 2010 in Kampala, President Museveni wasted little time getting to the point. Firmly backed by US Assistant Secretary of State for Africa Johnnie Carson and British Minister for Africa Henry Bellingham, Museveni and Sheikh Sharif Ahmed worked to formally change the mandate to allow AMISOM pre-emptive capability to go after al-Shabaab. Understandably, this was a paper exercise only. Retroactively, it would have provided AMISOM with the mandate that, for all practical purposes, was already being executed on the ground even as the summit got underway. Late Tuesday, July 27, 2010 following a day of straight talks involving the representatives from three permanent members of the UN Security Council (US, Britain and France), UN Special Representative for Somalia Augustine Mahiga refused to budge on changing AMISOM's mandate. As Johnnie Carson later characterized the closed-door meeting, "It was his [Mahiga's] view that under existing mandate, the forces on the ground could act in a more responsible but robust fashion."[94] Translation: AMISOM could go after al-Shabaab with strong force but needed to be careful to protect civilians and property from the crossfire. It was classic UN doublespeak that, at times, rendered its peacekeepers completely ineffective and, often, sitting ducks for predatory and violent groups like al-Shabaab. Museveni was not going to allow his troops to fall into that trap. However, Ambassador Mahiga was right. UNSC 1744 (2007) provided the mandate AMISOM needed, and did not require further augmentation at the UN level. Rather its interpretation at the AU level needed to be more flexible for the troops on the ground to do their work effectively. The summit approved the additional 2,000 troops recommended by IGAD to be deployed as soon as possible, noting it "deeply appreciates the regional initiative under the African Peace and Security Architecture to enable AMISOM reach its authorized 8,100 strength."[95]

Toward the goal of reaching maximum authorised troops strength, attempts were made to court Guinea, Djibouti and South Africa for the mission. Following the Kampala bombings, al-Shabaab sent a chill through the AU with dire warning of gruesomely bloody consequences for those foolhardy enough to join AMISOM. On Sunday, July 25, 2010, the day after African leaders arrived to red-carpet welcome at Entebbe Airport in Uganda, Sheikh Mohamed Ibrahim Bilal, one of many al-Shabaab leaders warned off any African nation thinking of sending troops to Somalia. "This is an American project, implemented through the AU. Our reaction will make people in other African capitals cry like those in Kampala."[96] After that, the African nations that came to Kampala seemed uninterested taking on the terror group that already claimed first blood outside Somalia. South African defense minister Lindiwe Sisulu, speaking to a South African parliamentary committee on Thursday, July 29, 2010, admitted that South Africa was under tremendous pressure from Southern African Development Community (SADC) to send troops to Somalia. Sisulu warned that her country could become vulnerable to terror attacks similar to what happened in Kampala.[97] Instead, she offered South African marine units to patrol Somali coastlines. Uganda and Burundi would have to go it alone. At least now, the troops in Somalia had a fighting chance, and they intended to fight to win.

# 12

# The War for Mogadishu

## The Ramadan Offensive

In mid-afternoon of Tuesday, August 17, 2010, from almost 30,000 feet, a chartered single engine Swiss-made Pilatus PC-12 NG aircraft, registration number N95NW, broke through puffs of white clouds and descended to within a few hundred feet above the Indian Ocean. The Pratt & Whitney Canada PT6 turboprop engine whined as the experienced pilot brought the plane so low the foaming ocean waves swelled as if to lick the bottom of the aircraft. Approaching Mogadishu from the air required extra precaution. Low flying aircrafts were vulnerable to rocket-propelled grenades and high-powered guns. Still keeping a safe distance from land, the plane began hugging the sandy coastline of south Somalia. The three passengers, a general, a colonel from a European country and a civilian, peered out the windows silently. They were near the end of a three and half hour flight from Kajjansi airstrip near Entebbe, Uganda.

After skimming the ocean top for what seemed like a long time, gracefully, the Pilatus turned inland and landed smoothly on the tarmac of Aden Abdulle Airport, rushing past the skeletal remains of the Ilyushin Il-76 aircraft that crashed in March 2007. The Pilatus slowed down before turning around to taxi toward the war-scarred terminal. A bevy of AMISOM senior officers gathered as the plane coasted to a stop in front of the terminal at Aden Abdulle Airport. The air stair door opened and, with a black travelling bag in hand, the Commander of Land Forces (CLF) of the UPDF, Lieutenant General Katumba Edward Wamala stepped out of the plane. He was casually dressed in a button-down collar short sleeve cream shirt and a pair of khaki chino pants. The uniformed officers on the tarmac snapped to attention, and saluted. On hand to receive the general was Maj. Gen. Nathan Mugisha, Colonel Michael Ondoga, Major Barigye Ba-Hoku, Captain Chris Magezi and others from Uganda and Burundi contingents.

The senior AMISOM officers were positively happy to see Gen. Wamala. To say the rank and file loved Wamala was an understatement. The general had built a solid respect among UPDF troops through sheer hard work, genuineness and down-to-earth approach of listening to concerns and finding immediate solution. From the beginning of the deployment of Uganda troops in Mogadishu in 2007, the general made it his business to visit often, every two weeks or sooner, meeting the troops at the frontline, sitting down with the commanders, consoling troops when tragedy struck as happened the previous year on September 17, boosting troops morale, and always finding time to speak to the soldiers at the lowest rank.

General Wamala's hands-on approach was very much a product of his humble upbringing. He was born on Monday, November 19, 1956 in the village of Bweeza, fifteen kilometers from Kalangala township on Bugala Island, one of a group of islands known as the Ssese Islands in the northwest corner of Lake Victoria in Uganda. His ancestors, the *ekika ky'Engonge*, Otter Clan, from the Bweeza area, were instrumental in the creation of Buganda Kingdom in the 1200s, and known for pioneering the making of bark-cloth and traditional herbal medicine.[1] As he narrated to Daily Monitor writer Ivan Okuda, Katumba, the last born in a family of nine siblings, grew up in the households of his older siblings who took turn to care for him in the absence of his mother.[2] Loved, and kept busy on the family farm, he learned to dig, take care of the family livestock and execute domestic chores including cooking. His father, a respected fisherman and trader on the Island, valued education and, when Katumba was of school age, moved the boy to the mainland for primary education. Through several primary schools in the Kampala-Jinja corridor and, finally, Old Kampala Secondary School, Katumba excelled at school. He recalled incidents when as a young boy he got into serious trouble, once for beating up a boy at the well, and another time at Kasubi Primary School when he lied to his teacher in order to escape the drudgery of class so he could sit under a tree to read his favourite novel. When discovered by the headmaster Mr. Wakatama, he was taken to the office where he received five hot *kiboko*, caning with a stick on the buttocks.[3]

Katumba's love of learning would take him to post-secondary education, studying agriculture at Bukalasa Agricultural College, International Relations at Nkumba University, and a Master of Science degree in Strategic Leadership at the US Army War College in Carlisle, Pennsylvania. After joining the army in 1979, Katumba quickly moved through the ranks, being commissioned to the rank of Second Lieutenant in 1980. Through the later part of the 1990s to mid-2000s, he solidified his leadership in the army by commanding military operations against the Lord's Resistance Army and other insurgents in northern Uganda, the Democratic Republic of Congo and, for five years between 2001 and 2005 as Inspector General of Police (IGP), before being promoted to Lieutenant General in 2005 and appointed commander of land forces.

The purpose of Wamala's visit to Mogadishu on that hot August afternoon was two fold. Aware that the real fight was about to begin, General Wamala wanted to raise the morale of AMISOM troops. After what was obviously a tough July, he planned to visit the troops in forward operating bases, and personally tell them they were doing a great job. More importantly, he also brought the message to the commanders that help was on the way. Another Uganda battalion was to be deployed shortly within a week, reinforcing the troops at the front for what was likely to be a deciding moment for AMISOM, whether the mission could withstand the assault from al-Shabaab or finally give up altogether, and go home in disgrace.

Gen. Wamala was quickly bundled into a waiting AMISOM armoured Toyota Land Cruiser and driven to the forces headquarters where a guard of honour mounted by Uganda troops was ready to be inspected. After shaking hands all around with the senior AMISOM officers from Uganda and Burundi, Wamala was led away by Gen. Mugisha for a briefing in the force commander's office.

Gen. Mugisha wasted little time getting to the status of the war against al-Shabaab. July had been a bruising month of non-stop fighting. Despite all the challenges, as it had done over the past three years, AMISOM had held its own. Eight of sixteen Mogadishu districts were now controlled by the TFG and AMISOM. Four districts were still being contested and the remaining four were controlled by al-Shabaab. The biggest loss for al-Shabaab in July was Hotel Jubba at the junction of Corso Somalia and Via Alto Guiba. The insurgents put up strong resistance but after serious losses, retreated, and its fighters were holed up nearby in the former Italian Embassy building, the Interior Ministry complex and Islamic Center. Meanwhile a fierce fight that started on Monday, August 9, 2010, pitting Burundi troops against al-Shabaab in Darkhenleey district concluded on the eve of Ramadan with Burundi troop wresting from the insurgents the Suuqa Kahda, a market located just west of Ex-Control Afgooye.

Then General Mugisha paused, the silence broken only by the whirring noise emitted by the small fan inside the digital projector he was using to project images on the opposite wall. Holy Ramadan in August was going to be a rough one, the general finally said. Believing the period of fasting for Muslims was a holy time to die fighting as martyrs, al-Shabaab fighters were planning a big Ramadan offensive on AMISOM, a war to end all wars. Somali Muslims began their month long fast on Wednesday, August 11, 2010 and, already, intelligence confirmed al-Shabaab was planning a massive attack, Gen. Mugisha added. On Friday, August 13, 2010, long convoys of trucks entered Mogadishu from Afgooye and other areas carrying young people brought to join the fight against AMISOM. On Sunday, August 15 and Monday August 16, the day before Gen. Wamala arrived, the insurgents attacked AMISOM positions in Hodan and Wardigley districts. AMISOM sustained no casualties. Still, Gen. Mugisha made it clear he was concerned about the size of his troops. "Because we did not have the capacity to meet the objectives set out in 2007, the mission has only grown more complex and delicate, and may now require up to 40,000 troops to get the job done properly," the commander said with obvious impatience in his voice.[4] In the general's shrewd assessment, at least 20,000 AMISOM troops were needed to support a similar number of Somali National Forces (SNF).

The rise of al-Shabaab as a powerhouse in Somalia obviously added to the complexity Gen. Mugisha was referring to. The insurgent group had the infrastructures to raise massive funds by taxing residents in vast swaths of Somalia under its control. Two weeks before Gen. Wamala arrived in Mogadishu, for instance, al-Shabaab ordered traders in Mogadishu, Afgooye and Baidoa to pay huge sums of money toward the war effort. On Monday, August 2, 2010, al-Shabaab officials went through Bakaara market telling traders what was expected of them. Bigger companies were ordered to pay for anti-aircraft guns mounted on four-wheeled trucks. In addition, al-Shabaab expected at least one million dollars from traders in Bakaara. "We were ordered to contribute $150,000. That is required from pharmacies in Bakaara Market only," Mohamed, a trader in Bakaara Market told Reuters.[5]

With AMISOM and TFG taking more ground in Mogadishu, various factions of the insurgency attempted once more to consolidate their fighters under one command. On August 1, 2010, representatives of al-Shabaab and Hizbul Islam met in a house in Mogadishu for talks to merge the two groups. There was no deal because the two sides could not agree on what to do with Hizbul Islam's weapons. al-Shabaab wanted HI to surrender all weapons, and take up low-level positions within al-Shabaab. HI commanders balked at the prospects of being left defenseless.[6] At a joint press conference on Tuesday, August 3, 2010, Hizbul Islam official Dr. Hassan Mahdi sat beside al-Shabaab's spokesman Sheikh Muktar Ali Robow to deny rift between the two organisations. Talks were still continuing, he said.[7] Yet, on Sunday, August 15, 2010, a top Hizbul Islam official Sheikh Mohammed Tahliil Warsame was shot at close range in Celaasha Biyaha, just on the outskirt of Mogadishu. An advisor to Sheikh Hassan Dahir Aweys, Sheikh Warsame was likely another victim of the continuing power struggle between al-Shabaab and Hizbul Islam.

Whatever feud lingered between the two major insurgent groups, Gen. Mugisha was positive that the expected al-Shabaab offensive could begin at any time. The only question left was when al-Shabaab would launch the assault. His troops were ready. Gen. Mugisha was especially happy to learn from Gen. Wamala that 1200 Uganda troops could start arriving as early as the weekend. The following day, Wednesday, August 18, 2010, Gen. Mugisha and Gen. Wamala headed out in a four Casspir convoy, first making a stop at al-Urubah Hotel, the headquarters for Uganda Battle Group V commanded by Lt. Col. Francis Chemo. The convoy then drove to Hotel Jubba where Major David Matua and his unit were engaged in a cat-and-mouse fight with al-Shabaab fighters. Matua pointed out for Gen. Wamala the location of the insurgents, some three hundred meters away at the Italian Embassy, and a bit further up at the Interior Ministry Building and the Islamic Center. "They will never come back here," Matua said.[8] As if to challenge that assertion, al-Shabaab gunners from the Italian Embassy let loose a few rounds directed at the fortified Hotel Jubba. An AMISOM machine gunner replied with a burst from his gun. Gen. Wamala quickly asked an AMISOM sniper to step aside from his Romanian-made PSL scoped semi-automatic sniper rifle propped against the sandbags.[9] The general took over and, peering into the scope, carefully calibrated it, aimed the gun at the Italian Embassy, his trigger finger waiting patiently for a suitable target. After ten minutes frozen in the same position, and no sign of al-Shabaab insurgents, Gen. Wamala returned the gun to the waiting soldier. "Those terrorists are lucky this time, but I will put a bullet through them the next time," the general remarked as others around him laughed.[10]

For the rest of the week while he stayed in Mogadishu, Gen. Wamala busied himself meeting with the commanders and troops, taking copious notes on what the troops needed to get the job done. Often, he would be found hunched in a corner, on a plastic chair or on the ground, looking at maps, discussing issues, finding solutions. He got along well with Gen. Mugisha with whom he shared the same quarters, and had breakfast and dinner together. The troops acknowledged the leadership by working harder, planning the next operations. al-Shabaab, meanwhile, seemed to take a few days off for Ramadan.

The arrival of promised additional troops from Uganda began on the morning Thursday, August 19, 2010, with more troops arriving the following day, Friday, August 20, 2010. Among the latter arrival was unit commander Major Anthony Mbuusi, a small man with glasses that gave him the appearance of a mild-mannered university professor, but which hid a brilliant military mind and fearless tactician. al-Shabaab would later get to know him as Four-Eyes.[11] Upon arrival, Mbuusi found one of his companies already deployed to support the Bondere operation commanded by the Second-in-Command of 41 Bn, Major David Opeero. On the same day, the calm was shattered in late afternoon by a huge explosion in a house near Shirkole in Bar Urbah neighbourhood. The next day it was established that al-Shabaab bomb makers putting final touches to a huge car bomb accidentally set it off prematurely.[12] The dead included three Pakistanis, two Indians, an Afghan national, an Algerian, two Somalis including a spiritual leader responsible for praying for suicide bombers before leaving on their mission.[13] Another al-Shabaab fighter was killed while planting a roadside bomb on Anzilotti Bridge.[14]

Two days later, on the morning of Sunday, August 22, 2010, Colonel Ondoga conferred with the commanders and decided to open a new detachment north of KM-4, the job falling on Major Mbuusi and troops under his command. The insurgents used the area to bombard KM-4 and other AMISOM locations. This would stop the attacks altogether. That same afternoon, in one fluid movement, Major Mbuusi, leading Uganda troops working with Somali militias belonging to General Indha Adde, opened the Tarabunka detachment, occupying four low rise white buildings clustered together. The insurgents camped just one building over could hardly believe such audacity and, through the afternoon, fought fiercely but failed to regain the captured buildings. The next morning, August 23, 2010, fortified in the new position, Mbuusi's forces took the next four buildings, only this time, instead of being exposed to heavy enemy fire, burrowed their way through the wall of one building to the next. By the time commander Mbuusi sent his situation report (SITREP) that evening, three more buildings adjacent to the old Coca-Cola plant were added under the control of Uganda forces. Moreover, there were no AMISOM casualties in the successful operations.

This was the beginning of the famed *mashimo ya panya*, 'mouse holes' where AMISOM forces carved holes in the walls of abandoned buildings to move troops forward. With the mouse holes came the tactic of 'creeping', sometimes called 'hugging' or 'kissing' that Col. Ondoga urged his commanders to adopt, ensuring the maximum protection of troops while facilitating slow forward movement to engage the insurgents. Uganda troops began creating mazes of aboveground tunnels that kept soldiers hidden from al-Shabaab for days on end until they were ready to spring a surprise attack. These intricate urban passageways gained legendary status in their use for ferrying ammunition and supplies to AMISOM troops in forward bases in Hodan, Wardigley, Hawl Wadaag, Abdi Aziz, Shibis and Karaan districts.

Often surprised to discover that Ugandan troops had closed in to within a few meters, al-Shabaab insurgents beat hasty retreat. The insurgents also learned to adapt. Upon realizing that the capture of a tall storey building said to belong to Sheikh Dahir Aweys or his relatives could give immense advantage to AMISOM troops to observe the movements of the insurgents, al-Shabaab fighters rigged the stairs of the building with explosives and blew them off. From then on, when a tall building was likely to fall into the hands of AMISOM, the insurgents used this tactic to destroy the building. If they could not use it, neither could AMISOM.

The same day while Major Mbuusi was busying taking new positions in Mogadishu, AMISOM spokesman Major Barigye Ba-Hoku who was in Nairobi spoke to the media about the situation in Somalia. AMISOM had brought the situation under control, Ba-Hoku said. Moreover, AMISOM was expanding in areas previously controlled by al-Shabaab in Shibis, Bondere, and Karaan districts. al-Shabaab often stirred trouble, although it never stayed long enough for the fight, Maj. Ba-Hoku explained, saying,

> They cause skirmishes for minutes then disappear but even those few minutes cause a lot of damage and deaths, and become the focus of the media, giving the impression that Mogadishu was the most dangerous place in the world. It scares countries that are potential contributors to peacekeepers.[15]

What was about to happen, however, was more than a skirmish. It was a full-scale war. On Monday, August 23, 2010, al-Shabaab formally announced the beginning of its long awaited Ramadan offensive. Spokesperson Sheikh Ali Mansour Robow 'Ali Dhere' called it the final phase of the war against the invaders. He declared, "We are launching a final war to terminate the invading infidels in Mogadishu and all forces from the Islamic provinces are going to take part and we will wipe out the enemies from Mogadishu."[16] Soon after the announcement, al-Shabaab fighters launched multiple attacks using mortars and artillery on AMISOM and TFG forces positions. By day's end, at least 20 people were reported killed and a further 100 taken to Medina hospital in South Mogadishu.[17] The violence spilled into Tuesday, August 24, 2010. Just before 11:00 a.m., a pair of al-Shabaab suicide attackers wearing Somali government forces uniforms attacked the lightly guarded Muna Hotel in Hamar Weyne district. By the time TFG forces secured the building in late afternoon, the death toll was at 18 including 10 members of parliament who were residing at the hotel. As world leaders including Barack Obama condemned the attack, Sheikh Ali Mohammed Rage boasted that al-Shabaab's special forces carried out the attack.[18] Using pictures taken after the attack, one of the dead hotel attackers was later identified as 16-year old Aden Hussein, a Rahanweyn from the southwestern town of Baidoa, and a former bodyguard to Sheikh Muktar Abu Mansour Robow.[19]

Even as the bloody drama at Muna Hotel was playing out, AMISOM engaged al-Shabaab in the Bermuda neighbourhood flanked by Hawl Wadaag Street to the east, Bakaara Street to the west and Maka al-Mukarama Road to the south. The insurgents' objective soon became clear. Their immediate plan aimed at entrapping units of Ugandan troops while pushing back the bulk of the AU forces further south toward the edge of the ocean. The bigger objective was to seize a piece of real estate on Maka al-Mukarama Road that linked the busy Aden Abdulle Airport, KM-4, the Seaport and Villa Somalia. Cutting off AMISOM's access to the road was a sure way to slowly squeeze the AU forces to the thin wedges of the Seaport and Aden Abdulle Airport. Split into two, and unable to get fresh supplies by road, AMISOM was very vulnerable at both ends. The insurgents reasoned that forced to choose between saving Villa Somalia and saving its own hide, AMISOM would take the latter option. Forces guarding Villa Somalia would melt into the Seaport, leaving the prize wide open.

Using a pincher movement, al-Shabaab attacked AMISOM troops from the side streets. Darting like skylarks between buildings, insurgent fighters worked to cut off the forward units of UGABAG V. For several hours lasting until the late morning of Wednesday, August 25, 2010, al-Shabaab forces relentlessly tried to overrun Maka al-Mukarama Road. Simultaneously, insurgents attacked AMISOM and TFG defenses around Villa Somalia, Hodan and Hawl Wadaag. The most vulnerable purchase was the front defended by the militias belonging to General Indha Adde. Although its commanders claimed the personnel numbered some 300 on the ground, it was a much thinner force. Worse, Major Mbuusi did not always know on whose side the Indha Adde men were fighting. There were moments when the militias blocked further progress of AU troops, arguing the area belonged to them and, as such, was out of bounds to all forces. During one such an argument with the militia next to a house along Tarehe Street, al-Shabaab fired an RPG that injured some of the Uganda troops, after which the troops branded the house 'RPG House'.

al-Shabaab engaged ASWJ militias through the night, pushing especially hard against the Sufi position in Sigaale, and finally overrunning it by morning when ASWJ fighters ran out ammunition, and were flushed out. The loss was significant for ASWJ fighters whose spiritual leader, Sufi cleric Mo'alin Nor was buried in the area at the Mowla Center. Sheikh Ali Mohammed Rage called it a victory for al-Shabaab. "We have advanced onto the enemy lines and taken control of their barracks near Maka al-Mukarama road...We have diluted their powers and forced them to retreat with the only road they were controlling becoming our frontline. It was cut off and the mujahideen will continue advancing if Allah says," he crowed.[20] al Kataib, the online propaganda media outlet for al-Shabaab declared victory, albeit prematurely, claiming, "Mujahideen fighters made new bases in areas they captured from Uganda, Burundi and stooges including Dabka Junction, Whelie Hotel and 15 May School which is very close to palace."[21]

So fierce was the battle that TFG soldiers fighting at the front were forced into a chaotic retreat. But Ugandan troops chose neither to retreat nor let up on al-Shabaab. Instead, Major Mbuusi quickly re-inserted ASWJ fighters into a building in Tarabunka, from where they could continue the battle. Almost immediately, the Indha Adde militias protested. They had no love for ASWJ and wanted them out of the area in a couple of hours. Temporarily distracted from the battle, Col. Ondoga and Major Mbuusi attempted to mediate between the two groups, but Indha Adde's Hawiye/Habar Gidir militias would not be appeased. The group had vested interest in the neighbourhood where they habitually collected money from homeowners whose home they guarded. In the end, Major Mbuusi took ASWJ under his wings and, working with their commanders Omar Moallin Nur and Abdullai Moallin Nur, went on later to recapture many areas including the Moallin Nur's Mosque in Sigaale, Shakara and Dhabka Junction.

Throughout the offensive, Uganda troops inched forward. Accompanying the booming guns were battle cries of *Endelea mbele!* Push forward. Crumbling TFG defenses were immediately shored up with AMISOM troops. Col. Ondoga, in the thick of it, called for reinforcement of fresh troops and fire support from the base at Halaane. Burundi forces also joined the fight from the northwest in Hodan district, hitting al-Shabaab forces from the rear. Along with as many as 25 fighters killed, al-Shabaab lost tactical commander Abdullahi 'Mortar', so named because of his deadly use of mortars against TFG, AMISOM and civilians.[22]

The tide turned late Saturday afternoon, August 28, 2010 when al-Shabaab retreated. AMISOM gave chase, pushing the rebels further north toward Sinai Road. Major Mbuusi's troops moved along Tarehe Street, edging the Fair Ground toward the fortified building from where al-Shabaab had fired heavily on AMISOM troops. Here AU troops discovered the cleverly disguised anti-tank ditches dug by the insurgents to deter tanks advancing along Tarehe Street. To the naked eye the road surface looked normal, but a closer inspection revealed a thin one-foot layer of soil covering a deep ditch taller than a man's head. The ditches were immediately filled up with sand by the Bancroft technical team working under Rocky Van Blerk.

The insurgents had left behind scores of their dead and wounded. The dead were buried and the wounded taken to the hospital. From inside Hawl Wadaag district, the insurgents regrouped on Sunday, August 29, 2010, putting a sustained fight. Again and again, rebels fighters attempted to break AMISOM defenses along Maka al-Mukarama Road. Through the night into Monday morning, showing little fear or concern for their safety, the young attackers came in waves, only to be pushed back each time by unyielding Ugandan troops. The morning of Monday, August 30, 2010, however, proved deadly for AMISOM. A mortar fired by insurgents from Bondere slammed into the perimeters of Villa Somalia. Four Ugandan soldiers were killed, and eight wounded. "We lost four Ugandan soldiers in mortar fire on Villa Somalia this morning," a somber Maj. Barigye Ba-Hoku told Reuters news agency.[23] Later in the day, reminiscent of the scenes from Black Hawk Down when bodies of American soldiers were dragged through dusty Mogadishu streets, young Somali boys were photographed dragging a body said to be an AMISOM soldier.[24]

It was not all bad news for AMISOM. According to Maj. Ba-Hoku, al-Shabaab had failed to capture the strategic Maka al-Mukarama Road. "Al Shabaab cannot come to the Maka Al Mukaraam (sic) Road as long as we are here. We chased them back yesterday. They had plans to come to this road but we did not allow them," he said. TFG and AMISOM also recaptured the Sigaale base that al-Shabaab seized from ASWJ militias two days earlier. Starting late Friday September 3, 2010 into early morning of Saturday, September 4, 2010, AU forces advanced, consolidated and fortified new bases along Maka al-Mukarama Road including at Villa Baydhabo in Wadajir, Banaadir High School in Hodan, the resident of former president Abdi Qasim Salad Hassan, and at Villa Somalia. Speaking from Nairobi, the Deputy Representative of the Chairman of AU Commission Wafula Wamunyinyi reported that as many as 300 insurgent fighters were killed during the Ramadan clashes.[25] In one of the fights, Pakistani-born al-Shabaab commander Al-Muhajir Al Mustafa was critically wounded, and died at Dayniile Hospital. A week earlier during the battle of Sigaale, al-Shabaab's foreign fighters lost Abu Ubayd, a Kenyan national active in the frontline.

The TFG had not faired well in the midst of the battle. Many TFG soldiers abandoned their positions at the frontline, fleeing ahead of advancing insurgents. AMISOM commanders complained that weapons as well as some TFG soldiers were likely moving to al-Shabaab. On Sunday, September 5, 2010, after investigation revealed that tons of heavy weapons were stolen from government armories, President Sharif Ahmed took the unusual step of firing the TFG military chief General Mohamed Gelle Kahiye, security officials and police commanders.[26] Yet, despite TFG's morale problems, the onslaught al-Shabaab imagined against AMISOM was turning into a nightmare for the insurgents. More problematic for the rebels, some units of TFG were beginning to put up a fight. On Sunday, September 5, 2010, al-Shabaab attacked TFG forces in Shibiis. Several rebel fighters were killed and the TFG recovered four PKM machineguns.[27] In heavy fighting in Hodan district on Tuesday, September 7, 2010, seven TFG soldiers and several insurgents were killed. On the same day, al-Shabaab spokesman Sheikh Ali Mohammed Rage told the media that there were more troops on the way to join the fight. "We shall chase AMISOM troops from our country and also those who are with them. We believe that they will take nothing from us," he said.[28]

There was no definitive date when the Ramadan Offensive was officially declared a failure for Somali insurgents, mainly because the daily attacks continued on TFG and AMISOM forces at various frontlines in Hodan, Wardigley, Hawl Wadaag, Shibis and Bondere. Instead there were signs, here and there, an utterance by an al-Shabaab official, or series of actions so out of touch with rebels' claims of victory on the battlefield. Sheikh Rage, while attempting to reassure the Somali people that al-Shabaab was still a viable force, inadvertently hinted at the turmoil the insurgents were encountering facing highly disciplined AMISOM troops. The first sign that al-Shabaab's Ramadan offensive was foundering appeared on Wednesday, September 9, 2010, two days before Eid al fitr, the Feast of Breaking the Fast, when Muslims around the world marked the end of Ramadan, commencing three days of joyous celebration. Information pointing to al-Shabaab resorting to asymmetric warfare, using suicide bombers and roadside IEDs against the TFG and AMISOM troops, first surfaced in the coastal town of Merka, south west of Mogadishu. According to the report, al-Shabaab officials visited the town's health centers, looking to recruit HIV/AIDS patients for use as suicide attackers.[29] The recruiters told potential recruits that volunteering for suicide missions was a religious duty that would cleanse the sins initially committed when the patients contracted HIV/AIDS. The report did not say whether volunteers stepped forward or whether they were promised blissful repose with Allah in the afterlife.

Coincidentally, perhaps, around 2:15 p.m. on the same day, two SUV vehicles carrying five suicide attackers attempted to breach the gate at Aden Abdulle International Airport guarded by AMISOM soldiers.[30] The first vehicle exploded at the first gate, located about 500 meters from the terminal. Two AMISOM soldiers were instantly killed and three were wounded.[31] The second vehicle was halted by machinegun fire before it got inside the gate. Two al-Shabaab fighters dressed in TFG uniforms then jumped out of the vehicle, ran through the gate firing AK-47 machineguns. Both were shot down before they could enter the terminal, and at least one managed to detonate his suicide vest. Later TFG Information Minister Abdirahman Omar Osman sent out a press release, saying "Somalia government regrets the sad loss of 3 civilians and 2 AMISOM soldiers in today's suicide attack in Mogadishu Airport...We greatly appreciate the support and sometimes the sacrifice of every African Union soldier who comes to Somalia to help us."[32] AMISOM spokesman Maj. Barigye Ba-Hoku also sent out a media release to reiterate AMISOM's determination to see the fight through. "This attack was in vain and will not deter us from our mission," he said.[33]

Around ten in the morning of the first day of Eid al Fitr, Saturday, September 11, 2010, a gunman commandeered a petrol tanker in south Mogadishu, and forced the driver to crash through the barriers at the checkpoint to the Seaport. TFG soldiers, unaware that the tanker was empty, shot out the tires, disabling the vehicle, and wounding both the gunman and the driver. A further search of the vehicle found explosive in a black bag. Later that same day, a massive roadside IED ripped into a government truck carrying TFG forces travelling in Wabeeri district, killing five soldiers and wounding several others.[34] In a separate incident, while driving in a neighbourhood in Hamar Weyn district in southern Mogadishu, an exploding grenade tossed at their vehicle wounded two TFG soldiers. On Tuesday, September 14, 2010, a roadside IED struck a TFG truck travelling in Hodan district, wounding three soldiers who were rushed to Medina Hospital.[35] al-Shabaab fighters also launched mortar attacks on Burundi forces based at Jalle Siyad Military Academy on Thursday, September 16, 2010, and caused casualties among the fishmongers in one of the corners of Bakaara Market.[36] Burundi forces responded with fierce fire.

The suicide attacks continued. On Monday September 20, 2010, a lone suicide attacker named Muse Ali Abdulla, a former TFG soldier and bodyguard to Interior Minister Abdulkadir Ali Omar, armed with a gun and grenade, sneaked through the gates of Villa Somalia, was spotted and shot dead by Uganda forces.[37] Abdulla managed to toss a grenade at the palace guards, slightly wounding two AMISOM soldiers. As in all previous suicide attacks, this had little effect on AMISOM's overall strategy to take control of Mogadishu. On Monday, September 20 and Tuesday, September 21, 2010, Uganda troops commanded by Major Mbuusi pushed al-Shabaab from El Hindi, moving the frontline to the former Coca-Cola Factory. On Tuesday, September 21, 2010, to demonstrate his confidence in his forces, and that he was not afraid to walk about in public, Force Commander General Mugisha attended the launch of mother-child healthcare initiative, and used the moment to call on the insurgents to "ceasefire for a day to give the Somali population a breathing space."[38] Mugisha did not expect the insurgents to take the extended olive branch. To the contrary, as the Somali say, *Gees lo'aad kulaylkaa lagu gooyaa*, 'Cut off the cow's horn while it is still hot,'[39] with the insurgents showing disarray, AMISOM pressed for more troops and resources to push the rebels out of Mogadishu. Wafula Wamunyinyi, happy with the way the fight was going in Somalia, declared, "We are making gains. The fact that we have contained the insurgents is evidence enough that if we receive everything we have been asking for, we should be able to respond to the situation effectively."[40] Maj. Ba-Hoku was more forceful, saying AMISOM needed as many as 20,000 troops to do the job properly, predicting that with a large force, AMISOM could take Mogadishu in two days. "We cannot continue advancing if we do not have enough troops because the first priority is our bases which must be fully guarded," he added.[41]

The shortage of boots on the ground, however, did not slow down AMISOM's forward march. Burundi forces, in a huge effort on Sunday, October 3, 2010 fought insurgents in Tarabunka in Hodan district and, by Monday morning, captured al-Shabaab's fortified bases at former National Forces Hospital, former meat processing industry, and former Russian base.[42] Around the same time, a platoon of Uganda's 69 Bn from Shakala detachment moved about 300 meters to successfully capture a strategic building along the June 23 Road, also known as Uganda Road. That same night, al-Shabaab mounted a heavy counter-attack using 'technicals', forcing the platoon to make a tactical withdrawal to another building 300 meters down the road. The house changed hands some more, earning the nickname from Uganda troops 'manyanga house', the house in vogue that all sides to the conflict eagerly anticipated occupying.

On the eastern side of Manyanga House, al-Shabaab had dug deep communication trenches used for ferrying fighters and supplies to the frontline. The Bancroft team consisting of Eugene and Fritz responded to call for support, bringing along a remote-controlled medium MineWolf (MW330) used to clear mines and move earth into the deep holes. As the team worked, al-Shabaab located at the former ASWJ base used a B10 recoilless rifle to knock out the signal receiver for the MW330, rendering the equipment inoperable from a distance. The blast also injured a UPDF WO2 and Eugene. Thankfully, the MW330 was eventually recovered.

When Gen. Wamala returned to Mogadishu in mid-October, the ill-fated Manyanga House was still controlled by al-Shabaab. The general ordered 69th Bn to switch position with Mbuusi's 19th Bn. Troops under Mbuusi's command took several streets over the next few weeks. At one point only June 26th Street separated the AU troops from al-Shabaab militias massed around Manyanga House but, for the time being, the building remained out of reach of AMISOM soldiers.

After the stalled Ramadan Offensive, however, the insurgent leadership desperately attempted to hide the growing cracks within their organisation. News emerged of a rift pitting al-Shabaab's second-in-command Sheikh Ali Mukhtar Robow against the leader Sheikh Mukhtar Abu Zubeyr, but Robow quickly denied any differences, saying, "The victory is close. We will continue our fight, and that's the end of the lies from our enemies."[43] al-Shabaab also resorted to bold-faced lies to target AMISOM's growing reputation as defenders and friends of Somali people. On Monday, October 11, 2010, Sheikh Ali Mohamed Hussein, al-Shabaab's governor for the Benadir region warned Somali people that medicine and drugs from AMISOM's medical clinics were infected with HIV virus. "We are telling the people not to use or visit AMISOM bases searching for drugs. Somali people must not be treated by them."[44] AMISOM responded the next day. Maj. Ba-Hoku denied the claims as unfounded, arguing, "The allegation means Al-Shabaab want to refuse the sick people to get our free medical care. We treat many different Somalis from morning until sunset. The people come from all areas in Somalia like Hargeisa, Kismayu and others."[45] A few weeks later, alarmed by the dwindling ranks of al-Shabaab fighters, Sheikh

Ali Mohamed Hussein ordered Mogadishu mothers to compel their children to join the insurgency's fight against AMISOM. "All those who are against al-Shabab mujahideen are very weak indeed. So we are required to come together and remove them," added the governor.[46] The report did not say if there were any takers.

More difficult for the insurgents to lie about was the growing alienation from the Somali populations that in the beginning was eager to support the insurgency but was growing more disillusioned and hostile following its failed Ramadan offensive. On Friday, October 16, 2010, Hizbul Islam militias fired into a crowd of onlookers enraged at the rebels for caning teenagers allegedly caught watching pornography on mobile phones, killing a pregnant mother and a child.[47] On Tuesday, October 19, 2010, as many as 20 al-Shabaab fighters were killed when gunmen using rocket-propelled grenades ambushed the vehicle the militias were travelling in between Mahas and Wabho districts in Hiraan.[48] al-Shabaab's growing paranoia and suspicion against the population, meanwhile, took a dark turn in the town of Beledweyne on Wednesday, October 27, 2010, when al-Shabaab regional commander Sheikh Yusuf Ali Ugas called for a public gathering and, as the assembled crowd watched, two young teenage girls, seventeen or eighteen years old, hands tightly bounded to their backs, were publicly executed by firing squad, allegedly for spying. "These women were spying for the enemy and were arrested by the mujahideen last week," Sheikh Ugas told the somber and fearful crowd.[49] One of the executed girls was due to travel to Bosaso to escape the Somali violence.

The fallout from the public execution of the girls, and simmering disputes within al-Shabaab leadership over strategy continued to distract the insurgents. On December 11, 2010, Major Mbuusi's troops retook Manyanga House. All efforts by al-Shabaab fighters to wrest the building from AU troops were futile. At the same time, the quarrel among insurgents finally spilled into the open. On December 20, 2010, while addressing worshippers at a mosque in Mogadishu, Sheikh Fuad Mohamed Khalaf 'Shongole' publicly condemned Ahmed Abdi Godane (Sheikh Mukhtar Abdirahman Abu Zubeyr) for having "hidden agendas".[50] Sheikh Khalaf was especially aggrieved by al-Shabaab's continuing hostility toward Hizbul Islam with repeated deadly clashes including earlier in December in the town of Burhakaba in Bay region that killed over 30 people. Later the same day, it emerged that Hizbul Islam's leader Sheikh Dahir Aweys surrendered his forces to al-Shabaab, ending the long disputes and uniting the insurgents.[51]

The marriage of convenience between the two sworn rivals came too little too late. The disastrous four-week Ramadan campaign yielded more tangible territorial gains for AMISOM than for the insurgents. If anything, for the remainder of December through the end of January 2011, the conflict settled into a predictable rhythm of urban warfare, the insurgents attacking TFG and AMISOM forces, causing the obligatory response from AU forces who, using superior equipment, discipline and organisation, poked the ribs of the insurgency, looking for weak spots, chipping away at the iron-grip the insurgents previously enjoyed over Mogadishu, and advancing at snail pace to occupy more areas in Hodan, Wardigley, Hawl Wadaag, Shibis, Karaan and Yaqshiid districts. The success of the AU forces brought in new allies including Nigeria. The country that could not contribute troops for the AU mission suddenly became one of the most vocal cheerleaders on the world stage for AMISOM. Speaking to the United Nations Security Council in New York on Thursday, September 16, 2010 on the situation in Somalia, Nigeria's Permanent Representative to the UN, Joy Ogwu pushed hard for improvement in the pay and welfare of AMISOM troops.

"Given AMISOM's commendable role, concerted effort should be made to provide support that is commensurate with operational mandates. It is a recipe for failure to deploy troops without giving them the requisite support particularly when the support is available," she demanded.[52] The UN Security Council responded positively to Ogwu's entreaties. On Wednesday, December 22, 2010, the world body adopted resolution 1964, in the process, "commending the contribution of the African Union Mission to Somalia (AMISOM) to lasting peace and stability in Somalia." The resolution instructed the UN Secretary General to provide a logistical package of equipment and services to AMISOM to a maximum of 12,000 troops.[53] The game had changed. AMISOM effectively had the world's backing to go after Somali insurgents. It did.

January 2011 started inauspiciously, with little action against the insurgents whose drive to expand was blunted by AMISOM, and also because it was distracted by its own internal politics. The publicised merger with Hizbul Islam in December 2010 brought little good to insurgency. Further complicating al-Shabaab's effort to replenish its rank by recruiting new fighters, raise money and continue the war was the onset of severe drought that killed livestock and crops in rural areas. Somalis, it seemed, were too hungry to fight an endless war. On December 1, 2010, December 20, 2010, and January 7, 2011, the government of Somalia issued warning about looming famine, asking the world to send food aid to avert a humanitarian disaster.[54] On Monday, January 10, 2011, speaking on Radio Mogadishu, the Chairperson of the Supreme Religious Council, Sheikh Bashir Ahmed Salad asked al-Shabaab to show mercy and allow food to be distributed to areas affected by drought.[55] al-Shabaab responded by asking wealthy Somalis to help drought victims. "Help your hungry brothers and sisters," said al-Shabaab's governor for Benadir, Sheikh Ali Mohamed Hussein.[56] al-Shabaab, for fear of appearing weak, could not relent on its orders blocking international aid agencies from distributing food to starving Somali people, a grievous tactical mistake that caused support to plummet for the insurgents. Sheikh Suldan Aala Mohamed articulated the group's suspicion, claiming, "What are called aid agencies or welfare agencies want to Christianize our people only. We will never accept that aid agencies come into the country pretending to help hungry people because they are deceitful."[57]

Despite appearances of iron grip on Somalia generally, and Mogadishu in particular, al-Shabaab was losing territory to AMISOM and TFG, a piece at a time. Somalia Prime Minister Mohamed Abdullahi Mohamed highlighted these gains to the UN Security Council in New York on Friday, January 14, 2011. "Our forces, with the support of AMISOM, are winning the security battle. Gradual and incremental though it may be, the secure space in Mogadishu grows daily. That is the nature of urban conflict when the protection of civilians is as important as expelling the insurgents."[58]

In fact while the insurgents feuded, AMISOM troops were completing their transformation into lethal urban warriors. With troop strength from Burundi and Uganda nearing 9,000 strong on the ground, and a battalion of EU-trained Somali soldiers expected from Uganda in February, Gen. Mugisha and his commanders began planning counter-offensive against al-Shabaab forces. The emerging strategy was a pincer movement with Uganda troops pushing northward and Burundi forces eastward, squeezing al-Shabaab into the small enclave of Bakaara market. General Mugisha reasoned that confined to a small part from which to fight either to the death, thereby wrecking the market in which they were heavily invested, or escaping, al-Shabaab would choose the latter option. Many in the senior leadership of al-Shabaab, after all, had too much at stake in Bakaara to see it destroyed.

At the contingent level, meanwhile, Colonel Michael Ondoga and Brigadier Maurice Gateretse reorganized the Uganda and Burundi forces respectively. Ondoga used the lull to review the positions of Uganda troops in various sectors of Mogadishu. He ordered 19th Bn to pull out of Urubah, Bondheere, Fisbaare, El Hindi and, instead, concentrate in Sigaale, Shakala and Dhabka area. Meanwhile 69th Bn moved back to nearby El Hindi sector. Perhaps the most visible change for the AU peacekeepers was the new paint job on most of its battlewagons, trucks, armoured carriers and tanks. As in other wars, colour mattered in this war. The white colour paint scheme used on UN vehicles in global hotspots mostly associated with benign and, in the case of Rwanda in 1994, unresponsive peacekeepers soon disappeared. White was no longer an option. al-Shabaab saw white as a symbol of weakness, never respecting AMISOM. The AU troops, meanwhile, saw white as an inescapable straitjacket limiting troops only to defensive rather than pre-emptive actions. With the choices of olive green and desert sand colours, AMISOM was ready for a hard battle with the insurgents.

Before the AU forces could launch an offensive, there were two minor setbacks to deal with. On the morning of Tuesday, January 25, 2011, a confrontation ensued between civilians and Uganda troops near Immigration on airport road. During the standoff, soldiers fired into the crowd, wounding several people who were rushed to Medina hospital. Gen. Mugisha was away in Uganda for a meeting. Sensitive to AMISOM's image as the people's friend, Deputy Force Commander Maj. Gen. Cyprien Hakiza apologized for the actions of the soldiers, two immediately placed into custody as investigation got under way to find out what happened. "I give my personal reassurance to the civilian in Mogadishu that AMISOM is their friend and we are striving to make the city a safer place," Hakiza said.[59] Seizing on the shooting incident to portray al-Shabaab in a better light than AMISOM, Sheikh Fu'ad Mohamed Shongole warned his militias against brutality and killing of innocent Somalis. "Don't kill Muslims because you suspect they are related to Somali Transitional government and the African Union peacekeeping force," he told his supporters after prayers in a Mogadishu mosque.[60] Sheikh Shongole's unusual exhortation for good behavior for al-Shabaab militias was largely a sham. Five days later, on Monday, January 31, 2011, an al-Shabaab Mogadishu district judge pronounced a Somali man named Ahmed Ali Hussein guilty of "spying for the CIA", and ordered his prompt execution.[61] The following week, on Sunday, February 6, 2011 in El Bur district of Galguudud region, an al-Shabaab judge recited a verse from the Quran, then ordered the right hand of a teenager chopped off for alleged theft as horrified residents watched.[62]

The much bigger headache for AMISOM commanders, however, started off innocently with a public demonstration on Sunday, February 13, 2011. Mogadishu residents, mostly students, fed up with the fighting between al-Shabaab and TFG and AMISOM forces, took to the streets between KM-4 and Benadir Junction, waving placards and chanting anti-war slogans. Two days later, a much larger anti-war demonstration once again took to the streets, condemning both TFG and al-Shabaab. Then shots rang out. Five people were killed and as many as seventeen wounded in the melee. The next day, Prime Minister Mohamed Abdullahi Mohamed, flanked by defense minister Abdihakim Hajji Fiqi and Interior Minister Abdishakur Sheikh Hassan Farah, told the media that the government had arrested the people behind the shooting of the demonstrators. They were former

Mogadishu mayor Mohammed Omar Habeb (Mohammed Dheere), former police chief Abdi Qeybdiid, Nur Ali Yalahow, Mohamed Rage Tifow and Ali Nur Mohamed.[63]

Although the affair was largely a Somali matter to be handled by the TFG, it spilled into the frontline. On Thursday, February 17, 2011, pro-TFG militias associated with one of the arrested men abandoned their positions in Bondheere and Abdi Aziz districts, vowing never to return until the men were released. AMISOM commanders scrambled to send replacement troops before the insurgents filled the void left by the feuding militias. It was a near disaster that almost played havoc with a major AMISOM offensive planned to begin in less than twenty-four hours. Luckily, the AU forces had learned to expect the unexpected from their Somali partners, and to plan for all contingencies.

A week before Valentine's Day 2011, the Ugandan contingent completed the repositioning of troops. To facilitate rapid movement of troops and vehicles, barriers placed along Maka al-Mukarama road were removed. Watching all the actions from a heavily fortified position a mere distance of 70 meters away, al-Shabaab fired at vehicles and pedestrians alike, causing mayhem along the section of the road. To counter the threat, under the cover of darkness, Uganda forces at Shakala were moved further into the valley, closing in unnoticed on al-Shabaab positions. On Valentine's Day, AMISOM launched assaults on al-Shabaab's positions barricaded with sand bags of more than a meter high. On Friday night, February 18, 2011, Ugandan troops began maneuvering into new positions around Sigaale and el Hindi areas of Hawl Wadaag. al-Shabaab countered head-on, concentrating heavy fire on the forward units of the continental force, hoping to cut them off from the main force concentrated along Maka al Mukarama Road. The fiercest battles were fought on Saturday, February 19 and Sunday, February 20 following the discovery of an intricate 4 kilometer-long trench communication system dug by the insurgents that ran eastward through Dhabka, el-Hindi into Wardhigleey neighbourhoods. al-Shabaab fighters used these trenches surreptitiously to move reinforcements closer to AMISOM frontlines. Their very survival pegged into protecting the trenches, insurgent fighters engaged with reckless abandon, some becoming unnecessarily exposed to AMISOM's withering return fire. By the end of day Sunday, AMISOM confirmed six foreign fighters killed and dozens of casualties among al-Shabaab fighters. The dead foreign fighters were listed as Magid al Yahya Abu Yaman (Hutiin clan, Yemen), Sahan Abdowr Barqish (nationality unknown), Abdi Rabi Mansuur (Pakistan), Amol Joorkay (India), Saman Bito (Kenya), and Abdi Magid Asad (Syria).[64] It was al-Shabaab's biggest loss since the failed Ramadan offensive. AMISOM lost two soldiers in the fight.

Under the gun, the insurgents countered with a vehicle suicide bomb attack on Darwish Police Training Academy on the morning of Monday, February 21, 2011. Around 8:30 a.m., as police officers lined up for morning routines, a car sped into the police compound and exploded, the powerful blast killing at least 14 and wounding 20 others.[65] The suicide attack, however, did little to slow the TFG and AMISOM offensive already on its seventh day of heavy fighting in Hawl Wadaag and Hodan districts.

As anticipated by AMISOM commanders, al-Shabaab poured hundreds of fighters to face Ugandan troops pushing toward the north of the city. With the northwest flank of the city exposed, Burundi troops decided to pounce on al-Shabaab positions east and northeast of Jalle Siyad Military Academy, the goal being to capture Gashaandiga, the former Ministry of Defense Headquarters. At 10:00 p.m. on February 22, 2011, General Nathan Mugisha informed the Bancroft team of the impending operations by the Burundi Forces, instructing the team to prepare AMISOM Engineer Unit for follow-up action to clear the building of improvised explosive devices and unexploded ordnance. At 3:00 a.m. on February 23, 2011, Burundi's 7th Bn commanded by Lt. Col. Pontien Hakizimana and 9th Bn commanded by Lt. Col. Pascal Hakizimana began moving on foot, Casspirs and UPDF T-55 tanks, taking a westerly route toward the main objective. To draw away al-Shabaab fire, a smaller force drawn from 10th Bn led by Egide Nitabara, 11th Bn commanded by Col. Gregoire Ndikumazambo and 12th Bn under Lt. Col. Richard Bimenyimana moved toward the Milk Factory and Somalia Barracks, quickly capturing the former Milk processing plant at the fork of the junction of Sodonka Street (Armed Forces Street) and Tarabunka Street (Via Lenin Street).

The battle grew intense. Through the night until early dawn of Wednesday, February 23, Burundi troops fought pitched battle for control of the former Ministry of Defense headquarters, Gashaandiga. Toward mid-morning, a TFG battalion replaced the BFDN stationed at Al Jazeera, the freed forces rushed to reinforce the battle already a few hours old at the Milk Factory, Somalia Barracks and the former Ministry of Defense (MOD).

The offensive proved costly for Brig. Gateretse's troops. al-Shabaab quickly brought reinforcement to Damanyo Military Camp (Sirkhole Offishale), just opposite Gashaandiga, cutting off the use of Warshadaha Road (October 21 Road, also Industrial Road), trapping and denying support to the forward units of Burundi troops already at Gashaandiga. At 2:00 p.m. in afternoon, with the battle growing more intense, BFDN attempted to use Casspirs and T55 tanks to resupply the troops holding the MOD behind insurgents' line. al-Shabaab put up a stiff resistance, concentrating so much fire that the operation took almost three and half hour to complete. Heavy fighting continued through the night, the insurgents working to deter reinforcement for the trapped BFDN/TFG troops at MOD, at the same time looking to annihilate the trapped troops. The following day, February 24 was critical for the troops at the front. Fresh supply of ammunition, food and water was urgently needed. al-Shabaab understood this, and concentrated all the big guns on the road approaching MOD.

The Bancroft team, once again, proved their immense worth in the heat of battle. Quickly bringing the aerial maps and photos of the MOD building and surrounding areas, planners were able to plot how to move around the insurgents. Under heavy fire, Bancroft crew furiously carved a new path through the thickets of thorn bushes, allowing relief supplies to reach beleaguered Burundi troops at Gashaandiga late in afternoon. To counter the intense fire from al-Shabaab fighters, TFG troops laid down some heavy fire of their own, from the north and west of the Military Camp where al-Shabaab was entrenched. The resupply took two hours and half, during which additional TFG fighters, about 200 men, joined the battle. By then there were AMISOM casualties including twelve wounded and a soldier missing in action. Throughout Wednesday afternoon and on Thursday, the insurgents reveled in parading bodies they claimed were dead Burundians and a man they claimed was a prisoner of war.[66] al-Shabaab spokesman Sheikh Abdiaziz Mus'ab was ecstatic, proclaiming victory to the crowd that gathered to see the alleged dead AU fighters. AMISOM, he said, announced the deaths of foreign insurgent fighters to divert attention from its own bitter losses. For his part, meanwhile, AMISOM spokesman Maj. Barigye Ba-Hoku was philosophical about the losses AMISOM incurred during the fighting, saying only, "You cannot go into a swimming pool and then come out dry. When there is fighting, death is possible, anything is possible."[67]

al-Shabaab's victory celebration, however, was premature. Heavy fighting started at midnight on Thursday and continued through the morning of Friday, February 25, 2011. Determined, Burundi troops worked Warshadaha Road and Sodonka Street with fire support to consolidate gains at Ganshandiga and the ex-Milk Processing Plant. Under the cover of darkness, Burundi troops moved on foot and resupplied the troops at the front, but took heavy fire from al-Shabaab. At 8:45 a.m. General Mugisha, Colonel Ondoga, Somalia Minister for Defense Abdihakim Mahmoud Haji-Fiqi and Deputy Prime Minister Dr. Abdiweli Mohamed Ali arrived at Jalle Siyad Military Academy. The troops needed morale boosting and the heavyweights were on hand to give it. This was war, after all.

Nobody said it out loud, but there was a sense that Brigadier Gateretse could have grossly underestimated the strength of the insurgents, and sent his men in harm's way. Casualties were mounting. Nobody had any idea how many soldiers had fallen to insurgent fire. One report put AMISOM losses at 53 troops, to hundreds of insurgents killed.[68] For the moment, however, the focus was on resupplying the troops hunkered down at the MOD. A total of 7 Bancroft engineers were at the ready with a front-end loader, but the fighting was too heavy to deploy the equipment. With T-55 tanks and Casspirs leading foot soldiers, another resupply operation was started at 2:20 p.m. As before, al-Shabaab expected the move and focused on stopping it from happening. Bullets poured on AMISOM like rain. AMISOM troops fought back with heavy support fire.

As the situation grew dire for Burundi troops behind enemy line, Gen. Mugisha called on Uganda troops along Maka al-Mukarama Road to reinforce Burundi troops in the fighting in the Dayniile neighbourhoods. In mid-afternoon, Colonel Ondoga sent elements of Uganda contingent and equipment to reinforce the Burundi troops. Four additional T-55 tanks for a total of seven, three 107 rocket launchers and 200 rockets – the rocket launchers remained on site at the Air base at the northern end of the runway, ready if needed. As well, Uganda dispatched four Forward Observation Officers and two armor commanders, complete with their equipment to provide additional support fire to Burundi forces, and a large truckload of ammunition for TFG fighting alongside the Burundi troops.

For the first time in three days, there was less fighting during the night. Burundi troops resupplied the MOD first thing on the morning of Saturday, February 26, drawing moderate fire from al-Shabaab. The resupply operation later in the day drew fairly heavy fire from the insurgents still lodged at Damanyo Military Camp, and showing no signs of quitting. The same routine was repeated the following morning at 7:30 a.m. when BFDN resupplied those at the MOD.

As he had done in the past when TFG and AMISOM took new grounds, President Sheikh Sharif Ahmed, General Mugisha, the Minister of Defense and deputy military chief General Abdikarim Yusuf Aden 'Dagha-badan' visited the Military Academy at 11:15 a.m. on Sunday, February 27, 2011. Sharif congratulated troops, and thanked AMISOM for the sacrifice made by the soldiers on behalf of the Somali people. Later in the day, around 3:00 p.m., Bancroft engineer Rocky van Blerk was injured by incoming mortar fire at the Military Academy and evacuated back to the Air base, accompanied by two members of the Bancroft team. van Blerk was extremely lucky. Moments before the mortar landed, he moved a few feet away before the bomb scored a direct hit at the exact spot where he stood fifteen seconds earlier.

The fighting finally petered out on Monday, February 28. A foot resupply to the MOD that morning at 7:00 a.m. drew feeble gunfire from al-Shabaab. A resupply later in the afternoon also saw little response from the insurgents. al-Shabaab had given it their best to stop the Burundi forces, exacting a huge toll on the AU. Burundi forces had persevered and taken the prize, the former Ministry of Defense firmly under their control.

It was a bittersweet victory, the triumph tempered by the lives lost by AMISOM. Ugandan troops, meanwhile, tasted one success after another, pushing insurgent fighters away from Hararyale base located near Florensa Hotel Junction, just north of Villa Somalia. Then, without pausing, Uganda troops dueled al-Shabaab to the edge of Wadnaha Street, along the way, finding more dead and wounded insurgent fighters. Ensuring overzealous TFG militias did not kill the wounded insurgents, they were evacuated by AMISOM medics for treatment.

Despite the successes in the field, in an unexpected shakeup on Monday, President Sheikh Sharif Ahmed fired the army top leadership, dropping Commander of National Army Maj. Gen. Ahmed Jim'ale Ghedi, commander of National Security Maj. Gen. Mohamed Sheikh Hassan Hamud, Commander of Disciplinary Army Maj. Gen. Abdullahi Ahmed Ali, and Commander of Somali Police Force, Maj. Gen. Ali Mohamed Hussein Layan. Unaffected by palace politics, by Wednesday, March 9, 2011, TFG forces began heading toward Bardhere town in al-Shabaab's stronghold in Gedo region. AMISOM, no longer willing to give breathing space to the insurgents in Mogadishu, from Friday through the following Wednesday, hit the insurgents in Hodan around Ex-Milk plant, in Deynile around Gashaandiga, Hawl Wadaag, focusing around Dabka Junction, and further northeast in Yaqshiid and Bondheere districts. By the second week of March, Major Mbuusi's units overran Sigaale market and Lower Shakala valley. In tandem with 69th Bn in el Hindi, the two battalions pushed al-Shabaab further into Bakaara.

Far away from Mogadishu, in Bay and Bakool region of southern Somalia, Sheikh Mukhtar Robow Abu Mansur and Sheikh Fu'ad Mohammed Khalaf Shongole were busy recruiting new fighters. Both al-Shabaab leaders attended a passing out parade of fresh fighters on Friday, March 4, 2011, in Baidoa town at which al-Shabaab's governor of Bay and Bakool, Sheikh Mahad Omar Abdikarim spoke. He told the gathered crowd that he was sending the graduates to reinvigorate the fighting in Mogadishu.[69] The war, though, had spread beyond Mogadishu with the TFG and Ahlu Sunna Walja'ama, over the weekend, capturing the town of Luq, 80 kilometers from Ethiopian border and El Wak closer to Kenya's frontier. On Wednesday, March 9, 2011, al-Shabaab concluded rushed training at Laanta-Buro, near Afgooye, for recruits from Lower Shabelle, some as young as thirteen. The young fighters were told they were being sent to participate in the war in Mogadishu. The same day, al-Shabaab officials ordered meat traders in Kismaayo to each pay $1500 in two days to finance the war, or else face serious consequences.[70]

In a measure of how desperate al-Shabaab had become, on Thursday, March 10, 2011, officials in Beledweyne paraded a group of some fifty Somali elders carrying spears, daggers, bows and arrows. The elders, according to the officials, were ready to confront the AU forces and TFG in Mogadishu. A 78-year old elder identified as Mohamed Mohamud Hashi said he was ready to meet the enemies of the Quran. "It is our turn," he said, "to combat the enemy alongside al-Shabaab fighters."[71] In the Somali culture where elders are respected, the ploy was likely aimed to shame young able-bodied men into stepping forward as volunteer fighters. Suffering from plummeting morale, the insurgents were having a tough time recruiting, let alone retaining young fighters. The very next day after the event in Beledweyne, Friday, March 11, 2011, news surfaced that 30 al-Shabaab fighters among whom was a man named Sheikh Mohamed Farah al-Ansari, defected to the TFG after strings of losses in Mogadishu. Foreign fighters cheated the youth, al-Ansari said, into fighting the TFG and AMISOM.[72] Bad luck added to the woes facing the insurgents. An explosion inside a vehicle carrying fighters near Laanta-Buro village in Lower Shabelle on Monday, March 14, 2011, killed five men, a loss al-Shabaab could barely afford. In an attempt to shore the flagging spirit of his fighters, Sheikh Abdiaziz Abu Mu'sab claimed on Wednesday, March 16, 2011 that his fighters had reclaimed the bases earlier taken by AMISOM and TFG. Gen. Abdikarim Yusuf Dhaga-badan laughed off the claim. "They sent us some of the lured young men to our military bases," he said, "but we forced them to run away from our bases."[73]

Unwilling any longer to give breathing space to al-Shabaab, for the remainder of March and to the end of April 2011, AMISOM and TFG continued to fight daily battles in Hodan, Hawl Wadaag, Wardigley, Yaqshiid, Bondere, Deynile and Shibis. Although al-Shabaab continued to deny it, Bondheere district fell to AMISOM and TFG on the early morning of Tuesday, March 22, 2011. On a working visit to Mogadishu for the week, UPDF Chief of Defense Forces, Gen. Aronda Nyakairima, accompanied by his Burundi counterpart, Maj. Gen. Godefroid Niyombare, pleased with the progress AMISOM had made, promised more boots to support the ongoing offensive. "There is no peace to keep here," Gen. Aronda said, "so each day and everyday our forces support TFG to expand their control of Mogadishu. We are making steady but consistent progress and we now have 60 percent territorial control as a result of the recently implemented offensive and we will continue to build on this."[74]

For General Nathan Mugisha, Colonel Ondoga and AMISOM spokesperson Major Barigye Ba-Hoku, though, the war was ending. On Monday, April 18, 2011, AMISOM announced that the officers would complete their tour of duty at the end of the month. After two years of overseeing the most difficult phase of AMISOM's evolution from a painfully restricted peacekeeping operation, vulnerable to insurgents, into confident and experienced peace warriors, Gen. Mugisha would hand the flag to countryman Major General Fred Mugisha in July. On Friday, April 29, 2011 at an elaborate ceremony at Halaane Base Camp, officiated by General Katumba Wamala, both Colonel Ondoga and Major Ba-Hoku were toasted by fellow officers for work well done. Returning for a second tour, and elevated to the rank of major, Paddy Ankunda replaced Major Ba-Hoku as AMISOM spokesperson. At the ceremony, Col. Ondoga imparted some Mogadishu wisdom to his replacement Col. Paul Lokech. "We have been planning and implementing together with unit commanders and the foot soldiers," he said. "When you make a military plan, you should implement with the foot soldiers, that's when their morale will be boosted and you see results."[75]

Lokech, a lanky six-foot tall man, was an experienced commander known for decisiveness and clarity of leadership. He needed little coaxing to get started on the job. His long march while leading a battalion through the jungles of the Democratic Republic of Congo in 2001 was the stuff of legend, taught to aspiring UPDF officers. Then, as commander of UPDF 65th Battalion, leading about 800 troops, Major Lokech faced off with Rwanda Patriotic Army in Kisangani. Congo was imploding under the despotic rule of President Laurent Kabila. Both Rwandan and Ugandan troops had crossed the border into the conflict-prone country in August 1998 to prevent DRC's expansive jungle from becoming the staging ground for insurgent planning to attack their respective countries. Although former allies during the Rwanda civil war of 1990-1994, and both eager to see

Kabila out of power, the two armies clashed violently in August 1999, May 2000 and, finally, for six days between June 5 and June 10, 2000. Once he tactically withdrew his forces out of Kisangani, yet denied the use of Bangoka, the only airport in the area, Major Lokech solved the dilemma facing his troops by electing to walk some 700 kilometers, in extremely rough jungle, for safe grounds in Uganda. He began the long jungle trek at the head of his soldiers on Monday, July 9, 2001. "It is hectic but we must go home," he said simply. "Where the road is bad I will detour and improvise."[76] After enduring almost twelve weeks of horrendous conditions of extreme humidity, rain, mosquitoes, malaria, leeches, snakes, and biting hunger, on Monday, October 15, 2001, a triumphant Major Lokech led his raggedly men into Mpondwe border post near Kasese town in southwestern Uganda, where he was welcomed home by President Yoweri Museveni.[77]

Earlier on Sunday, May 1, 2011, as Colonel Lokech and General Katumba Wamala toured various forward positions in Hodan, Hawl Wadaag, Dabka Junction, Sigaale, Maka al-Mukarama, they were trapped for an hour under intense shelling in Bondheere. The unit commander for the area Major Mbuusi ordered a tank to fire at al-Shabaab position barely 50 meters away, creating a passage for the general to leave the area unhurt.

Later that day, from the White House in Washington, US President Barack Obama announced to the world the killing of al-Qaeda's illusive leader Osama bin Laden in Abbottabad, Pakistan, sparking jubilation in the streets of Mogadishu and, inevitably, the promise of revenge from an extremely demoralized al-Shabaab leadership. The news of bin Laden's death came at the lowest moment for the insurgents group when foreign funding had all but dried up, and the organization was increasingly forced to raise funds from poor Somali and abduct young people to be sent to the war in Mogadishu. A week after bin Laden's death, on Tuesday May 10, 2011, al-Shabaab's governor for Lower Shabelle Sheikh Abu Abdalla used the death of the al-Qaeda leader to raise funds in the town of Merka. "It is essential for you, the people of Marka, and all Somalis to stand up and let your boys avenge our beloved leader Osama bin Laden's killing by infidels," he said.[78] The event raised around $6000 dollars and 80 pieces of armament including RPG, AK-47s and ammunitions.

In Mogadishu, however, the dynamics were changing almost by the day. Colonel Lokech was focused on ridding the city of al-Shabaab's odious presence once and for all. At the various battlefronts in Mogadishu, the insurgents still packed a punch, forcing AMISOM to move forward with caution. Still, when they could safely, the 19th and 69th Bn employed the fast manouver tactics where they moved fast into an area, kept a low profile, before repeating the same manouver. This way, the two battalions were able to capture the areas of Wadnaha Road. More importantly, the manouver did not give the insurgents enough time to dig new communications trenches that they had so effectively used earlier.

Starting late Wednesday, May 11, 2011, AMISOM squeezed al-Shabaab in Hodan and Hawl Wadaag, forcing the insurgents to relocate commanders, foreign fighters and hundreds of local fighters to the Bakaara enclave. In three days of fighting, close to three dozens al-Shabaab fighters perished to AMISOM's two. Burhan Ali 'Ayatulla', a skinny famed al-Shabaab commander with wild unkempt hair known for his daring exploit against AMISOM was killed during heavy fighting Thursday night, his dusty shirtless body paraded by TFG forces. al-Shabaab's commander for Bakaara Abdufita Mohamed was killed on Friday. Pakistani foreign fighters Hussein Abasi and Abdullahi Yalb, wounded in battle, were rushed to Dayniile hospital. West of Bakaara, the Burundians fought to within a few meters of al-Shabaab's base at African Village.

Late evening on Thursday, May 19, 2011, additional reinforcements arrived from Lower Shabelle, Bay and Bakool areas to support insurgent fighters in Hodan and Hawl Wadaag. Also 100 youth were reported abducted by al-Shabaab from Eel Erfid village, five kilometers from Mogadishu, for deployment at the fronts.[79] Steadily, over the next three days, AMISOM was licking at the gates of Bakaara and, on Sunday May 22, 2011, a Uganda unit from the 69th Bn commanded by Lt. Col. John Mugarula, became the first non-Somali force in almost eighteen years to reach Wadnaha Street between Hawl Wadaag and Shalalawi streets, the crash site of the second US Black Hawk helicopter, callsign Super 64, piloted by CW3 Michael Durant when it was shot down by an RPG. Psychologically al-Shabaab understood the significance of the moment, as a reversal of what happened almost two decades earlier when the Somalis had roundly defeated the world's superpower in these very streets. Spokesman Sheikh Ali Mohammed Rage was forced to issue a statement on radio, explaining that his fighters had withdrawn for tactical reasons. "We will attack the AU and TFG and we will stay in the market," he said defiantly.[80] At Villa Somalia, meanwhile, accompanied by minister of interior and national security Abdishakur Hassan Farah, an ebullient Defense Minister Abdihakim Hajji Mohamud Fiqi announced the taking of parts of Bakaara. "Our troops backed by African Union peacekeeping forces," he said, "have fully taken over Wadnaha road and the most important bases of al-Shabaab in Bakaara Market...We are asking our community to give us a hand to clean anti peace militias and foreigners who want to make Somalia a terrorism base."[81]

al-Shabaab, like a dying horse, still retained a vicious kick. A suicide squad in a white saloon car attacked AMISOM base at Shakala with assault weapons and body-packed bombs on Monday, May 30, 2011. The vehicle entered from Maka al-Mukarama road, the goal being to take out the 23mm anti-aircraft that Major Mbuusi had mounted on the top of a building. Two AU soldiers were shot dead by the insurgents, before they, in turn, were taken out. Bancroft engineers were called to the scene because the dead al-Shabaab fighters were rigged with body bombs. However, an Ahlu Sunna fighter named Giney foolishly kicked at the body of one of the al-Shabaab fighters sprawled on the ground causing it to explode. The ASWJ fighter was thrown back several meters, badly injured, losing two limbs.[82] The injured man was evacuated to AMISOM Level II hospital in Mogadishu.

The sense of the inevitable was slowly beginning to dawn on Mogadishu residents that al-Shabaab were on the losing end of the war. Bakaara market traders were the first to imagine the possibility of life after al-Shabaab. Concerned about the security of their investments in post al-Shabaab Mogadishu, thirty members from the business community calling themselves the Somali Central Non-State Actors (SOSCENSA) met on Thursday, June 2, 2011 to craft a petition calling on the warring parties to respect Bakaara as a "no war zone".[83] The 5-point petition, riddled with grammatical errors, focused on the behavior of the fighters and, poignantly, that of al-Shabaab in relation to the renowned market. Like a referee telling unruly little children the rules of the game, the second point of the petition says of Bakaara, "It has be a "no war zone" and the warring sides have to remain outside of market and not should [sic] ever fight inside the market." The fourth point repeats almost the same point noted in point two, except that it speaks directly to the insurgents, saying, "Harakat-al Shabaab has to work [sic] give hand on how to protect the market and properties and recognize the market to remain at No war Zone." Then to make sure everyone, without exception, understood the rules, point five repeats what the previous points already said. "All sides like Somali government, AMISOM, Ahlu-sunna and al-shabaab have the responsibility to take care of that market and its assets." Simple perhaps, but the traders understood better than most the fine balance of power that now teeter-tottered between al-Shabaab and the TFG backed by AMISOM. Aware that power was slipping from al-Shabaab, but sensitive that the government still was not fully in control, the five-point petition treated everyone with the same deference. In fact, some of the participants who came from areas still under al-Shabaab control preferred anonymity. "We are justifying that we cannot give journalists for our faces and the full names," said one businessman who did not want to be photographed, "because we came from Suuqa-Holaha district, which is controlled by al-Shabaab. If they get to know that we spoke about Suuqa-Bakarah then we will be harassed or killed by them for this."

There was wisdom in the sentiments expressed by the traders. al-Shabaab was not yet finished. The insurgents struck again with mortars on Saturday June 4, 2011 during exchange with Uganda troops at the frontlines in Bondheere. A shell ripped into an armoured vehicle killing Lt. Lawrence Tugume, Cpl. Abdullah Isabirye and Pte. Augustine Kuloba, all from Tank Battalion. In another incident in the same area, an al-Shabaab bullet hit the Commander of the 23rd Battalion, and deputy commander of Uganda Battle Group Six, Lt. Col. Patrick Tibihwa. He was the highest ranked Ugandan soldier killed in Mogadishu since the UPDF deployed to Somalia in 2007. On Thursday, June 9, 2011, blending with traders entering Mogadishu port, a suicide bomber fired from a pistol before detonating a body-packed bomb. The blast killed an old Somali man. The following day, at around four in the afternoon, Somalia interior minister AbdiShakur Hassan Farah was killed by a blast inside his home located in Soobe near KM-4. Farah's niece, according to a story that circulated later in Mogadishu, went to meet him to ask to be sponsored in school and, once in the presence of the minister, detonated a bomb hidden under her dress.[84] On Saturday, June 11, 2011, spokesman Sheikh Ali Dhere denied that a girl was behind the bombing, saying instead that al-Shabaab placed the explosive underneath the minister's bed. "We have prepared a mission to kill every so-called minister," warned Sheikh Dhere, "who are workers for the infidels. I am warning ministers that AMISOM tanks will not save you, we shall kill you in your offices, streets, and your houses, as we have done AbdiShakur."

## The Death of Fazul Abdullah

The bravado aside, al-Shabaab was bleeding badly. That very same afternoon, while Sheikh Dhere gloated about the killing of the interior minister, news surfaced of the death in Mogadishu of America's most wanted al-Qaeda terrorist Fazul Abdullah Mohammed. Fazul, on whose head rested a $5 million FBI bounty for his direct role in the 1998 US embassy bombing in Nairobi and Dar-es-Salaam, and Kenyan-born associate Musa Hussein were killed at a TFG roadblock three days earlier. Hassan Mohamed Abukar, the commander of the 21-soldier unit that killed Fazul, and Abdi Hassan, the young soldier who pulled the trigger, recounted the detailed story of the unlikely end of the illusive international terrorist to Somalia Report.[85] It was shortly after eleven on Wednesday night, June 8, 2011, a time when many Mogadishu residents knew better to stay at home. Bored and listless, Abdi Hassan was chewing *qat*. The green leaves used by some Somali men as a stimulant kept him awake. At some point, a dark blue 1995 model Toyota Surf with red decal running the length of the sides approached the roadblock where the soldiers were camped. The driver appeared to have lost his way. Abdi Hassan approached the driver side, and asked the driver to turn on the interior overhead light. The driver did as told and when asked to identify who was in the car, said simply that they were elders. The driver gave names that, thanks to the Somali clan affiliation where everyone knows everyone else, Abdi Hassan did not recognize. The soldier, now highly alert, noticed the men were younger than the elders they claimed to be. Abdi Hassan also noticed something else. The driver had a pistol on his lap. Significantly, the passenger, Fazul, had his hand on an AK-47. Then without warning, the driver switched off the light inside the car, pulled the pistol and fired at Abdi Hassan. The pistol jammed. Abdi Hassan shouted a warning. The men were armed, he yelled as he jumped backward, at the same time releasing the lock on his gun. Commander Hassan Abukar ordered the soldiers to open fire on the Toyota and not to stop until everyone in the car was dead.

After more than thirty bullets riddled the car, hitting the men inside many times, gingerly, the soldiers opened the car doors to see who the dead men were. They did not recognize the men, where they were coming from and where they were going. But the contents of the car told that these were no ordinary Somalis. "There were many things," said Hassan Abukar, "such as $40,000, four documents, one laptop, three AK-47s, three mobile phones, one pistol and a South African passport. We handed everything to senior government officials, except the money. We divided the money between troops before senior officials arrived." In fact, not knowing who the dead men were, the bodies were left by the roadside for several hours for curious passerby to see and photograph. Eventually the bodies were collected, and buried right away. Only later did news surface, likely from al-Shabaab itself, that one of the men killed at the roadblock was America's most wanted Comorian Fazul Abdullah Mohamed. He was exhumed. Forensic tests carried in Nairobi and United States confirmed the kill.

Coming barely a month after the killing of Osama bin Laden, the death of Fazul dealt further blow to the morale of the insurgent fighters in Mogadishu, for whom luck appeared to have vanished. At various fronts, with AMISOM and TFG troops racking up one victory after another throughout June 2011, a despondent feeling of doom settled on al-Shabaab fighters. The sense of defeat was hastened when, seemingly out of nowhere, US drones entered the fray on Thursday June 23, 2011, firing missiles at al-Shabaab training camp in Kismaayo, killing commander Ibrahim Hajj Jamaal 'Afghani', and wounding British jihadi Bilal el Berjawi.[86] The following week, the drones returned, firing at al-Shabaab leaders, wounding one.

On Sunday, July 3, 2011, a dozen al-Shabaab fighters handed their weapons to TFG troops in Dhobley in Lower Juba. One of the defectors, Abdlaahi Mohamed Abu Qudama narrated the harrowing tale of the drones wreaking havoc on al-Shabaab fighters. "Fear has gripped the fighters," he said, "all the leaders have disappeared and their whereabouts are still unknown. That's the main reason why we have surrendered ourselves."[87] The following day, Monday, July 4, 2011, al-Shabaab leaders Sheikh Ali Mohammed Rage and Sheikh Mukhtar Robow, desperate after failing to raise fighters through force, now tried gentle persuasion with Digil and Mirifle clan elders in Bay and Bakool regions. But the overtures were firmly rebuffed; the elders were no longer interested in a losing war. "We met with Sheikh Abu-Mansur and his men," said Suleiman Isse, an elder from Day-Nunaay, "and informed them that locals are not interested in the prolonged war."[88]

Humiliated on the battlefield by AMISOM and TFG who controlled most of Mogadishu, al-Shabaab tried to hang on. One of the last attempts at officialdom, the expression of formal power over all of Somalia by al-Shabaab occurred far away from

Mogadishu. On Tuesday, August 2, 2011, in the small village of Garas Bintow, near Aliyaale district in Middle Shabelle, a man in the village had died, presumably from natural causes. The villagers gathered to sympathize with the bereaved family and, as required by tradition and custom, to prepare the body for burial. That Tuesday morning, however, al-Shabaab's chairman for Aliyaale district Sheikh Ali Hoosh officiously informed the gathering to disperse. Funeral ceremonies were forbidden in areas controlled by al-Shabaab, said Sheikh Hoosh and he was there to enforce the law. The villagers never having heard of this law refused to disperse. The disagreement got loud and a militia that accompanied Sheikh Hoosh opened fire on the crowd, killing a member of the bereaved family. The villagers armed with knives, pangas (machetes) and spears no longer afraid of consequences, overpowered Sheikh Hoosh and stabbed him to death. "The people became angry and stabbed the officer and one of the militia," said a resident of Garas Bintow, "we don't know what they want from us. We were with a family whose father died last night, sharing their sorrow."[89]

Two days later, on Thursday, August 4, 2011, al-Shabaab fighters returned, burned twelve homes and detained seven people in Garas Bintow. Not satisfied with the action, on Friday, August 5, 2011, al-Shabaab officials drove to Kensaney Hospital in Mogadishu where Hassan Mohamed Hassan, one of the seriously injured residents of Garas Bintow was being treated, unhooked the sick man from life-support equipment and watched him die. The officials told hospital staff not to touch the body.[90]

That same afternoon, while vengeful al-Shabaab prowled the hospital corridors looking to take one more life, AMISOM was going through the changing of the guard at the headquarters in Halaane. After two years fighting the insurgents, a victorious Force Commander General Nathan Mugisha handed over the books to the incoming commander Major General Fred Mugisha. On hand to see the moment was AU Commission delegation led by Mr. El Ghassim Wane, Director, Peace and Security Department, TFG government and security officials, and AMISOM commanders. General Mugisha was awarded the AU Peacekeeping Medal. General Fred Mugisha meanwhile vowed to keep the pressure on the insurgents. When asked what he saw as the single biggest challenge in fighting al-Shabaab, the incoming Force Commander responded, "The single biggest challenge is that we are dealing with a terror group, bent on perpetuating hate and destruction. We are facing an increasing threat of al-Shabaab changing their tactics and resorting to unconventional warfare."[91]

al-Shabaab, no longer able to assert authority over a rebellious Somali population, had few options left. In the early hours of Saturday, August 6, 2011, after receiving yet further punishment from AMISOM and TFG forces through most of the night, al-Shabaab fighters began piling into every manner of vehicles, and streaming out of their bases at Mogadishu Stadium, Suqa-Holaha, Huriwa, Deynile, Warshada Basta, and so forth. al-Shabaab spokesman Sheikh Ali Mohammed Rage, summoning whatever dignity he had left, confirmed the withdrawal of his forces from eleven districts in north Mogadishu. "The enemy of Allah," he said in his grand style, "Burundi and Uganda, and those helping the so-called Somali troops will no longer gain joy from seizing our areas. Instead they will see hit and run attacks."[92] It was a peculiar way of saying al-Shabaab would no longer stick around to be the punching bag of AMISOM and TFG. More revealing, it was an admission that the territorial ambition al-Shabaab nurtured to hold physical space was no longer a tenable dream. Not when faced with an implacable force, like AMISOM, that learned to fight urban warfare that had never before been fought by a peacekeeping force in Africa. Mogadishu was finally liberated from the death-grip of al-Shabaab. Against all odds, the AU peace warriors and their TFG allies had prevailed in the battle for Mogadishu. Now, the time was right to extend the war elsewhere in Somalia.

After the midnight withdrawal of al-Shabaab on August 6, the war metamorphosed from an urban combat fought at close quarters in tight spaces between buildings to one where the theatre was the vast countryside, making it at once complex and just as dangerous. Planning what the new Force Commander Major General Fred Mugisha termed Phase Two, required additional troops on the ground. For one, without new troop count, the strategy that previously concentrated troops on one problem area in the city had to be abandoned in favour of spreading troops thinly to cover wider spaces. Essentially, the offensive and the consolidation of new territory recovered from al-Shabaab had become a big challenge. General Fred Mugisha and AMISOM commanders understood the challenge. They could not risk the concrete gains in Mogadishu. The insurgents would not be allowed to circle back into city, especially as the war moved away from the city, to cause mayhem.

al-Shabaab also understood the dilemma facing the AU forces, and stepped up the harassment of AMISOM and TFG. From their bases outside the city center, insurgents launched mortars almost daily into the city. The TFG following tips from civilians also uncovered several bomb plots and disrupted them. On September 19, 2011, there was some good news. Uganda's Minister for Defence, Dr. Crispus Kiyonga arrived with a delegation that included Gen. Wamala Katumba for a visit in Somalia. Met at Aden Abdulle Airport by Somalia Minister of Defense, Hussein Arab Isse, Kiyonga praised what he said were positive changes, and promised that Uganda would send additional 2,000 troops to Somalia.[93] The announcement could not come any sooner. On October 4, 2011, al-Shabaab carried out the deadliest attack since their ouster from Mogadishu. The attack came the day after the anniversary of the October 3, 2010 bombing of medical graduates. A truck bomb driven by a single suicide attacker named Bashar Abdullahi Nur exploded near a government building at KM-4, killing 65 and wounding over 100 civilians.[94] Many of the casualties were reportedly students registering for a scholarship offered by the government of Turkey.

Gen. Fred Mugisha condemned the attack as proof of "just how little the extremists value life".[95] But even he knew that the only language al-Shabaab understood was the gun, and to wait longer without attacking the insurgents could further embolden them. Behind the scene, Gen. Mugisha worked furiously to coordinate with the contingent commanders Colonel Lokech and Colonel Oscar Nzohabonimana, to expel insurgents from Mogadishu Stadium and the neighbourhood in Dayniile, Huriwa and Karaan where the insurgents were still entrenched.

An early morning offensive on October 8, 2011, by the combined TFG and AMISOM forces in Karaan district dislodged al-Shabaab from the strategic high grounds of Halima Haiti Hills. After almost 48 hours of fighting, the combined forces also took over former Arafat Hospital and Pasta Factory along Industrial Road, and the junction at Ex-Control Bal'ad on October 10, 2011. There were some setbacks. Burundi forces, especially the experienced and seasoned 7th Battalion that demonstrated fighting worth in the battle for Bakaara, were decorated with AU Peacekeeping Medal on September 10, 2011 at their base at Somali National University and, afterward, rotated out to allow for a new battalion to come in. Incoming Burundi forces, inexperienced and yet eager to move beyond

Gashandiga into the vast Deynile district in northern Mogadishu, ran into serious trouble. On Thursday, October 20, 2011, Burundi forces mounted a pre-dawn assault in the district, meant to push al-Shabaab further out from built-up areas. The battle lasted nearly half the day. al-Shabaab insurgents, showing it still retained formidable forces, used superior knowledge of the neighbourhood to surround a company of Burundi soldiers, inflicting casualties. Then using a well-worn propaganda routine, the insurgents displayed bodies they claimed belonged to dead AU soldiers at Alamada in the El Maan area, 18 kilometers from Mogadishu. "We can confirm that more than 150 Burundian soldiers were killed in the battle. We can confirm to you that 76 of the bodies are currently in our custody and the battle lasted for about six hours," an al-Shabaab commander Abu Omar told the gathered media.[96] Although AMISOM spokesperson Major Paddy Ankunda refused to speculate on casualties, those in the know later admitted that the AU did lose some good men that day.

Despite the setback, tenacious Burundi forces fought courageously and prevailed. By the end of the battle, Burundi held almost six kilometers of new territory that, according to AMISOM Spokesperson Major Ankunda, was "the largest swathe of territory to be taken by AMISOM in one single battle since its deployment in 2007."[97] The tenacity of al-Shabaab outside Mogadishu, elsewhere in Somalia, meanwhile, forced AMISOM to mostly hunker down in the Mogadishu area, with no fresh offensive planned for the rest of 2011. The outer provinces in Middle and Lower Shabelle, Galguudud, Bay and Bakool, and Jubba remained mostly in the hands of al-Shabaab. AMISOM needed to change to confront this reality. In October 2011, unrequested but not unexpected help came when Kenyan Defence Forces (KDF) entered Somalia, driving deep inland. The war had entered a new phase, one fought beyond Mogadishu.

# 13

# War Beyond Mogadishu

## Operation Linda Nchi

On the clear Saturday afternoon of September 10, 2011, the eve of the tenth anniversary of 9/11, Flight 051, a 12-seater Cessna Grand Caravan from Wilson Airport in Nairobi operated by Safarilink Aviation, touched down around 4:00 p.m. on the small airstrip on Kiwayu Island on the east coast of Kenya. Part of Lamu's spectacular archipelago, Kiwayu was the final destination for David Tebbutt and his wife Judith, the only passengers to get off Flight 051. For the English couple from the picturesque town of Bishop's Stortford in Hertfordshire, a one-hour drive north of London, it was like stepping into paradise on earth. Already into the second half of a two-weeks vacation that started in Masai Mara game reserve, the Tebbutts planned to conclude their dream holiday at the Kiwayu Safari Village, established in the early 1970s by Italian professional hunter and adventurer Alfredo Pelizolli. Simone, Alfredo's middle daughter, her husband George, and their four-year old daughter managed the rugged $1,700 per night resort. The large estate consisted of 18 palm-thatched no-door no-window huts known locally as 'bandas'.[1]

Of the island's unique beauty, Italian travel blogger Lorenzo Lovato described it in his native tongue this way,

Ambiente incontaminato, mare bellissimo, non stupisce che queste zone siano diventate fulcro di un turismo di lusso che fortunatamente si è dimostrato, almeno per ora, rispettoso dell'ambiente. Kiwayu oggi è quindi una destinazione esclusiva, isolata dal resto del mondo, ma sempre a misura d'uomo, e che dà la possibilità di trascorrere una vacanza indimenticabile a stretto contatto con la natura.[2]

Translated, it read just as beautifully,

An unspoiled environment, a beautiful sea: it is no surprise that this area has become the focus of luxury tourism that has remained, fortunately and at least for the moment, respectful of its surroundings. Today Kiwayu is an exclusive and secluded destination, far from the rest of the world, but capable of meeting peoples' needs, and a place that offers an unforgettable vacation close to nature.[3]

After being driven from the airstrip in style on a golf buggy across the sand dunes, the Tebbutts settled into the evening, spending time testing out the hammocks, taking a walk along the divinely beautiful sandy beach, dinning on fish and potatoes, washed down with their favourite gin and tonic, before settling in for the night in their banda, hands held lovingly as they drifted into blissful sleep.[4] A scant fifteen kilometers further north along the coast of the Indian Ocean was the southeastern tip of Somalia. Whatever suffering was going on in that troubled country seemed far removed from the tranquility, gentility and peacefulness of Kiwayu.

How long the Tebbutts slept was never established, and it did not matter. Judith woke up rudely to find intruders inside the open unprotected banda, already manhandling David. Yanked from the bed and half dragged across the sand, Judith was bundled on a speedboat and, soon, was headed northward toward the border of Somalia. Unknown to her at the time, her beloved husband lay dying, shot once in the chest by the intruders.

At that moment, as the nightmare of the Tebbutts played out, and Judith vanished into the darkness of terror, Marie Dedieu, 66, described as a former leading figure in the French feminist movement, was peacefully asleep at Ras-Kitau Bay on Manda Island, an hour and half southerly boat journey across the water to Lamu.[5] Rendered a tetraplegic after surviving a nasty car accident in her 30s and, later, cancer, Marie was planning to marry her much younger but very committed fiancé John Lepapa, 39. Far from Dedieu and Lepapa, much further inland to the northwest of Kenya, in the congested Dadaab Refugee Camp located near the Somalia border, two young Spanish women, Blanca Thiebaut, 30, and Montserrat Serra y Ridao, 40, were also fast asleep. The two women worked with Médecins Sans Frontières (MSF) since arriving in Kenya in July to establish a hospital unit to care for the sick in the camp.[6] Crammed with nearly a million Somali refugees in an impossibly tight space, Dadaab urgently needed the new hospital unit.

Strangers to each other in their separate worlds, the stories of the four European women—Judith, Marie, Montserrat and Blanca—would become intertwined a few weeks later with Kenya's largest post-independence military operation. As happened to Judith Tebbutt, heavily armed attackers kidnapped Marie in the early morning of October 1, 2011 quickly throwing her into a speedboat that sped away toward Somalia coast. Thirteen days later on October 13, 2011 at around one o'clock in the afternoon, as they were being driven between projects, gunmen abducted Blanca and Montserrat and shot their driver Hassan Borle. There were no obvious links between the kidnappings of the four women with the ongoing al-Shabaab insurgency inside Somalia. The Kenyan government immediately accused the Somalia insurgents of the kidnapping, saying the group posed serious threat to Kenya's security.[7] Less than twenty-four hours later, on October 14, 2011, Kenyan Defence Forces (KDF) launched Operation Linda Nchi, Kiswahili for *Protect the Nation*. The full-scale military offensive into southern Somalia involved air, naval and ground troops. It was the first cross-border incursion since Kenya gained independence on Thursday, December 12, 1963. Kenya's Minister for Defence Mohamed Yusuf Haji said at that time that KDF planned to fight al-Shabaab to its logical conclusion.[8]

In the emerging media narrative after Kenyan troops entered Somalia, adroitly hand managed by the Government of Kenya (GOK), the distinct impression created was that the series of kidnapping of foreigners precipitated spontaneous military operation into Somalia.[9] In fact, there was nothing spontaneous or spur-of-the-moment about Kenya's forces drive inside Somalia. Instead, Linda Nchi was the culmination of careful planning and coordination of all Kenya's military forces that dated back three years earlier. As far back as mid-July 2009, the US became aware of discussions held in Nairobi, and in Lower Juba in southern Somalia about just such a military mission. What's more, in those early days, the US encouraged the undertaking to push out al-Shabaab from Lower Juba. On July 24, 2009, US Representative for Somalia Bob Patterson met in Dubai with Somali businessman Mohamed Sheikh who was the Chairman of Somalia Telcom, the second largest telecommunication entity in Somalia.[10] Mohamed Sheikh was well connected within the TFG in Mogadishu, having bankrolled the former Islamic Courts Union

(ICU). During the meeting, Mohamed Sheikh revealed of a plan being hatched among the Darood/Ogaden clan in Lower Juba to muscle out Hassan Abdullah Hersi al-Turki, the aging commander of Ras Kamboni, an al-Shabaab affiliated militia in the Lower Juba. With the old leader ousted, Ibrahim Shukri and Ahmed Madobe, the younger commanders planned to deploy Ras Kamboni militias in direct campaign against al-Shabaab, aiming to push out the insurgents from the lucrative port city of Kismaayo. According to Mohamed Sheikh, a 27-member steering committee had been selected to handle precisely the detail of the project. In a secret cable to Washington on July 29, 2009, the US Deputy Ambassador to Kenya Pamela Slutz made it clear this was a positive development in the fight against al-Shabaab.[11] "We are encouraging various Juba leaders to work together to confront al-Shabaab and to continue dialogue with the TFG," wrote Slutz who was wrapping up her stay in Kenya to take up a new post as US Ambassador to Burundi.[12]

On August 12, 2009, Mohamed Sheikh met with US Ambassador Michael Ranneberger to provide update on progress of the Lower Juba plan.[13] According to Mohamed Sheikh, the plan was advanced for taking on al-Shabaab in Juba region, especially the control of Kismaayo port. Ahmed Madobe, one of the plotters was planning an offensive against the insurgents, taking over the Juba region and Kismaayo, forming a semi-autonomous state, but with allegiance to the TFG in Mogadishu. Barely concealing his growing excitement, Ambassador Ranneberger cabled the CIA, writing, "Madobe, Shukri, and their allies represent the most powerful subclan in Lower Juba."

Between August and October 2009, seeing an opportunity to finally control its national security from inside the Somalia border, the Government of Kenya became intimately involved with the planning of the offensive in Lower Juba, mostly undercutting the Americans. In the new plan, Kenya security forces would train as many as 2000 young Somali fighters recruited from refugee centers inside Kenya, mainly Dadaab Camp, to be used in the fight against al-Shabaab in Lower Juba. GOK called the project the Lower Juba Initiative, an idea that immediately alarmed the US government. For the Americans, the plan was good so long as it was confined to Somali people within Somalia organizing to fight al-Shabaab. The involvement of Kenya changed the equation, foremost, because it wrested the initiative away from US control. Secondly it created inside Somalia a proxy beholden to Nairobi rather than to Mogadishu and, by extension, Washington. Kenya needed to be stopped.

On October 16, 2009, Ambassador Ranneberger cornered President Sheikh Sharif Sheikh Ahmed while the Somali leader was in transit through Nairobi following the latter's successful visit to the US including trips to Washington, New York, Minneapolis and Chicago. Ranneberger went straight to the point.[14] The US was gravely concerned by Kenya's plan to train young Somalis recruited from northeast Kenya, especially from the Dadaab Refugee Camp to join anti al-Shabaab forces in Jubaland. The US categorically was opposed to the plan, Ranneberger said. Taken aback, Sheikh Sharif Ahmed responded, "No one should be recruited from the camps, and we will correct it if it happened." The president was also skeptical that a victorious Ahmed Madobe would choose to peg his rising stars onto the TFG in Mogadishu. To the disappointment of the American envoy, Sheikh Sharif Ahmed stopped short of condemning the entire Kenyan scheme.

Extremely unhappy with the Lower Juba Initiative, the US State Department decided it was time to play hardball with Kenyan authorities. The State Department drenched up an entirely separate matter which, given the timing could be interpreted as an attempt to strong-arm the Kenyan government to back off from the Lower Juba Initiative. In a secret cable to the US Embassy in Nairobi on November 27, 2009, US Secretary of State Hillary Clinton instructed embassy officials to confront senior Kenyan government officials with what the US claimed was undeniable evidence showing Ukrainian weapons bought by Kenya being transferred to the Government of South Sudan.[15] According to the cable, the US government had compiled this secret information beginning in 2007 when Kenya imported an assortment of weapons from Ukraine including 75 T-72 tanks, BM-21 multiple rocket-launchers, helicopters and other deadly combat materiel. All was above board so long as the weapons were destined for use in Kenya.

Clinton instructed that Kenyan officials be shown surveillance images, but not allowed to keep them, showing the Ukraine weapons being moved to South Sudan. Kenya, according to Clinton, had violated conventional arms End User Certificate (EUC) that dictated the weapons were not for resale anywhere. These weapons could fall into the hands of insurgents, some of them designated as terrorists under US laws. For its transgressions, Kenya could face possible US sanctions. Clinton was quick to end with a sweetener, writing, "These sanctions can be waived. A much stronger case can be made for a waiver if Kenya cooperates in this inquiry."[16] If Kenya played ball in this and other matters such as the Lower Juba Initiative, in other words, the US was willing to look the other way.

Kenya proved more stubborn than the US anticipated. To the deep annoyance of US officials, Kenyan officials stuck to the Lower Juba Initiative and, literally, thumped their noses at the mighty Americans. At a Nairobi meeting on January 26, 2010, US Assistant Secretary of Defence (ASD) Alexander Russell "Sandy" Vershbow met with defiant Kenya's delegation that included Prime Minister Raila Odinga, Defense Minister Mohamed Yusuf Haji, Chief of Defense Major General Jeremiah Kiaga, and Minister of Interior George Saitoti.[17] When the discussion turned to Somalia, the Yale-educated Vershbow acknowledged the threat that al-Shabaab posed to Kenya's security. But he was firm on the Lower Juba Initiative—the US had no use for it. Haji and General Kiaga strongly made the case for continuing with the initiative. Kenya needed to take active role in containing al-Shabaab, they pointed out. The two asked for "US understanding and support."[18] Vershbow showing little diplomatic niceties, and with a touch of arrogance, responded that while "you have our understanding, you do not yet have our support." This prompted the Sussex University educated Professor George Saitoti to retort in kind, pointing out that to date, the US had failed to propose a viable alternative to the Lower Juba Initiative. Vershbow had nothing to say.

The issue was left unresolved for another day. This came two weeks later on December 8, 2009 in Djibouti. Sitting down with Kenya's Minister for Foreign Affairs Moses Wetangula, US Deputy Assistant Secretary of State for African Affairs Karl Wycoff conveyed his country's strongest opposition to the Juba scheme. As Wycoff put it, the US government saw the Lower Juba Initiative as "a bad idea that would more likely add to Somalia's instability than to help stabilize the country."[19] Wetangula, however, was adamant. The initiative was the way to go, he told the US envoy. Wetangula blamed "some excited Kenyan military officers" for bungling the earlier phases of the operation, but planning was back on course. The initiative would create a strong Jubaland leading to the demise of al-Shabaab in southern Somalia. "I sincerely believe that good ideas should give way to better ideas," said Wetangula. He added that the GOK could "no longer afford to sit on the sidelines."[20] The two agreed to disagree. The matter was far from settled for the US. Kenya, too, was equally determined to hang tough.

Later the same day, Wycoff met with Djibouti President Omar Guelleh, and promptly complained about Kenya's Lower Juba Initiative. Guelleh listened sympathetically and offered his observations. Kenya's Minister of Defense, Mohamed Yusuf Haji "like the terrorist Hassan Hersi al-Turki, were both ethnic Ogadeni," Guelleh noted to Wycoff.[21] Moreover Guelleh agreed with Wycoff that the Kenyans playing the Ogadeni card in support of the TFG could backfire, causing chaos in the Ogadeni regions of Ethiopia and northern Kenya.

Aware that its plan to send Kenyan-trained forces into Somalia had raised America's deepest ire, the Government of Kenya went all out to sell the plan to US officials. On January 30, 2010, on the sideline of the AU Summit in Addis Ababa, Foreign Minister Moses Wetangula led a powerful Kenyan delegation to a meeting with Johnnie Carson, the US Assistant Secretary of State for African Affairs.[22] Accompanying Wetangula was Kenya's Defence Minister Mohamed Yusuf Haji, Director of National Security and Intelligence Services (NSIS), Major General Michael Gichangi and Chief of General Staff, General Jeremiah Mutinda Kianga. Carson's entourage included National Security Council (NSC) Senior Director for African Affairs, Michelle Gavin, ambassador to the African Union, Michael Battle, Charge d'Affaires in the US Embassy Addis Ababa, John Yates, Counselor for Somalia Affairs at the US Embassy Nairobi, Bob Patterson and Deputy Chief of Mission (DCM) US Mission to the African Union, Joel Maybury.

The Kenyans took to the offensive, highlighting the need for the Lower Juba initiative to move forward. Both the TFG and Ethiopian government of Meles Zenawi were in support of the initiative to send over 2,000 Kenyan-trained fighters into Lower Juba, Wetangula pointed out. Carson, unmoved, firmly rejected the idea, stating that the US government could not support such a scheme. It could be very expensive, for one, and, for another, could re-ignite clan and sub-clan rivalries and clashes. Moreover, even if it was successful, the Lower Juba entity could become a rival and a thorn to the TFG in Mogadishu. And who was to say that such an ambitious aspiration could not later nurture desire to create an autonomous and independent Lower Juba keen to break away from Somalia altogether?

The Kenyan delegation had not come to roll over and play dead while US officials took on an intimidating stance. Kenya was not planning to create a fiefdom in Lower Juba, they pointed out. It was all about the security of Kenya that needed to be confronted. To drive home the point, Major General Gichangi reasoned that AMISOM was slow in gaining traction and, in the meantime, al-Shabaab was strengthening ties with al Qaeda, and this needed to be tackled heads on. Wetangula concluded that the Government of Kenya did not need the participation of America, only its moral support for the project. "The threat is there," Wetangula pushed back, "We can see it, we can feel it."[23] Boxed in by the scrappy Kenyans who, like a pride of hungry lions in the tall grasses of Masai Mara, were relentless in the hunt, Carson gave a small hint of US flexibility. He suggested US technical staff could come to review Kenya's Lower Juba Initiative plan, see whether it was viable. It was the small victory the Kenyans were looking for, and they ran with it.

Before it was launched, the Lower Jubaland Initiative was christened Operation Linda Nchi. It was essentially the same plan with the added elements of including the offensive by Kenya's Defense Forces (KDF) into Somalia. In the official version of the invasion told by the Kenyan military in the book titled *Operation Linda Nchi, Kenya Military Experience in Somalia*, Kenya had suffered enough provocation from al-Shabaab, and decided to act.

Although at times it patriotically exaggerates and inflates Kenya's role in fighting al-Shabaab inside Somalia, the book provides key information and insight on how well planned the operation was to involve all the elements of the Kenya's armed forces including the army, navy and air force.[24] Despite an ill-fated start in which a helicopter ferrying ammunition to the front exploded on takeoff at Liboi Airstrip on Sunday October 16, 2011, killing all five KDF personnel on board,[25] the forward elements of the KDF, supported by Kenyan air force crossed into El Wak, Liboi and Ras Kamboni, meeting little resistance. By Tuesday, October 18, 2011, KDF troops had moved almost 100 kilometers inside Somalia, along the way capturing the towns of Dhoobley, Taabda, and Bilis Qooqani. Early KDF combat casualties included the wounding of two soldiers, one critically in a midmorning ambush by al-Shabaab on Thursday, October 27, 2011, as KDF convoy traveled between Taabda and Bilis Qooqani.[26] As they marked time around the two towns, Kenyan troops came under frequent attacks from al-Shabaab including in early November, though these were brief firefights that the KDF quickly suppressed.[27] Claims and counter-claims of casualties on either side were placed on social media, with KDF spokesperson Major Emmanuel Chirchir nimbly using Twitter to mount media offensive against the insurgents.[28]

At first, Kenya's military drive inside Somalia caused consternation with President Sheikh Sharif Sheikh Ahmed who condemned it as "inappropriate and unacceptable."[29] Over time, the TFG government saw the silver lining in aligning with Kenya to drive al-Shabaab out of Lower Juba. Following a daylong meeting in Nairobi involving Yoweri Museveni, Mwai Kibaki and Sheikh Sharif Sheikh Ahmed, a joint statement on Wednesday, November 16, 2011, endorsed Kenya's incursion in Somalia in pursuit of al-Shabaab, and "reaffirmed previous commitments to jointly pursue the objective of defeating Al-Shabaab and other militant groups to its logical conclusion."[30] Further high-level discussions began in Addis Ababa to align Kenya's offensive with AMISOM's objectives and, more importantly, to consider the formal integration of KDF into the AMISOM framework. Under the chairmanship of Prime Minister Meles Zenawi, the 19th Extra-Ordinary Summit Meeting of IGAD heads of state and governments held in Addis Ababa on Friday, November 25, 2011, welcomed the "joint security operation by Kenya Defense Forces (KDF) and TFG forces in pursuit of Al Shabaab in South and Central Somalia" and, formally, asked Kenya to "consider the prospects of integrating its forces to AMISOM and to consolidate security and stability in Somalia."[31] The following week at a meeting in Addis Ababa, on Friday December 2, 2011, the Peace and Security Council of the African Union backed IGAD's recognition of Kenya's involvement in Somalia, and also asked Kenya to consider integrating into AMISOM.[32]

President Mwai Kibaki did not need a third asking to join AMISOM. Linda Nchi was costing the Kenyan government a bundle of money. At a cabinet meeting the following Tuesday, December 6, 2011, Kibaki oversaw the approval of the AU request for the integration of KDF into AMISOM. A statement to the media read, "The Cabinet that met under the Chairmanship of President Mwai Kibaki at State House Nairobi also approved the re-hatting of the Kenya Defence Forces in Somalia to Amisom, subject to approval by Parliament."[33] The following day, Wednesday, December 7, 2011, the motion to move KDF under AMISOM's umbrella was unanimously rubberstamped by Kenya's Parliament.[34] The remaining formalities for the integration of KDF into AMISOM were set in motion when the AU Peace and Security Council on Thursday, January 5, 2012, asked the UN Security Council to raise the number of AMISOM troops from 12,000 to 17,731, "including 5,700 from the Djiboutian contingent and the re-hatted Kenyan troops."[35] The positive response from the UNSC came on Wednesday, February 22, 2012 in resolution 2036 (2012) which supported the increase in troops for AMISOM and, "on an exceptional basis and owing to the unique character of AMISOM," also authorized the reimbursement of contingent-owned equipment.[36] A ceremony ushering KDF into AMISOM took place at the Kenya Department of Defence headquarters in Nairobi on Friday, July 6, 2012, attended by among others, Lt. Gen. Andrew Gutti, the AMISOM Force Commander, Ambassador Boubakar Diarra, Special Representative of the chairman of the African Union Commission for Somalia, Ambassador Augustine Mahiga, the Special Representative of the Secretary General to the United Nations to Somalia, and General Julius W. Karangi, Chief of the Defence Forces of the Republic of Kenya.[37] In essence, the adoption of UNSC 2036 meant Kenya no longer needed to strain its own military budget while pursuing al-Shabaab deep inside Somalia. The international community took care of that part. What the KDF needed to do now was fight.

## Operation Free Shabelle

Beginning January 2012, AMISOM undertook the reorganisation of its forces necessitated by Kenya's entry into Somalia in the final months of the previous year. Following UNSC Resolution 2036 (2012) which raised troop ceiling to 17,731, AMISOM formally absorbed KDF troops, and reassigned contingent responsibilities to four different sectors of Somalia. Sector One and Four including Benadir, Lower and Middle Shebelle Regions went to Uganda and Burundi contingents. Sector Two including Lower and Middle Juba and part of Gedo was allotted to Kenya. Sector Three including Gedo, Bay and Bakool became the responsibilities of Ethiopian forces. Finally, Sector Four including Hiiran and Gulgudud regions were given to Djibouti. Fresh offensives began unfolding in the second week of January 2012. On January 20, 2012, after putting up a spirited fight, the insurgents were overwhelmed by the superior arms and numbers of the African Union forces, forcing them to relinquish the University of Mogadishu. The area under AMISOM control was extended to Maslah, a former training base and factory for manufacturing vehicle borne improvised explosive devices (VIED) on March 2, 2012. The main road at Ex-Control Balad was opened to troops movement for the first time. A week later, on March 16, 2012, Uganda troops extended their reaches to Galgato suburbs, along the way taking Suuqa Houlaha and Jetemirika Hill, north east of Mogadishu, marking the first time Mogadishu was totally under the control of AMISOM. The Burundi contingent, meanwhile, consolidated its hard-won success in Dayniile on March 30, 2012, flushing out the last remaining al-Shabaab fighters. Only four Burundi soldiers sustained injuries.

The planning for the big push to Afgooye and other towns outside Mogadishu began in earnest on the morning of April 29, 2012 at Mogadishu stadium. Codenamed Operation Free Shabelle (OFS), it brought together the contingent commanders of Ugandan forces Paul Lokech (now a brigadier), his Burundi counterpart Col. Oscar Nzohabonayo and his deputy Col. Dushimagize, and senior officers and unit commanders of the two forces.

Using a huge map and scaled three-dimensional shapes made from cardboard, the deputy contingent commander of Uganda forces, Lt. Col. Muhanga laid out the details of the operation, focusing on troops movements and the attack elements. Afgooye, situated at the junction of the Merka-Baraawe highway and Baidoa highway was critical to al-Shabaab as a resupply hub from the outlying districts. To wrestle Baidoa, Merka and beyond from al-Shabaab required that AMISOM offensive first deny the insurgents passage through Afgooye. The battle for Afgooye, therefore, incorporated two battalions of the Burundi National Army, a battalion of SNA, and five battalions drawn from Ugandan Battle Groups 8, 9 and 9 Plus. The plan was fairly straightforward. UGABAG 8, UGABAG 9 and 9 Plus and a battalion of the SNA would stage their movements from Dayniile Airstrip, keeping to the bushes on the north side of the Afgooye Road. Their tasks were to neutralize al-Shabaab at El-Shale before regrouping at Carbis. Taking Afgooye on the third day required Uganda troops to next deal with, according to intelligence report, a significant al-Shabaab threat at Lafole. The 33rd Battalion was assigned this responsibility.

On the south side of Afgooye Highway, meanwhile, the Burundi forces were to initiate movement from their base at Mogadishu University, splitting into two groups at Ex Control Afgooye, with a battalion supported by SNA taking on al-Shabaab at Garsbaley while the larger body of troops took on the significant threat at Celaasha Biyaha. Pushing through the bushes of Algaroba thicket, the Burundi forces were to link up with units from Uganda's UGABAG 9 and, together, block Merka-Afgooye highway, effectively sealing off insurgents' attempt to send reinforcement into Afgooye.

In the midst of all the battle preparation, on May 2, 2012, AMISOM bade goodbye to Gen. Fred Mugisha and welcomed the new force commander Lt. Gen. Andrew Gutti. A veteran of the 1980s wars in Uganda, Gutti came with the reputation of a genial fine-tuned diplomat who knew how to stitch differences, and get people working together, something his predecessors had worked hard to build in AMISOM. One of his very first challenges was to straighten some last minute wrangles between AMISOM commanders and UNSOA. Fixated on taking Baidoa first, UNSOA administrators were not keen to provide logistical support including fuel and food for troops for the battle for Afgooye. To AMISOM planners, however, it made absolutely no military strategic sense to take Baidoa first, only to risk the enemy still at large in Afgooye, cut off supplies to troops trapped behind al-Shabaab's lines. Brig. Lokech, not given to prolonged arguments, strictly rationed the troops and moved on without waiting for the full UNSOA support.[38]

On the early morning of Monday, May 21, 2012, just before dawn, Brig. Lokech began organising his troops for the capture of Deynile Airstrip. To confuse the insurgents, rehearsal for battle took place along the Balad Control Road, giving the appearance that AMISOM troops were poised to attack Balad. Intelligence suggested that the insurgents were laying in wait around the perimeter of the airstrip, anticipating Ugandan troops to mount a siege from a safe distance. In a protracted battle for the airstrip, al-Shabaab looked to gain the advantage over the UPDF. When the attack got underway, from his Gila command vehicle, Lokech employed the element of surprise. Already in fierce battle mode which at time required his subordinates to pile on him to physically restrain the commander from exiting the armoured vehicle to join the battle, Brig. Lokech directed his personal battlewagon to make a frontal charge at the enemy's defence, taking al-Shabaab fighters by surprise, some of whom were crushed under the heavy wheels of the Gila battlewagon. Generally disorganized, those insurgents lucky enough to escape with their lives fled in sheer panic. They had never seen anything like this, and would talk about it for sometime.[39]

As he always did on the eve of a major offensive, Brig. Lokech fired up his troops with patriotic UPDF songs. On one thing Lokech was very clear, troops were to act leniently with those fighters who surrendered. Those resisting were to be dispatched forthwith. At dawn of May 22, 2012, using Dayniile Airstrip as staging ground for the Afgooye offensive,

Lokech and his deputy Col. Muhanga led from the front. Under their command, UGABAG 8, 9 and 9 Plus moved in tandem, keeping off the Afgooye Highway. The insurgents had had time to anticipate AMISOM's attack, and planned its defence well along the main road to Afgooye, thinking the Ugandans would need the road to advance. Instead, cutting through terrains with thorny bushes and shrubs, Lokech forced al-Shabaab fighters to meet the assault in the bushy terrain. With firm sandy soil under the wheels of the mechanized battalion, Uganda troops possessed superior advantage over al-Shabaab, deploying experience and tactical knowledge from past bush warfare to overwhelm the insurgents with heavy support fire without risking civilian lives.

The troops, meanwhile, had help from American technology. Using the RQ-11 Raven, a hand-launched lightweight unmanned aircraft system (UAS) donated by the US Army, Uganda troops monitored the road and terrain ahead for real-time enemy activities, allowing troops to adjust battle plans accordingly. In the early dawn of Thursday, May 24, 2012, AMISOM troops engaged insurgents at Arbisca and took over the area. This was a former al-Shabaab training and torture centre where many innocent Somalis were murdered, its loss a huge psychological setback for the insurgents. On the same day, using a classic battle trick of appearing to by-pass an objective, Ugandan 33Bn circled back and took over Lafole. Meanwhile, after overrunning al-Shabaab defenses at Garsbaley and Tredisha, perhaps overwhelmed by the difficult Algaroba terrain, Burundi troops slowed down, crawling at snail pace toward Celaasha Biyaha. The planned link up with its Uganda counterparts for the march toward Afgooye-Merka highway never happened. Instead, the SNA and Uganda troops moved forward to take that objective.

On the third day of the march to Afgooye, Uganda troops faced stiff al-Shabaab offensive. Again, with fire support, the infantry prevailed over the insurgent fighters. In the ensuing fight, over 60 insurgents were killed, many left lying where they fell among the thorn bushes, the survivors fleeing toward Afgooye, and using the Merka highway to escape.[40] Had Burundi forces kept the pace as planned, the fleeing insurgents would have been easily intercepted by AMISOM troops.

Afgooye, formerly the stronghold of al-Shabaab, was liberated with hardly a shot fired just before 5:30 a.m. on May 25, 2012. At the head of Uganda battle troops from the 7th, 59th, and 53rd battalions, walking cane in hand, commander Lokech strolled through Afgooye town. Townsfolk gathered to cheer the liberators. The following day, May 26, 2012, the Burundi forces finally took Celaasha Biyaha, the last al-Shabaab stronghold along the Afgooye corridor.

With Afgooye in the bag, AMISOM commanders turned their attention to Balad, slightly to the north east of Afgooye, and 38 kilometers north of Mogadishu. The farm-rich area that supplied food to most of Somalia also teemed with a recalcitrant pocket of insurgents that openly used the town as a base for launching frequent attacks in Mogadishu. The preparation for launching an attack began on June 11, 2012. Tanks and artillery pieces moved north from Deynile and Maslah to the town of Garas Bintow, just nine kilometers shy of center Balad. To put pressure on the insurgents who vowed to defend the town, the allied forces put out news that the assault on the town was imminent within hours, but the appointed time came and went without a single shot fired. The actual capture of the town by 342nd battalion from UGABAG 9 Plus, came almost two weeks later, after a brief firefight, on the morning of June 26, 2012. Many al-Shabaab fighters fled into the water where they drowned. The rest chose to withdraw rather than face the formidably seasoned

Ugandan troops, who rolled into town amidst warm welcome.

What brief fight there was took place later in the afternoon.[41] As Commander Lokech and his deputy Col. Muhanga drove southward toward Mogadishu, their convoy encountered a number of TFG soldiers who frantically signaled that there was danger ahead. Lokech ordered the convoy to halt and to find out the nature of the problem. The TFG soldiers informed Lokech that al-Shabaab had laid an ambush and, just moments earlier, attacked civilian vehicles traversing that section of the highway, killing many. There was no way the convoy could pass through such an ambush, the men warned. But to those who knew Brig. Lokech, it was like waving a red flag in the face of a raging bull. Instead of retreating, Lokech ordered his convoy to drive straight into the ambush, anyway. The heavy fire from the convoy smoked al-Shabaab from their hideouts, forcing many into the open where they were killed. In the middle of the firefight, surrounded by Uganda soldiers, a young boy soldier inducted by al-Shabaab fighter threw up his gun and gave up. Excited SNA soldiers on the scene wanted the boy executed on the spot, but Brig. Lokech would have none of it. Moments later, like being united with a long lost little brother, Ugandan soldiers embraced the boy who, at first, was confused and bewildered by the attention and show of love showered on him by the soldiers whom al-Shabaab taught him were the enemies. Soon though, the boy calmed down enough to pose for pictures with his saviors, and answered questions from a gaggle of reporters who mobbed him for interview and photographs. All the lies al-Shabaab taught him about AMISOM were not true, he later said. AMISOM really loved Somali people.

The battle for the rest of the Lower Shabelle advanced fairly quickly. In many cases, as chronicled in his daily journal by Captain Henry Obbo, the spokesman and information officer for the Uganda contingent in Somalia, al-Shabaab no longer waited for a fight, instead melting away into the shadows ahead of the advancing AMISOM troops.[42] On July 6, 2012, a raid on Shabaab base at Mareerey led to recovery of several weapons and capture of insurgents. On July 11, 2012, UPDF captured Laanta-Buro, 12 km from Afgooye on Marka road. Laanta-Buro was training wing of al-Shabaab and an insurgent checkpoint to intercept and destroy humanitarian items meant for the Somali people. On July 15, 2012, Ugandan forces overran al-Shabaab hideout at Waraado, capturing many weapons and killing enemies. On August 4, 2012 KM-50 airstrip, located about 8 km from Laanta-Buro was taken. On August 27, 2012, Uganda forces captured the strategic port city of Merka and Shalambooti trading junction 105 km southeast of Mogadishu. And on September 4, 2012, Easley airstrip and El-Maan port 32 km north east of Mogadishu were added under the control of AMISOM forces. With Col. Stephen Mugerwa's UGABAG 9 Plus pushing hard into El Maan port, al-Shabaab had no time to properly bury their fallen fighters, instead ordering locals to hide bodies under the sand. The locals followed the orders but left the feet of some of the dead al-shabaab fighters sticking out of the sand.

As the Uganda contingent advanced southwest and westward, al-Shabaab fighters took to the vast space east of the Kenyan border and west of the Shabelle River and, in so doing, slowly, pulled Kenya into thick of the conflict. The toughest fights for the KDF came in the early weeks of 2012 before and after the capture of the town of Hoosingo. The march on the town began on Sunday, January 22, 2012, but was briefly halted by al-Shabaab attack in the night, killing two platoon commanders, Lieutenant Kevin Webi and Second Lieutenant Edward Okoyo, both from 1 Battlegroup. Another officer, Lieutenant Evans Ng'etich, was also killed in an ambush around the same time between Bilis Qooqani and Taabda.[43]

Considerably slowed down by extremely bad roads and active al-Shabaab harassment, the KDF took Hoosingo after a brief half-hour firefight on Sunday, March 1, 2012.[44]

Refusing to concede defeat, al-Shabaab reorganised for a counter offensive against the KDF. The big battle for Hoosingo occurred a month later on Wednesday, April 4, 2012, starting at early dawn around 5:30 a.m., and lasting until just after noon. Kenyan troops commanded by Lt. Col. G.M. Nyaga threw whatever they had at the insurgents that attacked again and again, in waves, looking to overrun KDF defences. The early morning entry into battle by a lone Kenyan attack jet piloted by Lt. Col. John Omenda turned the battle in favour of the ground KDF troops and, with additional support from four attack helicopters, al-Shabaab withdrew after sustaining heavy casualties. Estimated casualties ranged from a few to two hundred for al-Shabaab, and a few wounded for KDF soldiers.[45]

On Tuesday, May 15, 2012, KDF forces pushed for Afmadow, a town to the northeast of Bilis Qooqani, and considered crucial for the drive to Kismaayo. Two weeks later, on the afternoon of Thursday, May 31, 2012, the KDF successfully executed psychological operations (psyop) that caused al-Shabaab to believe simultaneous attacks on Kismaayo and Afmadow were about to begin. Forced to choose between defending Afmadow or Kismaayo, insurgent fighters rallied to defend the latter, leaving Kenyan forces to march into Afmadow with little opposition.[46]

The real jigger in the foot on the road to Kismaayo was the little town of Miido, just sixteen kilometers south between Afmadow and Bibi. On reaching the town shortly after 3:30 p.m. on August 30, 2012, KDF Battle Group 9 was welcomed by "mainly women, children and a few elderly men."[47] Less than half an hour later, and barely 800 meters on the edge of town, two KDF platoons conducting reconnaissance of the road ahead in preparation for the march the following day encountered a cleverly concealed insurgent ambush. In the ensuing firefight, al-Shabaab snipers shot out the tires of two armoured carriers with troop reinforcement, causing KDF soldiers to engage the insurgents from a distance while taking in mortar fires from all sides. Two and half hours later, as dusk approached, attempts by KDF troops to retrieve a 10-ton Isuzu truck and an APC from the ambush area were frustrated by relentless fire from the insurgents. The worse of it was the mounting KDF casualties—one KDF soldier was confirmed dead, fifteen wounded, while a platoon commander and five others were missing in action. The bodies of Lieutenant Francis Muthini, Corporal Charles Ndemo, Private Joseph Nditika Nyamu and Private Martin Kimngich were recovered the following morning from the battleground.[48] Early the same morning, September 1, 2012, al-Shabaab media propaganda went into high gear displaying the body of 23-year old Private Suleiman Adan and another, possibly that of Private George Karari Maina, 24. Accompanying the ghoulish images were several Twitter messages, including one that read, "Just like all invaders before them, #Kenyan soldiers were mercilessly dragged in the streets of Kismayu by an angry mob."[49]

Still pinned down two days later, KDF commanders ordered the destruction of the Isuzu truck and the APC "in order to deny the enemy their use."[50] Despite KDF's claim that the insurgents' losses included 150 killed in action, and assortment of weapons and ammunition captured, it was a bitter day for the AMISOM Kenyan contingent troops. But Miido also provided KDF with invaluable lessons on how cunning al-Shabaab could be, and the extra caution and discipline needed to fight the insurgents. Following a brief firefight in which KDF claimed "100 al-Shabaab lay dead and hundreds of others wounded," Harbole located six kilometers between Miido and Bibi was secured on Tuesday, September

11, 2012 and, three days later, BG 9 and SNA soldiers captured Bibi around noon.[51] On Sunday, September 16, 2012, as BG 9 left Bibi village, it ran into enemy ambush at around 10:00 in the morning and, again, with air support, KDF beat back the attackers, claiming 105 dead insurgents, 8 TFG and 5 Ras Kamboni Brigade killed. Five KDF personnel sustained injuries. The troops reached Sooyac on Monday, September 17, 2012 where it dug defence trenches and, at midnight on Wednesday, September 19, 2012, secured Janaay Cabdalla. Now, all of 50 kilometers lay between KDF and allied troops and Kismaayo.

First, KDF troops had to deal with water shortage at Janaay Cabdalla that grew so serious that a KDF soldier was killed by al-Shabaab fire as he desperately tried to get water, and another placed into AMISOM custody after villagers were fired upon, killing six.[52] The march on Kismaayo began on September 28, 2012 with BG 9, BG 5 and allied forces leading the way, reaching Saamoja on September 30, 2012, and departing on October 2, 2012 for the forty-kilometer trek to Kismaayo.

At around the same time, the final planning was under way for a top-secret parallel operation codenamed Sledge Hammer involving Kenyan Navy, Army and Air Force that aimed to approach Kismaayo from the Indian Ocean. Commanded personally by the Chief of Defence Forces Gen. Julius Waweru Karangi, the planning for the operation began in early September, with troops transported from Liboi to Manda Island near Lamu. A joint forces rehearsal at Mkunguni jetty on September 17, 2012 and a final one on September 24, 2012 were attended by Gen. Karangi, Airforce Chief Major General Samuel Ng'ang'a Thuita, Vice Commander of the Army Major General Maurice Otieno Oyugi, and Navy Commander Major General Ngewa Mukala.

Operation Sledge Hammer was formally launched by Gen. Karangi late in the evening of September 25, 2012, sending forth five Kenya Navy vessels led by the 19-year old Spanish-built KNS Tana that carried on board, among others, 19 vehicles, 6 ATVs, and 3 120mm artillery guns.[53] After several difficult attempts, the amphibious landing on the beaches of north Kismaayo occurred under the cover of darkness on September 28, 2012, allowing 80 KDF Special Forces to fan out ahead of the main landing party. On Saturday September 29, 2012, hemmed on all sides by approaching KDF and allied forces, al-Shabaab withdrew from their defenses in Kismaayo and, on October 2, 2012, BG 9 and BG 5 advanced into Kismaayo, securing Kismaayo University. KDF's preparation, planning and gamble had paid off. Al-Shabaab holdout in the biggest port town in Lower Juba was over. The only remaining major insurgent control along the east coast of Somalia was now the port town of Baraawe.

# 14

# War Without Frontier

The fall of Kismaayo to KDF and, the previous month, on August 27, 2012, Merka to Uganda troops, considerably narrowed the wiggle room for al-Shabaab along the coastal areas of Somalia. Inland, north of Kismaayo in Jilib, Buale and Gedo region generally, insurgents still held court. As well, still out of reach for AU troops was Jowhar, 90 kilometres to the north of Mogadishu, and most of Lower Shabelle including Quoryoleey, Buulomarer, Kurtunwaarey and Baraawe assigned to Uganda. al-Shabaab was also still comfortably ensconced further northwest of Afgooye in the Bay and Bakool region and almost all of Hiiran and Gulgudud regions. For the last quarter of 2012 and most of 2013, despite the fighting still left to do, AMISOM retreated into hibernation. As detailed in the Report of the Monitoring Group on Somalia and Eritrea pursuant to Security Council resolution 2060 (2012) released on July 12, 2013, with a force of about 5,000 fighters, the insurgents were as active as ever, continuing opportunistic attacks whenever there was an exposed flank, a weak defence or poorly defended military convoy.[1]

It was not by accident that the various AMISOM contingents were in idle mode, savouring past victories yet slow to recover new territories from al-Shabaab. Partly, it was the continuing effort by the AU Commission to gain additional support for AMISOM from the UN, which had been slow in coming. On April 10, 2013, the Military Coordination Committee (MOCC) recommended to the AU that AMISOM not undertake further expansion operations, having reached its operational limit.[2] In its report to the UN Security Council two months later on June 13, 2013, the AU Commission was candid. AMISOM lacked many of the promised force enablers including helicopters, APCs, engineering and logistical units and so forth. Moreover, the Somalia National Security Forces (SNSF) alongside whom AMISOM was fighting and to whom the AU force hoped to eventually relinquish security responsibilities for the country, were inadequately resourced, lacking logistical support including medical facilities.[3]

Further offensive against al-Shabaab was left to Uganda and Burundi with vast areas left to recover. Almost forgotten during this period of little action were the troops from tiny Djibouti. They had arrived in December 2011, and had not seen much action inside Somalia. Yet the US had poured a lot into courting and securing a battalion from Djibouti, a slow process that took the better part of two years of hard work and sweat in diplomacy. After initial attempts were rebuffed in early 2007, the US effort to secure Djibouti troops for the AU mission began afresh. US ambassador to Djibouti James Swan met with Djibouti officials on September 1, 2009 to discuss troops contribution to AMISOM and, at the time, left feeling positive that the government of President Guelleh was indeed serious about the commitment.[4] In a subsequent meeting with Guelleh on the morning of September 12, 2009, Ambassador Swan was expecting to hear more about troop contribution to AMISOM. Instead, the envoy got an earful from Guelleh who was incensed that the US had failed to follow through on the commitment to equip Djibouti-trained TFG troops who were ready to return to Mogadishu. "We can't just send them back with empty hands," Guelleh admonished Swan.[5] After the devastating Halaane bombings on September 17, 2009, more than ever, Swan needed to know the thinking of the Djibouti government, whether the tiny nation was still keen to contribute promised troops to AMISOM. On Tuesday, September 22, 2009, just five days after the suicide attacks on AMISOM headquarters in Mogadishu, Ambassador Swan met with Djibouti minister for foreign affairs Mahmoud Youssouf in Djibouti.[6] Youssouf, a genial man, told Swan not to worry himself. Djibouti was still committed to sending troops to Somalia. If anything, the meeting of the AU in Sirte, Libya in July 2009 had clarified something for Djibouti officials—there was nothing in the organisation's charter that specifically forbade frontline states like Djibouti and Kenya from contributing troops for peacekeeping in Somalia. What's more, the AU was pressing Djibouti to commit in writing to sending troops to Somalia. The only small impediment was some reluctance within the Djibouti military to move forward with the initiative.

Swan came away from the meeting with Youssouf convinced that Djibouti's commitment had not been "shaken by the bombing of the AMISOM compound in Mogadishu September 17." What remained unclear were the specifics of what Djibouti intended to do, and when it intended to do it. Youssouf was more forthcoming at the follow-up meeting on Thursday, October 29, 2009, also attended by MFA director for Bilateral Relations Mohamed Ali Hassan, US permanent representative to the African Union Ambassador Michael Battle, US Charge in Addis Ababa Roger Meece and Deputy Chief of Mission in Djibouti Eric Wong.[7] Djibouti, the foreign affairs minister told Ambassador Swan, was planning to deploy a battalion of 400 to 450 troops, perhaps as early as July 2010. In fact, he added, an AU team was coming to Djibouti the following week to discuss specifics.

This was the news the US team wanted to hear. Just to be sure Djibouti was on track, Deputy Assistant Secretary Karl Wycoff used his 90-minutes meeting with President Omar Guelleh on December 27, 2009 to talk about AMISOM.[8] Guelleh counseled that the TFG needed to begin replacing AMISOM in the interior areas, to take responsibility for the security of Somalia. Somewhat concerning for nervous Americans, Guelleh neither confirmed nor retracted Djibouti's commitment to send troops to Somalia and, for fear of eliciting a negative response, the Americans avoided asking the president directly. Instead, in a separate meeting later, Chief of Defense Staff, Major General Fathi Ahmed Houssein told the Americans that troops had been identified for the Somalia mission, but lacked equipment. Gen. Fathi promised to soon provide a list of the requirements for the troops in preparation for deployment.

Serious planning for the deployment of Djibouti troops began two weeks into the New Year. From January 11 to 15, 2010, senior members of the Djibouti Armed Forces (FAD), and US Africa Contingency Operations Training and Assistance (ACOTA) met at what was dubbed a Peace Support Operations (PSO) Training Strategy Conference.[9] The objective of the gathering was to develop Djibouti's strategy to participate in a multinational peacekeeping mission. Aware it was doing America a huge favour by agreeing to send troops to Somalia, Djibouti officials played it up for whatever it was worth. The list promised by Gen. Ahmed Houssein was long. It included a battalion headquarters with standard battalion staff, two infantry companies, a support company including a gendarme section, a six vehicle APC Platoon, a small motor transport section, a full complement of combat support section to support the contingent, and a headquarters company. The list also figured a liaison officer each to work with Uganda and Burundi contingents. To complete the list, a

Somali-speaking interpreter was required to support the Uganda contingent and, strongly suggested, a similar position to help Burundi. US assistance was needed immediately to facilitate the interpreter for Uganda to travel to Singo in Jinja, Eastern Uganda to train in February with Uganda Battle Group 5 preparing for deployment to Somalia. A similar arrangement was likely needed for the interpreter for Burundi to travel to Bujumbura to train with Burundi troops.

Reading the desperation in the US quest for troops for Somalia, Djibouti officials were not shy to push a hard bargain. The US was not in a position to start haggling with tiny Djibouti. So American officials listened and took notes. Two weeks later, on Thursday January 28, 2010, at a separate bilateral meeting focusing on security and counterterrorism, Djibouti officials came armed with still more demands for the US.[10] At the meeting was US Coordinator for Counterterrorism (S/CT) Ambassador Daniel Benjamin who came with an entourage that included Mark Thompson, Deputy Coordinator in the Bureau of Counterterrorism (Operations), Col. Richard D. Clarke, Director of Operations at Joint Special Operations Command at Fort Bragg, N.C. and Maj. Craig Miller, JSOC Liaison to Bureau of counterterrorism. Also present was Ambassador James Swan and DCM Eric Wong as note taker. The man the Americans needed to humour was Djibouti National Security Advisor Hassan Said Khaireh whose portfolio included the all-powerful position of Director of Djibouti National Security Service (DNSS) and Head of Military Affairs in the President's Office. Known as the 'president's man', having faithfully served the president long before Guelleh was sworn into office on Saturday, May 8, 1999, the grey-haired grandfatherly Hassan Said had the president's ears and was consulted by the Djibouti leader on almost all important decisions.[11] He came with his sidekick Abdillahi Mohamed Abdillahi and wasted little time coming to the point. President Guelleh directed him to educate the Americans on the threat Djibouti faced from terrorism. Having taken on many responsibilities, not the least of which was hosting America's military base at Camp Lemonnier, Djibouti was ripe for terrorists, especially al-Shabaab and other al-Qaeda affiliated elements. With limited resources, Djibouti could not fight terrorism alone, and called on the US to provide assistance in this matter. Boldly, Hassan Said told Benjamin to his face that the US was sometimes "tardy" when responding to urgent requests from the host country.[12] The ambassador admitted that was the case sometimes, especially since the US budgetary process had a way of meandering on forever. Hassan Said then laid out the list of what Djibouti wanted. It included equipment for border screening, laboratory for analysis, material for counterterrorism including vehicles, arms, and other equipment. Again, US officials dutifully took notes.

Three weeks after the meeting, Ambassador Swan dispatched a secret cable to Washington detailing the meeting. To make sure that the Djibouti requests got immediate attention, Swan wrote,

> A small country with limited resources, Djibouti has nevertheless placed itself at the forefront of international efforts to promote regional security. Djibouti's diplomatic and military support for Somalia's Transitional Federal Government (ranging from hosting UN-sponsored "Djibouti Process" peace talks, to training TFG troops, and publicly committing to deploy a battalion to support AMISOM); its hosting of international counterpiracy contingents (e.g., from the EU and Japan); and its hosting of U.S. and French bases, including Camp Lemonnier, the only U.S. military base in

Africa – underscore President Guelleh's active support for strategic goals that advance U.S. interests.[13]

Translation—whatever the Djiboutians wanted, just give it to them. Moreover, by committing to send troops to Somalia, Djibouti, indeed, was now the little tail of a pampered poodle wagging the American bulldog.

Djibouti's sense that it could get whatever it wanted from the US may have contributed to the little drama that played out when the first 100 Djibouti troops finally landed at Aden Abdulle Airport on the afternoon of December 20, 2011. At first, Djibouti Deputy Chief of Staff Major General Zakaria Sheikh Ibrahim was all smiles at the head of the advance troops in full combat gear including body armour as they were welcomed by the Somalia Prime Minister Abdiweli Mohamed Ali and AMISOM Deputy Force Commander Brigadier General Audace Nduwumusi. In a short welcome speech, Gen. Nduwumusi told the new arrivals, "Today's initial deployment of the Djiboutian contingent is a great step forward for the AMISOM Force in Mogadishu and for building stability in the country. The nine hundred extra troops will initially be based at Al Jazeera IV as they undergo specific, in theatre training."[14]

At the mention of Al Jazeera IV, there were quick glances of confusion among the Djibouti men who understood what Gen. Nduwumusi said. Al Jazeera IV was an active al-Shabaab playground in southern Mogadishu. The previous week, in characteristic fashion, al-Shabaab used Twitter to dismiss the news of Djibouti deployment, tweeting, "850 Djiboutian soldiers are ineffective where thousands of Kenyan, Ethiopian, Ugandan, Burundian and US mercenaries have miserably failed."[15] The stakes were a lot higher as the insurgents were more than likely to engage the Djibouti troops at Al Jazeera IV. Not amused, Gen. Sheikh Ibrahim asked to speak with the deputy, and soon his concerns became apparent. So far as he knew, said the Djibouti contingent commander, his men were supposed to deploy at the 'marina', a word he kept repeating.[16] The said marina was a scrub of bushes and sand located a mere 300 meters from the Aden Abdulleh airport runaway, and within the perimeters of Halaane Base, the headquarters for Uganda contingent.

Gen. Nduwumusi, a soft-spoken Burundi commander with calm demeanor, listened patiently to the issues. Finally, he spoke. The Djiboutian contingent was now in mission theatre, explained the Deputy Force Commander coolly, and the deployment of the contingent was at the pleasure of AMISOM Force Commander Gen. Fred Mugisha, the immediate and absolute superior to the contingent commander, but who was away on official duty on that day. A standoff ensued, the Djibouti troops refusing to leave the airport tarmac. Realizing that Gen. Nduwumusi would not budge on the matter, Gen. Sheikh Ibrahim backed down, instead asking permission for his men to stay at the marina to await the arrival of the main Djibouti force before relocating to Al Jazeera IV. Permission was granted.

Yet what was supposed to be a temporary stay in Mogadishu dragged on to the following year. Within AMISOM, it was no secret that the Djibouti contingent continued to use every excuse to stay in Mogadishu, at one time offering the argument that it spoke the same language as the Somali people and was robust enough to provide better protection for the presidency at Villa Somalia.[17] That job, however, was no longer available. The Ugandan contingent had taken it on and was extremely good at it.

Despite the inauspicious beginning, tinged with antipathy for deployment outside Mogadishu, the profile of the Djibouti contingent rose within AMISOM and internationally with the appointments of Djibouti's Brigadier General Osman Noor Soubagleh as AMISOM Chief of Staff, and the multilingual Colonel Ali Aden Houmed as the next AMISOM spokesperson, replacing Lt. Col. Ankunda whose term ended at the end of April 2012.[18] The Djibouti contingent finally moved out of Mogadishu, piecemeal, to Beledweyne to replace Ethiopian troops who captured the town from al-Shabaab on Saturday, December 31, 2011. A small number of officers arrived in the town on Wednesday, May 30 2012, to survey suitable base for the contingent. Two days later, on Friday, June 1, 2012, 50 Djibouti troops were airlifted in a UN plane to Ugas Khalif Airport, and were welcomed by the locals eager to see Ethiopian troops leave the area.[19] The next 300 troops arrived on Sunday, July 22, 2012 and, several weeks later, played a crucial role in evacuating and distributing food to some of the 3,200 families displaced during two days of flash flooding of the Shebelle River in Beledweyne on September 27 and 28, 2012.[20] In addition, from their base camp in Ceel Jaale in the northern section of the town, the troops filled the gap left by Ethiopian forces by patrolling the four major neighbourhoods in Beledweyne, focusing on Xaawotaako, Howlwadag, Buundoweyn and Kooshin. With the arrival of additional troops on November 16, 2012, Djibouti rounded the year helping to sort out inter-clan disputes in the area. For the remainder of 2012 and most of 2013, Djibouti as other contingents stayed away from fights with al-Shabaab. That changed with the terrorist attack at Westgate Mall in Nairobi at midday on Saturday, September 21, 2013, which shocked the transfixed world by its sheer brutality, and cajoled AMISOM back into action.

## Terror at the Mall

The mid morning drive through Nairobi's busy streets was mostly uneventful for French citizen Amber Prior, 35, and her two children Amélie, 6, and Elliott, 4, as they made their way to the Westgate Mall that opened in 2007 in the city's upscale suburb of Westlands. On this Saturday, September 21, 2013, as on other Saturdays, the mall was filled with shoppers, vendors, expatriates and middle-class Kenyans with money taking time for midmorning tea, snacks or lunch in the cafes. A cooking competition on the second floor brought in many parents with children to that area that morning. As detailed in the documentary *Terror at the Mall*, directed by British filmmaker Dan Reed, the Prior family was headed for Nakumatt Supermarket where Amber planned to buy grocery for the week ahead.[21] At 12:25 p.m., Amber had mostly completed her shopping at Nakumatt Supermarket. At the checkout, she remembered she needed a bottle of wine and went to pick one, leaving her children beside the cashier. While checking out the wine rack, she heard a loud bang, followed by what sounded like gunfire. As other shoppers ran deeper into the store, Amber raced back to her children. Amelie and Elliot were still hanging onto the shopping cart laden with grocery. The unmistakable sound of gunfire was persistent, growing louder. Amber took the children and hurried back inside the store, hiding behind the meat deli counter.

Amber did not know it yet, but four heavily armed al-Shabaab gunmen had entered the mall with only one mission in mind—to kill as many people as they possibly could inside the mall. According to Tristan McConnell in a graphic account of the incident titled *'Close Your Eyes and Pretend to be Dead'* written for the online magazine Foreign Policy, one of the gunmen was 23-year old Hassan Abdi Dhuhulow who lived for a while in Norway. The other three went by various names and aliases, and were identified as Ahmed Hassan Abukar, Mohammed Abdinur Said, and Yahya Ahmed Osman.[22] Survivors of the incident recalled that the young men of Somali heritage were exactingly methodical, calm, and relaxed as they shot at civilians cowering in tight spaces in the mall and inside the Nakumatt supermarket. Occasionally, one or the other gunman asked a victim whether he or she was a Muslim and, if quick witted enough to identify as a Muslim, was allowed to leave the blood bath, alive. Many were honest, revealing they belonged to other faiths, and did not make it, gunned down in cold blood, at close range.

One gunman finally approached the area where Amber, Amelie and Elliot Prior and almost two dozen others were huddled on the floor behind the deli counter, Amber draping her small body on top of her children to protect them from bullets. The gunman fired a volley of shots into the mass of bodies, women and children, alike, shot without pity. Amber was hit in the pelvis, but was alive. Beside her were the bodies of a Southeast Asian mother and her daughter, killed by the bullets. The dead Asian woman's son was also wounded, but he was alive. Also shot in the side was 15-year-old Makena Kinyua who lay next to Amber, alive. Amelie and Elliott were unhurt. Amber reached to the suffering boy, squeezed his hands reassuringly and told him, "Hold my hand, close your eyes, and pretend to be dead."[23] Amber used her mobile phone to send a succinct text message to her British husband, Daniel Prior, "I've been shot."

The gunman returned to the meat deli, asked whether there were women and children. When Amber Prior stood up to identify herself the gunman apologized to her. It was not personal, he said. "We just want people to understand that they can't come to our homes and kill us ... we will do the same to them," he said, speaking with a slight accent, but otherwise clear English. "I want you to forgive us," he added.[24] Amber asked if the little Asian boy whose sister and mother lay dead nearby could also leave, and the gunman said she could carry the boy out. Makena Kinyua also got up to leave. Amber discovered she was too weak from her own wound to carry the small boy, so she went to get a shopping cart. When she returned with the cart, the gunman had given Amelie and Elliott each two Mars bar chocolate. Elliott apparently took time to berate the gunman, telling him he was a bad man, and should let everyone go. Then, with an exaggerated show of concern as if to make sure nothing bad happened to the group, the gunman escorted the survivors as far as he could without exposing himself, allowing the five people to leave. Once outside, someone took a picture of the Priors, Makena Kinyua and the Asian boy emerging from the bloodied mall. Elliott, in his green 'I Heart NY' t-shirt, still clutching the Mars bar chocolate given by the terrorist, was photographed standing next to a dead man.

Almost forty-five minutes after the attack began, Kenyan security personnel had still to respond. A few good men including a brave Kenyan police officer of ethnic Somali named Corporal Nura Ali began to organise a rescue of those wounded on the rooftop, then moved to the body of the mall to do the same. Ali, himself, shot several times, survived. Befuddled, confused, and utterly lacking organised response, Kenyan securities finally entered the Mall around 4:00 p.m. The actual assault by the terrorists had long ended, the gunmen having withdrawn to a small room in the back of Nakumatt, calmly praying, eating a little and waiting for their own deaths, which they knew would come, but seemed to take a lot longer than they anticipated. A full day would pass before KDF blew up part of the mall with a rocket, starting a fire that burned for days, sending the upper concrete floors cascading into the ground, killing the four attackers. Altogether, 71 people died, and many were wounded. Video footage showed some KDF personnel looting the mall.

With the Westgate attacks still fresh, the world woke to the menace that al-Shabaab posed within and outside Somalia. The UN Security Council acted on November 12, 2013, passing resolution 2124 (2013).[25] The meeting lasting all of fifteen minutes, extended the mandate of AMISOM to October 31, 2014, and increased from 17,731 to a maximum of 22,126 uniformed personnel as part of "overall efforts to combat the increasingly asymmetrical tactics of Al-Shabaab rebels in the country."[26] The meeting also concurred with an early recommendation from the UN Secretary General that this was not the time to re-hat AMISOM into a UN operation because "conditions in Somalia were not yet appropriate for the deployment of a United Nations peacekeeping operation..." The further good news was the directive to United Nations Support Office for AMISOM (UNSOA) to support Somalia National Army with "food, water, fuel, transport, tents and "in-theatre" medical evacuation to front-line units...". The funding for the logistical supports would come from United Nations trust fund for Somalia. In one swift action, Resolution 2124, kick-started AMISOM's offensive posture in pursuit of al-Shabaab.

For Djibouti troops, finally, this meant getting out there to do some serious work. Under the command of Colonel Osman Doubad, Djibouti troops initiated aggressive westward campaigns against al-Shabaab in Bakool region beginning Thursday, March 6, 2014. The troops took over the towns of Tayeeglow, Xuddur and Rab Dhuure, to the west of Beledweyne.[27] Pushing on their successes, early on Thursday, March 13, 2014, the combined Djibouti and SNA troops took the villages of Raangoobo and Buq-Aqable and, in a hard fought battle that lasted half an hour, took the town of Buulo Barde later in the day.[28] A week later, in the early morning of Tuesday March 18, 2014, Djibouti troops suffered the largest casualties since deployment in Somalia. Suicide attackers used a car-bomb to ram into Hotel Amalow in Buulo Barde where some of the Djibouti and SNA troops were stationed, killing 20 people, including five Djibouti and eleven SNA soldiers. The wounded were first airlifted to Nairobi and, later, some were sent to South Africa for treatment.[29] A sixth Djibouti soldier, presumably wounded in the same attack, also died and was repatriated along with the others to Djibouti City on Thursday, March 20, 2014 where President Ismail Omar Guelleh received the bodies at Djibouti-Ambouli International Airport.[30]

Despite the setbacks, on June 6, 2014, Djibouti troops in Beledweyne and Buulo Barde proudly celebrated the 37th anniversary of the founding of Forces Armées Djiboutiennes (FAD) on the same day in 1977. Their capacity to contribute to an international peace effort in Somalia already established, Major Ali Dheere, acting Deputy contingent commander of Djibouti troops addressed his proud soldiers in Beledweyne. "Today is a very important day for the nation of Djibouti. We are celebrating the Djiboutian National Army. We are not only marking it here in Beletweyne but the Djiboutian contingent in Bulla Burde," he told them.[31] Two months later, on Thursday, June 26, 2014, two al-Shabaab suicide attackers disguised as SNA soldiers approached the gate of Hotel Amalow, hurled explosives, then exchanged fire during which two Djibouti soldiers and the attackers were killed. al-Shabaab spokesman Sheikh Ali Dheere, praised "our well armed mujahideen..." in a radio broadcast,[32] and vowed, "Our fighters will keep on attacking the Djiboutian troops until they withdraw their forces from Somalia."[33] The attack, however, had little impact on the morale of the Djibouti troops. The SNA and Djibouti commanders in Sector 4 were already busy planning their next advance on al-Shabaab stronghold towns, starting with the town of Jalalaqsi, south of Buulo Barde in Hiraan.[34]

## *Mpaka Baraawe,* Until Baraawe

On the evening of Thursday, July 31, 2014, following a satisfying dinner of *malakwang*, a sour green delicacy dressed in thick roasted *odii*, simsim and groundnut sauce from his hometown in northern Uganda, the contingent commander of Ugandan forces in Somalia Brig. Dick Olum was chatting with his compatriot and superior AMISOM Deputy Force Commander (Operations) Maj. Gen. Barnabas Muheesi. Within the Halaane Base in Mogadishu, the two shared the same house just around the corner from the 'White House', and deeply enjoyed each other's confidence and, whenever possible, had dinner together. Olum who believed in early to bed and first to rise was discussing plans for the following day. SNA and Ugandan troops had made excellent headway against the insurgents and, three months early, on March 23, 2014, taken the strategic town of Quoryoleey, and were now preparing for what AMISOM commanders and planners predicted would be the toughest, bloodiest and most perilous part of the campaign—liberating the southeastern coastal town of Baraawe from al-Shabaab fighters. With Kismaayo firmly under the control of SNA and Kenyan Defence Forces, Baraawe was the last al-Shabaab stronghold with access to the Indian Ocean. Moreover, intelligence reports indicated the top leadership of al-Shabaab was holed up in the town. The capture of the coastal town of 32,800[35] people would deny the insurgents not only the economic lifeline, but also the arms and personnel smuggled through the port to reinforce the insurgency. Brig. Olum, never one to idle, was way ahead of schedule in planning for the offensive to take the towns on the road to Baraawe. Already, he had written the operation orders and strategically repositioned Uganda's Battle Group 12 from Baidoa to Quoryoleey, Beled Amin and Shalambooti.

As Brig. Olum discussed his plans with Gen. Muheesi, his secure phone rang. On the line was the Commander-in-Chief President Yoweri Museveni. As he had done with all previous contingent commanders who served in Somalia, Museveni had hand picked Dick Olum to replace Col. Ondoga. On his second tour, Ondoga, then a brigadier, returned to Somalia in May 2013 to replace departing Brig. Paul Lokech, served briefly for a couple of months, was appointed Uganda's defense attaché to Kenya, but subsequently charged before a court martial on several counts including of failure to command.[36] Olum who greatly enjoyed Museveni's confidence had travelled with Col. Peter Elwelu and Inspector General of Police (IGP) Major General Kale Kayihura on a secret fact-finding mission to Baidoa in early November 2006. The trio was briefly trapped in Baidoa as fighting raged on the outskirt of town, but eventually made out safely. Olum's brief and insightful report on the situation on the ground shaped Museveni's decision to deploy Uganda troops to serve in Somalia in early 2007. The decision to send Brig. Olum to command Ugandan troops in Somalia was an easy one for Museveni. Olum was one of the highly educated young Turks in the UPDF who helped raise the professional standard within the force.

On the phone from Kampala, President Museveni wanted to know from the Commander what the situation on the ground was. Brig. Olum replied evenly. Other than the delay caused by uncertainty over logistics from UNSOA for items like dry rations, water, fuel and tires for the battlewagons, all the planning was in place to begin the next phase of the campaign toward Baraawe. President Museveni then told Brig. Olum of his visit to Kenya early that day to attend an informal meeting at State House in Nairobi of Heads of State of Kenya, Uganda, Ethiopia and South Sudan to discuss the Lamu Port Southern Sudan-Ethiopia Transport (LAPSETT) project.[37] On the side, he met privately with Kenya's President Uhuru Kenyatta to discuss security issues, and Somalia came up.

According to Museveni, Uhuru told him that Kenya was extremely concerned that al-Shabaab was using Baraawe to cause insecurity in his country. Since Baraawe was in Sector One and, therefore, the responsibility of Uganda to take on, President Kenyatta wanted Uganda to move more quickly to secure the town.

The apparent stab by Kenyan officials that Ugandan forces were dragging their feet and delaying the capture of Baraawe incensed Brig. Olum. "Mr. President, if I were to speak to His Excellency President Kenyatta, I would personally tell him that it is a lie that Baraawe is the cause of insecurity in Kenya." Brig. Olum responded with such firmness it caused Museveni to chuckle out loud. Olum explained that while Baraawe was an important economic and political seat for al-Shabaab, it defied military logic to think that securing the town would solve Kenya's insecurity problem. "Even with Baraawe under our control, al-Shabaab will still have plenty of playroom in Jilib, Bu'uale and Baardheere, all of which are closer to the borders of Kenya, to cause mayhem to our good neighbour." Brig. Olum added. President Museveni said he understood Brig. Olum's concerns and it would be beneficial for President Kenyatta to hear directly from the commander. Museveni added that he and President Kenyatta were travelling separately on Sunday, August 3 to attend the US-Africa Summit in Washington, from August 4 to 7.[38] In the meantime, his instructions were for Brig. Olum to travel to Nairobi the following week to meet security officials from Uganda, Kenya, Somalia, US and Britain to discuss the plan for an offensive on Baraawe. Brig. Charles Bakahumura, Uganda's Chief of Military Intelligence (CMI), would attend the meeting. The president wished Brig. Olum well, bade him goodbye and hung up.

Brig. Olum travelled to Nairobi for the meeting scheduled for Thursday, August 7, 2014. The meeting discussed the operational modalities for moving on Baraawe that, according to available military intelligence, could take up to three months to capture, maybe longer. The US promised to position maritime assets near Baraawe when the time was right but, because this was not a US-led mission, these would be for show of force only with no shots fired. Kenya offered air assets, specifically helicopter gunships and transport to support the SNA and Uganda troops on the ground. British officials at the meeting were skeptical, suggesting Ugandans were way over their heads taking on Baraawe. Subsequently, the British did not endear themselves to Brig. Olum who had no problem "telling them off."[39] A second meeting took place the following week. Kenya now seemed to backtrack on their commitments. Getting the operational orders for air support could take time, Kenyan officials at meeting informed Brig. Olum. Given its strategic importance to al-Shabaab, taking Baraawe could be bloody, the Americans cautioned. Sensing he could face indefinite delay waiting on partners to show up, Brig. Olum stunned the meeting. He planned to take Baraawe within thirty days, "Look, my soldiers are used to walking, and with or without you, we are walking to Baraawe." On returning from Nairobi, Brig. Olum immediately summoned Col. Emmy Mulindwa, Commander of UGABAG 12, and battalion commanders Major Lugira, Major Ojuga and Major Ankankunda. In the next few days, he told them, he planned to make a move on Buulo Mareer, the first in a string of towns on the road to Baraawe where al-Shabaab was expected to put up a show of force. He needed to know that the troops were ready. The commanders responded they were ready to move.

On the afternoon of August 23, 2014, seemingly unconcerned about the looming battles to start within days with al-Shabaab, Brig. Olum took time from war planning to receive medical supplies donated by the US Department of State for use by AMISOM troops to treat Somali civilian patients. "We have been doing this in so many areas so we think up to the time we will go to Barawe, even when we pass through Kurtunwaaray, Bula Marer, Goliweyn we shall continue treating the people and this is one of the efforts we have been getting from the government of the United States and it continues to give us support with other partners," Olum informed the gathered media.[40] Then the Brigadier jumped into a 40-ton GILA fighting vehicle that he rustled from Villa Somalia "because President Hassan did not need it," and joined the convoy of armoured vehicles heading out for the war front to link up with UGABAG 12.

Operation Indian Ocean, the codename given the offensive, began on the evening of August 29, 2014, with Olum strictly rationing his troops to three days worth of dry food. Over the past months, because he was not assured that UNSOA would come through with food supply for his troops when he needed it, Olum carefully stashed away the dry goods whenever he could feed his troops cooked foods such as beans, maize meals and the like. "When you are poor, you learn how to make do and, so that's what you need for the next few days," Olum told his troops. Then, like all Uganda commanders, he fired the men up with patriotic UPDF songs and, soon, the vehicles were heading out toward the first objective— Buulo Marer.

The planned offensive was fairly straightforward. The 37th Bn of Maj. Lugira would move from Shalambooti and block off any rear reinforcement for al-Shabaab. Maj. Akankunda's 43rd Bn would converge from Quoryoleey on the right flank and, along with a unit of SNA, Maj. Ojuga's 61st Bn was the main attack force on the town. The march through the night was at first uneventful until the forward group reached Golweyn at dawn, a mere 8 kilometers from the objective, and began encountering some fire. A sniper shot and killed a member of the Special Forces but before he could hit again an artillery shell hit the window where the fire came from and silenced the killer. Further on, at the outskirt of town, the fighting intensified. Ojuga's big guns softened enemy positions, while the infantry inched closer within gun range. For six hours, fighting raged. al-Shabaab brought fresh fighters to support sagging defense lines, but Ojuga's troops relentlessly marched forward. Two AMISOM soldiers were injured, but there were no more deaths.

At 1:30 p.m. on August 30, 2014, the SNA supported by 61st Bn took Buulo Mareer and, although sporadic resistance popped up here and there, by 2:00 p.m. the 37th Bn had mostly completed the mop-up of the town. At 3:30 p.m. Brig. Olum called Deputy Force Commander Gen. Muheesi to tell him about the capture of Buulo Mareer. "You, what is wrong with you, what is the hurry?" Gen. Muheesi said in admiration. Brig. Olum had one more surprise for Gen. Muheesi. "In the next half hour, I am going to capture Kurtunwaarey," the commander said. "Are you out of your mind? You are going to be court-martialed for reckless endangerment of troops, that is sheer suicide," Gen. Muheesi cautioned.

Brig. Olum's mind was made up. He had carefully studied the way al-Shabaab fought. The insurgents often tried to overwhelm the opponent with concentrated fire but were unable to withstand prolonged fights. More importantly, whenever there was the element of surprise, the insurgents ran away in disarray. In al-Shabaab's thinking, Uganda troops took almost three months to move 30 kilometers from Quoryoleey to Buulo Mareer and, after the big fight in Buulo Marer that morning, it would be at least a few days or even a week before Uganda troops were expected in Kurtunwaarey. This was the optimal opportunity to attack the next town, Olum reasoned, and it was best to travel very light, with a small, fast but lethal attack force.

On the radio, Olum summoned Lt. Col. Don Williams Nabasa, commander of the Special Forces, and asked for the number of fighting vehicles Nabasa could assemble within a quarter hour. Twenty, Lt. Col. Nabasa answered. "Good, leave the mop-up of Buulo Marer to 37th Bn, and take 18 vehicles, each with 12 Special Forces. We are moving into Kurtunwaarey within the hour."

Lt. Col. Nabasa quickly assembled his men, and told them to board the South African and US-made APCs. The 15 kilometers drive to Kurtunwaarey began almost right away. Brig. Olum ordered his driver to break away from the vehicle formation, and pull ahead of the convoy. The commander insisted on leading from the front in his Gila fighting vehicle. At the edge of town, the convoy encountered firing. At first puzzled because the guns did not seem to be directed at the AU forces, it soon became apparent to Olum that posted lookouts were firing the shots. Completely surprised by the sudden appearance of AMISOM troops, the sentries were more concerned with warning residents of the town to flee than to stand and fight. Indeed, from a kilometer away, AMISOM troops could see a long lines of sleek looking SUVs, some with doors swinging open, hurriedly leaving center town in a cloud of dust. The mad dash on the road toward Baraawe was evidence that al-Shabaab was caught completely unaware and, rather than stand and fight, preferred quick exit to safety elsewhere.

Brig. Olum directed his vehicles toward a row of low buildings that appeared to have active insurgents. As the GILA approached, it encountered some fire from a particular building. The return fire set afire the shanty building that later was discovered to house several brand new, never driven motorcycles. An insurgent fighter emerged, machinegun in hand, dashing to gain cover from which to shoot at the oncoming AMISOM troops. Olum ordered his rooftop gunner to use the 12.7mm machinegun to take out the resistor. The gunner obliged and, with a quick burst of fire, the lone al-Shabaab fighter dropped to the ground, shattered into pieces. With the one-man resistance of Kurtunwaarey quickly dispatched off, the final push into the center of town was mostly quiet. The time was 4:30 p.m.

Brig. Olum again called Gen. Muheesi. Kurtunwaarey was liberated, the commander told his superior. "Dick, you are a complete mad man, of that I am convinced," said Gen. Muheesi, who then alerted the Force Commander Maj. Gen. Silas Ntigurirwa who was away in Burundi, and also informed the head of security for President Hassan. President Hassan called Brig. Olum within a few minutes, and asked if it was really true that Kurtunwaarey was in hand. Brig. Olum assured the Somalia president that, yes, the Ugandan forces had taken Kurtunwaarey and, even as he spoke, were already focusing their attention on Baraawe.

Unbeknown to Brig. Olum and his forces, the surprise takedown of Kurtunwaarey shook loose a much bigger prey. From a secret hideout in the town where he had been monitoring the fight in Buulo Marer early that day, al-Shabaab leader Abdi Godane was caught unprepared by the sudden entry of Uganda forces into the town, forcing him to flee, helter-skelter in the convoy of shiny SUVs seen speeding toward Baraawe. Godane, angry with his commanders for not anticipating the Uganda attack on Kurtunwaarey, activated his emergency phone to berate them, demanding to meet them immediately at a pre-arranged location. US intelligence had known for sometime from a paid informer that Godane owned this particular phone and, only in the very direst circumstances such as the sudden attack on Kurtunwaarey, would use it to communicate with his most trusted associates. Instantly alerted when Godane turned the phone on, US surveillance began tracking the device and, within minutes, the order for a hit was relayed to US warships in the Indian Ocean. On Monday evening at around 7:20 p.m. local time, September 1, 2014, loud explosions were head when US laser-guided Hellfire missiles struck a vehicle and buildings inside a compound in Dhay Tubaako neighbourhood (also called Dhayo) in Sablaale district, about 30 kilometers northwest of Baraawe, killing Godane and several al-Shabaab commanders gathered for a meeting.[41]

In the meantime, Brig. Olum rested his troops in Kurtunwaarey for a couple of weeks as he prepared the logistics for the final assault. The take down of Baraawe was anti-climactic. This time, keen to be part of the action, UNSOA opened the store to Brig. Olum. He could have whatever he needed to get the job done. There was a sense of excitement, and the soldiers told the commander they wanted to move on Baraawe quickly and return home to Uganda. The final preparation for taking Baraawe began on Tuesday, September 30, 2014. As troops amassed at Mojemereer, the order for the 37th Bn was to flank the north side, and position itself between Sablaale and Baraawe, cutting off possible reinforcement by the remnants forces of killed al-Shabaab leader Godane. Reinforced by 43rd and SNA troops, 61st Bn was the main attack force on Baraawe. Before attacking, Olum first sent out feelers to Baraawe to determine the level of resistance. Early Saturday, October 4, 2014, a team of Somali elder from Baraawe sought out the AMISOM commander. Baraawe, they told Brig. Olum was ready to receive AMISOM peacefully because al-Shabaab fighters had mostly withdrawn from the town, starting the previous day, Friday, October 3, 2014. Olum promised that with no resistance, there was no point destroying the town. AMISOM would only fight heavy resistance while avoiding civilian casualties.

Troops began moving toward Baraawe on the early morning of Sunday, October 5, 2014, making contact with the enemy at Mudule Baraawe, the junction where the road forked right toward Kismaayo, and left into the valley town of Baraawe. The high point gave the insurgent a vantage point to aim mortar, anti-aircraft and heavy machine gun fire at AMISOM troops. The following day, as the battle intensified, and al-Shabaab gunners seemingly untouchable, American MQ-1C Gray Eagle unmanned combat aircraft joined the fray, helping AMISOM artillery section to aim and deliver deadly volley of mortars that silenced the opposition. At 5:00 a.m. on Monday, October 6, 2014, AMISOM troops began marching down the valley into Baraawe.[42] There was no opposition. The only drama came later in midmorning at Sheikh Mahmoud Stadium where thousands of jubilant residents had gathered to welcome and dance with the liberators. Brig. Dick Olum summoned Abdikadhir Sheikh Mohammed Nor, the Governor of Lower Shabelle, to sit down and, to the howling delight of 15,000 Baraawe residents assembled in the town's square, used a pair of scissors to cut off the hair from the Somali leader's head. The Governor had wagered to cut off his hair if Baraawe was liberated within a month after the capture of Kurtunwaarey. It was, and the Governor was happy to lose his hair. Olum made a short address to the gathered crowd, saying, "AMISOM has come to make your children go to school, give you peace and...your wives to get good medical treatment. If AMISOM and SNA steal your property, report to us, we are here."

Brigadier Olum left shortly after, travelling by road back to Mogadishu where he caught a plane to Nairobi, and then travelled to South Africa. The purpose of his trip to Mandela's country was to respond to allegations by Human Rights Watch (HRW) of rapes and sexual exploitations of Somali women by AMISOM soldiers. Although the allegations contained in the report titled, *The Power these Men Have Over Us*," focused on Burundi forces and a few Ugandan soldiers, the report created the impression of an epidemic of sexual exploitation that tarred the reputation of all AMISOM troops.[43] Brig. Olum intended to confront Human Rights Watch to produce specific evidence so that alleged offenders could be brought to justice. The one thing he was not prepared to accept was a blanket accusation from the human rights agency against the entire force. The democratic principles that allowed the authors of the report to write whatever their imagination fancied should be extended to the soldiers to defend themselves. Instead, abandoning all principles of fair play, HRW chose to be the judge, jury and executioner. It was not right.

It was a different fight, in a different forum, one that AMISOM needed to get used to. Having demonstrated in the battlefield what peacekeeping looked like in the era of well-armed, well-resourced, well-educated and media-savvy insurgents, and how to confront, engage and contain them, AMISOM commanders like Brigadier Olum needed to learn to speak to the larger world audience about what really goes on in the battlefield, and why the old notion of peacekeeping where blue-hatted soldiers rattled around in white-painted vehicles no longer worked. The world needed to be educated that the new African peace warriors as abundantly demonstrated by AMISOM forces, unlike indisciplined militias and insurgents with no respect for authority and civilians lives, are professionals whose approach to peacemaking is based solidly on deep regards for all humans to live in peace.

AMISOM had redefined peacekeeping.

# AMISOM as a Template for Future Missions

Through the absence of war is not the same as the presence of peace. It is a reality that continental Africa retains many simmering conflicts, dormant like sleeping volcanoes, yet capable of exploding with such ferocity to claim lives and property within a short time span. The Democratic Republic of Congo, Central African Republic, Mali, Nigeria, South Sudan, Libya, Burundi, are some of the latest hotspots in the news cycle. Kenya's electoral violence in January 2008 was unprecedented by its magnitude and intensity. The world was equally unprepared for the violence that swept through South Sudan in January 2014, leaving more than 2007 people butchered in Bor town, north of Juba between January 10 and January 20, 2014. Ugandan troops finally intervened with swift force to end the bloodshed. A potential genocide was averted only because the UPDF separated the warring factions from further killing each other. Of course, Rwanda's 1994 genocide remains one of the most heinous crimes committed against humanity in modern times.

Simply, it is never too early to prepare for the next conflict on continental Africa with the potential to cause untold human suffering. As a template upon which to model future continental, even global peace missions, AMISOM offers enormous learning opportunity. The peace mission evolved over time into a success story. The crucial contributing factors included decisive African leadership, responsive and flexible UN support, and involvements of committed international partners including the EU, AU and permanent members of UNSC like the US. Other important considerations include willingness to contribute troops, clarity of mission, and command and control over multinational troops on the ground.

## Decisive African Leadership

Uganda's President Yoweri Museveni is known for his decisiveness as illustrated in this short anecdote. Around noon on Monday August 12, 2013, after officiating at the laying of the foundation stone at the proposed 600 megawatts (MW) Karuma hydro power project near Karuma Falls in northern Uganda, President Museveni took a short car ride back to his helicopter which sat waiting on the grass at a local primary school ground.[1] The president was pressed for time to get to his next appointment to address a rally in Mukono, in south central Uganda. Once inside the Russian-made MI17 helicopter, the president settled into his seat, and quietly waited for the familiar distinctive whine when the pilot fired up the chopper's engine. A minute went by. Nothing. There was complete silence. The president's security detail looked down at their shiny black military boots. Nobody spoke. Tension built. Then the pilot, a Ugandan, emerged into the cabin, saluted and addressed the leader.

"Mr. President, the helicopter will not start," said the pilot.

"What is the problem?" Museveni asked.

"Mr. President, I don't know. This has never happened before," replied the pilot.

"Do we have a back-up helicopter at Entebbe?" Museveni asked.

"No, Mr. President, we do not have one."

"Why not?"

"The back-up helicopter is currently being serviced, and will not be ready for a few days," the pilot responded.

"Okay," Museveni said calmly, "No problem, we go by road. Get the convoy to turn back," he ordered, before disembarking and walking to the shade of mvule trees where he stood, alone, waiting for the presidential motorcade rushing back to pick him for the 300 kilometer rough road trip to Mukono.

It was a small thing. But the incident provided a glimpse of how President Museveni confronts problems and issues that arise. Whether they are malfunctioning choppers or large scale airlifting of troops for continental peace missions, clear, practical and decisive leadership style has served him since assuming office in January 1986 as a fresh revolutionary who fought his way into power. These were the same qualities that Museveni employed in supporting the first successful African-led continental force whose intervention in Somalia prevented a potentially catastrophic conflict with consequences echoing Rwanda's 1994 genocide.

Indeed, a serious evaluation of the achievements of AMISOM in Somalia cannot overlook the leadership and contributions made by President Museveni. In the absence of formal frameworks and processes for compelling AU members to contribute troops for the mission, it was Museveni's forceful and unbending commitment that nurtured AMISOM, the concept peace-making vehicle, into a robust continental force that, at long last, is pacifying Somalia after decades of deadly internal conflicts. He deftly translated what was, until his involvement, a paper exercise into practical actions that included training the forces designated to serve in Somalia, selecting the best qualified, tested and experienced military commanders to lead the troops, and persuading Ugandans and other African leaders that this was a cause worthy of support.

Understandably, Museveni often reacted with anger when Ugandans suffered serious casualties as happened on May 1, 2007, September 17, 2009, July 11, 2010, December 25, 2014 and, the most grievous for Ugandan contingent serving in Somalia, the early morning al-Shabaab attack on Ugandan troops based in Janaale in Lower Shabelle on Tuesday, September 1, 2015. In all the cases, the setbacks served to reinforce Museveni's conviction, making him to double down, as it were, in the belief that AMISOM was the right vehicle for fighting al-Shabaab as a global terror group. "The responsibility of bringing peace to our region, the continent, is not one we should take lightly, especially when people are dying in conflict, then we need to act with resolve, fortitude and determination to do everything to bring a resolution," he said when asked about the motivation behind his commitment to AMISOM.[2]

Indeed, Museveni demonstrated flexibility for compromise and statesmanship at critical moments in the evolution of AMISOM into a viable and potent continental peace-force. He was widely consulted as part of the joint African Union-United Nations planning meetings of December 5-17, 2011 that developed the new AMISOM Concept of Operations (CONOPS).[3] Among the main recommendations arising from these meetings was the consolidation of all separate military operations in Somalia under a coordinated centralized command. Effectively, Kenyan and Ethiopian forces were invited to integrate and submit to AMISOM's command and control.[4] This arrangement also meant Uganda giving up the command of AMISOM. Until this point, by virtue of providing the bulk of AMISOM's force and as pioneer troop contributing country, AMISOM's force commanders came from Uganda—Gen. L. Karuhanga, Gen. F. Okello, Gen. N. Mugisha, Gen. F. Mugisha, and Gen. A. Gutti. Uganda lawmakers and military commanders had lobbied Museveni to specifically reserve the post for a Ugandan general.[5] But, prior to the meeting of ministers of defence and chief of defence staffs of troop contributing countries (TCC) in Nairobi on January 17, 2012, Museveni quietly instructed Uganda's representatives to support a sustainable structure that allowed leadership of AMISOM to rotate among the TCC. This was one way of building and strengthening AMISOM for the long run, Museveni later said.[6] The meeting decided that two deputy force commanders, one for Operations and Plans, and another for Support would deputize the Force Commander.[7] The next force commander, to be rotated in 2013, would come from Burundi, followed by a Kenyan and so on.

It was, however, in his role as statesman-mediator that President Museveni proved invaluable in preventing the unraveling of AMISOM in August 2013. Friction had developed between the Government of Somalia and Kenya over the latter's deep involvement in the regional politics of Lower Juba region. Since the liberation of Kismaayo in September 2012, Kenya mostly had free hand in strengthening the powers of its ally Sheikh Ahmed Mohamed Islam, better known as Ahmed Madobe, something the Americans feared could happen. This arrangement worked so far as Sheikh Madobe did not challenge the central authority of Mogadishu, which he did with a series of declarations for autonomy of Juba region from Mogadishu culminating with his election as President of Jubaland State on May 15, 2013.[8] Somalia's President Mahmoud Hassan, fairly new on the scene, was left with two choices; either keep quiet and watch Ahmed Madobe become a regional power house or assert the position of Mogadishu. He chose the latter option by appointing Col. Abbas Ibrahim Gurey (Abbas Dheere) as Division 43 SNA Commander responsible for the Kismaayo area. Col. Gurey came from the Gedo region in 2013, leading a militia group aligned with the SNA. On the morning of Friday, June 28, 2013, Col. Gurey was arrested by Kenya Defence Forces in Kismaayo and was rumoured taken to Wajir in Kenya.[9] By afternoon the same day, forces loyal to the colonel were engaged in a firefight with KDF-backed forces of Ahmed Madobe.

On Sunday, June 30, 2013, with the situation in Kismaayo escalating into a bigger conflict, Somalia Deputy Prime Minister and Minister for Foreign Affairs, Fawzia Yusuf Haji Adan, known in the local media as the "Iron Lady" of Somalia,[10] fired off a toughly worded three-paged letter to Ambassador Ramtane Lamamra, AU Commissioner for Peace and Security. With a subject line that read 'Extremely Urgent—Kismaayo conflict', the words "Extremely Urgent" appearing in red fonts, the letter was copied to the AU Special Representative of the Chairman of the Commission (SRCC) for Somalia, Ambassador Mahamat Saleh Annadif, Chairperson for AU Commission Dr. Nkosazana Dlamini Zuma, and AMISOM Force Commander Lt. Gen. Andrew Gutti.[11] The minister pulled no punches, accusing KDF in Kismaayo of not being neutral, in effect, backing one Somali faction over another, thereby causing an outbreak of fighting with preliminary death toll at 65 and 155 injured. What's more, the letter went on, all these was due to the "incompetence" and "poor judgment" of the KDF Commander Brig. Gen. Anthony Ngere whose interference with Somalia Government initiative for SNA forces in Juba region caused the arrest of Col. Abbas Ibrahim Gurey. As redress, Deputy Prime Minister Fawzia Adan sought the immediate removal of KDF forces from Kismaayo, to be replaced by a neutral AMISOM force. Without naming names, Somalia Deputy Minister for Information, telecommunications and Postal Services Abdishakur Ali Mire, reiterated the same talking point to the media later the same day.[12] Somalia President Mahmoud Hassan also expressed his own frustration, acknowledging the drastic step taken to write the letter, saying, "In ten months, we have never complained, now we are forced to write a letter to the AU."[13]

Amplified by sensational media headlines in Kenya,[14] the conflict threatened to kill the budding relationship between Kenya and Somalia and, with it, Kenya's participation in AMISOM. Playing the statesman, President Museveni arranged a summit at Speke Resort and Conference Centre, Munyonyo, Kampala, starting with a ministerial level meeting on Saturday, August 3, 2013 and culminating with heads of state summit on Sunday, August 4, 2013. The conference themed "Towards a Harmonized Approach by the Stakeholders in Building a Peaceful Somalia," barely hinted at the gravity of the situation in Juba region. With President Museveni as host and chair, the meeting brought all the key players under one roof including Hailemariam Desalegn, Prime Minister of Ethiopia, Uhuru Kenyatta, President of Kenya, and Hassan Sheikh Mohamud, President of Somalia. The Minister of Defence, Hassan Darar Houfaneh, represented the Government of Djibouti. Gabriel Nizigama, Minister of Public Security represented the Republic of Burundi and, Permanent Representative to the AU Andrew Gbebay Bangali, represented the Government of Sierra Leone. Ambassador Mahamat Saleh Annadif, Special Representative of the Chairperson of the Commission (SRCC) and Head of Mission, AMISOM, represented the African Union.

Tension and hostility was discernible during the Saturday morning ministerial session between, on the one side, the Kenyan delegation led by Secretary of Defence Rachel Awuor Omamo and Secretary of Foreign Affairs Amina Mohamed and, on the other, Somalia Deputy Prime Minister and Minister for Foreign Affairs, Fawzia Yusuf H. Adan and her delegation. The Deputy Prime Minister wasted little precious time getting to the heart of the matter. Kenya was meddling in Kismaayo and, by supporting one clan, turned the port city into a serious conflict zone.[15] The list of grievances was long, but, in not so many words, Kenya had to get out of Kismaayo, concluded Fawzia Adan.

Scandalised by the accusation of KDF's meddling in Kismaayo, Kenya's Defence Secretary Omamo, supported by Foreign Affairs Secretary Amina Mohammed, a Somali by descent, shot back with barely concealed contempt, leaving the strong impression that should matter become physical she could take on anyone in the Somali delegation. Were it not for the timely intervention of Kenya's Defence Forces, Kismaayo and all of Juba would still be in the hands of al-Shabaab.[16] By the time recess was called, the atmosphere had degenerated into finger pointing between the Kenyan and Somalia delegations.

No doubt briefed about what happened in the morning, President Museveni kept out of sight the three heads of state. Joined by representatives from Burundi, Djibouti and Sierra Leone, away from the raucous gathering, the leaders crafted a win-win plan that saw Kenya continue to play important military role in the pacification of Somalia, but essentially reduced KDF's dominancy in Jubaland by bringing Ethiopia to the Gedo region and Sierra Leone troops into Sector Two. With the draft agreement already finalized behind the scene, the leaders emerged into the conference hall, unified in front of cameras, only for the reading of the communiqué by Uganda's minister for foreign Affairs, Sam Kutesa. The language was unequivocally clear. Foremost, "the control of the Kismaayo seaport and airport should be handed over to the Federal Government of Somalia (FGS)."[17] Asserting FGS's control over Somali militias, the communiqué required that "all militias should be integrated into the Somalia National Security Forces," and for AMISOM to "urgently work out the modalities and operationalization of an AMISOM multinational force to be deployed in Kismaayo."

A full conflict between two AU neighbours was averted. Later that Sunday evening after President Uhuru and Prime Minister Desalegn had returned home, President Museveni invited President Hassan and a few guests to State House, Nakasero. The tension of the weekend gone, a jovial Museveni spent time mentoring Hassan on the art of building a national, unified and professional armed forces. Most important of all considerations, he told Hassan, is the recruiting, training and retaining of well-educated officers corps.[18] Possibly, this was nothing new to President Hassan, but it was an opportunity too good to pass for the two leaders to build rapport and, for President Museveni to use his experience and skills as the commander-in-chief of one of Africa's most professional forces, to support the rebuilding of Somalia National Army with the support of AMISOM. There was genuine respect and friendship between the two men.

Listening to the two men converse, the observer could not help thinking how Somalia, from a nation that was given up for dead had, like the Greek's mythical phoenix bird, risen from the ashes to this moment when its leader could sit, talk and laugh about endless possibilities. The first instinct to yell out aloud—AMISOM made this possible!- was immediately tempered by the recognition that the pioneering architecture of African leaders like President Museveni who believed in the abilities of African troops to bring change in Somalia, ultimately, were proven right because the international community through various institutions and agencies rallied around with firm commitments in funding and resources.

In time, naturally, the conversation of the two presidents drifted to the continued support of AMISOM and Government of Somalia by the international community. Both leaders felt positively good that the world continued to rally around the progress in Somalia—the AU, UN, EC, US, even the Gulf States were working together to lift Somalia from its former misery into a place of hope. President Hassan revealed he was keenly looking forward to attend the "New Deal Compact" for Somalia conference organised by the European Union in Brussels, the following month on September 16, 2013. The EU was committed to contributing funds and resources toward the five peace and state building goals articulated by Somalia government including building inclusive politics, security, justice, economic foundations and revenue collections and provision of services.[19] Since April 2010, the European Union Training Mission (EUTM) under successive commanders—Colonel Ricardo Gonzalez Elul (Spain), Colonel Michael Beary (Ireland) and, starting February 1, 2013, Brigadier General Gerald Aherne (Ireland)—used Bihanga military training school in Ibanda District in western Uganda to train Somalia security forces, focusing on non-commissioned officers (NCOs), junior officers, specialists and trainers.[20] EU was also contributing to fighting piracy at sea using EU Naval Force (EU NAVFOR), training of women leaders, supporting agriculture and schools.

But as both Hassan and Museveni knew well, the Peace and Security Commission, hitherto little known AU department deserved recognition for the Somalia mission. To be fair, IGAD was instrumental in laying the groundwork and, presumptively, insisting that an African-led mission could intervene to reverse Somalia's worsening crisis. Instead of being seen as emblematic of the failure of African nations to act in crisis situations, the demise of IGASOM should be viewed as the necessary step that gave birth to the creation of AMISOM.

The leadership and sophistication required for moving the Somalia mission concept onto the operational stage was beyond what Ambassador Attalla and IGAD could provide. Instead, PSC was instrumental in developing AMISOM and, in turn, being transformed in stature as an indispensable agency of the AU with the experience, skills and expertise to manage and support peace missions on the continent. Under Algerian diplomat Said Djinnit, the department oversaw the creation and deployment of AMISOM in 2007. On March 6, 2007, the first day AMISOM deployed to Somalia, Ambassador Djinnit brimmed with optimism as he welcomed into his office in Addis Ababa, Somalia representative to the AU, Abdikarin Farah, for the signing of the Status of Mission Agreement (SOMA).[21] Djinnit expressed confidence that other AU members would step forward quickly to contribute troops to support the mission. By the time he left a year later, with the exception of Burundi that sent a small force in December 2007, it had not happened.

Instead, the building of the infrastructure elements to support the struggling mission fell to Djinnit's successor Ambassador Ramtane Lamamra, also an Algerian. Sworn on April 28, 2008, Lamamra quickly pushed the department to oversee AMISOM's evolution from a peacekeeping role to robust and lethal peacemaking one that took on Somali insurgents. Under Lamamra's leadership, the AU Peace and Security Commission became a highly responsive bureaucracy capable of making quick decisions, pulling together at short notice various stakeholders under one roof in Addis Ababa, writing critical reports on the progress in the field, liaising with various AU members, troops contributing countries and the Somalia government, and keeping connected with the all-important United Nations Security Council on whose directives AMISOM was being funded and provided the resources it needed to do its work. Lamamra developed a close working relationships with various UN leaders over the year, often making the trips to New York to personally brief UNSC on progress on the ground in Somalia and, naturally, ask for more funds for the mission as he did on October 21, 2010.[22] In the wake of the devastating twin bombing in Halaane Base in Mogadishu in September 2009, the Peace and Security Commission led the debate and the drafting of outline of what AMISOM needed to become if it were to survive long enough to support Somalia's TFG.

Along the way as the mission grew more complex, in size of troops, the number of troops contributing countries, and operational decisions, the AU created the ministerial level Joint Coordination Mechanism (JCM). At its inaugural meeting in Addis Ababa on April 11, 2012, the advisory body was defined as supporting the AU Commission on strategic and political issues regarding the deployment and operations of AMISOM, reviewing progress of the military effort in Somalia and providing advice on how to enhance the effectiveness of the campaign toward a successful conclusion.[23] The Military Operations Coordination Committee (MOCC, meanwhile, brought chief of defence staffs to tackle practical issues relating to operations in the field and outside of it.[24]

On October 12, 2013 in Addis Ababa, following his appointment as the Foreign Minister of Algeria on 11 September 2013, Ambassador Lamamra was succeeded by, yet another Algerian, Ambassador Smail Chergui.[25] At the helm Ambassador Chergui supported AMISOM's coordination and training of Somali troops and police,[26] and civil outreach programs including the empowerment of Somali women. On November 12, 2012,

AMISOM Gender Office organised in Mogadishu a one-day workshop with the theme 'Empowering Somali Women and Engaging Elders and Politicians', enabling the voices of Somali women to be heard.[27] The success of AMISOM, more importantly that of the AU itself in managing the mission, was celebrated by none other than the Special Representative of the Chairman of the Commission (SRCC) Ambassador Maman Sidikou who has established his offices in Mogadishu. Writing in the opening remarks for the glossy 16th edition of *AMISOM Magazine: On the Edge of Success* (May-August 2015), Ambassador Sidikou beamed, "We are looking at an exciting future for Somalia. I acknowledge effort by all who work tirelessly to contribute to Somalia's success story. Together we are re-writing this country's history."[28] Glowingly mentioned by name was United Nations Assistance Mission in Somalia (UNSOM), underscoring the good working relationship between the UN and AU in Somalia. And, of course, the United States of America as well.

## International Sponsor and Cheerleader

Few in the international community could foresee the success that AMISOM later became. Instead, the efforts of the United States of America, a powerful member of the UN Security Council, was crucial in engaging the UN and the international community on Somalia generally and AMISOM specifically, ensuring that the mission did not remain mere framework of naked ideas looking for an opportunity to be implemented. To be sure, the US is no fan of UN-style peacekeeping and has long quietly complained about the cost of UN peacekeeping operations. A year into his tenure as the US Ambassador to the United Nations, Zalmay Khalilzad wrote to his bosses at the State Department, on February 29, 2009, looking to rally them to confront what he saw as escalating cost and lack of accountability in peacekeeping. The cable titled, "Strategy for more effective peacekeeping operations", openly griped about "unprecedented 90,883 peacekeepers deployed across seventeen peacekeeping operations" at the staggering cost of $7 billion for the financial year 2008, of which the US was footing $2.2 billion.[29]

It was time, Ambassador Khalilzad argued, to look at each operation to determine its viability and, where there is none, terminate it altogether. "Instead of rubber-stamping existing PKOs, the Security Council needs a mandate renewal process that...emphasizes accountability within a strategic framework, and, where appropriate, seriously considers termination of PKOs," he wrote. Khalilzad had a clear mind on where the axe should fall. "USUN requests an update on Department thinking as to a strategy towards the closure of UNFICYP and MINURSO....MINURSO mandate renewal is 30 April. UNFICYP mandate renewal is 15 June," the diplomat wrote.

Ambassador Khalilzad had a point. United Nations Peacekeeping Forces in Cyprus (UNFICYP) was a dinosaur created in 1964 to keep the Greek Cypriot and Turkish Cypriot communities from killing each other. Four decades after its creation, UNFICYP had outlived its usefulness. The two sides are not fighting any more. Then there was United Nations Mission for the Referendum in Western Sahara (MINURSO), established on April 29, 1991 to support the people of Western Sahara to decide through a referendum whether to integrate with Morocco or go their separate independent ways. The referendum never took place. Instead, the entire decade was frittered away working to determine who was who within the various tribes through a very complicated identification process of individuals.[30]

Ambassador Khalilzad did not say it in the cable, but the UN had a knack for harvesting bitter outcomes on continental Africa even in cases where success was fairly attainable. Rwanda 1994 was an apocalyptic failure to act by United Nations Assistance Mission in Rwanda (UNAMIR).[31] United Nations Advance Mission in the Sudan (UNAMIS) established in 2004, and transformed in March 2005 to United Nations Mission in the Sudan (UNMIS) barely functioned to keep warring factions apart.[32] In moments of utter despair over UN lack of actions in such cases, one imagined UN bureaucrats in suits, working in air-conditioned offices in New York and drinking café lattes, doing everything possible to maintain the UN brand as a peace promoting world body, not worrying about the lives of folks facing possible genocide. Moreover, one further imagined, when thing went wrong and all else failed, the motto of these UN bureaucrats is CYB (Cover Your Butt), and ensure the inevitable reports indicate that all protocols were observed.

That seems to be the case with United Nations Organization Stabilization Mission in the Democratic Republic of the Congo (MONUSCO). After taking over from its equally impotent predecessor the United Nations Organization Mission in the Democratic Republic of the Congo (MONUC), on May 28, 2010, MONUSCO was, among others, mandated "to the protection of civilians, humanitarian personnel and human rights defenders under imminent threat of physical violence and to support the Government of the DRC in its stabilization and peace consolidation efforts."[33]

From a mere 5,537 troops in March 2000, the mission had by May 2010 ballooned to 19,000 military personnel. Despite MONUSCO's superior firepower, at the collosal operational cost of $1.4 bn a year,[34] on Tuesday, November 20, 2012, the UN force stood aside while M23 rebels commanded by General Bosco Ntaganda sauntered into Goma town in Eastern DRC.[35] Ntaganda had a reputation for mass killings, and was indicted of war crimes by the International Criminal Court (ICC) on January 12, 2006.[36] The UN history in Africa was a mess and, on that day, MONUSCO did little to improve that image.

But with AMISOM, it was different. The US, guided by what it did not want AMISOM to become—another expensive UN-sponsored peace mission on continental Africa with little to show for it—hand managed many of the Security Council resolutions on AMISOM, guided the debates in different fora including the International Contact Group and took leadership when it mattered to round up support and resources from reluctant or indifferent members. Discussions to turn AMISOM into a UN peacekeeping operation, while not completely discouraged (resolutions 1772 (2007) and 1814 (2008)), were politely parried aside. On January 16, 2009, the Security Council passed Resolution 1863, for instance, directing the Secretary-General to "submit a report for a United Nations Peacekeeping Operation by 15 April 2009, to include developments in the situation in Somalia, progress towards the full deployment and strengthening of AMISOM with a view to transition to a United Nations Peacekeeping Operation..."[37]

However, with the helping hand of the US all over it, in his report to the Security Council on April 16, 2009, the Secretary General made it clear that the situation in Somalia was "extremely volatile and unpredictable."[38] The report noted that a contingency plan for re-hatting AMISOM into a UN peacekeeping operation existed and was reviewed in February 2009. The SG cautioned, however, that the deployment and the transfer of authority from AMISOM to the United Nations operation "not be determined arbitrarily, but should be contingent on critical factors including availability of the essential military capabilities." To that point, the report revealed that on February 19, 2009, the Office of Military Affairs in the Department of Peacekeeping Operations sent "notes verbales" to

60 Member States to determine whether there was an appetite for contributing troops for a mission should the Security Council decide to establish a United Nations peacekeeping operation for Somalia. "Only 10 Member States responded, all in the negative," the report revealed. It is a safe bet that if the US threw its weight behind the idea such lack of enthusiasm could be reversed. Understandably, America's only focus was ensuring a responsive and flexible UN support to make AMISOM a successful mission.

## Responsive and Flexible UN Support

Ban Ki-moon, the outgoing Secretary General of the United Nations, was barely three weeks into the job as the head of the UN in January 2007 when the concept of an African-led peace mission, later AMISOM, took practical shape on January 19, the day AU PSC adopted the decision for "deployment of an AU peace support mission" in Somalia.[39] Boosted by strong support from the AU, US and EU, under Ki-moon the UN became a tacit backer of the mission to Somalia from its infancy, along the way, overseeing the passing of important resolutions starting with Resolution 1744 (2007) that gave AMISOM the Chapter 7 mandate to operate in Somalia. In essence, with strong urging of the US, the UN focused on supporting AMISOM, to make it succeed. Using its existing Nairobi-based United Nations Political Office for Somalia (UNPOS), at the time, led by Ambassador Ahmedou Ould-Abdallah (Mauritania) as Special Representative of the Secretary-General (SRSG) for Somalia and, in June 2010, by Dr. Augustine P. Mahiga (Tanzania), the UN pushed for and organized high level international conferences involving International Contact Group (ICG), donors and contributors in support of Somalia and AMISOM including the Djibouti Peace Agreement in June 2008,[40] Brussels on April 23, 2009,[41] and the First and Second Istanbul conferences on Somalia in May 2010[42] and June 2012[43] respectively. To effectively manage funds, resources, equipment and logistics slated for AMISOM, United Nations Support Office for AMISOM (UNSOA) was created under Resolution 1863 on January 16, 2009.[44]

With time, it was important that funding was assured through assessed contributions of UN members. On May 26, 2009, the Security Council took the boldest step by passing resolution 1872 which guaranteed a logistical support package of equipment and services for the mission, and encouraged members to contribute to the United Nations Trust Fund for AMISOM.[45] The funds and corollary support were to be administered by UN Support Office for AMISOM (UNSOA) based, at first, in Nairobi and subsequently moved to Mogadishu. It was the booster AMISOM needed to transform into a robust force capable of taking on al-Shabaab. Meanwhile, to broaden and strengthen direct on-the-ground international support for Somalia generally and AMISOM specifically, the UN phased out UNPOS, replacing it with United Nations Assistance in Somalia (UNSOM) on May 2, 2013.[46] In a letter to the UN Security Council dated April 19, 2013, in anticipation of the new agency, Secretary General Ban Ki-moon wrote that Somalia needed a "one-door" approach from its international partners, making sure to avoid "fragmented, duplicative efforts at international assistance."[47] "I am determined to reinforce coherence and close cooperation through the United Nations system to ensure focused, effective support," Ki-Moon wrote.

On April 29, 2013, putting his words into action, the Secretary General appointed as the new Special Representative of the Secretary General (SRSG) to Somalia and head of UNSOM, Ambassador Nicholas Kay. A veteran of diplomacy in some of Africa's and world's toughest neighbourhoods, Kay had served as the UK ambassador to the Democratic Republic of Congo from 2007 to 2010, and in the Republic of Sudan from 2010 to 2012. Before that, he worked in Helmand Province, Afghanistan, from 2006 to 2007 as Regional Coordinator for Afghanistan and head of the Provincial Reconstruction Team.[48] Immediately likable, energetic, genuine and down-to-earth,[49] Ambassador Kay's immediate action was to move UN staff from Nairobi to Mogadishu in June 2013. Kay then embarked on broadening support and building capacity for the Government of Somalia, meeting on a regular basis with President Mahmoud Hassan, local, provincial, national and international Somalia leaders and civil population. All the while, Kay ensured that UNSOA, now absorbed into UNSOM, continued to provide the support AMISOM needed in its drive to expand and consolidate territory under the control of the Government of Somalia.

It was no easy task for Ambassador Kay to coordinate the diverse UN-supported Somalia initiatives in a fast changing, even dangerous political and social landscape. On Wednesday June 19, 2013, as his staff began unpacking in Mogadishu, the United Nations Development Programme (UNDP) base was attacked, first, by a car bomb, and then by gunmen. Ambassador Kay spoke out against the violence, saying, "The UN is here to help and we are here to stay."[50] Two months later, on Monday September 2, 2013, Ambassador Kay addressed a large section of Somalia society and international delegates at the successful Mogadishu conference themed Vision 2016, and declared "UNSOM is based in Somalia. I have no house in Nairobi. You are not alone. We are here to help and we are here to stay as long as we're needed."[51] Five days later, on Saturday, September 7, 2013, there was a double suicide attacks that began with a car bomb at the Village Restaurant in Mogadishu. As by-standers gathered at the chaotic scene, a second suicide-bomber blew up in the crowd, leaving over 20 dead and over 50 wounded.[52] Many condemned the savagery of the terror actions. Ambassador Kay also added his indignant voice as the UN representative to Somalia. In the face of terror, Kay put out a fresh statement, saying, "I am appalled by this act of savagery and condemn it in the strongest terms. I offer my sincere condolences to the families and friends of those killed and wish a speedy recovery to the injured".[53]

Occasionally, Ambassador Kay's sincere efforts were misread or misunderstood. Brig. Dick Olum recalled how, shortly after arriving on September 23, 2013, taking over from Acting Contingent Commander Brigadier Deus Sande, as the new contingent commander for Ugandan forces, his first meeting with Ambassador Kay began on the wrong footing. Olum recalled, "After a bomb blast in Mogadishu killed many people a UN official had cancelled a planned trip abroad to return to Mogadishu."[54] Brigadier Olum saw the action by the UN official whom he had not met as an empty grandstanding, even self-promotion. "After the bomb blast, some UN official said he was cancelling his trip to return to Mogadishu, just what exactly did he think he was coming back to do here?" Olum recalled saying out aloud at his first interagency meeting between AMISOM and the UN. There was silence in the room. An elbow away, Ambassador Kay sat quietly. Later, Brigadier Olum recalled with much laughter, it dawned on him that the "UN fellow" he referred to was the Boss, Ambassador Nicholas Kay.

By the time Brigadier Olum returned home to Uganda in November 2014, triumphant after capturing large territory from al-Shabaab including Baraawe, friction between UN personnel and AMISOM commanders were far in between. Ambassador Kay's patience toward consensus building, and never-ending international lobbying efforts on behalf of

AMISOM had helped build a stronger, enduring and robust mission to meet the changing nature of terror, build the security sector in Somalia and support the political and social rehabilitation of the once shattered nation, now on the mend. His skills in working with partners came in handy in the creation of the United Nations Guard Unit (UNGU) in Mogadishu, consisting of 410 personnel drawn from the ranks of Uganda Peoples Defense Forces (UPDF), and inaugurated on May 18, 2014. UNGU ensured that the UN could continue supporting the rebuilding of Somalia with meaningful work within the communities.

## Other Considerations

With international support assured, the effective continental peace mission modeled on AMISOM must necessarily confront and overcome some of the issues that slowed down AMISOM. Clarity of mission, for instance, plagued AMISOM's from the start. Was it a peacekeeping or a peacemaking mission? The goal of any peace mission should be crystal clear to everyone, from the top commander to the lowest rank and file, what is to be achieved and how information is transmitted to the boots on the ground. In the case of AMISOM, clarity of the mission evolved with time, almost three years in the making, before troops were able to start making progress in controlling the environment in Mogadishu and, subsequently, elsewhere in Somalia. Once the troops understood what was needed, namely, to make peace happen because there was none to keep, they were able to do their job, taking Mogadishu and expanding the area of control to the rest of Somalia.

Consideration at the AU level must also look at the mechanism for troop contribution. This important element of peace missions cannot be left to the whims and preferences of each member nation. After Ugandan troops deployed in March 2007, it was an uphill battle getting other African nations to join the mission. Despite the US practically sleeping on the doorsteps of many nations, begging for troops, only Burundi initially stepped forward. The rest trickled in almost four years later.

Rather, responding to crisis such as Rwanda's 1994 genocide and South Sudan in 2013 is the duty of each AU member nation. Just as the United Nations has a system of assessing funding contributions from member states for peacekeeping operations, the AU must operationalize a mechanism for assessing member states to contribute troops for various missions. Of course such a process must take into account factors such as frontline states, past history of conflicts between troop contributing members and receiving nation.

Equally imperative, the men and women deployed in peace missions must be well-trained professionals with experiences as soldiers. The rigorous trainings, combat experience and, most important, the ideological conditioning of troops from Uganda Peoples Defence Forces (UPDF) provided the character strength upon which AMISOM's success was built. Every soldier in the UPDF, from the highest to the lowest ranked, understood the commitment and sacrifice needed to do the job right in Somalia. It was never about the money. This was part of their duties as Africans, a mantra drilled again and again at every opportunity where two or three soldiers were gathered. The professionalism displayed by Ugandan troops enabled, at long last, for ordinary Somali people to learn that the army uniform can bring peace and development that helps people.

That said, casualties registered by some of the contingents over the last eight years were due to avoidable mistakes, mostly because of lack of experience and training. The most practical step toward a professional and ideologically committed peace force is to make it a requirement for future African forces to train together. Such trainings cannot be relegated to weekend exercises that peremptorily bring soldiers of different nations together to present 'trooping the colour', before dispersing them on their separate journeys. Viable training must be scheduled for longer periods, two to three months, where soldiers from different nations bunk, train, and plan together, learning from each other, and taking orders from a single command structure. Such a force, at least five to six battalion strong, could be the tip of the spear, the leading African force that moves with efficient speed to intervene wherever needed on continental Africa, or elsewhere on the globe.

## Command and Control

According to David Alberts and Richard Hayes clear command and control involves establishing goals, determining roles and responsibilities, establishing rules and constraints, and monitoring and assessing the situation and progress.[55] In AMISOM, the Force Commander under whom all the contingents work is the overseer of operational plans. It is his responsibility to work with the contingent commanders to plan and execute a coherent plan involving all the elements and resources required for success. While this was not a huge problem in AMISOM, mainly because the force commanders were strong, effective and successful leaders with established experiences, there were hints of potential problems lurking just beneath the surface. During Operation Free Shabelle to capture Afgooye in May 2012, for example, Burundi forces failed to move forward as agreed forcing Ugandan forces to improvise to fill the gap. The Kenyan Defense Forces (KDF) worked almost autonomously in Lower Juba, far away from Mogadishu. Djibouti arrived in December 2011, did not begin to work until early 2014, and seemed to take its cues from Djibouti. Ethiopia almost the lone wolf, operated from the fringes, doing its own thing.

Any peace mission fashioned on AMISOM will have to evaluate the issue of command and control. Foremost, the mission must augment the command and control of the Force Commander (FC) whose authority should be implemented by the contingent commanders. The contingent commanders must have autonomous control over their troops in the course of executing the task/mission ordered by the FC, but not the freedom to choose whether they will or will not participate in a mission.

To be fair, some of the problems of command and control had to do with language barrier. The Tower of Babel syndrome, where communication is limited among troops and commanders from different nations, could critically cripple the rapid transmission of operational information and command. On a number of occasions during the battle for Mogadishu, there were moments of anxieties when Uganda troops could not determine the movements or plans of the Burundi forces operating to the northwest of Bakaara. Following an incident in which his troops almost fired on a Burundi unit because of lack of communication, a Uganda commander became extra careful, even hesitating from engaging the insurgents for fear of causing casualties from friendly fire.

While translators could be deployed among the thousands of troops working in close proximity to one another, this is not efficient or practical. Instead a peacekeeping mission fashioned on AMISOM must explore the possibility of bundling together troops that speak similar languages such as Kiswahili, English, and French on a mission. Although they operated in different sectors, Uganda and Kenya use Kiswahili as common *lingua franca*. Somalia and Djibouti troops, with shared kinship, communicate fairly easily in Somali and, to a limited extent, in Afar language also spoken in Ethiopia. Such linguistic fusions support better communication, clear command, and efficient execution of mission.

All the foregoing observations boil down to the necessity for a strong standby African peace force mandated by the UN, supported by the international community and led by Africans. Understandably, the Bangladeshis, Pakistanis, Indians, Paraguayans and Fijians troops have established track records as peacekeepers with the UN. What they lack, however, is the visceral commitment to intervene effectively in African conflicts. They are not in it because they deeply feel the commitment to lay down their lives for the suffering Africans. They are in the Democratic Republic of Congo, South Sudan and elsewhere on the continent to do a job for which they are paid handsome salaries. That needs to change in a hurry.

Without starting from scratch, there already exists five African regional standby forces that make up the African Standby Force (ASF), including the North Africa Regional Capability (NARC),[56] Economic Community of West African States (ECOWAS),[57] Economic Community of Central African States (ECCAS), and Southern Africa Development Community (SADC), and the Eastern African Standby Force (EASF). Both EASF and SADC are making some progress. Formerly East African Standby Brigade (EASBRIG) created in February 2004 in Jinja, Uganda,[58] and renamed in 2011, EASF has established a planning element (PLANELM) and Eastern Africa Standby Force Coordination Mechanism (EASFCOM) based in Nairobi, Kenya. Supported by the UN, EU, AU, France, Norway, Netherlands, Japan, Germany and the US, it has field-tested troops training on several occasions, in Uganda, Comoros, and Kenya. It also ran a Command Post Exercise (CPX) in Adama, Ethiopia from November 13-24, 2014, which brought together troops from 10 East African countries.[59] While a start, with AU and international support, it needs to be expanded into a true standing force, fully trained and equipped to respond with resolve in crisis.

SADC contingent, launched on August 17, 2007 in Lusaka, Zambia, with South Africa as the lead force, has also established planning elements, and made steady progress toward operationalizing the troops.[60] As the main force, it hosted as many as 5,000 personnel from around Africa for training at the South African Army Combat Training Centre in Lohatlha, Northern Cape from October 19 to November 7, 2015.[61]

Of course, such large standby forces require huge logistics, funding and equipment dedicated specifically for their use. The blessing and support of the United Nations and the international community are foundational and irreplaceable. However, when viewed as an investment in peace, and that the cost of doing nothing is higher when human lives are at stake as happened in Rwanda, creating and supporting such a force is the least expensive option. AMISOM offers the template on which to build future peace missions that successfully resolve conflicts on continental Africa, and elsewhere on the globe before they get out of hand.

# Notes

## Preface

1   Kerry A. Trask, *Black Hawk: The Battle for the Heart of America* (New York: Henry Holt and Company, 2007).

2   Wild Life Campus, "Credo Mutwa" (blog), Birds, beautiful fertilisers of earth, http://www.wildlifecampus.com/Help/PDF/Folklore_Birds.pdf

3   Jenny Hill, "Horus", Ancient Egypt (blog), http://www.ancientegyptonline.co.uk/horus.html; Also see Dr. Zahi Hawass, "Horus: The Falcon God" (blog), http://www.guardians.net/hawass/horus.htm

## Introduction

1   **Introduction:** Creighton Peet, "They Keep the Tower Clock Running," *Popular Mechanics*, 106, no.6 (1956), 82-84.

Also see "346 Broadway Tower Clock," (blog) http://www.clocks.org/new_york_state/ny_manhattan_broadway_346_index.html,

2   Also see David W. Dunlap, "A Tower Clock in Danger of Losing its Purpose," *New York Times*, November 12, 2014, http://www.nytimes.com/

The immediate death toll including the 19 hijackers was 2996. However, since the events of 9/11, many more deaths including among first responders have been recorded and attributed directly to the events of that day.

3   National Commission on Terrorist Attacks, The 9/11 Commission Report: Final Report of the National Commission on Terrorist Attacks Upon the United States (New York, NY: W.W. Norton & Company, 2004).

4   *ibid.*,4

5   Al-Itihaad al-Islamiya (AIAI), an international Muslim brotherhood with an offshoot in Somalia, was listed under "Terrorists and Groups" in the original Executive Order 13224 signed by President George W. Bush on September 23, 2001, http://www.state.gov/j/ct/rls/other/des/122570.htm

6   See example in Lucy Hannan, "City Life: Mogadishu: Mobiles Mean Business Amid the Ruins," *The Independent*, Monday, May 17, 1999, http://www.independent.co.uk/news/city-life-mogadishu-mobiles-mean-business-amid-the-ruins-1094216.html

7   "Films set in Somalia," Wikipedia, "https://en.wikipedia.org/wiki/Category:Films_set_in_Somalia

## Chapter 1

1   "Welcome to Prime Minister Abdirashid of Somalia," Papers of John F. Kennedy. Presidential Papers. President's Office Files. November 27, 1962, doi:JFKPOF-041-032

2   John F. Kennedy, "Remarks of Welcome at the White House to the Prime Minister of the Somali Republic," November 27, 1962. Online by Gerhard Peters and John T. Woolley, The American Presidency Project. http://www.presidency.ucsb.edu/ws/?pid=9028.

3   Tom Cooper, Wings over Ogaden War, the Ethiopian-Somali War, 1978-1979, (Solihull, West Midlands: Helion & Company, 2015). Also see Tom Cooper and Gianfranco Lanini, "Air Combat Information Group (ACIG)," Online publication www.acig.info/

4    Christian A. Herter, "Telegram from the Department of State to the Embassy in Italy," US Department of State: Foreign Relations of the United States, April 15, 1960, 1958-1960, 14, no. 48, https://history.state.gov/historicaldocuments/frus1958-60v14/d48

5    Robert Patman, The Soviet Union in the Horn of Africa: The Diplomacy of Intervention and Disengagement (New York: Cambridge University Press, 1990).

6    John F. Kennedy, "Desk Set: Box with Crest of Somali," John F. Kennedy, Presidential Library and Museum, doi:JFKSG-MO-1963-506e

7    US Department of State, "Memorandum of Conversation," Office of the Historian, Foreign Relations of the United States 1961-63, (Africa)21, no. 285, https://history.state.gov/historicaldocuments/frus1961-63v21/d285#fnref1

8    "Photograph of Prime Minister of the Somali Republic Dr. Abdirashid Ali Shermarke," John F. Kennedy Presidential Library and Museum, doi:JFKSG-MO-1976-300

9    Tom Cooper, 2015, ibid.

10   Until that date, and even after, Siad Barre had consistently denied that the SNA was involved in military operations inside the disputed territories in Ethiopia. See also Human Rights Watch, "Evil Days. Thirty Years of War and Famine in Ethiopia." (New York: Human Rights Watch, 1991) 73—76

11   Podgorny had visited Tanzania to discuss the liberation of former Rhodesia, but suddenly switched his schedule to visit Somalia on April 3, 1977. See "Podgorny Extends Trip to Somalia," Sydney Morning Herald, Monday, April 4, 1977, 3.

12   "Brezhnev Blasts Somalia," Lodi (CA) News Sentinel, Friday, September 30, 1977.

13   Brian Jeffries, "Somalia expels Soviets," The Free Lance-Star, (Fredericksburg, Virginia), November 14, 1977, 93, No. 268, 1

14   Nederlandse Organisatie voor Internationale Bijstand (NOVIB), "War and Famine in Ethiopia and Eritrea: An Investigation into the Arms Deliveries to the Struggling Parties in Eritrea and Tigray," Zeist, 1991.

15   Research on Islam and Muslims in Africa (RIMA), Somali Proverb, June 2013, https://muslimsinafrica.wordpress.com/2013/06/26/somali-proverbs/

16   Associated Press, "US, Soviets, Italy helped arm Somalis," Register Guard (Eugene, Oregon), November 2, 1993, 5 http://news.google.com/newspapers

17   Peter Bridges, "Safirka, the Envoy in Somalia," Michigan Quarterly Review, 37, 1, Winter, http://hdl.handle.net/2027/spo.act2080.0037.101

18   Ibid.

19   Mohamed Barud Ali, The Mourning Tree—An Autobiography and A Prison Memoir, (Ponte Invisible/Red Sea Press), http://www.redsea-online.com/books/

20   Roobdoon Forum, "The 1978 Attempted Coup," (blog) http://biyokulule.com/1978_coup.htm. Also see Helen Chapin Metz (ed), Robert Rinehart, Irving Kaplan,Donald P. Whitaker, Jean R. Tartter, and Frederick Ehrenreich, "Somalia: A Country Study," (Washington: GPO for the Library of Congress, 1992), http://countrystudies.us/somalia/

21   Charles Kingsley, A Vet in Somalia (Bloomington, Ind.: Xlibris Corporation, 2012)

22   Roobdoon Forum, "The Somali Manifesto I," Biyokulule, http://www.biyokulule.com/Somali%20Manifesto%20I.htm

23   Human Right Watch, "Somalia", Human Right Watch World Report 1990, http://www.hrw.org/reports/1990/WR90/index.htm#TopOfPage

24   Immigration and Refugee Board of Canada, "Somalia: Information about a Massacre at a Football Match in Somalia between 4 and 8 July 1990, 1 July 1990," SOM6462, http://www.refworld.org/

docid/3ae6aac64.html

25    James K. Bishop, "Meeting with President Siad Barre," December 27, 1990, doi:90MOGADISHU11295_a,

26    James K. Bishop, "More on Massacre at Animal Market," December 9, 1990, doi:90MOGADISHU10663_a,

27    Bishop, "Meeting with President Siad Barre."

28    Joseph P. Englehardt, "Desert Shield and Desert Storm: A Chronology and Troop List for 1990-1991 Persian Gulf Crisis," Strategic Studies Institute (SSI) Special Report, March 25, 1991, http://www.dtic.mil/dtic/tr/fulltext/u2/a234743.pdf

29    Research on Islam and Muslims in Africa (RIMA), Somali Proverb, June 2013, https://muslimsinafrica.wordpress.com/2013/06/26/somali-proverbs/. With additional translation from Hussein Adani Bilan, Toronto.

30    Bishop, "Meeting with President Siad Barre."

31    Ibid.

32    Adam B. Siegel, "Eastern Exit: The Noncombatant Evacuation Operation (NEO), from Mogadishu, Somalia in January 1991," Center for Naval Analyses (CNA), October 1991, doi:ADA445517

33    Ibid.

34    Didrikke Schanche, "Somali Dictator Flees to Kenya," Associated Press, April 30, 1992, http://www.apnewsarchive.com/

35    Blaine Harden, "Only Sharks Offshore are Frisky in Somnolent Somalia," The Montreal Gazette, Saturday, July 13, 1985, http://news.google.com/newspapers

36    ibid

37    Daniel Compagnon, "Somali Armed movements: The Interplay of Political Entrepreneurship and Clan-based Faction," in African Guerrillas ed. Christopher Clapham (Oxford, UK: James Currey), 73-90. Also see Desert News, "Somalian Rebels Name President; Siad Barre Seeks Asylum in Kenya," http://www.deseretnews.com/

38    Ibid.

39    Ibid.

40    Médecins Sans Frontières (MSF), "Somalia 1991-1993 Civil war, famine alert and UN 'Military Humanitarian' intervention 1991-1993," MSF Speaks Out, 2013, doi: PPP_SomalieVA PDF_0.pdf

41    Ibid.

42    United Nations, "Resolution 733 (1992) of January 23, 1992," http://www.un.org/

43    United Nations, "Resolution 746 (1992) of 17 March 1992," http://www.un.org/

44    United Nations, "Resolution 751 (1992)," S/RES/751 http://www.un.org/

45    Stephen Smith, "Drugs and the Security of Foreigners, Mothers of the War in Somalia," Libération (France), March 3, 1992 (French).

46    United Nations, "Resolution 794 (1992)," S/RES/794 http://www.securitycouncilreport.org/

47    George H. Bush, "Address on Somalia," (Transcript) December 4, 1992, Miller center, University of Virginia, http://millercenter.org/president/bush/speeches/speech-3984

48    United Nations, "Somalia: UNOSOM II, Mandat," http://www.un.org/en/peacekeeping/missions/past/unosom2mandate.html

49    United States Institute of Peace, "Addis Ababa Agreement Concluded at the First Session of the Conference on National Reconciliation in Somalia," March 27, 1993, http://www.usip.org/publications/peace-agreements-somalia

50    "Thomas M. Montgomery: Awards and Citations," Hall of Valor, Military Times, www.projects.militarytimes.com/

51   United States Forces, "Somalia (USFORSOM) After Action Report," Center of Military History, United States Army, Washington, www.history.army.mil/html/documents/somalia/SomaliaAAR.pdf

52   Ibid.

53   United Nations, "Resolution 837 (1993)," S/RES/837 (1993), http://www.un.org/

54   USFORSOM, After Action Report

55   Ibid.

56   Ibid.

57   Ibid.

58   Ibid.

59   Ibid.

60   Ibid.

61   Research on Islam and Muslims in Africa (RIMA), Somali Proverb, June 2013, https://muslimsinafrica.wordpress.com/2013/06/26/somali-proverbs/. With additional translation from Hussein Adani Bilan, Toronto.

62   BBC World Service, "Aidid Aide, Ato Interviewed on Aidid's Death," Focus on Africa, August 3, 1996, In Zooming into the past, Biyokulule, http://biyokulule.com/August_1990s(1).htm

63   Hrvoje Hranjski, "Aidid's Bloody Legacy," Associated Press/Tampa Tribune, August 3, 1996 in Zooming into the past, Biyokulule, http://biyokulule.com/August_1990s(1).htm

64   William J. Clinton, "Press Briefing by David Johnson, Senior Director for Press and Public Policy, N.S.C.," August 2, 1996. Online by Gerhard Peters and John T. Woolley, The American Presidency Project. http://www.presidency.ucsb.edu/ws/?pid=58852

## Chapter 2

1   George W. Bush, "Address to a Joint Session of Congress and the American People," United States Capitol, Washington, September 20, 2001, http://georgewbush-whitehouse.archives.gov/news/releases/2001/09/20010920-8.html

2   US Department of State, "Executive Order 13224," September 23, 2001, http://go.usa.gov/3pnqh

3   US Department of State, "Appendix E: US Processes, Program, Policy," May 21, 2002, http://go.usa.gov/3dkzR

4   Duale A. Sii'arag, "The Birth and Rise of al Ittihad al-Islami in the Somali Inhabited Regions in the Horn of Africa," *Maanhadal*, http://www.maanhadal.com/maanhada/Al-Ittihad%20_maanhadal.html

5   Lara Loewenstein, "Al Ittihad Al-Islamiyya and Political Islam in Somalia," *The SAIS Europe Journal*, April 2010, http://www.saisjournal.org/posts/al-ittihad-al-islamiyya-and-political-islam-in-somalia

6   "UNDP Horn of Africa," *The Monthly Review*, August 28—September 23, 1996, http://www.africa.upenn.edu/eue_web/hoa0996.htm

7   Robert F. Baumann, Lawrence A Yates and Versalle F. Washington, *My Clan Against the World: US and Coalition Forces in Somalia*, 1992-1994 (Fort Leavenworth, Kansas: Combat Studies Institute Press, 2003). Also see Ioan M. Lewis, *Understanding Somalia and Somaliland: Culture, History and Society* (New York, NY: Columbia University Press, 2008).

8   James Phillips, "Somalia and Al-Qaeda: Implications for the War on Terrorism," April 5, 2002, Heritage Foundation, http://www.heritage.org/research/reports/2002/04/somalia-and-al-qaeda-implications-for-the-war-on-terrorism

9   William Bellamy, "Somali Policy Considerations," December 5, 2005, doi:05NAIROBI5019_a

10 Jonathan Fighel, "Al-Qaeda-Mombasa Attacks, November 28, 2002," The Meir Amit Intelligence and Terrorism Center, June 16, 2011, http://www.terrorism-info.org.il/data/pdf/PDF_19300_2.pdf

11 Frontline, "The Journey of Haroun Fazul," *PBS*, http://www.pbs.org/

12 Angel Rabasa, *Radical Islam in East Africa* (Santa Monica, CA: Rand Corporation), 56.

13 Sheikh Sharif Sheikh Ahmed, interview at Villa Somalia, July 19, 2012,

14 Stig Jarle Hansen, *Al Shabaab in Somalia: The History and ideology of a Militant Islamist Group, 2005-2012* (New York, NY: Oxford University Press, 2013).

15 Angel Rabasa, Peter Chalk, Kim Cragin, Sara A. Daly, Heather S. Gregg, Theodore W. Karasik, Kevin A. O'Brien and William Rosenau, *Beyond al-Qaeda: Part 1, The Global Jihadist Movement* (Santa Monica, CA: RAND Corporation, 2006), 133, http://www.rand.org/pubs/monographs/MG429.

16 Thomas P.M. Barnett, "The Americans have Landed," *Esquire*, June 2007, http://www.esquire.com/news-politics/a3083/africacommand0707/

17 Shashank Bengali, "US military Investing Heavily in Africa," *LA Times*, October 20, 2013, http://www.latimes.com/world/la-fg-usmilitary-africa-20131020-story.html

18 Jeremy Scahill, "Blowback in Somalia: How US Proxy Wars Helped Create a Militant Islamist Threat," *The Nation*, September 07, 2011, http://www.thenation.com/article/blowback-somalia/

19 Ibid. See also Emily Meehan, "Notes from a Failed State: America's Warlord," *Slate*, August 19, 2008, http://www.slate.com/

20 LA Times, "Working with Warlords," May 26, 2006, http://articles.latimes.com/2006/may/25/opinion/ed-somalia25

21 Ibid.

22 Stig Jarle Hansen, 32-34

23 Guled Mohamed, Mogadishu-based journalist and writer, interview by author in Mogadishu, July 21, 2013.

24 Mohamed interview.

25 James Phillips, *ibid.*

## Chapter 3

1 Marguerita Ragsdale, "A/S Frazer and IGAD Executive Secretary on Somalia," July 13, 2006, doi:06DJIBOUTI831_a,

Also of note, the new US Embassy Compound Complex in New Haramous neighbourhood was completed in 2011, and opened on December 7th 2011 by U.S. Ambassador to Djibouti Geeta Pasi.

2 National Climatic Data Center, "Weather Data for Djibouti, June 2006, http://www.geodata.us/

3 South Sudan was admitted as a member of IGAD on Friday, November 25, 2011. See Reuters, "East African Bloc Admits South Sudan as member," Friday, November 25, 2011, http://www.reuters.com/

4 The Big Bethel Baptist Church, "Church History," http://www.thebigbethelbaptistchurch10.com/

5 108th Congress, 1st Session Issue,149, No. 144 — *Congressional Records Daily Edition*, October 15, 2003.

6 US Congress, "Congressional Record—Daily Digest," November 5, 2003, https://www.congress.gov/congressional-record/2003/11/5/daily-digest

7 Marguerita Ragsdale, "IGAD Executive Secretary Sees no Conclusive Outcome for March 22 Djibouti Ministerial Meeting," March 21, 2004, doi:04DJIBOUTI413_a.

8 Ibid.

9 Marguerita D. Ragdale, "IGAD Executive Secretary Briefs Ambassador on March 22 Ministerial

Meeting, March 25, 2004," doi:04DJIBOUTI437_a.

10    Ibid.

11    "Somalia National Peace Conference, Arta, Djibouti, April 20—May 5, 2000," (blog) http://www.banadir.com/whatisthere.htm

12    Also see IRIN News, "In-depth: Somali National Peace Conference," *Online publication*, http://www.irinnews.org/in-depth/72039/54/somali-national-peace-conference    Lt.    Col.    Paddy Ankunda, interview by author, Kampala, Uganda, July 30, 2015.

13    "The Transitional Federal Charter of the Federal Republic of Somalia, February 2004," Nairobi, http://www.ilo.org/dyn/travail/docs/2177/Transitional%20Federal%20charter-feb%20 2004-English.pdf

14    IGAD, "Proceedings of the Meetings of the Eastern Africa Chief of Defence Staff on the Establishment of the Eastern Africa Standby Brigade (EASBRIG)," February 2004, https://www.issafrica.org/AF/RegOrg/unity_to_union/pdfs/igad/easbrigfeb04.pdf

15    IGAD, "Joint Communique issued by the IGAD Special Summit on Somalia," October 15, 2004, http://reliefweb.int/report/somalia/joint-communiqué-issued-igad-special-summit-somalia

16    African Union, "Report of the Chairperson of the Commission on the Outcomes of the Fact-finding/reconnaissance Mission to Somalia and the IGAD military planning meetings," African Union Peace and Security Council, http://www.peaceau.org/

17    African Union, "Decisions and Declaration (Assembly/AU/Dec.65(IV))," Assembly of the African Union, Fourth Ordinary Session 30-31 January 2005, January 31, 2005, Abuja Nigeria, http://www.peaceau.org/uploads/communiqueeng-24th.pdf

18    African Union, "Decision on Somalia," January 31, 2005, http://www.peaceau.org/uploads/assembly-au-dec-65-iv-e.pdf

19    African Union, Report of the Chairperson of the Commission on the outcomes of the factfinding/Reconnaissance,

20    Ibid.

21    Ibid.

22    Ibid.

23    Irin News, "Somalia: IGAD to Deploy Peacekeepers Despite Opposition by Faction Leaders," March 15, 2005, http://www.irinnews.org/fr/report/53418/somalia-igad-to-deploy-peacekeepers-despite-opposition-by-faction-leaders

24    Ibid.

25    IGAD, "Communiqué of the 24th Ordinary Session of the IGAD council of Ministers on Somalia," 18th March 2005, Nairobi, Kenya, March 18, 2005, http://reliefweb.int/

26    IGAD, "Statement of the IGAD Council of Ministers of Foreign Affairs 18th March 2005," Nairobi, Kenya, http://www.aigaforum.com/Documents_on_Somalia.pdf

27    Joyce Mulama, "Somalia: Talks About a Peacekeeping Force Prove Disruptive," *Inter Press Service News Agency*, March 18, 2005, http://www.ipsnews.net/2005/03/politics-somalia-talks-about-a-peacekeeping-force-prove-disruptive/

28    Ibid.

29    Panapress, "US Opposes Somalia Troops Deployment, Threatens Veto," *Panapress*, March 17, 2005, http://www.panapress.com/

30    Rockwell A. Schnabel, "Demarche Response: Somalia IGAD Peace Support Mission," February 16, 2005 doi: 05BRUSSELS672_a.

31    Ibid.

32    Ibid.

33   Ibid.

34   William L. Lyons Brown, "Somalia-IGAD Deployment: Austria's Response," March 18, 2005, doi:05VIENNA907_a.

35   Mel Sembler, "Somalia-Italians Share Concerns over IGAD Troop Deployment," March 21, 2005, doi:05ROME950_a.

36   Mel Sembler, "Somalia-Italy Requests USG View on the Situation; IGAD Amended Peace Plan," March 24, 2005, doi:05ROME1012_a.

37   Michael P. McKinley, "TransAtlantic Consultations on Africa," Wednesday, May 4, 2005 doi:05BRUSSELS1734_a.

38   Research on Islam and Muslims in Africa (RIMA), *Somali Proverb*, June 2013, https://muslimsinafrica.wordpress.com/

39   McKinley, TransAtlantic Consultations

40   William Bellamy, "Somali Policy Considerations," Monday, December 5, 2005, doi:05NAIROBI5019_a.

41   "Jendayi Frazer," *Wikipedia*, https://en.wikipedia.org/wiki/Jendayi_Frazer

42   James Ainsworth, "A Peacemaker in Africa's Brave New World," *An Eye on Africa*, Denver: Co, Wednesday, March 12, 2008, http://aneyeonafrica.blogspot.ca/2008/03/peacemaker-in-africas-brave-new-world.html

43   University of Cape Town, "Monday Paper Archives,"24, no. 06, April 11, 2005, http://www.uct.ac.za/mondaypaper/archives/?id=5045

44   US Department of State, "President Thanks Secretary of State Rice at Swearing-in Ceremony," January 28, 2005, http://20012009.state.gov/

45   Jendayi Frazer, "Remarks at press conference, Nairobi, Kenya," June 21, 2006, U.S. Department of State, http://2001-2009.state.gov/p/af/rls/rm/2006/68405.htm

46   Marguerita Ragsdale.

## Chapter 4

1   Vicki Huddleston, "Ethiopia: Samora Reiterates GOE Policy on Somalia to General Abizaid," Wednesday, June 21, 2006, doi:06ADDISABABA1708_a.

2   Conversation with US official, July 28, 2011

3   General Samora Yonus said as much the following day, June 20, 2006 in conversation with the US Defense Attache (DATT) in Addis Ababa, see doi:06ADDISABABA1708_a

4   Vicki Huddleston, "Meles/Frazier Review Approach to Somalia," June 29, 2006, doi:06ADDISABABA1783_a.

5   Ibid.

6   Ibid.

7   Conversation with US official, July 28, 2011

8   Janet Wilgus, "Ethiopia: Deputy Minister Talks Somalia, Regional Issues with DAS Yamamoto," September 16, 2006, doi:06ADDISABABA2526_a.

9   Ibid.

10   Vicki Huddleston, "Ethiopia: Deputy FM talks on Eritrea Incursion, Somalia Contact Group," October 18, 2006, doi:06ADDISABABA2818_a.

11   Ibid., Also note, Donald Yamamoto was appointed US Ambassador to Ethiopia on October 4, 2006, https://history.state.gov/departmenthistory/people/yamamoto-donald-y

12   Rory Carroll, "Mogadishu's New Rulers Reassure West," *The Guardian*, June 14, 2006, http://www.theguardian.com/world/2006/jun/14/rorycarroll

13    Vicki Huddleston, "Ethiopia: Meles Hopes to Delay Somalia Intervention until Mid-November," October 26, 2006, doi:06ADDISABABA2872_a.

14    Ibid.

15    Ibid.

16    Conversation with US official, July 28, 2011.

17    Yoweri Museveni, interview, State House, Kampala August 2012

18    Keymedia history Clip, "General M. Farah with Yoweri Museveni and Amb. Sahnoun, 1992," Youtube, http://www.youtube.com/watch?v=mwpYbNqNYkk

19    Robert H. Tuttle, "Somalia: Museveni Tells A/S Frazer Ugandan Troops Can Guard Baidoa," November 22, 2006, doi:06LONDON8066_a.

20    Ibid.

21    Robert H. Tuttle, "A/S Frazer Discusses Sudan and Somalia with FCO, DFID," November 26, 2006, doi:06LONDON8106_a.

22    Ibid.

23    "Hansard Parliamentary Debates," Lords, November 20, 2006, Column 119, http://www.publications.parliament.uk/pa/ld200607/ldhansrd/ldallfiles/peers/lord_hansard_4335_od.html

24    Hansard Parliamentary Debates, Lords, November 20, 2006, Column 219, http://www.publications.parliament.uk/pa/ld200607/ldhansrd/ldallfiles/peers/lord_hansard_4335_od.html

25    Ibid.

26    Ibid.

27    Tuttle, A/S Frazer Discusses

28    Hansard Parliamenary Debates, House of Commons, December 6, 2006, Column 289, http://www.publications.parliament.uk/pa/cm200607/cmhansrd/cmallfiles/mps/commons_hansard_3953_od.html

29    United Nations, "Security Council Approves African Protection, Training Mission in Somalia, Unanimously Adopting Resolution 1725 (2006)," December 6, 2006, http://www.un.org/press/en/2006/sc8887.doc.htm

30    Nabeel A. Khoury, "Somalia's Sheikh Sharif Ready for Dialogue, But on His Own Terms," March 27, 2007, doi:07SANAA451_a.

31    Hansard Parliamentary Debates, Lords, January 30 & 31, 2007,http://www.publications.parliament.uk/pa/ld200607/ldhansrd/ldallfiles/peers/lord_hansard_4335_od.html

32    11 September is Ethiopia's New Year. The New Year signals the end of the big rains. The day is called *Enkutatash,* 'gift of jewels.'

33    Janet Wilgus, "Ethiopia: PM Meles Reports to Parliament on Successful Somalia Operation," January 4, 2007, doi:07ADDISABABA18_a.

## Chapter 5

1    Donald Yamamoto, "Somalia: PM Meles Affirms Need for Ethiopian Troops to Withdraw," January 8, 2007, doi:07ADDISABABA40_a.

2    Richard Appleton, "Communique of January 5 International Contact on Somalia," January 5, 2007, doi:07NAIROBI91_a.

3    Ibid.

4    SABA, "President Talks with US State Official on Somalia," January 6, 2007, *SABANET,* http://www.sabanews.net/en/news124570.htm

5    Thomas Krajewski, "Saada: Casualties Mount, Saleh Prepares for Offensive," February 6, 2007, doi:07SANAA221_a.

6   SABA, "US Official Leaves Aden," January 6, 2007, *SABANET*, http://www.sabanews.net/en/news124588.htm

7   Associated Press, "Somalia May Fall Back to Chaos," *Sudan Tribune*, January 9, 2007, http://www.sudantribune.com/

8   Eric M. Bost, "No South African Troops for Somalia," January 26, 2007, doi:07PRETORIA300_a. Also see David Masango, "South Africa will not Send Troops to Somalia, January 30, 2007, *BuaNews*, http://www.southafrica.info/news/international/somalia-300107.htm

9   Eleneus Akanga, "Rwanda Requested to Deploy in Somalia," January 13, 2007, *The New Times*, http://allafrica.com/stories/200701130024.html

10  Ann Talbot, "Somalia: African Union Force Agreed," January 23, 2007, *WSWS*, https://www.wsws.org/en/articles/2007/01/soma-j23.html

11  Agence France Presse, "Somalia: African Union to Deplot Peacekeepers," January 19, 2007, *AFP*, http://reliefweb.int/report/somalia/somalia-african-union-deploy-peacekeepers-0

12  Joseph Stafford, "The Gambia: Possible TCC for AU Peacekeeping," January 5, 2007, doi:07BANJUL7_a.

13  Joseph Stafford, "The Gambia: An Irascible President Jammeh in Year-end Interview," January 9, 2007, doi:07BANJUL11_a.

14  Joseph Stafford, "The Gambia: Troop contributions to Darfur," March 7, 2007, doi:07BANUL120_a.

15  Michael R. Arietti, "Rwanda Will not Send Troops to Somalia," January 24, 2007, doi:07KIGALI73_a.

16  Ibid.

17  Donald Yamamoto, "Somalia: PM Meles Highlights Land Reform as Key to Clan Reconciliation and Political Stability in Somalia," February 1, 2007, doi:07ADDISABABA311_a.

18  Ibid.

19  Donald Yamamoto, "A/S Frazer Meeting with Ugandan President Museveni Focuses on Somalia, Darfur and Chad," February 1, 2007, doi:07ADDISABABA312_a.

20  On January 1, 1902, King's African Rifles was formed. It comprised of six battalions: 1st and 2nd Battalion Nyasaland, 4th Battalion Uganda, 3rd and 5th Battalion Kenya, and 6th Somaliland. The first and longest war fought by KAR was against Seyed Mohamed Abdullahi Hassan, the "Mad Mullah" in Somaliland. It lasted from 1900 to 1920. All the KAR Battalions were engaged in the war (except 4 KAR).

21  Tim Cocks, "African Peace Mission Won't Fail in Somalia: Uganda," January 6, 2007, *Reuters*, http://uk.reuters.com/article/2007/01/06/us-somalia-conflict-uganda-idUKL0576014620070106

22  African Union, "Decisions and Declarations", Assembly of the African Union Eighth Ordinary Session, 29—30, January 2007, Addis Ababa, Ethiopia, http://www.au.int/en/sites/default/files/ASSEMBLY_EN_29_30_JANUARY_2007_AUC_THE_AFRICAN_UNION_EIGHTH_ORDINARY_SESSION.pdf

23  Steven A. Browning, "Uganda: Vote on Approval of Somalia Deployment Initiated," February 1, 2007, doi:07KAMPALA193_a.

24  Ibid.

25  Steven A. Browning, "Uganda: Parliamentary Defense Committee to Recommend Somalia Deployment," February 12, 2007, doi:07KAMPALA238_a.

26  Steven A. Browning, "Uganda: Parliament Approves Somalia Deployment," February 13, 2007, doi:07KAMPALA254_a.

27  United Nations, "Security Council Authorizes Six-Months African Union Mission in Somalia, Unanimously Adopting Resolution 1744 (2007), February 20, 2007, http://www.un.org/press/

en/2007/sc8960.doc.htm

28 Steven A. Browning, "Uganda: Action Items on Somalia from EUCOM Deputy Commander General Ward's Visit," February 28, 2007, doi:07KAMPALA342_a.

29 Ibid.

30 United States Congress, "Text of the Somalia Stabilization and Reconstruction Act of 2007," February 6, 2007, 110th Congress, https://www.govtrack.us/congress/bills/110/s492/text

31 Jendayi E. Frazer, "Testimony by Assistant Secretary for African Affairs Jendayi E. Frazer: Establishing a Comprehensive Stabilization, Reconstruction and Counter-terrorism Strategy for Somalia," Senate Foreign Subcommittee Hearing, February 6, 2007, http://www.foreign.senate. gov/imo/media/doc/FrazerTestimony070206.pdf

32 Ibid.

33 Colonel Ddamulira Sserunjogi, interview by author, Serena Hotel, Kampala, July 20, 2015.

## Chapter 6

1 Brigadier Peter Elwelu, interview by author, Serena Hotel, Kampala, July 20, 2015.

2 Ali Abdi Musa, "African Union Peacekeepers Arrive in Somalia," *Agence France Press*, March 6, 2007, http://reliefweb.int/report/somalia/african-union-peacekeepers-arrive-somalia

3 John Mackinlay and Abiodun Alao, "Liberia 1994:
ECOMOG and UNOMIL Response to a Complex Emergency," (1995), http://archive.unu.edu/ unupress/ops2.html#Ecomog

4 Opiyo Oloya, "African Force in Somalia Doomed to Fail," *New Vision*, February 20, 2007, http:// www.newvision.co.ug/PA/8/20/550133

5 David Morgan, "Uganda Denies Peacekeepers in Somalia," *CBS News/Associated Press*, March 1, 2007, http://www.cbsnews.com/news/uganda-denies-peacekeepers-in-somalia/

6 United Nations Security Council, "Resolution 1744, Adopted by Security Council at its 5633rd Meeting," S/RES/1744 (2207), February 20, 2007, http://www.un.org/en/ga/search/view_doc. asp?symbol=S/RES/1744(2007)

7 Ibid.

8 Colonel Ddamulira Sserunjogi interview.

9 Karen Allen, "Uganda Troops not 'peacemakers'," *BBC News*, March 1, 2007, http://news.bbc. co.uk/2/hi/africa/6409167.stm

10 Mohamed Olad Hassan, "African Peace Keepers Arrive in Somalia," *Washington Post/Associated Press*, March 1, 2007, 1http://www.washingtonpost.com/wp-dyn/content/article/2007/03/01/ AR2007030100619.html

11 Jeffrey Gettleman, "Insurgents Shell Somali Airport as Peacekeeps Arrive," *New York Times*, March 6, 2007, http://www.nytimes.com/2007/03/06/world/africa/06cnd-somalia. html?pagewanted=print&_r=0

12 Ali Abdi Musa, "African Union Peacekeepers Arrive in Somalia," *Agence France Press*, March 6, 2007, http://reliefweb.int/report/somalia/african-union-peacekeepers-arrive-somalia

13 Karen Allen, "Ugandan Troops Leave for Somalia," *BBC News*, March 2, 2007, http://news.bbc. co.uk/2/hi/africa/6411105.stm

14 Michael Ranneberger, "Somali Insurgents Attack Arriving Ugandans," March 9, 2007, doi:07NAIROBI1127_a

15 BBC, "African Force Ambushed in Somalia," March 8, 2007, *BBC News*, http://news.bbc.co.uk/2/ hi/africa/6428969.stm

16 Martin Plaut, "AU Troops 'may spark Somalia War'," *BBC News*, March 9, 2007, http://news.bbc.

co.uk/2/hi/africa/6436263.stm

17 In interview, Col. Ddamulira narrated that his intelligence team gathered information indicating that highly skilled Eritrean artillery officers were training the insurgents in the use of artillery and mortars.

18 Brigadier Elwelu interview.

19 Michael Ranneberger, Somali Insurgents.

20 Henry Mukasa, "Eritrea Warns Uganda to Leave Somalia," *New Vision*, March 10, 2007, http://www.hiiraan.com/news4/2007/Mar/2378/_eritrea_warns_uganda_to_leave_somalia__.aspx

21 Ali Musa Abdi, "12 Killed in Somalia as AU Deploys Fresh Troops," *Agence France-Presse*, March 8, 2007, http://reliefweb.int/report/somalia/12-killed-somalia-au-deploys-fresh-troops

22 Aviation Safety Network, "Criminal Occurrence Description," March 9, 2007, http://aviation-safety.net/database/record.php?id=20070309-0

23 Michael Ranneberger, "AMISOM Equipment Plane Afire on Mogadishu Landing," March 9, 2007, doi:07NAIROBI1132,

24 Col. Ddamulira Sserunjogi and Lt. Col. Paddy Ankunda, interview

25 Ibid.

26 Lt. Col. Dr. Ambrose Oiko, interview by author, Halaane Base, Mogadishu July 22, 2015.

27 When asked about the event that had a clear impact on the mission, all UPDF officers including General Katumba Wamala, Brig. Elwelu, Col. Ddamulira, Lt. Col. Ankunda, Lt. Col. Dr. Ambrose Oiko and others pointed to this incident as the most significant.

28 Variants of this story, all not true, had a very sick old man abandoned at the Halaane base, while another had a woman being brought by relatives, but both leaving the base cured. As the physician in charge at the time, Lt. Col. Dr. Oiko was able to clear up the mystery, narrating exactly what happened.

29 Update: Hassan, studying in London, England, visited Dr. Ambrose Oiko's clinic in Mogadishu on Saturday, October 10, 2015 to meet the doctor who saved his life. Dr. Oiko was away at the time, so Hassan left a crate of soda for the good doctor as a token of his gratitude. Dr. Oiko provided this update on Sunday, October 18, 2015 via Skype from Mogadishu.

30 Oiko interview.

31 The author named the Outpatient Clinic on August 19, 2010 as the Gate of Hope, a name that stuck.

32 Michael Ranneberger, "Somali Insurgents Switch to Assassination," March 1, 2007, doi:07NAIROBI990_a.

33 Mohamed Olad Hassan, "Somali Troops Enter Mogadishu to Cheers," *Associated Press,* December 28, 2006, http://www.washingtonpost.com/

34 Mohamed Olad Hassan, "African Peace Keepers Arrive in Somalia," *Associated Press/Washington Post*, March 1, 2007, http://www.washingtonpost.com/

35 Emmy Allio, "General Aronda Flies to Ethiopia," *New Vision*, March 2, 2007, http://www.newvision.co.ug/D/8/12/552339

36 Jeffrey Gettleman, "Chaos in Somalia as Fighting Intensifies and Death Toll Rises," *New York Times*, April, 23, 2007, http://www.nytimes.com/

37 AFP, "Somali, AU troops Secure Mogadishu Port Ahead of Deployment," *Agence France-Presse*, Monday, March 19, 2007. http://www.hiiraan.com/

38 Mustafa Haji Abdinur, "Heavy Mortar Fire Rocks Somali Capital, *Agence France Presse*, March 19, 2007, http://reliefweb.int/report/somalia/heavy-mortar-fire-rocks-somali-capital.

39 Michael Ranneberger, "TFG Plans to Disarm Mogadishu," March 13, 2007, doi:07NAIROBI1173_a.

40 Michael Ranneberger, "Somali TFG Arms Sweep Begins—heavy Fighting," March 21, 2007,

doi:07NAIROBI1302_a

41    Ibid.

42    Human Rights Watch, "Shell-shocked: Civilians Under Siege in Mogadishu," (August 2007) 19, No. 12(A), 36, http://www.hrw.org/sites/default/files/reports/somalia0807webwcover.pdf

43    Michael Ranneberger, "Somali Clan Warfare Threatens Reconciliation," March 22, 2007, doi:07NAIROBI1322_a

44    Michael    Ranneberger,    "Somalia—Hawiye/Ethiopian    'truce'," March    23,    2007, doi:07NAIROBI1335.

45    Michael Ranneberger, "Somali Insurgents Attack Ethiopians, February 26, 2007, doi:07NAIROBI905,"

46    Michael Ranneberger, "Ambassador's Call to Somali TFG President Yusuf," March 23, 2007, doi:07NAIROBI1336_a.

47    Ibid.

48    Aviation Safety Network, "Criminal Occurrence Description," Friday, March 23, 2007, *Flight Safety Foundation*, http://aviation-safety.net/database/record.php?id=20070323-0; Also see Ambassador Ranneberger, "Somalia—Belarus IL-76 Probably shot down," March 26, 2007, 07NAIROBI1359.

49    "2007 Mogadishu TransAVIAexports Airlines Il-76 Crash," *Wikipedia*. https://en.wikipedia.org/

50    Stig Jarle Hansen, "Revenge or Reward. The Case of Somalia's Suicide Bombers," *Journal of Terrorism Research*, (2011) 1, no. 1, http://ojs.st-andrews.ac.uk/index.php/jtr/article/view/165/169

51    Michael    Ranneberger,    "Somali—Heavy    Fighting    Continues,"    March    30,    2007, doi:07NAIROBI1440_a

52    Elwelu interview.

53    Michael    Ranneberger,    "Somalia—Meeting    with    President    Yusuf,"    May    15,    2007, doi:07NAIROBI2069_a.

54    Ibid.

55    Michael    Ranneberger,    "Somali—Meeting    with    Solana    Envoy,"    May    16,    2007, doi:07NAIROBI2098_a.

56    Ibid.

57    Ibid.

58    Col. Dr. Kiyengo and Major Dr. Ibrahim Kimuli described the function of the OPD and also gave me an exclusive tour of the facility on Wednesday, August 18, 2010. As I watched, desperately ill Somali patients were brought in, screened by TFG forces for possible weapons and IEDs hidden in clothings, and then ushered into the clinic for treatment.

59    Guled Mohamed, "Bomb Kills Four Ugandan Peacekeepers," *Reuters*, May 16, 2007, http://www.reuters.com/

60    Gerald Businge, "Uganda's Peacekeeping Mission in Somalia: Not so Peaceful Keeping Peace in Somalia," *UGPulse*, July 7, 2007, http://www.ugpulse.com/government/uganda-s-peace-keeping-mission-in-somalia/650/ug.aspx

61    Michael Ranneberger, "Somalia—Attempt on PM's Life," May 18, 2007, doi:07NAIROBI2135_a

62    Ibid.

63    Businge, Uganda Peacekeepers.

64    Elwelu interview.

65    Mohamed, Bomb Kills Four Ugandans.

## Chapter 7

1    Cynthia Grissom Efird, "No Troops for Somalia, Door Open for Other Aids," January 22, 2007,

doi:07LUANDA57_a

2    Cynthia G. Efird, "Angolan Government Warmly Receives A/S Frazer," June 21 2007, doi:07LUANDA624_a,

3    Ibid.

4    Michael L. Retzer, "Tanzania: Moving Closer to Committing PKO Troops," December 20, 2006, doi:06DARESSALAAM1951_a

5    Ibid.

6    Ibid.

7    Michael L. Retzer, "Tanzania: No Decision Yet on Somalia Troops," January 19, 2007, doi:07DARESSALAAM93,

8    Michael L. Retzer, "Tanzania: President Kikwete on Deployment to Somalia and Darfur," February 2, 2007, doi:07DARESSALAAM158

9    Ibid.

10   Michael L. Retzer, "Tanzania: A/S Frazer and President Kikwete Discuss Somalia, Darfur and Eritrea-Ethiopia Boundary Dispute," February 28, 2007, doi:07DARESSALAAM260_a.

11   Michael L. Retzer, "Tanzania: Start of ACOTA Training Delayed till August," May 4, 2007, doi: 07DARESSALAAM660_a

12   Ibid.

13   Ibid.

14   Mark A. Green, "ACOTA: Tanzania indicates Readiness to Get Peacekeeping Training Back on Track," October 4, 2007, doi:07DARESSALAAM1348_a.

15   Donald Yamamoto, "Somalia: PM Meles Highlights Land Reform as Key to Clan Reconciliation and Political Stability in Somalia," February 1, 2007, doi:07ADDISABABA311_a.

16   John Campbell, "PDP candidate Yar'Adua Gravely ill, Possibly Dead," March 07, 2007, doi:07ABUJA431_a.

17   John Campbell, "Nigerian "election" a Charade," April 23, 2007, doi:07BAUJA766_a.

18   John Campbell, "A/S Frazer Visit Update," May 23, 2007, doi:07ABUJA1020_a.

19   John Campbell, "Nigeria: Scenesetter for A/S Frazer May 28-30 Visit," May 25, 2007, doi:07ABUJA1056_a.

20   John Campbell, "A/S Frazer May 29 Meeting with Nigeria President Yar'Adua," June 18, 2007, doi:07ABUJA1265_a.

21   John Campbell, "Nigerian Request for a Meeting by President Yar'Adua with President Bush on the Margins of the G8," June 1, 2007, doi:07ABUJA1081_a.

22   Ibid.

23   John Campbell, "Nigeria: Senator Nelson Meets with President Yar'adua," June 08 2007, doi:07Abuja1157_a.

24   John Campbell, "Nigeria Struggles to Meet AMISOM Commitment," June 21, 2007, doi:07ABUJA1320_a.

25   Ibid.

26   Ibid.

27   John Campbell, "Nigeria: Ambassador's Farewell Meeting with President Yar'Adua," July 20, 2007, doi:07ABUJA1544_a.

28   George W. Bush: "Nominations Sent to the Senate," July 11, 2007. Online by Gerhard Peters and John T. Woolley, The American Presidency Project. http://www.presidency.ucsb.edu/ws/?pid=83358.

29   Robert E. Gribbin, "Nigeria: Congress Payne Meets with President, MFA, and new Minister of Foreign Affairs Ojo Maduekwe," August 30, 2007, doi:07ABUJA1876_a.

30   Ibid.

31   Robert E. Gribbin, "A Strategy for Getting Nigerian Troops to Somalia," August 22, 2007, doi:07ABUJA1826_a.

32   Ibid.

33   Lisa Piascik, "Nigeria: Deputy Secretary's meeting with President Yar'Adua, November 12, 2007," November 15, 2007, doi:07ABUJA2382_a.

34   Ibid.

35   Renee Sanders, "Nigeria: AFRICOM Leadership Visit Abuja," December 3, 2007, doi:07ABUJA2497_a

36   Lisa Piascik, "Nigerian Military Delivers its AMISOM Equipment Wish List," January 10, 2008, doi:08ABUJA64_a

37   In the early evening of September 29, 2007, forces of Justice and Equality Movement (JEM) and Sudanese Liberation Army (SLA) operating in Darfur area, attacked African Union Mission in Sudan (AMIS) forces base in Haskanita town. The attack lasted through the night until four in the morning. 12 AMIS peacekeepers, the majority Nigerian, were killed. The attackers also looted 17 vehicles, food, weapons, ammunition communication equipment and fuel, See Alberto M. Fernandez, "AMIS Investigation Report on Haskanita Attack," October 31, 2007, doi:07KHARTOUM1684_a.

38   Lisa Piascik, "Nigerian Military Delivers its AMISOM Equipment Wish List," January 10, 2008, doi: 08ABUJA64_a.

39   Robin R. Sanders, "Nigeria: DAS Moss's Meeting with MOD and NSA," February 4, 2008, doi: 08ABUJA219_a.

40   Robin R. Sanders, "Nigeria: An Analysis—Yar'Adua and His Government at Eight Months," February 22, 2008, doi:08ABUJA345_a.

41   Renee R. Sanders, "Nigeria: Tribunal Upholds Presidential Election," February 26, 2008, doi:08ABUJA364_a

42   Robin R. Sanders, "Nigeria: Army Claims Somalia-bound Battalion Nearly Ready," July 15, 2008, doi:08ABUJA1338_a

43   Robin Renee Sanders, "Nigeria: Codel Berman Meeting with Vice President Goodluck Jonathan," July 3, 2008, doi:08ABUJA1294_a.

44   Lisa Piascik, "Sweeping Changes in Nigeria's Military," August 22, 2008, doi: 08ABUJA1671_a.

45   Oil "bunkering" refers to hacking into the national crude oil pipeline to steal millions of liters of crude, to refine or sell. Only powerful Nigerians with clout can protect the bunkering sites from government inspectors.

46   Walter Pflaumer, "Nigeria: Kingibe out, DEFMIN in as Secretary to Government of Federation," September 9, 2008, doi:08ABUJA1829_a

47   Walter Pflaumer, "DRL A/S Kramer Meets Nigerian FONMIN Maduekwe," September 11, 2008, doi:08ABUJA1844_a

48   Robin R. Sanders, "Nigeria: Reinforcing AMISOM," December 31, 2008, doi:08ABUJA2541_a

49   Ibid.

50   Robin R. Sanders, "Nigeria: Ambassador Discusses AMISOM with Foreign Minister," March 10, 2009, doi:09ABUJA417_a

51   Ibid.

52   Ibid.

53   Robin Renee Sanders, "Nigeria: Foreign Minister Sets up Surprise Encounter with EFCC Chairwoman," March 17, 2009, doi:09ABUJA458_a.

54    Human Right Watch, *Corruption on Trial: The Record of Nigeria's Economic and Financial Crimes Commission*, (New York, NY: HRW, 2011).

55    René Lemarchand, "The Burundi Killings of 1972," *Online Encyclopedia of Mass Violence*, 27 June 2008, http://www.massviolence.org/The-Burundi-Killings-of-1972, ISSN 1961-9898

56    Boniface Fidel Kiraranganya, *La Verite sur le Burundi: Temoignage* (Sherbrooke, Quebec: Editions Naaman, 1985)

57    Rene Lemarchand, *Burundi: Ethnic Conflict and Genocide*, (New York, NY: The Woodrow Wilson Center Press and Press Syndicate of the University of Cambridge, 1996). Also see Nigel Watt, *Burundi: Biography of a small country*, (London, UK: Hurst Publishers Ltd., 2008); Amnesty International, Burundi, *Locked Down: A Shrinking of Political Space*, (London, UK: Amnesty International Publications, 2014), http://www.amnesty.ca/sites/default/files/burundlockeddownfinal.pdf

58    United Nation, "International Commission of Inquiry for Burundi," April 13, 1996, http://www.usip.org/sites/default/files/file/resources/collections/commissions/Burundi-Report.pdf

59    Ibid.

60    Accord, "South Africa's peacekeeping role in Burundi: Challenges and Opportunities for Future Peace Mission," *Occasional paper series*, (2007) 2, No. 2. http://www.accord.org.za/publications/occasional-papers/492-south-africas-peacekeeping-role-in-burundi

61    Patricia Moller, "DAS Swan Visit to Burundi: Tackling Obstacle to Progress," March 21, 2007, doi:07BUJUMBURA201_a

62    Condoleeza Rice, "Burundi-USUN Instruction Cable on BINUB Resolution," December 19, 2007, doi:07State168497_a

63    Human Rights Watch, "Burundi: Bring Muyinga Murder Suspects to Trial," September 25, 2007, *Human Rights Watch*, https://www.hrw.org/news/2007/09/25/burundi-bring-muyinga-massacre-suspects-trial

64    Patricia Moller, "Burundi President Being Advised by High Level Military Quartet," August 17, 2007, doi:07Bujumbura574_a.

65    Ann Breiter, "Burundi's Defense Minister: Troops in Somalia Within two Months?" March 22, 2007, doi:07BUJUMBURA206_a.

66    Anne Breiter, "Burundi Renews Appeal for U.S Support for Troops Deploying to Somalia," March 26, 2007, doi:07BUJUMBURA215_a.

67    Ibid.

68    Ibid.

69    Cindy Courville, "Meeting with Burundi's Foreign Minister on AMISOM Deployment," April 4, 2007, doi:07ADDISABABA999_a

70    Eric. M. Bost, "SAG Open to Cooperating on Burundi AMISOM Deployment," April 16, 2007, doi:07PRETORIA1288_a.

71    Ann Breiter, "AU Assesses Burundi's Capabilities for Somalia Deployment," June 15, 2007, doi:07BUJUMBURA460_a.

72    Ibid.

73    Ibid.

74    Wayne J. Bush, "Support for AMISOM: Belgian Engagement with Burundi military—Question of Burundi's Capability Remains," August 23, 2007, doi:07Brussels2675_a.

75    Ibid.

76    Mark Pekala, "AMISOM: French MFA says new Resources not Likely to Assist Burundi Concerning Somalia," August 8, 2007, doi:07PARIS3342_a

77    Patricia Moller, "DAS Swan Urges Dialogue to Resolve Burundi's Political, Financial, and Military

Problems," September 25, 2007, doi:07BUJUMBURA682_a.

78   Aweys Yusuf and Abdi Sheikh, "Burundi Peacekeepers Deploy in Mogadishu," *Reuters*, December 24, 2007, http://mg.co.za/article/2007-12-24-burundi-peacekeepers-deploy-in-mogadishu

79   Aweys Yusuf and Abdi Sheikh, "Burundi sends 92 more peacekeepers to Somalia," *Reuters*, December 24, 2007,

80   Ibid.

81   Edmund Sanders, "In Somalia, Troops for Peace end up at War," *LA Times*, August 29, 2009, http://articles.latimes.com/2009/aug/29/world/fg-somalia-peacekeepers29

## Chapter 8

1    Human Rights Watch, "Report: Mogadishu under Siege," 2007, http://www.hrw.org/reports/2007/somalia0807/4.htm

2    Human Rights Watch, "Shell-shocked: Civilians Under Siege in Mogadishu," August 2007, 19, No. 12(A), http://www.hrw.org/sites/default/files/reports/somalia0807webwcover.pdf

3    Stig Jarle Hansen, *al-Shabaab in Somalia*,

4    United Nations, "Final Report of the Monitoring Group on Somalia pursuant to Security Council Resolution 1676 (2006)," November 27, 2006, S/2006/913, http://www.un.org/sc/committees/751/mongroup.shtml, p.11-14

5    Ibid.

6    Andrew McGregor, "The leading factions behind the Somali insurgency," *The Jamestown Foundation, Terrorism Monitor*, (April 26, 2007) 5, No. 8. http://www.jamestown.org/

7    Human Right Watch, 2007.

8    Ibid.

9    Guled Mohamed, Mogadishu resident and reporter for AP, interview, July 2013.

10   Ibid.

11   Hansen

12   Ibid., 80.

13   Scott Baldauf and Ali Mohamed, "Somalia's al Shabaab Recruits 'holy warrior' with $400 Bonuses," *The Christian Science Monitor*, April 15, 2010, http://www.csmonitor.com/World/Africa/2010/0415/Somalia-s-Al-Shabab-recruits-holy-warriors-with-400-bonus

14   MEMRI, "Bin Laden's Speeches 2003-2006," Special Dispatch No. 1286, September 8, 2006, http://www.memri.org/report/en/print1872.htm

15   Hansen, p.64.

16   Dina Temple-Raston, "Minesotan Sheds Light on Somali Terrorist Group," *NPR*, July 29, 2009, http://www.npr.org/templates/story/story.php?storyId=111341852, also see Dina Temple-Raston, "'Jihadi Pipeline' Stirs In Minneapolis," NPR, August 4, 2009,

17   Raveena Aulakh, "Did Five Torontonians Join Jihad in Somalia," *Toronto Star*, December 12, 2009, http://www.thestar.com/

18   Chris Welch, "Minnesota men Charged in Somali Recruiting," *CNN*, Thursday, July 16, 2009, http://www.cnn.com/

19   Dina Temple-Raston, "Somali-American Pleads Guilty in Terrorism case," *NPR*, August 12, 2009, http://www.npr.org/

20   Anti-Defamation League, "Al Shabab's American Recruits," updated February 2015, http://www.adl.org/assets/pdf/combating-hate/al-shabaabs-american-recruits.pdf; Also see Michael Daly, "American Jihadis Douglas McCain and Troy Kastigar: From Losers to Martyrs," The Daily Beast, August 28, 2014, http://www.thedailybeast.com/

21   Ibid.

22   Former al-Shabaab members, interviews by author, Mogadishu, July 2014.

23   al-Kataib Foundations for Media Production, "The Path to Paradise: From the Twin City to the Land of Two Migrations," August 7, 2013, http://jihadology.net/

24   Jessica Mador (June 7, 2009). Missing Somali teen reportedly killed in Mogadishu. http://www.mprnews.org/story/2009/06/06/somalideath

25   al-Kataib Foundations for Media Production.

26   The reference to the "seventeenth day of Ramadhan" as the date of the deaths of Kastigar and Mohamud is also mentioned in the video information put out by al-Kataib titled, *The Path to Paradise: From the Twin City to the Land of Two Migrations*. As Ramadhan began in Mogadishu on August 20, 2009, this pinpoints the date of the demise of two men as Saturday, September 5, 2009. Independent informants put the deaths of the men on late Saturday, September 5, 2009 or early hours of Sunday, September 6, 2009. The al-Shabaab offensive against the Jalle Siad Academy started on Thursday, September 3, 2009, and fighting carried on through Sunday, September 6, 2009.

27   In the video "The Path to Paradise: From the Twin Cities to the Land of Two Migrations", the purported blessing is shown of the two dead men as they lay side by side.

28   al-Shabaab interviews.

29   Rashid Nuune, "Assasination in Somalia: Security Ministers are key Targets," *Somalia Report*, October 7, 2011,http://www.somaliareport.com/

30   Hansen, 44

31   Jeffrey Gentleman, "Somalia's Prime Minister Survives Attack; 7 Others Die," *The New York Times*, June 4, 2007, http://www.nytimes.com/

32   Hussein Ali Noor, "Suicide Bombers Kill at Least 28 in Somalia," *Reuters*, Wednesday, October 29, 2008, http://www.reuters.com/

33   Ibid.

34   Donald Yamamoto, "FORMIN Details Effort at Somali Stabilization, Reconcilliation," March 13, 2008, doi:08ADDISABABA718_a.

35   Condoleezza Rice, "Somalia—Talking Point for March 5 Briefing," March 5, 2008, doi:08STATE22378_a.

36   Ranneberger, "Somalia—Conversation with TFG President Yusuf," March 14, 2008, doi:08NAIROBI734_a.

37   Ronald K. McMullen, "ARS on Al Shabab, Somali Reconcilliation," March 24, 2008, doi:08ASMARA155_a.

38   Ibid.

39   Michael Ranneberger, "Alliance for Re-Liberation of Somalia," April 4, 2008, doi:08NAIROBI902_a.

40   Michael Ranneberger, "Scenesetter for Somalia President Yusuf Visit," April 16, 2008, doi:08NAIROBI1013_a.

41   Michael Ranneberger, "Somalia—Meeting with President Yusuf," May 14, 2008, doi:08NAIROBI1257_a.

42   Robert H. Tuttle, "Somalia: UN Special Rep Calls for International Support for Djibouti Agreement," June 20, 2008, doi:08LONDON1666_a.

43   Donald Yamamoto, "Ethiopia: TFG President Must Go, All Options on the Table," October 15, 2008, doi:08ADDISABABA2848_a.

44   Michael Ranneberger, "Somalia—ARS Chairman Leads Delegation into Somalia," November 4, 2008, doi:08NAIROBI2543_a.

45   Michael Ranneberger, "A/S Frazer Tells President Yusuf to Get Behind Djibouti Process," December

31, 2008, doi:08NAIROBI2901_a.

46    Michael Ranneberger, "Somalia—TFG President Resigns," December 29, 2008, doi: 08NAIROBI2879_a.

47    Michael Ranneberger, "Somalia—Sheikh Sharif Elected President," February 2, 2009, doi:09NAIROBI172_a.

48    Donald Yamamoto, "Ethiopia Will Provide Full Support for AMISOM Until ENDF Departure, Meles," December 19, 2008, doi:08ADDISABABA3393_a.

49    Edris Kiggundu, "Angry Museveni Overhauls UPDF's Somalia Command," *The Observer*, July 5, 2009, http://www.observer.ug/

50    al-Shabaab interview.

51    Except for Omar Mahmoud and Mohamed Abdullahi, there were conflicting information about the names and identities of the other three operatives, and the names used here could be pseudonyms or aliases.

52    C. August Elliott, "Istishhad and Suicide Bombings in Contemporary Conflict: Sacred or Profane?," January 31, 2015, https://caugustelliott.wordpress.com/

53    al-Shabaab interview.

54    UN, "Statement from the UN in Somalia on the Looting of UN Compounds," July 20, 2009, http://www.undp.org/

## Chapter 9

1     US official conversation, Friday, January 3, 2014

2     Kenya Daily Nation, "al-Qaeda Threat to Peace in East Africa," *Daily Nation*, June 21, 2009, http://www.nation.co.ke/

3     Barack Obama, "Obama's Speech at Woodrow Wilson Center," August 1, 2007, http://www.cfr.org/

4     Kate Phillips, "Palin: Obama is 'Palling Around with Terrorists," *The Caucus/New York Times*, October 4, 2008, http://thecaucus.blogs.nytimes.com/

5     Mark Mazetti, *The way of the knife: The CIA, A secret Army, and a war at the ends of the earth*, (New York, NY: Penguin Press, 2013), 246

6     al-Shabaab interview.

7     Eyewitness accounts, July 22, 2015.

8     Jeff Zeleny and Sewell Chan, "Obama and Bill Clinton have Lunch in the Village," *Blog, The New York Times*, September 14, 2009, http://cityroom.blogs.nytimes.com/

9     BBC, "Saleh Ali Saleh Nabhan," September 15, 2009, http://news.bbc.co.uk/2/hi/8256024.stm

10    Barack Obama, "Press Gaggle by Press Secretary Robert Gibbs," September 14, 2009, Online by Gerhard Peters and John T. Woolley, *The American Presidency Project*. http://www.presidency.ucsb.edu/ws/?pid=86627.

11    Research on Islam and Muslims in Africa (RIMA), Somali Proverb, June 2013, https://muslimsinafrica.wordpress.com/2013/06/26/somali-proverbs/

12    Mohamed Diriye Abdullahi, *Culture and Customs of Somalia*, (Westport, CT: Greenwood Press, 2001), p. 68

13    Ambassador Nathan Mugisha, interview by author, July 2013.

14    Xan Rice, "Somali Insurgents Pledge Revenge After US Kills al-Qaida Militant," *The Guardian*, September 15, 2009, http://www.theguardian.com/

## Chapter 10

1     Now Lt. Col. Rugumayo, Uganda People's Defense Forces

2    United States Army, "United States Forces, Somalia After Action Report and Historical Overview: The United States Army in Somalia, 1992—1994," *Center of Military History*, http://www.history. army.mil/html/documents/somalia/SomaliaAAR.pdf

3    Ibid.,131-2

4    Ridley Scott, *Black Hawk Down*, Motion Picture, 2002

5    Contrary to media reports, while the two vehicles were indeed stolen from the UN, the white Land Cruisers did not have the familiar black UN markings on the sides.

6    Pieter D. Wezeman, "South African Arms Supplies to Sub-Saharan Africa," *SIPRI Stockholm International Peace Research Institute,* January 2011, www.sipri.org

7    Former AMISOM soldier, interview, July 2013

8    When Gen. Niyoyunguruza died in the suicide blast, all the media mistakenly identified him as AMISOM's Deputy Force Commander. In fact, Gen. Hakiza was effectively the new deputy force commander. Gen. Hakiza who was with Gen. Nathan Mugisha walking toward the door, narrowly escaped with his life when the bomb went off that morning.

9    Summary report of the Burundi Senate plenary session of April 16, 2009 relating to the approval of appointments for the positions of Governors of provinces, ambassadors and heads of Defense and Security Corps. www.senat.bi

10   Leslie Crawford, "Troops Overthrow Burundi President," *The Financial Times*, October 22, 1993

11   International Commission of Inquiry for Burundi, "Letter of 25 July 1996 from the UN Secretary-General to the President of the Security Council," UN document S/1996/682. August 22,1996 report established that on the critical night of October 21, 1993, Gen. Niyoyunguruza, then a Major in command of the 1er Bataillon Parachutiste, claimed he was locked in a garage while the coup took place.

12   Nathan Mugisha, interview, Kampala, July 25, 2013.

13   David Matua, interview, Mogadishu, July 22, 2013

14   There were reports that the young men were shot by soldiers just before the car exploded, but the evidence points to shrapnel from the bomb killing them.

15   Col. Dr. Kiyengo, interview by author, July 2012

16   Ibid.

17   Major Dr. Ibrahim Kimuli, interview, August 5, 2013

18   Ibid.

19   Captain Dr. Ronald Mukuye, interview, August 19, 2010

20   Kimuli interview.

21   Somalia Deputy Police Commissioner General Mohamed Nur died ten days later, on Saturday, September 26, 2009, from his wounds at Aga Khan Hospital in Nairobi, Kenya. His body was flown back to Somalia for a state funeral.

## Chapter 11

1    Charles H. Twining, "Aftermath of Somalia Death; Burundi Will Stay in Somalia," September 21, 2009, doi:09BUJUMBURA508_a

2    AFP, "Burundi Opposition Seeks Troops Recall from Somalia," Friday, September 19, 2009, http://www.hiiraan.com/

3    Twining, Aftermath.

4    Al Jazeera News, "Deaths in West Somalia Fighting," September 21, 2009, http://www.aljazeera.com/

5    Susan Rice, "Uganda to Consider Sanction Resolution which Covers Djibouti; Remains Committed

to AMISOM," September 29, 2009, doi:09USUNNEWYORK861_a.

6    BBC News, "AU Urges More Weapons for Somalia," September 18, 2009, http://news.bbc.co.uk/2/ hi/africa/8262310.stm

7    Susan Rice, "Ambassador Rice's Meeting with Ethiopian Prime Minister Meles Zenawi on September 21 2009," September 28, 2009, doi:09USUNNEWYORK857_a.

8    Twining, *ibid.*

9    Twining, *ibid.*

10   Jerry Lanier, "Uganda outlines AMISOM Requirements After Suicide Bombing," September 22, 2009, doi:09KAMPALA095_a.

11   Ibid.

12   Hillary Clinton, "Assistant Secretary Carson's Participation in the Contact Group on Somalia— September 23, 2009," September 30, 2009, doi:09STATE101610_a.

13   Ibid.

14   Susan Rice, "President Obama's September 23 Meeting with Top UN Troop Contributing Countries," October 1, 2009, doi:09USUNNEWYORK866_a.

15   United Nations, "Security Council Told of Some Progress in Somalia Situation, with Many Challenges Still Needing International Attention," October 8, 2009, http://www.un.org/press/ en/2009/sc9761.doc.htm

16   Jerry P. Lanier, "Uganda: Assistant Secretary Carson's Meeting with President Museveni," November 4, 2009, doi:09KAMPALA1276_a.

17   Ibid.

18   United Nations, "Security Council 6206th meeting," Monday October 26, 2009, S/PV.6206, http://www.un.org/

19   Ibid.

20   Susan Rice, "AU-UN: Security Council Divided on UN Assessed Contributions as a Funding Option," November 2, 2009, doi:09USUNNEWYORK979_a.

21   Ibid.

22   Ibid.

23   Tulinabo Salama Mushingi, "USAU: Synopsis of AMISOM Meeting with TCCs and Partners," November 6, 2009, doi:09ADDISABABA2642_a.

24   Ibid.

25   Ibid.

26   Al Shahid Webmaster, "Hizbul-Islam, Al Shabaab is Our Number One Enemy," November 18, 2009, http://english.alshahid.net/archives/2545

27   Herve Bar, "Ahmed Seeks Backing from Abroad," November 24, 2009, *AFP*, http://www.iol.co.za/

28   Hassan Osman Abdi, "Somalia: President Sharif Visits Military Centers in South Mogadishu," December 1, 2009, *Shabelle News Network*, http://allafrica.com/stories/200912010999.html

29   Nasib Farah and Søren Steen Jespersen (doc.) Warriors from the North," Motion Picture, October 12, 2014, Copenhagen, Denmark.

30   Mohamed Olad Hassan, "My Experience at the Deadly Hotel Shamo Bombing," *BBC/Associated Press*, December 17, 2009, https://cpj.org/blog/2009/12/my-experience-at-the-deadly-hotel-shamo-bombing.php

31   *ibid.*

32   Hamsa Omar, "Somali Islamists Deny Responsibility for Suicide Bomb Attack," *Bloomberg*, December 4, 2009, http://www.bloomberg.com/apps/news?pid=newsarchive&sid=a9Y6HHORr46M

33   Hassan Osman Abdi, "Somalia: Islamist Leader Calls Fresh Fighting Against AMISOM," *Shabelle*

*News Network*, December 5, 2009, http://allafrica.com/stories/200912070836.html

34   Hassan Ali, "Insurgents Fire Mortar at Somali Police, 13 Dead," *AFP/Somalilandpress*, December 20, 2009, http://www.somalilandpress.com/insurgents-fire-mortars-on-somali-police-13-dead/

35   Abdikarim, Al Shahid, "Islamic Rebels Fail to Agree in Somalia," *AlShahid*, December 18, 2009, http://english.alshahid.net/archives/3178

36   Alshahid, "Somali Islamist Rebels Force Men to Grow Beards," *Al Shahid*, December 20, 2009, http://english.alshahid.net/archives/3226

37   Abdihakim, "Al Shabaab Confirms their Ties with al Qaeda," *Al Shahid*, December 31, 2009, http://english.alshahid.net/archives/3436

38   Abdihakim, "Al Shabaab Bans Listening to Radio Mogadishu," *Al Shahid*, December 30, 2009, http://english.alshahid.net/archives/3406

39   AFP, "Somali's Shebab Says Will Send Fighters to Yemen," *Wardheer News*, January 1, 2010, http://wardheernews.com/News_10/01_alshabab_yemen.html

40   Abdihakim, "Hundreds of al-Shabaab Recruits Complete Training," *Al Shahid*, January 2, 2010, http://english.alshahid.net/archives/3481

41   Mohamed Hussein, "We will Recapture Mogadishu Districts; Somali Government," *Al Shahid*, December 29, 2009, http://english.alshahid.net/archives/3399

42   Abdiaziz Hassan, "Interview—Somali PM See Rebel Rout from Capital This Month," *Reuters*, January 3, 2010, http://uk.reuters.com/

43   African Union, "Report of the Chairperson of the Commission on the Situation in Somalia," PSC/PR/2(CCXIV), January 8, 2010, http://www.peaceau.org/

44   There were unsubstantiated claims that Somali State Minister for Defense Yusuf Mohamed "Indha Adde" Siyad was always an insider informing the insurgents on what the government was planning and doing. Many Somali I spoke to in Mogadishu believe Siyad was behind the twin bombing of AMISOM base on September 17, 2009; they claim, without providing evidence, that he provided the intelligence, giving the precise time and location when the meeting was taking place. While there is no direct evidence of Siyad's involvement in that tragedy, there is enough to suggest someone from the inside gave vital intelligence that enabled the bombing to occur when it did.

45   Abdihakim, "Alshabab and Hizbul Islam Warn the TFG Against Planned Offensive," *Al Shahid*, February 10, 2010, http://english.alshahid.net/archives/4276

46   Abdihakim, "Fighters Pour into Somali Capital," *Al Shahid*, February 11, 2010, http://english.alshahid.net/archives/4300. Also see Mohamed Olad Hassan, "Somali Rebels 'pour into Mogadishu'," *BBC*, February 10, 2010, http://news.bbc.co.uk/2/hi/8508176.stm

47   Abdihakim, "Somali Government Downplays Rebel Groups' Threat," *Al Shahid*, February 14, 2010, http://english.alshahid.net/archives/4380

48   Abdihakim, "The TFG Averts Planned Assassination," *Al Shahid*, February 17, 2010 http://english.alshahid.net/archives/4459

49   Herve Bar, "No Peace for Peacekeepers in Somalia," The Telegraph, December 2, 2009, http://www.telegraph.co.uk/

50   Abdihakim, "Somalia: Government Signs Agreement with Moderate Islamists," *Al Shahid*, February 20, 2010, http://english.alshahid.net/archives/4515

51   Voice of America (VOA), "Somali Government, Moderate Islamists Sign Power-sharing Deal," *VOA*, March 14, 2010, http://www.voanews.com/

52   Mohamed Abdi, "Alshabab and Hizbul Islam Leaders Meet," *Al Shahid*, Thursday, March 11, 2010,

53   Abdihakim, "Alshabab Destroy Grave of Renowned Cleric," *Al Shahid*, Wednesday, March 24, 2010, http://english.alshahid.net/archives/5442

54   Ali Musa Abdi, "Somalia's Sufis Organise in Face of 'existential' Threat," *The Telegraph*, November 5, 2009, http://www.telegraph.co.uk/

55   Mohamed Abdi, "Alshabab Bans BBC and VOA from Operating in Areas Under Alshabab's Control," *Al Shahid*, Friday, April 9, 2010, http://english.alshahid.net/archives/6051

56   Shafi'i Mohyaddin Abokar, "Extremist Rebels Invite Bin Laden to Somalia," *News Blaze*, April 4, 2010, http://newsblaze.com/

57   Wilfred Mulliro, "Alshabab Fighters Take Over Three Towns from Somalia Government," *Al Shahid*, April 24, 2010, http://english.alshahid.net/archives/6357

58   Lt. Col. Francis Chemo, interview with author, Mogadishu, August 18, 2010.

59   Wilfred Mulliro, "Uganda Soldiers Injured by Alshabab in Somalia Airlifted to Nairobi for Treatment," *Al Shahid*, Thursday, April 29, 2010, http://english.alshahid.net/archives/6457

60   CBS/AP, "Explosion in Somali Mosque Kills at Least 30," *CBS/AP*, May 1, 2010, http://www.cbsnews.com/

61   AFP, "Somali Islamists Threaten Reprisal After Blasts," *AFP*, May 2, 2010, http://www.hiiraan.com/

62   Shabelle Media Network, "Somalia: Hizbul Islam Officer Killed Between Mogadishu and Afgoi," *Shabelle Media Network*, May 5, 2010, http://allafrica.com/

63   Wilfred Mulliro, "AU Somalia Mission Warns of Planned Coordinated Suicide Attacks in Mogadishu," *Al Shahid*, May 6, 2010, http://english.alshahid.net/archives/6641

64   Mohamed Abdi, "Alshabab Accuses AMISOM of Planning Suicide Attacks," *Al Shahid*, May 10, 2010, http://english.alshahid.net/archives/6736

65   Abdihakim, "Al-Shabab Told to Seize President's Villa," *Al Shahid*, Tuesday, May 25, 2010, http://english.alshahid.net/archives/7049

66   Wilfred Mulliro, "Somali Gov't Denies Reports of Attack on Presidential Villa Somalia," *Al Shahid*, May 26, 2010, http://english.alshahid.net/archives/7095

67   Wilfred Mulliro, "Somalia Defense Minister Survives a Roadside Blast That Kills Three Somalis, *Al Shahid,* May 28, 2010, http://english.alshahid.net/archives/7181

68   Abdihakim, "Somali Minister Accuses Presidential Palace for Attack," *Al Shahid*, May 29, 2010, http://english.alshahid.net/archives/7238

69   Mustafa Haji Abdinur, "Somali Insurgents Parade Bodies After Mogadishu Battle, *Agence France Presse/Daily Star*, June 5, 2010, http://www.dailystar.com.lb/

70   Bancroft Global Development, "About Bancroft," http://www.bancroftglobal.org/about-bancroft-global/

71   Jeffrey Gettleman, Mark Mazzetti and Eric Scmitt, "U.S. Relies on Contractors in Somalia Conflict," *New York Times*, August 10, 2011, http://www.nytimes.com/

72   Abdi Guled and Abdi Sheikh, "Somali Rebels Kills Two AU Peacekeepers—AMISOM," *Reuters*, June 5, 2010, http://uk.reuters.com/article/2010/06/05/idUKLDE6540A4

73   Abdihakim, "Algerian Fighter Killed in Somalia Battle," *Al Shahid*, June 5, 2010, http://english.alshahid.net/archives/7485

74   Abdihakim, "Hizbul Islam Calls for Unity of Somali Mujahideens," *Al Shahid*, May 27, 2010, http://english.alshahid.net/archives/7173

75   Wilfred Mulliro, "Somali Rebel Leader Aweys Defends Decision to Vacate Central Town, *Al Shahid*, June 21, 2010, http://english.alshahid.net/archives/8056

76   Wilfred Mulliro, "Somali President Takes AK47 and Joins Troops Against Rebels," *Al Shahid*, July 1, 2010, http://english.alshahid.net/archives/8432

77   Mohamed Abdi, "Blast in Somalia's Presidential Palace, *Al Shahid*, July 1, 2010, http://english.alshahid.net/archives/8422

78   Mohamed Abdi, "Two AMISOM Soldiers Killed in Mogadishu," *Al Shahid*, July 4, 2010, http://
     english.alshahid.net/archives/8562

79   Mohamed Abdi, "Two AMISOM Soldiers Killed in Mogadishu," *Al Shahid*, July 4, 2010, http://
     english.alshahid.net/archives/8562

80   Wilfred Mulliro, "Somalia: Alshabab Rebels Mobilize Protests Against IGAD Meeting," *Al Shahid*,
     July 7, 2010, http://english.alshahid.net/archives/8697

81   Wilfred Mulliro, "Somali Rebels Protest Against the Presence of Foreign Troops in the Country,"
     *Al Shahid*, July 8, 2010, http://english.alshahid.net/archives/8748. Also see "Burqa-clad Women
     Wielding   AK-47s   Seen,"   http://islamizationwatch.blogspot.ca/2010/07/burqa-clad-women-
     wielding-ak-47s-seen.html

82   Medeshi News, "Somalia's Islamist Leader Threatens Ugandans, Burundians with Revenge,"
     *Medeshi News*, July 5, 2010, http://www.medeshivalley.com/

83   Abdulkadir Khalif, "Somalia: Al-Shabaab Urges Attacks on Diplomats," *Daily Nation on web*, July
     8, 2010, http://allafrica.com/

84   Steven Candia and Agencies, "Uganda Detains Top al-Shabaab Commander," *Africa News Online*,
     September 24, 2010, http://africanewsonline.blogspot.ca/

85   Francis Mugoga, "Re: God Protected Me During the Bomb Blast," *Testimony Share*, October 31,
     2011, http://www.testimonyshare.com/bomb-blast/

86   Xan Rice, "Uganda Bomb Blasts Kill at Least 74," *The Guardian*, January 12, 2010, http://www.
     theguardian.com/

87   Paul Fletcher, July 11, 2010, BBC Sport, Netherlands 0-1 Spain (aet), http://news.bbc.co.uk/sport2/
     hi/football/world_cup_2010/matches/match_64/default.stm

88   Stephanie Condon, "Obama, Clinton, Condemn Uganda Bombing, Offer Help," *CBS*, July 12,
     2010, http://www.cbsnews.com/

89   Ibid.

90   United Kingdom, "Press Release, Prime Minister's Office, Bomb attacks in Kampala," July 12, 2010,
     https://www.gov.uk/

91   Wilfred Mulliro, "Uganda Blasts: It is a Terrorist Attack, condemns AU," *Al Shahid*, July 12, 2010,
     http://english.alshahid.net/archives/8931

92   Herbert Ssempogo, "Museveni Declares Seven Days of Mourning," *New Vision*, July 12, 2010,
     http://www.newvision.co.ug/D/8/12/725617

93   The Daily Monitor, "Museveni Declares War on Al Shabaab," *The Daily Monitor*, July 15, 2010,
     http://www.monitor.co.ug/News/National/-/688334/958308/-/x245yh/-/index.html

94   Risdel Kasasira and Solomon Muyita, "United Nations Block Change of Amisom Mandate," *The
     Daily Monitor*, July 28, 2010, http://www.monitor.co.ug/

95   African Union, "Decisions, Declaration and Resolutions Adopted by the Fifteenth Ordinary
     Session of the Assembly of the Union," July 27, 2010, http://www.au.int/

96   Abdulkhadir Khalif, "Hands Off Somalia, Shabaab Warns AU, *The Citizen/Hiiraan Online*, July
     26, 2010, http://www.hiiraan.com/news2/2010/july/hands_off_somalia_shabaab_warns_au.aspx

97   Linda Ensor, "South Africa: Sisulu Warns of "Terror" Threats for Joining AU Forces," *Business Day*,
     *Hiiraan Online*, July 30, 2010, http://www.hiiraan.com/

## Chapter 12

1    Neil Kodesh, *Beyond the Royal Gaze: Clanship and Public Healing in Buganda*, (Charlottesville, VA:
     University of Virginia Press, 2010),75-81.

2    Ivan Okuda, "Lt. Gen. Katumba Wamala: From an Aspiring Doctor to an Army General," *Daily

*Monitor*, Sunday, September 16, 2012, http://mobile.monitor.co.ug/

3    Ibid.

4    Mogadishu field notes, Tuesday, August 17, 2010, Mogadishu.

5    Mohamed Ahmed and Abdi Sheikh, "Somali Islamists Demand Cash and Jewelry for Holy War," *Reuters*, Tuesday, August 3, 2010, http://ca.reuters.com/

6    Also see report by Mohamed Abdi, "Alshabab and Hizbul Islam Fail to Agree on Power Sharing Deal," *Al Shahid*, August 1, 2010, http://english.alshahid.net/archives/10522

7    Wilfred Mulliro, "Somalia Rival Rebel Groups Hold Joint Press to Deny Divisions," *Al Shahid*, August 3, 2010, http://english.alshahid.net/archives/10598

8    Mogadishu field notes.

9    See Wikipedia, The PSL (*Puşcă Semiautomată cu Lunetă model 1974*) 7,62 x 54mm is a variant of the Soviet-made Dragunov sniper rifle, and goes by various names including PSL-54C, Romak lll, FPK, FPK Dragunov and SSG-97. http://en.wikipedia.org/wiki/PSL_(rifle)

10    Field notes.

11    Former al Shabaab operatives, interview, July 2013.

12    Mohamed Abdi, "Alshabab Bomb Experts Die in an Explosion, *Alshahid*, August 22, 2010, http://english.alshahid.net/archives/11581

13    Ministry of Information, "Somalia: Failed al-Shabab Attack Proves Ramadan Terror Threat," August 22, 2010, http://www.duhur.com/

14    Named after Italian administrator in Somalia Enrico Anzilotti (1957 to July 1958), one of the last colonial administrators in Somalia before independence. See Associated Press, "Somali Serves as an Example to African Nations," *The New London, Conn. Evening Day Newspaper*, April 28, 1956.

15    Fred Oluoch, "Peacekeepers Say al-Shabaab Under Control," *Hiiraan Online*, August 22, 2010, http://www.hiiraan.com/

16    CNN, "Fighting in Somalia's Capital Kills at Least 20," *CNN*, August 23, 2010, http://www.cnn.com/

17    Ibid.

18    VOA, "Alshabab Claims Responsibility for Somalia Hotel Bombing," *Hiiraan News*, August 25, 2010, http://www.hiiraan.com/

19    VOA News, "Hotel Suicide Bomber Linked to al-Shabaab's Senior Leader, *VOA News*, August 24, 2010, http://www.voanews.com/

20    Agence France-Presse, "Somalia: 11 Civilians Dead in Fresh Mogadishu Fighting," *Agence France-Presse*, August 28, 2010, http://reliefweb.int/report/somalia/somalia-11-civilians-dead-fresh-mogadishu-fighting

21    Ibrahim Mohamed, "Somalis Flee Fourth Day of Violence in Mogadishu," *Reuters*, May 26, 2010, http://af.reuters.com/

22    Government of Somalia, "Press Release," Thursday, August 26, 2010, http://terrorfreesomalia.blogspot.ca/2010/08/somali-government-says-killed-25-al.html

23    Abdi Sheikh, "Islamist Rebels Kill Four AU Peacekeepers, *Reuters*, August 30, 2010, http://reliefweb.int/

24    Stringer/AFP/Getty Images, "Somali Boys Drag the Body of an Alleged AU Fighters Through the Streets of Mogadishu on August 30, 2010," http://www.vancouversun.com/

25    AP, African Peacekeepers Open 9 More Bases in Somalia," September 3, 2010, http://www.arabnews.com/node/354329

26    Press TV, "Somali President Fires Top Commanders," *Hiiraan Online*, September 6, 2010, http://www.hiiraan.com/

27 Wilfred Mulliro, "Somali Govt Kills Several Alshabab Rebels in Capital," *Alshahid*, September 6, 2010, http://english.alshahid.net/archives/12361

28 Wilfred Mulliro, "Somalia Rebels to Bring Hundreds of Troops Soon," *Alshahid*, September 7, 2010, http://english.alshahid.net/archives/12393

29 Wilfred Mulliro, "Somalia Terrorists Alshabab Recruit AIDS Victims as Suicide Bombers," *Alshahid*, September 9, 2010, http://english.alshahid.net/archives/12540

30 al kataib, "AMISOM: The Inevitable End Chronicles the Preparation for This Attack," *Alshahid*, September 9, 2010.

31 Barigye Ba-Hoku, "We Foiled Planned Vast Airport Suicide Attack," *AMISOM Press Release*, September 10, 2010, http://english.alshahid.net/archives/12567

32 Horseed Media, "Somalia Government Condemns Strongly Today's Suicide Bombers Attack in Mogadishu Airport," September 9, 2010, http://horseedmedia.net/

33 Ba-Hoku Barigye, *ibid*

34 AFP, "Five Somali Soldiers Killed in Bomb Blast," Saturday, September 11, 2010, http://en.starafrica.com/

35 Wilfred Mulliro, "Somalia Govt Soldiers Hit by Landmine Blast," *Alshahid*, September 14, 2010, http://english.alshahid.net/archives/12752

36 Katherine Houreld, "Somalia: Mogadishu Shelling Kills 12 Civilians," *AFP*, September 16, 2010, http://reliefweb.int/

37 Abdi Sheikh, "Suicide Bomber Attacks Somali Presidential Palace," Reuters, Monday, September 20, 2010, http://www.reuters.com/. Also see, Somalionline, "Villa Somalia: Suicide Bomber was Bodyguard of Interior Minister Abdulkadir Ali Omar," *Somalia Online*, http://www.somaliaonline.com/

38 Mareeg.com, "For Immediate Release: Extremists Asked to Give Peace a Chance," *Mareeg*, September 21, 2010, http://www.mareeg.com/

39 Research on Islam and Muslims in Africa (RIMA), Somali Proverb, June 2013, https://muslimsinafrica.wordpress.com/2013/06/26/somali-proverbs/

40 PANA, "Uganda Boosts African Union Force in Somalia," *Hiiraan Online*, September 18, 2010, http://www.hiiraan.com/news2/2010/sept/uganda_boosts_african_union_force_in_mogadishu.aspx

41 Risdel Kasasira, "Memo From Mogadishu," *Daily Monitor*, September 30, http://www.monitor.co.ug/

42 Wilfred Mulliro, "AU Burns 3 Armored al-Shabab Vehicles, Fighting Continues 2nd Day in Mogadishu," *Alshahid*, October 4, 2010, http://english.alshahid.net/archives/13555

43 Mohamed Ibrahim, "In Somalia, Signs of Discord Appear in Militant Group," *New York Times*, October 8, 2010, http://www.nytimes.com/

44 Abdi Hajji Hussein, "AlShabab Rebels Warn Somalis That Medicine From AU Mission Has HIV Virus," *Allheadlinenews.com,* October 12, 2010, http://english.alshahid.net/archives/13918

45 Wilfred Mulliro, "Somalia: AMISOM Dismisses Alshabab's Claims Over Infected Medicine," *Alshahid*, October 13, 2010, http://english.alshahid.net/archives/13933

46 Nasongo Willy, "Somalia Al-Shabab Rebel Ask Women to Order Their Children to Join Fighting," *Alshahid*, November 3, 2010, http://english.alshahid.net/archives/14698

47 Wilfred Mulliro, "Somalia Militants Open Fire on Crowd that Revolted Teenage Public Beating," *Alshahid*, October 16, 2010, http://english.alshahid.net/archives/14111

48 Wilfred Mulliro, "Somalia: Gunmen Ambush Alshabab Rebels' Vehicle, Killing About 20," *Al Sshahid*, October 19, 2010, http://english.alshahid.net/archives/14193

49    Al Jazeera, "al Sbabab Executes Two Girl "spies"," *Al Jazeera*, October 28, 2010, http://www.aljazeera.com/

50    Nasongo Willy, "Somalia: al Shabaab Leaders Condemn Each Other Publicly," *Al Shahid*, December 20, 2010, http://english.alshahid.net/archives/16426

51    Mareeg Online, "Hassan Dahir Aweys of Isbul Islam Leader Joins Al-Shabab Militias," *Mareeg*, December 20, 2010, http://www.mareeg.com/

52    United Nations Security Council, "6386th Meeting," Thursday, S/PV.6386, September 16, 2010, http://www.securitycouncilreport.org

53    United Nations Security Council, "Resolution 1964 (2010)," S/Res/1964(2010), December 22, 2010, http://www.securitycouncilreport.org

54    Nasongo Willy, "Somalia State Govt Issues Emergency Drought Appeal," Press release," *Alshahid*, January 7, 2011, http://english.alshahid.net/archives/16890

55    Nasongo Willy, "Allow Aid for starving Somalis, Al-Shabab Urged," *Alshahid*, January 10, 2011, http://english.alshahid.net/archives/17012

56    Nasongo Willy, "Somalia Al-Shabab Now Calls for Help Over Biting Drought," *Al shahid*, January 10, 2011, http://english.alshahid.net/archives/17017

57    Nasongo Willy, "Al Shabab Blocks Food Aid Agencies From Drought Stricken Somalis," *Alshahid*, January 12, 2011, http://english.alshahid.net/archives/17113

58    United Nations Security Council, Friday, January 14, 2011, S/PV.6467, http://www.securitycouncilreport.org/

59    AMISOM, "AMISOM Investigates Shooting Incident in Mogadishu," January 25, 2011, *Hiiraan Online*, http://www.hiiraan.com/news2/2011/jan/amisom_investigates_shooting_incident_in_mogadishu.aspx

60    Nasongo Willy, "Al-Shabaab Leader Warns His Group Against Brutality and Killing People," January 28, 2011, *Alshahid*, http://english.alshahid.net/archives/17720

61    Abdulkadir Khalif, "Somali Militant Group al-Shabaab Executes 'CIA spy'," *Africa Review*, January 31, 2011, http://www.africareview.com/

62    Nasongo Willy, "Somalia Al-Shabaab Rebels Cut a Boy's Hand Over Theft," *Al Shahid*, February 8, 2011, http://english.alshahid.net/archives/18020

63    Shabelle Media Network, "Somali Govt Seizes Person Linked to Mogadishu Demonstrators Deadly," *Shabelle Media Network*, February 17, 2011, http://allafrica.com/stories/201102170764.html

64    Barigye Ba-Hoku, "AMISOM Claims Smashing AlShabaab Urban Trench System," *Mareeg*, February 20, 2011, http://www.mareeg.com/

65    Hamsa Omar, "Somali Police Station Hit by Suicide Bomber; 18 People Dead," *Bloomberg News*, February 21, 2011, http://www.bloomberg.com/

66    Abdi Guled and Malkadir M. Muhumed, "Clashes in Somalia as Gov't Begins Long Awaited Offensive, Takes Key Positions in Mogadishu," AP/Biyokulule, February 24, 2011, http://www.biyokulule.com/. Also see Somaliland Press, "At Least 7 AU Troops Killed and More Captured," http://www.somalilandpress.com/

67    Also see Views from the Occident, blog, February 24, 2011,
http://occident.blogspot.ca/2011_02_01_archive.html
Patrick Nduwimana, "Somali Militants Kill Six Peacekeepers in a Single Day," *Reuters*, February 24, 2011, http://af.reuters.com/article/topNews/idAFJOE71N0IA20110224

68    Katherine Houreld, "53 peacekeepers Killed in Somalia Offensive," *Associated Press/Washington Post*, March 4, 2011, http://www.washingtonpost.com/

69    Shabelle Media Network, "Al Shabaab Deploys More Fighters to War-torn Mogadishu," *Shabelle*

*Media Network*, March 4, 2011, http://www.tmcnet.com/

70  Abdifitah Ibrahim, "Somalia: Al-Shabaab Asks Kismayo Traders to Pay Money," Wednesday, March 9, 2011, *Sunatimes*, www.sunatimes.com/view.php?id=874

71  Abdulkadir Khalif, "African Review, Al-Shabaab Recruits Elders in War Against Somalia Government," *Africa Review*, March 11, 2011, http://www.africareview.com/

72  Aweys Mohamed, "Somalia: Fighters Defecting from Al-Shabaab," *Sunatimes/Ethiopian Times*, Friday, March 11, 2011, https://ethiopiantimes.wordpress.com/

73  Shabelle Media Network, "Al-Shabaab Claims Victory Over Mogadishu Fighting; Govt Denies," *Shabelle Media Network*, March 17, 2011, http://baidoanews.com/

74  Barigye Ba-Hoku, "Press Release: Burundi and Uganda Defence Force Chiefs Visit Mogadishu, Somalia and Commit Additional Troops to AMISOM," *Horseed Media*, March 26, 2011, http://horseedmedia.net/

75  James Kabengwa, "UPDF Shuffles Somalia Command," *New Vision*, May 3, 2011, http://www.newvision.co.ug/D/8/13/753834

76  Felix Osike, "Congo UPDF Start Six Week Trek," *New Vision*, July 12, 2001, http://allafrica.com/

77  Grace Matsiko and John Thawite, "Uganda: Museveni Receives Troops from DRC," *New Vision*, October 16, 2001, http://allafrica.com/

78  Mohamed Ahmed, "Al-Shabaab Starts bin Laden Revenge Drive," *Somalia Report*, May 10, 2011, http://www.somaliareport.com/

79  AK and Rashid Nuune, "Al Shabaab Reinforces Mogadishu," *Somalia Report*, May 19, 2011, http://www.somaliareport.com/index.php/post/792/Al-Shabaab_Reinforces_Mogadishu

80  Mohamed Odowa, AK and Rashid Nuune, "TFG Enter Bakaara Market," *Somalia Report*, May 22, 2011, http://www.somaliareport.com/

81  Ibid

82  Lt. Col. Anthony Lukwago Mbuusi, interview, July 22, 2015

83  Mohamed Odowa, "Bakaara Market Business People Make Demand," *Somalia Report*, June 2, 2011, http://www.somaliareport.com/

84  Rashid Nuune, Mohamed Odowa and Yusuf Hagi, "Blast Kills Interior Minister," *Somalia Report*, June 10, 2011, http://www.somaliareport.com/

85  Mohamed Odowa, "Fazul's Last Moment," *Somalia Report*, Thursday, June 16, 2011, http://www.somaliareport.com/

86  Aweys Cadde and Mohamed Ahmed, "Airstrikes Hit al-Shabaab Camp near Kismayo," Somalia Report, June 24, 2011, http://www.somaliareport.com/index.php/

87  Aweys Cadde, "12 Al-Shabaab Fighters Surrender to TFG," *Somalia Report*, July 3, 2011, http://www.somaliareport.com/

88  Mohamed Odowa, "Al Shabaab Tries to Regain Popularity," *Somalia Report*, July 4, 2011, http://www.somaliareport.com/

89  Aweys Cadde, "Angry Residents Kill al-Shabaab Leader," *Somalia Report*, Agust 2, 2011, http://www.somaliareport.com/

90  Aweys Cadde, "Al Shabaab Burns 12 homes; Kill Civilian," *Somalia Report*, August 5, 2011, http://www.somaliareport.com/

91  African Union, "Close up with Major General Fred Mugisha, AMISOM Force Commander," *Peace and Security*, No. 3, 3, August 2011, http://www.peaceau.org/uploads/august-newsletter.pdf

92  AK, Mohamed Odowa and LMO, "Al Shabaab Quits Mogadishu," *Somalia Report*, August 6, 2011, http://www.somaliareport.com/

93  Abdi Abtidoon and Jama Deperani, "Uganda to Send 2,000 More Troops to Somalia," *Somalia*

*Report*, September 19, 2011, http://www.somaliareport.com/

94    Abdi Abtidoon, Abdirashid Abdi and Mohamed Odowa, "Blast in Mogadishu Kills at Least 65," *Somalia Report*, October 4, 2011, www.somaliareport.com

95    AMISOM, Press Release, October 4, 2011, AMISOM condemns cowardly attack in Mogadishu. www.amisom-au.org

96    Al Jazeera, Al Shabaab Claims Peacekeepers' Killings," October 21, 2011, http://www.aljazeera.com/

97    Paddy Ankunda, "Talking Mogadishu," *AMISOM Review*, No. 6, January 2012

## Chapter 13

1    Charlotte Metcalf, "Catch It While You Can," *Spectator*, July 15, 2009, http://www.spectator.co.uk/

2    Lorenzo Lovato, blog, December 5, 2009, Isola di Kiwayu: Vacanza di lusso nella Kiunga Marine Reserve, http://www.ilturista.info/

3    Translation by Dr. Roberta Iannacito Provenzano, York University, August 2015.

4    Judith Tebbutt and Richard Kelly, *A Long Walk home: One Woman's Story of Kidnap, Hostage, Loss—and Survival*, (London, UK: Faber and Faber, 2013); Also see Kira Cochrane, "Judith Tebutt: My Six Months as a Hostage of Somali Kidnappers," *The Guardian*, July 9 2013, http://www.theguardian.com/world/2013/jul/09/judith-tebbutt-hostage-somali-kidnappers.

5    Xan Rice and Kim Willsher, "French Woman Kidnapped by Somali Militants Dies," *The Guardian*, Wednesday, October 19, 2011, http://www.theguardian.com/world/2011/oct/19/french-woman-kidnapped-somalia-dies; Also see Mike Pflanz and Henry Samuel, "French Woman Held Hostage in Somalia Dies," October 19, 2011, *Telegraph*, http://www.telegraph.co.uk/

6    Catalan News Agency, "The Two Spanish MSF Workers Kidnapped in Kenya 21 Months Ago are Released," July 18, 2013, http://www.catalannewsagency.com/society-science/item/the-two-spanish-msf-workers-kidnapped-in-kenya-21-months-ago-are-released; Also see BBC Report, "Kenya-Somalia Abductions: Profiles," October 19, 2011, http://www.bbc.com/news/world-africa-15332410

7    Humphrey Malalo, "Kenya Says Kidnapping Provocation by al-Shabaab," *Reuters*, October 3, 2011, http://www.reuters.com/article/2011/10/03/us-kenya-kidnap-idUSTRE7924OK20111003; Also read excellent article on the topic by Margot Kiser, "How Somali Pirates and Terrorists Made Bank off Two Western Hostages," *Vocativ*, August 6, 2013, http://www.vocativ.com/money/uncategorized/how-pirates-and-terrorists-made-bank-off-hostages/

8    Boniface Ongeri and David Ochami, "Kenyan Troops Close in on Somali's Second Key Town," *Standard Media*, October 18, 2011, http://www.standardmedia.co.ke/

9    Jeffrey Gettleman, "Kenyan Forces Enter Somalia to Battle Militants," October 16, 2011, *The New York Times*, http://www.nytimes.com/2011/10/17/world/africa/kenyan-forces-enter-somalia-to-battle-shabab.html; Also see Associated Press, "Kenyan Troops Move Into Somalia," Sunday, October 16, 2011, http://www.theguardian.com/

10    Pamela J. H. Slutz, "Somalia—Lower Juba Forces Stepping Up Anti-Shabaab; Jubaland Steering Committee Formed," July 29, 2009, doi:09NAIROBI1648_a.

11    Ibid.

12    Barack Obama, "President Obama Announces More Key Administration Posts, 6-11-09," White House, June 11, 2009, https://www.whitehouse.gov/

13    Michael Ranneberger, "Somalia: Madobe Preparing Juba Offensive; Gedo Issue Unresolved," August 12, 2009, doi:09NAIROBI1710_a.

14    Michael Ranneberger, "Somalia—TFG President on Recruitment in Kenya and Political Outreach," October 21, 2009, doi:09NAIROBI12203_a.

15    Hilary Clinton, "Kenya's Conventional Arms End-user Certificate Violation," November 27, 2009, doi:09STATE122115_a.

16    Ibid.

17    Michael Ranneberger, "ASD Vershbow Visit Highlights Regional Security Issues," February 11, 2010, doi:10NAIROBI159_a.

18    Ibid.

19    James Swan, "Somalia: Kenyan Foreign Minister Pushes Lower Juba Initiative," December 10, 2009, doi:09DJIBOUTI1391_a.

20    Ibid.

21    James Swan, "DAS Wycoff Discusses Regional Security Challenges With Djibouti's President Guelleh," December 27, 2009, doi:09DJIBOUTI1423_a.

22    John M. Yates "Assistant Secretary Carson's January 30, 2010 Meeting with Kenyan Foreign Minister Wetangula," February 2, 2010, doi:10ADDISABABA166_a.

23    Ibid.

24    Titus T. Migue et al, *Operation Linda Nchi: Kenya's Military Experience in Somalia*, (Nairobi, Kenya: Kenya Ministry of Defence, 2014). The book overstates certain facts, including making the wild claim that, "Operation Sledge Hammer that saw the fall of Kismayu to the KDF was a turning point in the peace effort in Somalia..." (p. 38), and that in Kismayo, "The fighters were armed with surface to air missiles, SAM-7 and a surface-to-air gun ZU23 with orders to bring down..." (p.205). While it makes for exciting reading in fiction, in reality, the turning point in the war against al-Shabaab was the failed Ramadan Offensive in Mogadishu from July to October 2010 which, eventually, led to the collapse of the insurgents in August 2011. As far as claims of SAM-7, no evidence exists that al-Shabaab was in possession of the fairly sophisticated shoulder-fired weapon. If the group did have, they would have gladly used them to bring down planes in Mogadishu and elsewhere where there were daily flights by regular commercial and military chartered planes.

25    Abdi Guled and Katherine Houreld, "Kenya Helicopter Crashes; Push into Somalia Begins," *Associated Press*, October 16, 2011, http://news.yahoo.com/kenya-helicopter-crashes-push-somalia-begins-181411202.html

26    Peter Leftie and Issa Hussein, Kenya Troops Kill 9 Al Shabaab Troops," *Africa Review*, October 27, 2011, http://www.africareview.com/

27    For excellent summary of daily chronology of KDF actions in Somalia from October 2011 to March 2012, see Katherine Zimmerman and Kennan Khatib, "Timeline: Operation Linda Nchi," *Critical Threats*, March 9, 2012, http://www.criticalthreats.org/

28    Alice Klein, "Kenya Denies al-Shabaab Ambush Casualties," *The Telegraph*, November 2, 2011, http://www.telegraph.co.uk/

29    Associated Press/CBS News, Two explosions Rock Nairobi, at Least 1 Dead," *Associated Press/CBS News*, October 24, 2011, http://www.cbsnews.com/news/two-explosions-rock-nairobi-at-least-1-dead/

30    Peter Leftie, "Kenya and Amisom to Join Forces in al Shabaab fight," *Africa Review*, November 16, 2011 http://www.africareview.com/

31    IGAD, "Communique of the 19th Extra-Ordinary Session of the IGAD Assembly of Heads of State and Government on the Situation in Somalia and a Briefing on the Outstanding Issues of Sudan Comprehensive Peace Agreement," November 25, 2011, http://igad.int/

32    African Union, "Communique of the 302nd Meeting of the Peace and Security," Peace and Security Council 302nd Meeting, Addis Ababa, December 2, 2011, http://www.au.int/

33    Daily Nation, "Cabinet Approves AU Request on Kenyan Troops," December 6, 2011, http://www.

nation.co.ke/

34    BBC, "Kenya Troops to 'join Somalia's African Union Force'," December 7, 2011, http://www.bbc.com/news/world-africa-16077642

35    African Union, "Peace and Security Council 306th Meeting," January 5, 2012, Addis Ababa, Ethiopia, http://www.peaceau.org/

36    United Nations, "Security Council Requests African Union to Increase Troop Level of Somalia Mission to 17,700, Establish Expanded Presence in Keeping with Strategic Concept: Resolution 2036 (2012) Adopted Unanimously; Also Expands Support Package," February 22, 2012, http://www.un.org/press/en/2012/sc10550.doc.htm

37    Embassy of Republic of Kenya, "Kenya Troops Re-hat Into AMISOM, Nairobi," http://www.kenyaembassyaddis.org/

38    Maj. George Katabu, conversation with author on the morning of August 5, 2015, Obo, Central African Republic. Maj. Katabu was integral part of the planning team of Operation Free Shabelle.

39    al Shabaab interview. The former insurgents talked about Brig. Lokech and Col. Muhanga, his deputy with a great deal of respect and awe as very tough generals to fight against. Some of their toughest fights were during the period between April 2012 and August 2012, they intimated in anecdotal conversations.

40    Major Henry Obbo, email to author, November 13, 2015. Until May 22, 2012, al Shabaab took away all their casualties, leaving little or no signs of casualties. With so many casualties on this date, there was no time to take the dead.

41    Cpl. Robert Amia and Brig. Kayanja Muhanga, interviews, July 14, 2015 in Juba, South Sudan. Both were present and part of the said convoy from Bal'ad.

42    Captain Henry Obbo, now Major Henry Obbo, personal diary made available July 22, 2015 at UPDF Information Center, Mbuya, Kampala.

43    Karanja Njoroge and Edwin Makiche, "Families of Soldiers who Perished in Somalia Say Seeking Benefits has Been a Frustrating Affair," *Standard Digital*, October 6, 2013, http://www.standardmedia.co.ke/

44    Note that two dates are supplied in the book *Operation Linda Nchi*, the official account of the Kenyan military, one saying that the town of Hoosingo was captured on Sunday, March 1, 2012 (p. 176), and another saying the town was taken on Wednesday, April 1, 2012 (p. 177). I have used the former date because it is supported by other key information including the deaths of Lieutenant Kevin Webi, Lieutenant Evans Ng'etich, Second Lieutenant Edward Okoyo, all of 1 Battlegroup (p. 176) killed at the start of the march toward Hoosingo on January 22, 2012. Also a night attack by al-Shabaab on March 8, 2012, is said to have occurred after the capture of the town (p. 176).

45    See account of the battle (p.176-183) in Titus T. Migue et al, *Operation Linda Nchi: Kenya's Military Experience in Somalia*, (Nairobi, Kenya: Kenya Ministry of Defence, 2014).

46    Titus T. Migue et al, 189-191.

47    Ibid. 193

48    Paul Wafula and Nyambega Gisesa, "The Day They Dragged my Son's Body in the Streets of Kismayu," *Daily Standard*, Wednesday, April 30, 2014, http://www.standardmedia.co.ke/

49    *ibid*. See also Paul Wafula and Nyambega Gisesa, "The Day al Shabaab Called," Standard Online, Tuesday, April 29, 2014, http:www.standardmedia.co.ke/ Also see Somalia News Index, Shabaab Displays Bodies of Kenyan Soldiers Near Kismayo," September 1, 2012, http://somalianewsindex.blogspot.ca/2012/09/shabaab-displays-bodies-of-kenyan.html

50    Titus T. Migue et al, *Operation Linda Nchi,* 194

51    Ibid.,197

52 David Smith, "Kenyan Amisom Peacekeeper Held 'after Shooting Dead Six Somali Civilians'," *The Guardian*, September 25, 2012 http://www.theguardian.com/

53 Titus T. Migue et al, 202-211.

## Chapter 14

1 United Nations, "Report of the Monitoring Group on Somalia and Eritrea pursuant to Security Council resolution 2060 (2012): Somalia (S/2013/413)," July 12, 2013, http://www.un.org/sc/committees/751/mongroup.shtml

2 African Union, "Report of the Chairperson of the Commission on the Joint AU-UN Benchmarking Exercise and the Review of the African Union Mission in Somalia," October 10, 2013, http://www.peaceau.org/uploads/psc-rpt-399-amisom-09-10-2013.pdf

3 African Union, "Communique," PSC/PR/COMM(CCCLXXIX, June 13, 2013, http://www.peaceau.org/uploads/psc-379-com-somalia-13-06-2013-3-2-.pdf

4 James Swan, "Djibouti/Somalia—Senior GODJ Officials on Somalia Developments," September 8, 2009, doi:09DJIBOUTI1089_a.

5 James Swan, "Djibouti President Appeals Again for USG to Equip Somali Trainees," September 12, 2009, doi:09DJIBOUTI1103_a.

6 James Swan, "Djibouti: Foreign Minister on Possible AMISOM Deployment," September 23, 2009, doi:09DJIBOUTI1147_a

7 James Swan, "Djibouti/Somalia—Contribution to AMISOM," October 29, 2009, doi:09DJIBOUTI1247_a.

8 James Swan, "DAS Wycoff Discusses Regional Security Challenges with Djibouti's President Guelleh," December 27, 2009, doi:09DJIBOUTI1423_a.

9 James Swan, "Djibouti Planning for AMISOM Contingent," January 19, 2010, doi:10DJIBOUTI52_a.

10 James Swan, "Djibouti: S/CT Ambassador Benjamin and GODJ National Security Advisor Discuss Eritrea, Yemen and Somalia," February 22, 2010, doi:10DJIBOUTI199_a.

11 Cherif Ouazani, February 4, 2003, Jeune Afrique, L'homme du president, http://www.jeuneafrique.com/132180/archives-thematique/l-homme-du-pr-sident/

12 James C. Swan, US Ambassador to Djibouti, Monday, 22 February 2010, Djibouti: S/CT Ambassador Benjamin AND GODJ National Security Advisor Discuss Eritrea, Yemen, And Somalia, doi:10DJIBOUTI199_a.

13 Ibid.

14 New Vision, "Djibouti Bolsters Peacekeepers in Somalia," *New Vision*, December 20, 2011, http://www.newvision.co.ug/

15 Mohamed Abdiwab, "First Djibouti Troops Join AU Somalia Force," *AFP*, December 21, 2011, http://www.modernghana.com/

16 Brig. Gen. Audace Nduwumusi in conversation, Thursday, July 19, 2012 at 11:00 a.m. in his office at Halaane Base, Mogadishu. Lt. Col. Paddy Ankunda, AMISOM's spokesman in Mogadishu at the time of the event, corroborated the story in a phone conversation from his home in Kajjansi, Uganda, on Friday, August 20, 2015.

17 Lt. Col. Paddy Ankunda, phone conversation, Friday, August 20, 2015.

18 Somalilandpress, "Somalia: Djiboutian Colonel appointed Spokesperson of AMISOM," *Somaliland Press*, July 8, 2012, http://www.somalilandpress.com/

19 Somalilandpress, "Djibouti Peacekeepers Arrive in Central Somalia," *Somaliland Press*, June 1, 2012, http://www.somalilandpress.com/djibouti-peacekeepers-arrive-in-central-somalia/

20    Irin News, "Floods Displace Thousands in Beletweyne," October 2, 2012, http://hiiraan.com/news4/2012/Oct/26217/floods_displace_thousands_in_beletweyne.aspx. Also see UNOCHA and other agencies Report, October 15, 2012, "Multisectoral Assessment on the Impact of Floods in Beletweyne," https://docs.unocha.org/

21    Dan Reed, Terror at the Mall. Motion Picture. Directed by Dan Reed. New York, NY: HBO, 2014.

22    Tristan McConnell, "Close Your Eyes and Pretend to Be Dead: What Really Happened Two Years Ago in the Bloody Attack on Nairobi's Westgate Mall," *Foreign Policy*, September 20, 2015, http://foreignpolicy.com/

23    Zoe Flood, "Kenya Mall Attack: Mother Who Negotiated with Terrorist to Spare Children Tells of Ordeal", The Telegraph, October 5, 2013, http://www.telegraph.co.uk/. Also read Tom Palmer, Rakesh Ramchurn and Jonathan Brown "Kenya Shopping Mall Attack: Stories of the Heroes and the Victims," September 25, 2013, *Independent*, http://www.independent.co.uk/

24    *ibid*. Tom Palmer, Rakesh Ramchurn and Jonathan Brown.

25    United Nations, "Security Council Extends Mandate of African Union Mission in Somalia, Requests Increase in Troop Strength," November 12, 2013, http://www.un.org/press/en/2013/sc11172.doc.htm

26    Ibid.

27    Shafi'i Mohyaddin, "Somali Army and AMISOM Forces Seize Five Strategic South-western Somali Towns," *Hiiran Online*, March 8, 2014, http://hiiraan.ca/

28    Shafi'i Mohyaddin, "Somali Govt and Amisom Troops Seize Strategic Towns in Central Somalia," *Hiiraan Online*, March 13, 2014, http://hiiraan.ca/

29    Dalsan Radio/All Africa news, "Somalia: Death Toll of Buloburte Hotel Car Bomb Rises to 20, Officials Said," March 18, 2014, http://allafrica.com/stories/201403181732.html.

Also see Xinhua News, "Djibouti Confirms 5 Soldiers Killed in Somalia Attack," March 19, 2014, http://news.xinhuanet.com/english/africa/2014-03/19/c_133198476.htm

30    Xinhua News, "Bodies of 6 Soldiers Killed in Somalia Repatriated to Djibouti," March 21, 2014, http://news.xinhuanet.com/english/africa/2014-03/21/c_133204209.htm

31    Dateline, June 6, 2014, posted on Youtube by Elmi Dhigal on June 9, 2014, https://www.youtube.com/watch?v=QwlR5-7v-mk

32    Al Jazeera, "Al-Shabab Gunmen Attack Hotel in Somalia," June 26, 2014, http://www.aljazeera.com/

33    Abdulkadir Khalif, "Al-Shabaab Vows to Intensify Attacks on Djibouti," *Africa Review*, June 27, 2014 http://www.africareview.com/

34    Alshahid Webmaster, "AMISOM Troops in Central Somalia Promises New Advance to Al-Shabab Stronghold Towns," April 8, 2014, http://english.alshahid.net/archives/date/2014/04/08

35    Tageo.com, "Somalia City and Town Population," http://www.tageo.com/index-e-so-cities-SO.htm

36    Ekimeeza, "Brig. Ondoga, Two Others, Remanded Over Somalia Food Theft," Ekimeeza, November 2, 2013, http://www.ekimeeza.com/2013/11/02/brig-ondoga-two-other-officers-remanded-over-somalia-food-theft/. Note that the General Court Martial sitting in Kampala completely acquitted Brig. Ondoga of all charges on May 8, 2015. See Michael Odeng, Barbra Kabahumuza and Innocent Anguyo, "Brigadier Michael Ondoga Finally Freed by General Court Martial," New Vision, May 8, 2015, http://www.newvision.co.ug/

37    Muthoki Mumo, "East Africa Plans United Front in Search of Shs2trn Lapsset Funding," *Daily Nation*, July 31, 2014, http://mobile.nation.co.ke/

38    PSCU, "President Uhuru Kenyatta Leaves for US-Africa Summit to be Held in Washington, DC," Standard Media, August 3, 2014, http://www.standardmedia.co.ke/. Also see, Uganda

Media Centre, "President Leaves for US-Africa Summit," Sunday, August 3, 2014, http://www.mediacentre.go.ug/

39 Brig. Dick Olum, Interview, Kampala, July 11, 2015

40 AMISOM Public Information, "AMISOM Receives Drugs From American Government," *Dateline*, August 23, 2014, https://vimeo.com/104302305

Also see, AMISOM Public Information, "AMISOM Receives Medical Supplies," August 23, 2014, https://www.flickr.com/photos/au_unistphotostream/sets/72157646774515225/detail/

41 Abdalle Ahmed Mumim and Julian E. Barnes, "Al Shabaab Leader Targeted in US Airstrike, Not Known if Killed," *The Wall Street Journal*, September 2, 2014, http://www.wsj.com/

42 BBC, "Somali Troops in 'full control' of Barawe," October 6, 2014, http://www.bbc.com/news/world-africa-29510216

43 Human Rights Watch, "The Power These Men Have Over US: Sexual Exploitation and Abuse by African Union Forces in Somalia," HRW, September 8, 2014, https://www.hrw.org/

## Chapter 15

1 Author's field notes traveling with President Museveni on Monday, August 12, 2013.

2 President Yoweri Museveni, Interview, Thursday, August 23, 2012, State House, Nakasero.

3 African Union, "Communique of the 306th PSC on the Situation in Somalia," January 5, 2012, http://amisom-au.org/2012/01/commuique-of-the-306th-psc-meeting-on-the-situation-in-somalia/

4 United Nations, "Special Report of the Secretary-General on Somalia, S/2012/74," January 31, 2012, http://www.un.org/

5 Conversations with two senior UPDF commanders, and three senior cabinet ministers July 2015 in Kampala, Uganda

6 President Yoweri Museveni, Interview, Thursday, August 23, 2012, State House, Nakasero.

7 Ibid.

8 Garowe Online, "Somalia—Ahmed Madobe Elected First President of Jubaland in Landslide Victory," May 15, 2013, http://allafrica.com/stories/201305160045.html

9 Garowe Online, "Somalia: Jubaland Forces Clash with Illegal Militias and Al Shabaab in Kismayo," June 28, 2013, http://allafrica.com/stories/201306290008.html

10 Qalinle Hussein, "Tough Foreign Policy Challenges for Somalia's "Iron Lady"," November 21, 2012, http://www.somalilandpress.com/tough-foreign-policy-challenges-for-somalia's-"iron-lady"/

11 A senior AU official provided author with a copy of the Letter written by the Deputy Prime Minister and Minister for Foreign Affairs Fawzia Yusuf Haji Adan on the letterhead of the Federal Republic of Somalia, Ministry of Foreign Affairs and International Cooperation, dated 30th June 2013, Mogadishu, REF: MFA/OM/13/2013, addressed to Ambassador Ramtane Lamamra, AU Commissioner for Peace and Security, Addis Ababa.

12 Cyrus Ombati, "Somali Government Wants Kenya Defence Forces out of Kismayo, Calls for Neutral Force," *Standard Online*, July 1, 2013, http://www.standardmedia.co.ke/

13 H.E. Mahmoud Hassan, conversation with the President of Somalia at Villa Somalia, Mogadishu at 2:00 p.m. on July 22, 2013.

14 Malkhadir M. Muhumed, "Mogadishu Plots to Eject Kenya Defence Forces out of Somalia," *Standard Online*, July 6, 2013, http://www.standardmedia.co.ke/

15 Author's personal notes as delegate, Speke Resort and Conference Centre, Munyonyo, Kampala, Saturday, August 3, 2013.

16 Ibid. Also see Emmanuel Toili, "Somalia Wants Kenya Defence Force out of Kismayu," *Africa*

*Review*, July 1, 2013, http://www.africareview.com/

17    Horseed Media.net, "Somalia: Final Communique on TCC's," August 4, 2013, http://horseedmedia.net/

18    H.E. President Yoweri Museveni and H.E. President Mahmoud Sheikh Hassan, in conversation, involving author and others, at State House, Nakasero, 8:30 p.m. Sunday, August 4, 2013.

19    EU Mission to Somalia, "European Union Supporting the Somali New Deal, Booklet," http://www.eeas.europa.eu/

20    The Council of European Union Decision 2010/96/CFSP of 15 February 2010 on a European Union military mission to contribute to the training of Somali security forces, http://eur-lex.europa.eu/

21    African Union, "The Commissioner for Peace and Security of the African Union signed the Status of Mission Agreement (SOMA) for the AU Mission in Somalia with the Ambassador of Somalia," March 6, 2006, http://reliefweb.int/

22    United Nations, "AU Peace and Security Commissioner Briefs Council on Somalia," October 15, 2010, http://www.unmultimedia.org/

23    Abdul Karim Koroma, "Defence Minister Attends JCM Meeting in Ethiopia," *Information Attache, Embassy of Republic of Sierra Leone*, Addis Ababa, http://africayoungvoices.com/

24    African Union, "Opening Remarks by Ambassador Ramtane Lamamra, Commissioner for Peace and Security, at the 2nd Ministerial Meeting of the Joint Coordination Mechanism on Somalia on the Preliminary Outcome of the AU Strategic Review of AMISOM," January 14, 2013, http://www.peaceau.org/uploads/jcm-2nd-meeting.pdf

25    African Union, "Swearing in of Amb. Smail Chergui as Newly Elected Commissioner for Peace and Security of the African Union," October 13, 2013, http://www.au.int/

26    AMISOM Magazine, "At the Helm of AMISOM Police," May-August 2015, No. 16, 26-27, http://issuu.com/amisom/docs/amisom_mag_may_2015_finale

27    AMISOM News, "AMISOM Gender Office/Unit Event on Empowering Somali Women and Engaging Elders and Politicians," November 12, 2012, http://amisom-au.org/2012/11/amisom-gender-officeunit-event-on-empowering-somali-women-and-engaging-elders-and-politicians/

28    Maman Sidiku, "Message From the SRCC," May 2015, http://issuu.com/amisom/docs/amisom_mag_may_2015_finale

29    *ibid*. Zalmay Khalilzad, USUN.

30    United Nations, "MINURSO: United Nations Missions for the Referendum of Western Sahara," http://www.un.org/en/peacekeeping/missions/minurso/background.shtml

31    United Nations, "Report of the Independent Inquiry into the Actions of United Nations During the 1994 Genocide in Rwanda," December 16, 1999, http://www.un.org/

32    United Nations, "UNMIS, United Nations Mission in the Sudan," http://www.un.org/en/peacekeeping/missions/past/unmis/background.shtml

33    UN, "MONUSCO, United Nations Organization Stabilization Mission in the Democratic Republic of the Congo," http://www.un.org/en/peacekeeping/missions/monusco/mandate.shtml

34    United Nations, "Approved Resources for Peacekeeping Operations for the Period from 1 July 2014 to 30 June 2015, http://www.un.org/

35    Pete Jones and David Smith, "Congo Rebels Take Goma With Little Resistance to Little Cheer," *The Guardian*, November 20,2012, http://www.theguardian.com/

36    BBC, "Hague Hears DR Congo's Bosco Ntaganda 'ordered killings'," February 10, 2014, http://www.bbc.com/news/world-africa-26114895. Also see, International Criminal Court, "The Prosecutor V. Bosco Ntaganda," ICC-01/04-02/06, http://www.icc-cpi.int

37    United Nations, "Security Council Expresses Intention to Establish Peacekeeping Mission in

Somalia, Subject to Further Decisions by June 1, Unanimously Adopting Resolution 1863," *UN Press Release*, January 16, 2009, http://www.un.org/press/en/2009/sc9574.doc.htm

38   United Nations, "Report of the Secretary-General on Somalia Pursuant to Security Council Resolution 1863 (2009)", April 16, 2009, S/2009/210, http://www.un.org/

39   African Union, "Communique of the 69th Meeting of the Peace and Security Council," November 12, 2012, http://www.ausitroom-psd.org/Documents/PSC2007/69th/Communique/CommuniqueEng.pdf

40   United Nations Political Office for Somalia (UNPOS), "Agreement between Transitional Federal Government of Somalia (TFG) and The Alliance for the Re-Liberation of Somalia (ARS)," http://unpos.unmissions.org/

41   United Nations Political Office for Somalia (UNPOS), "SRSG Calls for Successful Follow up to Brussels Meeting on Somalia," Press Release 015/2009, http://unpos.unmissions.org/

42   UNPOS, "Istanbul Conference on Somalia is A Breakthrough for All Stakeholders," May 24, 2010, http://reliefweb.int/report/somalia/istanbul-conference-somalia-breakthrough-all-stakeholders

43   Republic of Turkey, "The Second Istanbul Conference on Somalia, Final Declaration," Ankara, June 1, 2012 http://www.mfa.gov.tr/the-second-istanbul – conference-on-somalia_-final-declaration_-1-june-2012_-istanbul.en.mfa

44   United Nations, "Resolution 1863 (2009)," http://unsoa.unmissions.org/sites/default/files/s-res-1863.pdf

45   United Nations, "Resolution 1872 (2007)," S/RES/1872 (2009), http://www.securitycouncilreport.org/

46   United Nations, "Resolution 2102 (2013)," http://www.un.org/

47   United Nations, "Letter Dated 19 April 2013 From the Secretary-General Addressed to the President of the Security Council," April 19, 2013, http://www.securitycouncilreport.org/

48   United Nations, "Secretary-General Appoints Nicholas Kay of United Kingdom as Special Representative for Somalia,"
http://www.un.org/press/en/2013/sga1401.doc.htm

49   Ambassador Nicholas Kay, Meeting via video-link, Friday, August 9, 2013.

50   Abdi Sheikh, "UN Compound in Somalia Attacked", *Reuters*, June 19, 2013, http://www.thesudburystar.com/2013/06/19/un-compound-in-somalia-attacked

51   Ambassador Nicholas Kay, "SRSG Kay's Speech at the "Vision 2016" National Conference," *Hiiraan Online*, http://www.hiiraan.ca/

52   Abdirahman Hussein and Abdi Sheikh, "Al Shabaab Bombers Strike Mogadishu Restaurant, 15 Dead," *Reuters*, September 7, 2013, http://www.reuters.com/

53   UNSOM, "UN Secretary General's Special Representative for Somalia, Nicholas Kay, on terrorist attack in Mogadishu," *Reliefweb*, September 7, 2013, http://reliefweb.int/

54   Brigadier Dick Olum, interview, July 11, 2015 Kampala, Uganda. Brig. Olum did not specify whether Amb. Kay was reacting to the June or the September 2013 bomb attacks in Mogadishu. The author assumed the latter since it was the closest to the date of Olum's arrival in Mogadishu.

55   David S. Albert and Richard E. Hayes, Understanding Command and Control, DoD Command and Control Research Program, http://www.dodccrp.org/files/Alberts_UC2.pdf

56   Europafrica.net, "North Africa Regional Capability signs the MoU between AU, Regional Economic Communities and Regional Standby Brigades of East and North Africa", June 1, 2010, http://europafrica.net/

57   Peter Clottey, "ECOWAS, Mali settle dispute over standby force," *Voice of America*, September 6, 2012, http://www.voanews.com/content/ecowas-mali-settele-disagreement-over-standby-

force/1503343.html

58   IGAD, "Draft protocol for the establishment of the Eastern Africa Standby Brigade", February 2004, https://www.issafrica.org/

59   Panapress, "Ethiopia: East African Force Reaches Full Military Deployment Capability", November 22, 2014, http://www.panapress.com/

60   Hussein Solomon, "Critical reflections of African Standby Force: The case of its SADC contingent," *Southern Africa Peace and Security Studies*, Vol. 1 No. 2, http://www.saccps.org/

61   Peter Fabricius, "Is African Standby Force nearly Ready for Action," *Global Observatory*, July 30, 2015, http://theglobalobservatory.org/

# Bibliography

Abdullahi, D. Mohamed. *Cultures and Customs of Somalia*. Westport, CT: Greenwood Press, 2001.

Ali, B. Mohamed. *The Mourning Tree—An Autobiography and A Prison Memoir*. Ponte Invisible/Red Sea Press. http://www.redsea-online.com/books/

Baumann, Robert, Lawrence A. Yates and Versalle F. Washington. *My Clan Against the World: US and Coalition Forces in Somalia, 1992-1994*. Fort Leavenworth, Kansas: Combat Studies Institute Press, 2003.

Bowden, Mark. *Black Hawk Down: A Story of Modern War*. New York, NY: Grover Press, 1999.

Compagnon, Daniel. "Somali Armed Movements: The Interplay of Political Entrepreneurship and Clan-based Faction." In *African Guerrillas*. Edited by Christopher Clapham. Oxford, UK: James Currey, 1998.

De Waal, Alex. *The Real Politics of the Horn of Africa: Money, War and the Business of Power*. Malden, MA: Polity Press, 2015.

Englehardt, P. Joseph. "Desert Shield and Desert Storm: A Chronology and Troop List for 1990-1991 Persian Gulf Crisis." *Strategic Studies Institute (SSI) Special Report*, March 25, 1991, http://www.dtic.mil/dtic/tr/fulltext/u2/a234743.pdf.

Fallin, Don. *Somalia: Hidden Threat to Our Homeland*. Norfolk, VA: Joint Forces Staff College, 2014.

Farah, Nasib and Søren Steen Jespersen (doc.) "Warriors from the North." October 12, 2014, Copenhagen, Denmark. Motion Picture.

Hansen, J. Stig. *Al Shabaab in Somalia: The History and ideology of a Militant Islamist Group, 2005-2012*. New York, NY: Oxford University Press, 2013.

Hirsch, L. John and Robert B. Oakley. *Somalia and Operation Restore Hope: Reflection on Peacemaking and Peacekeeping*. Washington, DC: The Endowment of the United States Institute of Peace, 1995.

Human Rights Watch. *Evil Days. Thirty Years of War and Famine in Ethiopia*. New York: Human Rights Watch, 1991.

Kaptejins, Lidwien. *Clan Cleasing in Somalia: The Ruinous Legacy of 1991*. Philadelphia, PA: University of Pennsylvania Press, 2013.

Kingsley, Charles. *A Vet in Somalia*. Bloomington, Ind.: Xlibris Corporation, 2012.

Kiraranganya, F. Boniface. *La Verite sur le Burundi: Temoignage*. Sherbrooke, Quebec: Editions Naaman, 1985.

Kodesh, Neil. *Beyond the Royal Gaze: Clanship and Public Healing in Buganda*. Charlottesville, VA: University of Virginia Press, 2010.

Laitin, David and Said Samatar. *Somalia: A Nation in Search of State*. Boulder, CO: Westview Press, 1987.

Lemarchand, Rene. *Burundi: Ethnic Conflict and Genocide*. New York, NY: The Woodrow Wilson Center Press and Press Syndicate of the University of Cambridge, 1996.

Lewis, M. Ioan. *Understanding Somalia and Somaliland: Culture, History and Society*. New York, NY: Columbia University Press, 2008.

Lewis, M. Ionian. *A modern History of the Somali: Nation and State in the Horn of Africa*.

Athens, OH: University of Ohio Press, 2003.

Mazetti, Mark. *The way of the knife: The CIA, A Secret Army, and a War at the Ends of the Earth.* New York, NY: Penguin Press, 2013.

Médecins Sans Frontières (MSF). "Somalia 1991-1993 Civil war, famine alert and UN 'Military Humanitarian' intervention 1991-1993." *MSF Speaks Out*, 2013. doi: PPP_SomalieVA PDF_0.pdf

Meehan, Emily. "Notes from a Failed State: America's Warlord." *Slate*, August 19, 2008. http://www.slate.com/

Metz, Helen (ed), Robert Rinehart, Irving Kaplan, Migue, Titus et al. *Operation Linda Nchi: Kenya's Military Experience in Somalia.* Nairobi, Kenya: Kenya Ministry of Defence, 2014.

National Commission on Terrorist Attacks. *The 9/11 Commission Report: Final Report of the National Commission on Terrorist Attacks Upon the United States.* New York, NY: W.W. Norton & Company, 2004.

Nederlandse Organisatie voor Internationale Bijstand (NOVIB), "War and Famine in Ethiopia and Eritrea: An Investigation into the Arms Deliveries to the Struggling Parties in Eritrea and Tigray,"*Zeist*, 1991.

Oloya, Opiyo. "African Force in Somalia Doomed to Fail." *New Vision*, February 20, 2007. http://www.newvision.co.ug/PA/8/20/550133

Osman, A. Abdulahi. "Cultural Diversity and the Somali Conflict: Myth or Reality?" *African Journal on Conflict Resolution 7*, no. 2 (April 2008): 93—133

Patman, Robert. *The Soviet Union in the Horn of Africa: The Diplomacy of Intervention and Disengagement.* New York: Cambridge University Press, 1990.

Phillips, James. "Somalia and Al-Qaeda: Implications for the War on Terrorism." *Heritage Foundation*, April 5, 2002. http://www.heritage.org/research/reports/2002/04/somalia-and-al-qaeda-implications-for-the-war-on-terrorism

Rabasa, Angel. *Radical Islam in East Africa.* Santa Monica, CA: Rand Corporation, 2009.

Rabasa, Angel et al. *Beyond al-Qaeda: Part 1, The Global Jihadist Movement.* Santa Monica, CA: RAND Corporation, 2006. http://www.rand.org/pubs/monographs/MG429.

Reed, Dan. Terror at the Mall. Directed by Dan Reed. Aired September 17, 2014. New York, NY: HBO, 2014. Motion Picture.

Scahill, Jeremy. *Dirty Wars: The World is A Battlefield.* London, UK: Serpent's Tail, 2013.

Scahill, Jeremy. "Blowback in Somalia: How US Proxy Wars Helped Create a Militant Islamist Threat." *The Nation*, September 07, 2011. http://www.thenation.com/article/blowback-somalia/

Siegel, B. Adam. "Eastern Exit: The Noncombatant Evacuation Operation (NEO), from Mogadishu, Somalia in January 1991," *Center for Naval Analyses (CNA)*, October 1991, doi:ADA445517

Solomon, Hussein. "Critical Reflections of African Standby Force: The case of its SADC contingent." *Southern Africa Peace and Security Studies 1*, no. 2 (September 2012).

Tebbutt, Judith and Richard Kelly. *A long Walk Home: One Woman's Story of Kidnap, Hostage, Loss—and Survival.* London, UK: Faber and Faber, 2013.

United Nation. "International Commission of Inquiry for Burundi." *United Nations*, April 13, 1996. http://www.usip.org/sites/default/files/file/resources/collections/commissions/Burundi-Report.pdf

United States Forces. "Somalia (USFORSOM) After Action Report." Washington, DC: US Army Center of Military History, 2003. www.history.army.mil/html/documents/

somalia/SomaliaAAR.pdf

Wasdin, E. Howard and Stephen Templin. *Seal Team Six: Memoir of an Elite Navy Seal Sniper.* New York, NY: St. Martin's Griffin, 2012.

Whitaker, P. Donald, Jean R. Tartter, and Frederick Ehrenreich. *Somalia: A Country Study.* Washington: GPO for the Library of Congress, 1992.

# Index

## Index of People

## Index of Places